The social science
imperialists

The social science imperialists

G.C. Harcourt

Edited by Prue Kerr

Routledge & Kegan Paul

London, Boston, Melbourne and Henley

To Joan

First published in 1982
by Routledge & Kegan Paul Ltd
39 Store Street, London WC1E 7DD,
9 Park Street, Boston, Mass. 02108, USA,
296 Beaconsfield Parade, Middle Park,
Melbourne, 3206, Australia, and
Broadway House, Newtown Road,
Henley-on-Thames, Oxon RG9 1EN
Set by Hope Services, Abingdon and
Printed in Great Britain by
Redwood Burn Ltd
Trowbridge, Wiltshire

Library of Congress Cataloging in Publication Data

Harcourt, Geoffrey Colin.
The social science imperialists and other
essays.
Bibliography: p.
Includes index.
1. Economics – Addresses, essays, lectures.
2. Social sciences – Addresses, essays, lectures.
I. Kerr, Prue, 1931–   .   II. Title.
HB171.H2733   300   81-17842

ISBN 0-7100-9064-1   AACR2

Contents

v

Preface

It is twenty-five years since I published my first paper and I was 50 in June 1981. So I was pleased when Routledge & Kegan Paul asked me whether they could publish a collection of my essays; and I was delighted when a former research student of mine from Adelaide, Prue Kerr, agreed to edit the collection.

I have been most fortunate with my students, my teachers and my colleagues. I hope that they approve of the collection for it bears the stamp of their influence and their guidance. I would like to thank all my students and I would like especially to mention the following friends: Keith Frearson, Doug Hocking, Joe Isaac, Wilfred Prest, Ken Rivett (my teachers at Melbourne); Phyllis Deane, Ronald Henderson (my Cambridge supervisor), Richard Kahn, James Meade, Luigi Pasinetti, Brian Reddaway, Joan Robinson, Piero Sraffa, Geoff Whittington (colleagues at Cambridge); John Grant, John Hatch, Russell Mathews, Bob Wallace (colleagues, or former colleagues, at Adelaide); Jon Cohen, Lorie Tarshis (colleagues at Toronto). I wish also to pay a tribute here to the late Eric Russell, who for nearly twenty years was a close friend and mentor at Adelaide, and to the late Maurice Dobb.

When I started teaching and writing I tried to be a straight-laced scientist – my Ph. D. dissertation and early papers were written in the third person. But the Vietnam war together with the writings of Noam Chomsky and Hugh Stretton changed that. They made me realize that ideology and analysis are indissolubly mixed and that we must always tell our students and our contemporaries where we stand. Where *I* stand has caused some problems and raised suspicions in conservative quarters, but it has also, I like to think, made me more alive and my work, I dare to hope, more relevant.

Most important of all I have been blessed with a happy marriage and a loving family. It is with gratitude and love that I dedicate this collection of essays to Joan Harcourt.

G.C.H.
Cambridge

Introduction

The essays collected together in this volume are grouped under seven headings with, however, overlapping themes. It will be seen that I have become increasingly dissatisfied with orthodox neoclassical analysis and more and more committed to what is sometimes called modern classicism: an amalgam of the theories and approach of the classical political economists and Marx with those of Keynes, Kalecki, Sraffa and Joan Robinson.

I Inflation, accountants' procedures and company behaviour

One virtue of an Australian degree in economics is that students have to take at least one course in accounting. I believe that it is not possible properly to understand the workings of capitalism unless you have a nodding acquaintance with accountants' conventions and procedures. Certainly the best economists – Marx, Keynes and Hicks, for example – knew this. My Ph.D. dissertation at Cambridge was on the implications for economic activity in a period of inflation, of using historical cost accounting procedures to measure income for taxation and dividend purposes, and in order to set prices. The research was done in the mid to late 1950s and inflation then proved disobliging by going away so that my predictions were not borne out immediately; the 1970s, though, have provided ample evidence with which to support my earlier speculations. They are reported in the first three essays of Part I, in the second one of which the influence of Joan Robinson's contributions in *The Accumulation of Capital* (Robinson, 1956) is evident also. The other two essays arise from a puzzle which was first posed to me by Harold Lydall in 1962: why don't accountants and economists get the same answer for the rate of profit in a situation of realized expectations? The answers contained in 'The Accountant in a Golden Age' (Harcourt, 1965b) still seem to me definitive despite John Kay's attempts to rescue the accountant: see Kay (1976), also Wright (1978), Kay (1978). The last paper in Part I shows what might have happened to investment–labour ratios in the Soviet Union if the accountant's measure of the rate of profit had been used as the basis for deciding bonus payments to Soviet managers.

II Post-Keynesian theory

Part II contains examples of what we now call Post-Keynesian theory. The first essay is a critique of Kaldor's theory of income distribution and economic growth (1950s, 1960s vintage), asking, in effect, what microeconomic foundations would give his macroeconomic results. The essay is critical of certain details in Kaldor's approach – in particular, the unsatisfactory nature of either his assumption of full employment or his demonstration that it must exist in a growing capitalist economy, and the constraints which this imposes on the analysis. Nevertheless, I want to place on record my admiration for his incredibly fertile and inventive contributions and to say that I really *am* on his side whether he likes it or not.

The immediate inspiration for the second essay was hearing Solow's 1963 Marshall Lectures (on a mythical creature called Nicky and another called Joan). They stimulated me to set out a positive approach to some of the issues to which Kaldor also had addressed himself. It incorporated in particular the insights of Michał Kalecki, Joan Robinson, Wilfred Salter and Piero Sraffa, in order to provide a model of the distribution of income and the level of activity which did not necessarily have to be a full-employment one.

The third essay (written jointly with another former research student from Adelaide, Peter Kenyon) is from a much later period but is included here as an example of Post-Keynesian theory. It gathers up for one precise question, the determination of the mark-up and the level of investment in oligopolistic firms, strands from parts I, II, III and IV, and especially those associated with the contributions of the late Wilfred Salter. I first had a 'go' at this particular problem in 1966 but could not get it right. I did not get the problem and approach into the present form until Peter and I worked together on it in late 1974. I would like to record here my indebtedness to J. W. Ball (1964), whose work in this area has not received the recognition which it should have.

III Salter's contributions, investment-decision rules, investment incentives and related econometric issues

Wilfred Salter's death in 1963 was a tragic loss for Australian economics, indeed, economics generally. Though I only met Wilf a few times, the fates decreed that I should have something to do with virtually all his published work, and his contributions, especially in *Productivity and Technical Change* (1960), have inspired and guided much of my own work. I reprint here my review article of his 1960 book; my only excursion ever into the pages of the Green Horror, which derives directly from Salter's work on vintages and which was the foundation of my critique (1964) of Minhas's book (1963) and related papers; and a paper on investment incentives, taxation and the choice of techniques which is an extension of Salter's insights into areas of policy, together with an attempt to theorize about businessmen's actual behaviour.

IV Sraffa's production of commodities and Marxian economics

When I returned to Cambridge in 1963 for, I thought, a year's study leave from Adelaide (in fact I stayed for three and a half years) I intended to work on Sraffa's 1960 classic, *Production of Commodities by Means of Commodities.* Very early on I met an American scholar, Vincent Massaro, of like intent and so we worked together. We read *Production of Commodities* . . . and did not allow ourselves to go on to the next sentence until we had convinced ourselves that we had understood the preceding one. We also had many illuminating and enjoyable discussions with Piero Sraffa himself. We wrote two papers which are reprinted here: one, an expository piece on Sraffa's ingenious device of sub-systems, the other, our review article of the book (which was originally published in the *Economic Record* in 1964 and which benefited from the detailed scrutiny of the author himself). Though I think that this essay is worth reprinting, I would like to draw the attention of readers to my essay, 'The Sraffian Contribution: An Evaluation', in Howard and Bradley (1981), for my current views. I also include a light-hearted review of Ian Steedman's important *Marx after Sraffa* (1977), written for *Nation Review*, the Australian surrogate for the *New Statesman*, and one of my latest papers, commissioned for the session celebrating the 90th anniversary of the publication of Marshall's *Principles* at the Eastern Economic Assocation Meeting in Montreal in May 1980, 'Marshall, Sraffa and Keynes: Incompatible Bedfellows?' (Perhaps the organizers feared A.M. would not survive the nervous 90s?) It concerns an issue which is currently being fiercely debated: how useful is the concept of a centre of gravitation in an analysis of modern capitalism?

V The capital theory controversies

I suppose that if I have any claim to recognition in the trade (apart from my many years as an Australian Rules footballer, where I played left of centre), it is in the area of capital theory and the Cambridge controversies therein. I therefore have selected four papers on these issues, the first of which is an infant's guide and the second and third, in effect, are sequels to my 1972 book, *Some Cambridge Controversies in the Theory of Capital* (Harcourt, 1972). I have tried to put the modern controversies in an historical context and to discuss the conceptual issues involved as well as to give simple expositions of the purely analytical puzzles associated with this literature. The fourth essay outlines the characteristics of non-neoclassical capital theory. The fifth (and the third, too) shows, I hope, that being a Post-Keynesian *and* a capital theorist are not bars to making useful interventions in the area of macroeconomic policy.

VI Intellectual biographies

In recent years I have become interested in the problems of writing intellectual biographies and I reprint here three – on Eric Russell, Joan Robinson and Lorie Tarshis – which I have written myself. It will become obvious that I am attracted to the contributions of these economists because they all belong to the classical-cum-Keynesian-Kaleckian tradition, the tradition which forms the background to the essays in this volume.

I am especially glad now to be able to publish (in a more accessible form than the Newcastle Research Report or Occasional Paper series) my account of the contributions of Eric Russell to Australian political economy. I wish to add that while in the essay I am critical of the views of another old friend, Donald Whitehead, alas now dead, our friendship survived this, and indeed Donald's views and mine on the causes of stagflation and what should be done about it were in the end very close.

I leave the essay on Joan Robinson to speak for itself (perhaps I could say that it is my tribute to a very great economist and a valued and trusted friend).

Finally, it has been my good fortune, since I began to spend regular periods in Toronto, to get to know Lorie and Inga Tarshis. I hope that my admiration and affection for them are reflected in the notes of the conversation which I had with Lorie on Friday 13 June 1980 which closes the section.

VII Conclusion: The social science imperialists

I have chosen to conclude the collection with the name essay 'The Social Science Imperalists' (which was the Academy Lecture of 1978), because it gave me a chance to roam far and wide through our discipline as it stood at the end of 1978. I have much enjoyed giving this paper in various places since then and my one regret is that a threatened airstrike (which never eventuated) prevented many of my so-called friends in the Academy of the Social Sciences in Australia from hearing me give the lecture in Canberra in November 1978. If I were to write it today, I would devote some space to the rational expectations school, who in recent years have become exceptionally influential, indeed dominant, especially on the North American continent, and I would pay an explicit tribute to the influence of Ken Arrow.

Part I

Inflation, accountants' procedures and company behaviour

1 The quantitative effect of basing company taxation on replacement costs*

The differences between company profits reckoned as revenues less historical costs, and company profits reckoned as revenues less replacement costs, have been considerable in many of the post-war years, mainly because of the neglect of stock appreciation and the inadequate allowance by historical cost depreciation allowances for durable capital consumption in the former reckoning.[1] In consequence, many writers have been led to call for reforms both in accounting procedures and in the methods of estimating company profits for taxation purposes.[2] Generally, the accounting profession has not been in favour of any of the suggested schemes that attempt to replace historical cost accounting by replacement cost accounting (for example, the use of L.I.F.O. methods for stock valuation and the adjustment of historical cost depreciation allowances by indices of the prices of fixed assets), nor did the Millard Tucker Committee or the Royal Commission on the Taxation of Profits and Income suggest reforms incorporating such principles. The granting of initial allowances (and, later, investment allowances) for expenditure on plant and machinery did, in effect, compensate for (sometimes more than compensate for) the inadequate allowance by historical cost depreciation allowances for durable capital consumption;[3] but this result was a by-product of their main purpose, which was to encourage investment expenditure, and, moreover, the result depended upon companies spending the same or an increasing amount on durable assets in future years.[4]

It is not proposed to advocate either historical cost or replacement cost accounting principles here or to debate the desirability or otherwise of using profits reckoned as revenues minus replacement costs as the measure of profits for taxation. The purpose of this article is to estimate what would have been the quantitative effects of changing the tax base to such a measure of profit in 1950 and 1951, the two post-war years when stock appreciation was greatest:[5] specifically, to estimate the size of additional company taxes that would have had to be raised in order to bring in the same revenue from the changed tax base,

9

and the changes in the incidence of company taxation, because of the reform, on companies in various United Kingdom manufacturing industries.

The article is in four sections. Section 1 sets out the assumptions that are used in the subsequent analysis. Section 2 contains estimates of the new rates of taxation that would have been levied. Section 3 sets out the conditions under which a company, after the reform, paid more tax, the same tax or less tax than previously. Estimates of the values of these conditions for 1950 and 1951 are shown. Section 4 contains an analysis of the changes in the incidence of company taxation on companies in various manufacturing industries that would have occurred in 1950 and 1951.

I

The estimates of the effects of a reform in the tax base are for 1950 and 1951 only; the greatest stock appreciation of the post-war period occurred in these years, so these are estimates of the *maximum* changes in tax rates and incidence that could have occurred. It is assumed that the reform in the tax base would not have altered the aggregate amount of revenue that the government intended to raise from company taxation; and that the companies would have distributed the same amount of dividends, despite the reform in the tax base. The first assumption, that the reform in the tax base would not have altered the aggregate amount of revenue that the government intended to raise from company taxation, is reasonable, provided that the required increase in tax rates are not too great.[6] The important decision that the government has to make is the amount of revenue that it wishes to raise from each particular source; then it can decide the appropriate rates of taxation (see Grant and Mathews, 1957, pp. 158-9). The second assumption, that companies would have distributed the same *amount* of dividends rather than the more plausible assumption that the companies would have distributed the same *proportion* of their (now lower) profits, is used because dividend restraint was in operation in these years and it is probable that companies on the whole did not distribute as much as they would have in the absence of this restraint.

Though initial allowances plus annual statutory depreciation allowances were greater than durable capital consumption, they were not greater than capital consumption and stock appreciation combined; so aggregate taxable company profits in 1950 and 1951 were considerably greater than they would have been, had there been this reform in the tax base.[7] Therefore, income and profits tax at the rates current in 1950 and 1951 would not have brought in as much revenue as before. It is assumed that the government imposed a supplementary tax on taxable profits (as reckoned after the reform) at a rate which would bring in an amount equal to the amount by which the yields of the other two taxes on the new tax base fell short of the total amount of company tax the government wished to raise. The method of estimating these rates is shown in the next section.

II

The assumptions are that the total amounts of company taxation and dividends and the rates of income and profits tax remain unchanged, but that the tax base is changed to profits reckoned as revenues less replacement costs. Therefore, the rate of supplementary tax is the difference between total taxation and the combined yields of the income and profits taxes from the new tax base, divided by that base.

The standard rate of income tax was 9s. 6d. in the pound in 1950 and 1951; the profits tax was 30 per cent in 1950 and 50 per cent in 1951 on distributed profits and 10 per cent in both years on undistributed profits.[8] Estimates of the aggregate profits of United Kingdom companies less stock appreciation and durable capital consumption in 1950 and 1951 were prepared (see Table 1.1).

Table 1.1   Aggregate taxable company profits before and after the assumed reform in the tax base, 1950 and 1951

	1950 £m	1951 £m
Gross trading profit of companies operating in the United Kingdom	2,131	2,489
Non-trading profit	363	391
TOTAL PROFITS	2,494	2,880
Less capital consumption	329	376
Less stock appreciation	440	465
'TRUE' PROFITS	1,725	2,039
Less interest payments	31	36
TAXABLE PROFITS AFTER REFORM	1,694	2,003
TAXABLE PROFITS BEFORE REFORM	1,989	2,352
(Total profits *less* annual statutory and initial depreciation allowances, and *less* interest.)		

Source: *National Income and Expenditure, 1957*, Tables 26, 47, 57, p.71.

Taxable profits, after the assumed reform, would have been 15 per cent less than the actual taxable profits of both 1950 and 1951.[9]

Gross dividends – that is, dividends before payment of income tax – are shown in Table 1.2. Using these gross dividends, the estimates of taxable profits given above, and the income and profits tax rates of 1950 and 1951, the combined yields from these two taxes following the reform were estimated (see Table 1.2). The differences between these yields and the actual tax paid (also shown in Table 1.2) are the amounts that would have had to be raised by the supplementary tax; the rates of supplementary tax are those amounts divided by company profits less capital consumption and stock appreciation. The rates of supplementary tax would have been 9 per cent in 1950 and 12 per cent in 1951 (see Table 1.2); both rates are lower than the rates of the Excess Profits Levy introduced in 1952 and 1953.[10,11]

Table 1.2 Estimates of supplementary tax, 1950–1

		1950	1951
1 Taxable profits after reform	£m	1,694	2,003
2 Gross dividends	£m	597	641
3 Yield from income tax $(1) \times 0.475$	£m	805	951
4 Yield from profits tax $(2) \times \dfrac{0.1575\,(1950)}{0.2625\,(1951)} + (1-2) \times 0.0525$	£m	152	240
5 Total yield from income and profits taxes $(3) + (4)$	£m	957	1,191
6 Total tax raised before reform	£m	1,103	1,433
7 SUPPLEMENTARY TAX	£m	146	242
8 RATE OF SUPPLEMENTARY TAX	percentage	9	12

Sources: *National Income and Expenditure, 1957*, Tables 26, 47, 57; Prais (1955, p.200).

III

In section 2 the aggregate changes in the rates of taxation made by the reform in the tax base were discussed. The purpose of this and the succeeding section of the article is to discuss the implications of the reform for tax payments by individual companies (and by the companies in particular industries).

First, individual companies. What are the formal conditions under which a company would pay more, the same or less tax than before? What conditions are most favourable to its paying less?

The conditions are deduced for two models, one assuming that the company distributes the same amount of dividends after the reform as it did before, the other assuming that it distributes the same *proportion* of a (now lower) profit.

Let Taxable profit	$= Y$
Tax	$= T$
Gross dividends (dividends before income tax)	$= G$
Undistributed profit $(Y - G)$	$= U$
Standard rate of income tax	$= S$
Rate of profits tax on distributed profit	$= P$
Rate of profits tax on undistributed profit	$= p$
Rate of supplementary tax	$= e$

Subscript $_1$ indicates before reform
Subscript $_2$ indicates after reform

First model
Assumptions: $Y_1 > Y_2, G_1 = G_2, S, P, p =$ constants.

Aim: To find the conditions under which $T_1 \gtrless T_2$

$$T_1 = S\,Y_1 + P\,G_1 + p\,U_1$$
$$T_2 = S\,Y_2 + P\,G_2 + p\,U_2 + e\,Y_2$$

$$\begin{aligned}
T_1 - T_2 &= (S\,Y_1 - S\,Y_2) + (P\,G_1 - P\,G_2) + (p\,U_1 - p\,U_2) - e\,Y_2 \\
&= S(Y_1 - Y_2) + p(U_1 - U_2) - e\,Y_2 \text{ (as } G_1 = G_2, \text{ the second} \\
&\qquad\qquad\qquad\qquad\qquad\qquad\qquad\qquad\qquad\quad \text{term cancels out)}
\end{aligned}$$

Now $U_1 = Y_1 - G_1$
and $U_2 = Y_2 - G_2 = Y_2 - G_1$ as $G_1 = G_2$
$\therefore\ U_1 - U_2 = Y_1 - G_1 - (Y_2 - G_1) = Y_1 - Y_2$
$\therefore\ T_1 - T_2 = S(Y_1 - Y_2) + p(Y_1 - Y_2) - e\,Y_2$
$\qquad\qquad\ \ = (S + p)(Y_1 - Y_2) - e\,Y_2$
i.e. $T_1 < T_2$ if $(S + p)(Y_1 - Y_2) < e\,Y_2$
$\qquad T_1 = T_2$ if $(S + p)(Y_1 - Y_2) = e\,Y_2$
$\qquad T_1 > T_2$ if $(S + p)(Y_1 - Y_2) > e\,Y_2$

The corresponding conditions for the **second model** (where $G_1 > G_2$ $= \dfrac{Y_2}{Y_1}\,G_1$) are:

$T_1 < T_2$ if $M < e\,Y_2$
$T_1 = T_2$ if $M = e\,Y_2$
$T_1 > T_2$ if $M > e\,Y_2$
$\qquad\qquad\qquad$ where $M = \left\{1 - \dfrac{Y_2}{Y_1}\right\}\{Y_1(S + p) + G_1(P - p)\}$[12]

Whether a company would pay more, the same or less taxation than before depends directly on the rates of income and profits tax, the difference between taxable profits before and after reform, and inversely upon the rate of supplementary tax and the level of taxable profits after the reform.[13]

The conditions most favourable to a company paying less tax than previously are moderate stock appreciation and increases in the prices of durable assets for the economy as a whole, combined with severe stock appreciation and increases in the prices of durable assets for the company itself. In these circumstances the difference between taxable profits before and after reform will be large, and the level of taxable profits after reform and the rate of supplementary tax will be small – that is to say, the left-hand side of the third inequality will be large, the right-hand side will be small, so that T_1 will be very much greater than T_2. Conversely, severe stock appreciation and increases in the prices of durable assets generally, combined with moderate stock appreciation and increases in the prices of durable assets (or, worse still, stock *depreciation* and price falls) for the particular company, would lead to considerably heavier tax payments than previously.

What are the sizes of the differences between taxable profits before and after the reform which at the tax rates of 1950 and 1951 would cause a company to pay the same, or more or less tax than before? And, assuming that annual statutory and initial depreciation allowances combined were equivalent to durable capital consumption, so that the difference between taxable profits can be regarded as due to stock appreciation only, what levels of stock appreciation do these differences imply for 1950 and 1951?

The answers to these questions are shown in Table 1.3. The calculations are made on the assumptions that the company distributed the same amount of dividends as previously and that the amount of tax paid before the reform was 55 per cent of taxable profits in 1950 and 61 per cent of taxable profits in 1951. These proportions are those that were in fact borne in these years by aggregate tax payments in relation to aggregate taxable company profits.

To have paid the same amount of tax after the reform as before, the difference between the taxable profits of a company before reform and after reform had to be 17 per cent in 1950 and 23 per cent in 1951 (implying stock appreciation equivalent to 17 per cent of taxable profits after reform in 1950 and 23 per cent in 1951).[14]

For all reasonable values of the difference in taxable profits (where taxable profits *after* reform are less than taxable profits before reform)

Table 1.3 Change in the tax payments, implied stock appreciation levels at the tax rates of 1950 and 1951 (all columns show percentages)

	1950			1951		
$\dfrac{Y_1-Y_2}{Y_2}$	$\dfrac{T_1-T_2}{Y_2}$	$\dfrac{T_1-T_2}{T_1}$	Stock appreciation as percentage of Y_2	$\dfrac{T_1-T_2}{Y_2}$	$\dfrac{T_1-T_2}{T_1}$	Stock appreciation as percentage of Y_2
1	2	3	4	2	3	4
−50	−35.4	−128.7	−50	−38.4	−125.9	−50
−35	−27.5	−76.8	−35	−30.5	−76.8	−35
−20	−19.6	−44.5	−20	−22.6	−46.3	−20
−10	−14.3	−28.9	−10	−17.3	−31.5	−10
−5	−11.6	−22.2	−5	−14.6	−25.2	−5
0	−9.0	−16.4	0	−12.0	−19.7	0
5	−6.4	−11.1	5	−9.4	−14.7	5
10	−3.7	−6.1	10	−6.7	−10.0	10
15	−1.1	−1.7	15	−4.1	−5.8	15
17	–	–	17	−3.0	−4.2	17
20	1.6	2.4	20	−1.4	−1.9	20
23	3.1	4.6	23	–	–	23
25	4.2	6.1	25	1.2	1.6	25
35	9.5	12.8	35	6.5	7.9	35
50	17.4	21.1	50	14.4	15.7	50

Y = taxable profits   Subscript $_1$ indicates before reform
T = tax   Subscript $_2$ indicates after reform
Column 2 calculated by letting $Y_2 = 100$, $Y_1 - Y_2 =$ the values in column 1, substituting these values in $T_1 - T_2 = (S + p)(Y_1 - 100) - e\,100$ and solving for $T_1 - T_2$.
Column 3 calculated by dividing columns 2 by $0.55\,\{100 + (Y_1 - 100)\}$ in 1950 and by $0.61\,\{100 + (Y_1 - 100)\}$ in 1951.
Column 3 shows the change in tax payments (as a percentage of actual tax payments) that would result if the differences between taxable profits were the values shown in column 1.

the changes in taxation payment are surprisingly small. A difference of 10 per cent implied an *increased* payment of 6 per cent in 1950 and 10 per cent in 1951; a difference of 25 per cent implied a *decreased* payment of 6 per cent in 1950 and 2 per cent in 1951. Even with a difference of 50 per cent (which implies a very severe amount of stock appreciation, at least double the amounts for all companies in those years), the decreases in payments would have been only 21 per cent in 1950 and 16 per cent in 1951. On the other hand, increased tax payments would have been very heavy; thus a company with no stock appreciation would have paid 16 per cent more tax in 1950 and 20 per cent more in 1951; and even a moderate amount of stock *depreciation* –

for example, 10 per cent of new taxable profits – would have led to increased tax payments of 29 per cent in 1950 and 32 per cent in 1951. Stock depreciation of 50 per cent would have more than doubled tax payments in both years.

IV

Suppose taxable profits had been reckoned on the new base in 1950 and 1951: what companies would have been favoured by the reform (would have paid less tax) and what companies would have paid more tax? An exact answer cannot be given as there are no available figures for the stock appreciation and capital consumption of companies in individual industries. But by using the techniques of the previous section, the amounts of stock appreciation implied by assuming that the companies paid the same amount of tax after the reform can be estimated.[15] An examination of these amounts in conjunction with the investment in stocks by companies in 1950 and 1951, and in the light of what is known of each industry, then shows whether they are reasonable amounts, or too large, or too small. If they are too large, the inference is that the companies concerned would have paid more tax than before as a result of the reform; if too small, that they would have paid less.

The companies examined were the quoted public companies in the following United Kingdom manufacturing industries: chemicals and allied trades, iron, steel and non-ferrous metals, shipbuilding and non-electrical engineering, electrical engineering and engineering goods, vehicles, other metal goods, cotton, wool, other textiles, clothing and footwear, food, drink, tobacco, paper and printing, and other manufacturing industries.[16] First the actual taxable profits of these companies in 1950 and 1951 were estimated;[17] next the taxable profits after the reform on which the companies would have paid the same aggregate amount of tax were estimated by dividing the actual taxable profits of 1950 by 117 and that of 1951 by 123.[18] The differences between the two estimates of taxable profits were expressed as percentages of the increases in the value of the stocks of the companies in 1950 and 1951, giving estimates of the amounts of stock appreciation that would have been necessary if the companies were to have paid the same amount of tax as previously. These estimates were examined to see if they could be considered reasonable, or too large, or too small. If too large, it was assumed that the companies in that industry would have paid more tax than previously. On this basis, the companies in each

Table 1.4 Possible and probable gainers and losers from the assumed reform in the tax base, 1950 and 1951 (quoted public companies in fifteen manufacturing industries in the United Kingdom)

Industry	1950		1951	
	Implied stock appreciation $(Y_1 - Y_2)^{(a)}$ increase in value of stocks	G = gainer Gp = probable gainer L = loser	Implied stock appreciation $(Y_1 - Y_2)^{(a)}$ increase in value of stocks	G = gainer Gp = probable gainer L = loser
	1 percentage	2	1 percentage	2
1 Chemicals and allied trades	54	L	20	G
2 Iron, steel, non-ferrous metals	73	L	118	L
3 Shipbuilding and non-electrical engineering	260	L	47	L
4 Electrical engineering and engineering goods	76	L	22	G
5 Vehicles	128	L	32	Gp
6 Other metal goods	86	L	45	L
7 Cotton	44	L	38	L
8 Wool	11	G	–	L
9 Other textiles	47	L	40	Gp
10 Clothing and footwear	37	Gp	18	G
11 Food	36	Gp	22	G
12 Drink	80	L	50	L
13 Tobacco	21	G	26	G
14 Paper and printing	70	L	33	Gp
15 Other manufacturing	23	G	16	G

(a) Y = taxable profits. Subscript $_1$ indicates before reform. Subscript $_2$ indicates after reform.

Sources: *Company Income and Finance, 1949-1953: 96th and 97th Reports of the Commissioners of Her Majesty's Inland Revenue* (years ending 31 March 1953 and 1954).

See Appendix I for the derivation of column 1.

industry were classified as probable or possible gainers or losers from the assumed reform in the tax base (see Table 1.4).

Had their taxable profits been reckoned as revenues less replacement costs in 1950, the wool, tobacco and other manufacturing companies would certainly have paid less tax and the clothing and footwear companies and food companies probably would have paid less. The chemical, iron and steel, shipbuilding, electrical engineering, vehicles, other metal goods, cotton, other textiles, drink, and paper and printing companies would have paid more tax. In 1951 the companies in the chemical, electrical engineering, clothing, food, tobacco and other manufacturing industries would certainly have paid less tax and the companies in the vehicles, other textiles and paper and printing probably would have paid less. The companies in the iron and steel, shipbuilding, other metal, cotton, wool and drink industries would have paid more.

There are three factors which could explain why the companies in ten manufacturing industries in 1950 and in six manufacturing industries in 1951 would have paid more tax in those years (would have been losers), had the reform been in operation. The first factor is that the losers may have experienced relatively less stock appreciation (as a percentage of their taxable profits before the reform) than did all companies. In these circumstances the differences between the losers' taxable profits before the reform and their taxable profits after the reform would be such that the decrease in tax because of the lower tax *base* after the reform would be less than the increase in tax because of the higher tax rates[19] after the reform – on balance the losers would have paid more tax.

The second factor is that the losers may have spent proportionately more than all companies on durable assets. In these circumstances the initial allowances received because of this expenditure would so narrow the differences between their taxable profits before and after reform that again the decrease in tax because of the lower tax base would be less than the increase in tax because of the higher tax rates. The third factor is that the secular rise in the prices of the durable assets of the losers may have been less than that of all companies. In these circumstances the differences between profits reckoned as revenues less historical costs and profits reckoned as revenues less replacement costs (*ceteris paribus*)[20] would be proportionately less than those of all companies.

The factors which could explain why the companies in five manufacturing industries in 1950 and in nine manufacturing industries in 1951 would have paid less tax (would have been gainers) are the converse of the above three. The companies in these industries may have experienced relatively greater stock appreciation (as a percentage of their taxable profits before reform) than did all companies; they may have spent relatively less on durable assets; and the secular rise in the prices of their durable assets may have been greater than the rises in the prices of the durable assets of all companies.

Some very rough tests (which are described in Appendix II) suggest that the first factor, the stock appreciation experienced by the losers and the gainers, is the most *general* explanation of why the losers would have paid more tax, and the gainers would have paid less, than previously. With rapidly expanding industries – for example, chemicals and allied trades and vehicles – the second factor, relatively greater expenditure on durable assets, is important also.

In view of the importance placed in 1950 and 1951 on the development of the basic and export industries of the United Kingdom, it is interesting to note that the tax reform would not have been favourable in 1950 to these very industries (with the exception of the textile industries). This conclusion is not so true of 1951, for in that year companies in three important industries – chemicals, electrical engineering and vehicles – would have been either probable gainers or possible gainers. However, as has been shown above, unless their stock appreciation was very severe, the decrease in their tax payments would not have been very significant. Similarly, increases in tax payments were also unlikely to have been severe, unless the companies concerned had experienced stock *depreciation* while the remainder of the economy experienced stock appreciation.[21] And if this is true of the years when stock appreciation was greatest, it is even more true of years when it was not so great. Thus a reform of the tax base to include what from the economist's viewpoint is a more logical measure of profits was unlikely in those years to have altered significantly the incidence of company taxation on the companies in different industries. In reaching this conclusion it must be remembered that the initial allowances of 1950 and 1951 had reduced by about half[22] the differences between profits reckoned as revenues less historical costs and profits reckoned as revenues less replacement costs.

Summary and conclusions

This article examines the quantitative effects of a reform to make the measure of taxable company profits the difference between revenues and replacement costs instead of the difference between revenues and historical costs. The two bases were compared for the years 1950 and 1951, the years with the greatest amounts of stock appreciation since the war. It was found that this reform would have made necessary the introduction of a 9 per cent supplementary tax in 1950, and a 12 per cent supplementary tax in 1951 if the same amount of revenue were to have been raised in those years. Whether a company would pay more tax, the same tax or less tax after the reform depended upon the difference between its taxable profits before and after the reform, the level of taxable profits after the reform, and the rates of income, profits and supplementary tax. The conditions most favourable to a company paying less tax were for it to have considerable stock appreciation and increases in the prices of its durable assets, and for the economy to have mild stock appreciation and inflation generally, so that the rate of supplementary tax would be small. To have paid the same amount of tax after the reform as before, the difference between the taxable profits of a company before and after reform had to be 17 per cent in 1950 and 23 per cent in 1951.

Had the reform been in operation in 1950 and 1951, the companies in five manufacturing industries in 1950 and in nine manufacturing industries in 1951 would have paid less tax than previously. The companies in ten manufacturing industries in 1950 and in six manufacturing industries in 1951 would have paid more tax than previously.

Three factors explain why the companies in particular manufacturing industries would have been gainers or losers in those years from the assumed reform. These factors were the stock appreciation of the companies, their expenditure on durable assets and the secular rises in the prices of their durable assets. Probably the most *general* explanation was their stock appreciation. Expenditure on durable assets was important for companies in rapidly expanding industries.

Had the reform been in operation in 1950 and 1951, many of those companies most important to the prosperity of the economy, that is, companies in the basic and export industries, would probably have been adversely affected – they would have had to pay more tax; but it is unlikely that these additional payments would have been very significant.

Whatever may have been the theoretical desirability of such a reform, its practical effects on the incidence of taxation between different industries were unlikely to have been significant in 1950 and 1951. And what is true of those years is even truer of years with milder price changes. This is not to deny that, when considered in relation to profits reckoned as revenues less replacement costs, the incidence of company taxation generally is too great, but to suggest that if this is so, *rates* of taxation are more in need of reform than the tax base itself.

Notes

* *Accounting and Business Research*, vol. 9, no. 1, January 1958, pp. 1–16.

1	1948 £m	1949 £m	1950 £m	1951 £m
Gross trading profit of companies operating in United Kingdom *plus* non-trading profit *less* annual statutory allowances for depreciation (but not initial allowances)	1,924	1,966	2,247	2,626
Gross company profits *less* stock appreciation and capital consumption	1,637	1,719	1,725	2,039

Source: *National Income and Expenditure, 1957*, Tables 26, 47, 57, p. 71.

2 For a discussion of the first subject and a bibliography of recent writings on it, see Prest (1950). For a discussion of the reform in the methods of estimating company profits for taxation purposes, see Wiles (1951). For a discussion of the treatment of depreciation by the taxation authorities of various countries, see Davidson (1957).

3		1948	1949	1950	1951	1952	1953	1954	1955	1956
Annual statutory allowances for depreciation[a]	£m	208	220	247	254	287	303	357	435	486
Initial allowances[b]	£m	95	185	227	238	111	104	156[d]	181[d]	208[d]
Total	£m	303	405	474	492	398	407	513	616	694
Capital consumption[c]	£m	295	297	329	376	416	455	499	567	615

[a,b] *National Income and Expenditure, 1957*, p. 71
[c] *National Income and Expenditure, 1957*, Table 57.
[d] Includes investment allowances.

While capital consumption was greater than the statutory allowances for depreciation every year, it was less than these allowances *plus* initial allowances every year except 1952 and 1953 – in the economy at large, but not necessarily for every company.

4 No doubt the clamour by business men and financial journalists for some allowance in the estimates of taxable profits for the war and post-war rises in the prices of durable assets did influence the government decision to grant initial allowances and, in particular, to increase them to 40 per cent in 1949.

5	1950	1951
Stock appreciation (£ million)	440	465
As percentage of company profits *less* stock appreciation and capital consumption	26	23

Source: *National Income and Expenditure, 1957*, Tables 26, 47.

6 It is shown below that the increase in rates that would have been needed was relatively small.

7	1950 £m	1951 £m
1 Stock appreciation and durable capital consumption	769	841
2 Annual statutory allowances and initial allowances	474	492
3 Difference	295	349
4 Taxable profit before reform [a]	1,989	2,352
5 Taxable profit after reform [b]	1,694	2,003
6 Difference	295	349

[a] Company profits *less* statutory allowances and initial allowances and interest payments.
[b] Company profits *less* stock appreciation, capital consumption and interest payments.

Source: *National Income and Expenditure, 1957*, Tables 26, 47, 57, p. 71.

8 Profits tax was a deductible expense for tax purposes in 1950 and 1951. A device suggested by Dr S. J. Prais (see S. J. Prais, 'The Measure of Income for Shareholders and for Taxation', *Accounting Research*, vol. 6, no. 3, 1955, pp. 187–201, particularly Appendix B, p. 200) was used to avoid making this deduction in the calculations of the income and profits tax yields. It consists of charging profits tax on taxable profit at lower rates than the published ones, rates which are equivalent to charging the published rates on taxable profits *less* profits tax.

9 It will be seen that the initial allowances granted in 1950 and 1951 had, in conjunction with the annual statutory depreciation allowances, already gone a long way towards closing the gap between profits reckoned as revenues less historical costs and taxable profits as reckoned after the assumed reform. Had there been no initial allowances in these years, taxable profits after the reform would have been 22 per cent less in 1950 and 21 per cent less in 1951. (These figures were calculated from the ratio $\frac{Y_1 - Y_2}{Y_1}$, where Y_1 is taxable profits before reform plus initial allowances less the *difference* between the statutory depreciation allowances that would have been received had no initial allowances been given, and actual statutory depreciation allowances; Y_2 is taxable profits after reform.)

10 The rates of the Excess Profits Levy were 15 per cent on taxable profits or 30 per cent on excess profits, whichever was lower.

11 Had the companies distributed the same *proportion* of their (lower) profits, the rates of supplementary tax would have been 10 per cent in 1950 and 14 per cent in 1951.

12 These are not the *only* conditions, but those most relevant for an economist. The only general conditions are $T_1 \leftrightharpoons T_2$ if $(S + p)(Y_1 - Y_2) - e\, Y_2 \leftrightharpoons 0$ (first model) and if $M - e\, Y_2 \leftrightharpoons 0$ (second model). These can be expressed as different inequalities from those shown in the text.

13 In the second model, the amount of gross dividends and the ratio of taxable profits after reform to taxable profits before reform are relevant also. Only the first model will be used in this article as its assumption that $G_1 = G_2$ is the appropriate one for 1950 and 1951. The first model is a special case of the (more general) second model.

14 That is to say, it is assumed that the annual statutory and initial depreciation allowances granted the company in 1950 and 1951 were equal to its durable capital consumption. As was shown above, this assumption is unlikely to be true unless the company spent very little on durable assets in those years. Thus the differences between taxable profits underestimate the amount of stock appreciation implied by the assumption that the company paid the same amount of taxation as previously.

15 It was pointed out in note 14 that by this assumption the actual amount of stock appreciation is probably underestimated.

16 The information on these companies is taken from *Company Income and Finance, 1949–53*, National Institute of Economic and Social Research, London, 1957.

17 Actual taxable profits were taken as gross trading profits before depreciation allowances by the companies, plus income from other sources, less interest on long-term loan capital and depreciation allowances, including initial allowances, granted by the Board of Inland Revenue. The first three figures are given in *Company Income and Finance, 1949–53*. The last figure was estimated as follows. The reports of the Board of Inland Revenue gave the ratios of depreciation allowances to gross trading profits for each industry and it was assumed that these ratios were the same for all the companies of that industry. Depreciation allowances granted by the Board of Inland Revenue to the companies were estimated by multiplying their gross trading profit by these proportions. The figures for trading profits in the reports of the Board were exclusive of profits tax, while those of the companies included profits tax. It was possible to estimate the amounts of profits tax for the industries from the ratios of profits tax to turnover given for each industry in the appendices to the reports; the ratios of depreciation allowances to trading profits were adjusted for these amounts of profits tax.

18 As shown above, to have paid the same amount of tax after reform, the difference between the taxable profits of companies before reform and after reform had to be 17 per cent in 1950 and 23 per cent in 1951.

19 The imposition of a supplementary tax together with unchanged rates of income and profits tax is equivalent to a higher tax rate.

20 The other things which have to be equal include the age structure and expected lifetimes of the durable assets, and the profitability of the losers and all companies. (See Appendix II.)

21 Thus the wool companies would have paid considerably more taxation in 1951, for raw wool prices tumbled in that year, when stock appreciation was greatest for the economy generally.

22

	1950 £ million	1951 £ million
Difference between taxable profits and taxable profits after reform	239	249
Difference between taxable profits, had no initial allowances been given, and taxable profits after reform	481	527

Appendix I

Industry	1950				1951			
	Y_1	Y_2 $(=Y_1)$ $\overline{117}$	S	$\dfrac{Y_1-Y_2}{S}$	Y_1	Y_2 $(=Y_1)$ $\overline{123}$	S	$\dfrac{Y_1-Y_2}{S}$
	£m	£m	£m	Percentage	£m	£m	£m	Percentage
Chemicals	97	83	26	54	119	97	106	20
Iron and steel	73	62	15	73	107	85	17	118
Shipbuilding	91	78	5	260	111	90	46	47
Electrical engin.	67	57	13	76	85	69	74	22
Vehicles	65	56	7	128	74	60	44	32
Other metals	39	33	7	86	55	45	22	45
Cotton	49	42	16	44	61	50	29	38
Wool	23	20	26	11	16	13	–	–
Other textiles	64	55	19	47	75	61	35	40
Clothing	18	15	8	37	16	13	17	18
Food	37	32	14	36	43	35	37	22
Drink	57	49	10	80	66	54	24	50
Tobacco	32	27	24	21	36	29	27	26
Paper	49	42	10	70	83	67	48	33
Other	40	34	26	23	44	36	51	16

Y_1 = actual taxable profits;
Y_2 = taxable profits after reform on which companies would have paid the same amount of tax, and
S = increase in the value of stocks.

Appendix II

The first factor was the stock appreciation experienced by the companies. A rough measure of whether the companies in a particular industry experienced more or less stock appreciation (as a percentage of their taxable profits before reform) than did all companies is a comparison of the ratios:

$$\frac{S_1/Y_1}{S_0/Y_0} \quad \text{and} \quad \frac{S_1'/Y_1'}{S_0'/Y_0'}$$

where S = the increase in the value of stocks;
  Y = taxable profits before reform;
  Subscripts $_{0,\,1}$ indicate years $_{0,\,1}$;
  S, Y without primes indicate the companies concerned; and
  S, Y with primes indicate all companies.

If $\frac{S_1/Y_1}{S_0/Y_0} \lessgtr \frac{S_1'/Y_1'}{S_0'/Y_0'}$

the stock appreciation experienced by the companies concerned probably was less than, equal to or greater than that for all companies. These ratios were calculated for the companies in the fifteen manufacturing industries and compared with the corresponding ratio for all companies. If the companies in a particular industry were losers/gainers and their ratio was less/greater than that of all companies, the first factor was regarded as part of the explanation of why they were losers/gainers.

The second factor was the expenditure on durable assets. A rough measure of whether the companies in a particular industry spent relatively more or less than all companies on durable assets is a comparison of the ratios:

$$\frac{i}{I} \text{ and } \frac{y}{Y}$$

where i = expenditure on durable assets;
   y = profits reckoned as revenues less historical costs;
  and small letters indicate the companies concerned; and
    capital letters indicate all companies.

If $\frac{i}{I} \lessgtr \frac{y}{Y}$, the companies probably spent more than, the same amount, or less than all companies on durable assets. These ratios were calculated for the companies in the fifteen industries and for all companies. If the companies in a particular industry were losers/gainers and i/I was $>y/Y$ (losers), $<y/Y$ (gainers), the second factor was regarded as part of the explanation of why they were losers/gainers.

The third factor was the secular rise in the prices of durable assets. This is the hardest factor to isolate from the available statistics because its effect can be outweighed by other factors. For example, if in the past the stock of durable assets of a company has grown faster than that of all companies, *ceteris paribus* the average age of its assets will be less than that of all companies. If there has been a secular rise in the prices of durable assets the *increase* in the replacement value of the average asset in its stock will be less than the increase for all companies. But its annual depreciation allowances on historical costs will be relatively greater than those of all companies. If replacement cost depreciation is measured by multiplying the annual historical cost depreciation allowances by the ratio $\frac{p_c}{p_a}$, where p is the price index of durable assets, and subscripts c, a indicate the current year and the year of acquisition respectively, then the higher multiplicand may outweigh the effect of a lower multiplier – that is, the third factor may be an explanation but its effect can be outweighed. Only if the rate of growth and the expected lifetimes of the durable assets of the company and the profitability of the company are the same as those of all companies, can the effect of a lower secular rise in the prices of durable assets definitely be isolated. For then both the multiplicand and the multiplier will be less: the multiplicand, because the historical costs of the assets and therefore the annual historical cost depreciation allowances are less; the multiplier, because the rise in prices of durable assets and therefore the ratio $\frac{p_c}{p_a}$ are less.

A very rough measure of whether the secular rises in the prices of durable assets of the companies in a particular industry were less than or greater than those of all companies is a comparison of the ratios:

d/p and D/P

where d = historical cost depreciation allowances;
$\qquad\quad p$ = profits reckoned as revenues less historical costs;
and   small letters indicate the companies concerned; and
$\qquad\quad$ capital letters indicate all companies.

If the companies in a particular industry were losers/gainers and $d/p \leqslant D/P$ (losers) $\geqslant D/P$ (gainers), the third factor was regarded as part of the explanation of why they were losers/gainers. If $d/p > D/P$ (losers) or $< D/P$ (gainers), the third factor might or might not have been part of the explanation.

1950	Losers 1st factor	2nd factor	3rd factor	1950	Gainers 1st factor	2nd factor	3rd factor
Chemicals	yes	yes	*indef.	Wool	yes	yes	indef.
Iron and steel	yes	yes	indef.	Clothing	no	yes	indef.
Shipbuilding	yes	no	indef.	Food	no	no	yes
Elect. engin.	no	no	indef.	Tobacco	yes	yes	indef.
Vehicles	yes	yes	indef.	Other	yes	indef.	yes
Other metals	yes	yes	yes				
Cotton	yes	no	yes				
Other textiles	yes	no	indef.				
Drink	yes	yes	yes				
Paper	no	no	yes				

1951				1951			
Iron and steel	yes	yes	indef.	Chemicals	yes	no	indef.
Shipbuilding	no	yes	indef.	Elect. engin.	yes	indef.	yes
Other metals	no	indef.	yes	Vehicles	yes	no	yes
Cotton	yes	no	yes	Other textiles	no	yes	indef.
Wool	yes	indef.	yes	Clothing	yes	yes	indef.
Drink	no	yes	yes	Food	yes	no	indef.
				Tobacco	no	yes	indef.
				Paper	yes	yes	indef.
				Others	yes	indef.	yes

* indef. = indefinite.
This factor may or may not have been part of the explanation.

STANDARDS (RATIOS, ETC.) FOR ALL COMPANIES

		1950	1951
$\dfrac{S_1'/Y_1'}{S_0'/Y_0'}$		2.6	1.8
I	£m	628	631
Y	£m	2020	2388
D/P	percentage	12	11

Sources: *National Income and Expenditure, 1957*, Tables 26, 47, 57, p. 71; *Company Income and Finance, 1949–53*, pp. 26–54.

2 Pricing policies and inflation*

1. Professor Mathews and Mr Grant argue that historical-cost accounting and pricing are more expansionary than current-cost accounting and replacement-cost pricing in times of inflation. 'With historical-cost accounting and pricing, aggregate demand in real terms will be higher than with current-cost accounting and replacement-cost pricing, to the extent that real consumption is greater because of lower prices' (Mathews and Grant, 1958, p. 163). That is, if prices are cost-determined and there is excess demand in the economy, queues for goods are likely to be greater, at any moment of time, with historical-cost pricing and accounting than with current-cost accounting and replacement-cost pricing. Similarly, if prices are rising and there is unemployment, it is likely to be less with historical-cost pricing. With historical-cost pricing, the rate of change of prices is determined by the changes in costs of the preceding stock-turnover period; with replacement-cost pricing it is determined by the changes in costs of the current stock-turnover period. Therefore, if costs are rising, price levels will be higher, at any moment of time, with replacement-cost pricing. The purpose of this note is to derive these results from a combination of the models of profits and income under alternative pricing policies of *Inflation and Company Finance* and the model of *The Accumulation of Capital* (Mathews and Grant, 1958, pp. 165-6; Robinson, 1956, pp. 63-71).

2. Consider two economies which are alike in every respect except that the firms in one use historical-cost accounting and pricing and in the other, current-cost accounting and replacement-cost pricing. In the historical-cost economy, profits are regarded as the differences between revenues and historical costs and prices are set by adding a constant percentage mark-up to historical (F.I.F.O.) costs. In the other economy, profits are regarded as the differences between revenues and current costs, and prices are set by 'marking up' replacement (L.I.F.O.) costs (Mathews and Grant, 1958, pp. 150-1. The mark-up could be a constant absolute margin, also).

28

3. Assume that the economies produce one type of capital good and consumption good only; that all raw materials are imported; and that there are fixed coefficients of production.[1] Wage earners consume all their income. A fixed proportion of profits (revenues less historical costs in the historical-cost economy and revenues less current-costs in the current-cost economy) is distributed to rentiers, who consume a fixed amount in real terms. For the moment, assume there is some unemployment in the economies.

4. The profits of the firms in the two economies will be approximately equal (op. cit., p. 163), and if the investment plans of the firms are related to the *prevailing concepts* of profits in their respective economies, investment plans are likely to be the same in both economies. For the moment, assume that real gross fixed capital formation each stock-turnover period is constant and the same in both economies.

5. There is perfect competition in the capital and labour markets of the economies, so that money wage rates and profit margins are the same in the capital goods and consumption goods sectors. In the historical-cost economy, changes in raw materials and wage costs are reflected in the prices of capital and consumption goods *only after a lag of one stock-turnover period*; in the current-cost economy they are reflected immediately.

6. Suppose raw material prices and money wages have been steady for many periods, so that prices, employment, monetary and real expenditures are the same in both economies. At the beginning of a particular stock-turnover period, raw material prices increase and workers succeed in raising money wages by the same amounts in both economies.[2]

7. Real gross fixed capital formation will remain the same as will employment in the capital goods sectors. The price of consumption goods will not change in the historical-cost economy but will rise in the current-cost economy, where the raw materials and wages cost components of prices and the absolute value of the mark-up have risen.[3] Whether the real wage rises in the current-cost economy (it obviously rises in the historical-cost economy) depends upon whether the relative rise in the money wage rate is greater than the rise in the price of consumption goods.[4]

8. Total employment in each economy is equal to the number of men employed in the capital goods sector, plus the number of men necessary to produce consumption goods for the workers in the capital goods sector, rentiers and themselves. That is, employment in the consumption goods sector depends upon the productivity of workers in this sector, the real wage and rentiers' consumption.[5] As the real wage of the

historical-cost economy has risen more than the real wage of the current-cost economy, and as employment in the capital goods sectors and rentiers' consumption have not changed in either economy, employment in the consumption goods sector and aggregate real consumption expenditure must be greater in the historical-cost economy in the stock-turnover period in which the rises in costs occur. Total employment and real national output will be greater, also. Should the rises in costs continue in succeeding periods, aggregate real consumption, total employment and real gross national output will always be greater, at any moment of time, in the historical-cost economy. If there is excess demand in the two economies, queues for goods will always be greater, at any moment of time, in the historical-cost economy. In the historical-cost economy, the rate of change of prices in any stock-turnover period is determined by the changes in costs of the preceding stock-turnover period and in the current-cost economy, by the changes in costs of the current stock-turnover period.[6] Therefore, if costs are rising, the level of prices must be higher at any moment of time, in the current-cost economy.

9. If investment in the economies is related to changes in the level of consumption expenditure, real gross fixed capital formation will tend to be less, at any moment of time, in the current-cost economy. Also, it is only when the physical turnovers of firms are the same in both economies that the profits of firms in the two economies are approximately equal (op. cit., pp. 165–6). Once costs and prices start to rise, aggregate physical turnovers will be less in the current-cost economy and, therefore, its aggregate profits will be less than those of the historical-cost economy. If the prevailing concepts of profits affect investment demands in the two economies, aggregate fixed capital formation again is likely to be less in the current-cost economy. Finally, the prices of consumption goods in this model do not contain any depreciation components, that is to say, they are assumed to be unaffected by the prices of capital goods. The inclusion of depreciation, at *historical cost* in the historical-cost economy and at *current cost* in the current-cost economy, in these prices would further increase the differences, at any moment of time, between the prices of consumption goods and the real consumption expenditures of the two economies. These are further reasons for expecting that current-cost accounting and replacement-cost pricing will be less expansionary than historical-cost accounting and pricing. However, the conclusions of this note do not apply when prices are demand-determined.

Notes

* *Economic Record*, vol. 35, no. 70, April 1959, pp. 133–6. The author is indebted to the members of the Departments of Economics and Commerce of the University of Adelaide for reading and commenting upon a draft of this note.

1 This rules out any substitution between inputs when their relative prices change, in order to bring out the effects of aggregate demand on the employment of inputs.

2 How they are able to do this is not relevant to the present argument. It is assumed that they are able to do so, in order to analyse the effects on prices and employment of internal as well as external, rises in costs.

3 The prices of the consumption goods in the economies in the period in which the rises in cost occur can be written as

$$p_1{}^h = (1 + v) \left(a r_0 + \frac{m_0}{x} \right) \quad \text{(historical-cost economy)}$$

and $p_1{}^c = (1 + v) \left(a r_1 + \frac{m_1}{x} \right)$ (current-cost economy)

where p = price, $v\%$ = profit margin, r = price of raw materials per unit, m = money wage, a = raw material input per unit of output, x = output of consumption goods per man, and subscripts 0, 1 refer to stock-turnover periods. Obviously, $p_1{}^c > p_1{}^h$.

4 It can be shown that real wages will rise if the relative increase in the money wage rate is greater than the relative increase in raw material prices.

5 These conditions can be written as

$$N = N^i + N^{ii}; N^i = k, N^{ii} = \frac{N^i w}{x - w} + \frac{R}{x - w}$$

and $w = \dfrac{m}{p}$

where $N \doteq$ employment, k = a constant, w = the real wage, R = rentiers' consumption, x = output of consumption goods per man, m = money wage, p = price of consumption goods, and primes i,ii refer to the capital goods and consumption goods sectors respectively.

6 The rate of change of prices in stock-turnover period 2 can be written as

$$\frac{p_2{}^h - p_1{}^h}{p_1{}^h} = \frac{a(r_1 - r_0) + \frac{1}{x}(m_1 - m_0)}{a r_0 + \frac{m_0}{x}} \quad \text{(historical-cost economy)}$$

and $\dfrac{p_2{}^c - p_1{}^c}{p_1{}^c} = \dfrac{a(r_2 - r_1) + \frac{1}{x}(m_2 - m_1)}{a r_1 + \frac{m_1}{x}}$ (current-cost economy)

where p = price, a = raw material input per unit of output, x = output per man, r = price of raw materials per unit and m = money wage.

If the relative increases in raw material costs and money wages become greater each succeeding stock-turnover period, the rate of increase of prices will be greater in the current-cost economy than in the historical-cost economy. If the relative increases in costs remain the same, prices will increase at the same rate in both economies (after the first stock-turnover period).

3 Pricing policies and earning rates*

1. The purpose of this note is to show that in a period of rising costs, historical-cost pricing policies mean lower real earning rates than those existing when costs were constant and those which would be obtained with replacement-cost pricing, whether physical sales are constant or rising; to argue that the real earning rates of certain United Kingdom companies[1] fell in the years of the period 1949-53 when costs were rising, even though there is some evidence that the percentage mark-ups on costs were lengthened over the same period, so that apparent earning rates were maintained or increased; and that historical-cost pricing policies could explain these falls. The apparent earning rate is defined as the ratio of accounting profit to the historical cost value of funds employed, that is, the historical cost value of net assets. The real earning rate is defined as the ratio of current income[2] to the current value of funds employed, that is, net assets valued at current replacement prices. If production and investment decisions are based on apparent earning rates, low real earning rates could lead in the long run to misallocation of resources, and distributions based on accounting profit could lead to a deterioration in the financial structures of the companies concerned.[3]

2. There are three pricing policies relevant to the discussion – replacement-cost pricing, F.I.F.O.-cost pricing and average-cost pricing. As a first approximation replacement-cost pricing is pricing by adding a constant percentage margin to costs, including stocks valued by the L.I.F.O. method, which are regarded as approximations to current replacement costs. F.I.F.O.-cost pricing is the process of marking-up costs, including stocks valued by the F.I.F.O. method, and average-cost pricing is the process of marking-up costs, including stocks regarded as coming from a common pool. The latter two methods are historical-cost pricing policies; all are cost-determined pricing policies. The main empirical study in the United Kingdom covering the period 1949-53 suggests that the pricing policies of manufacturing companies were mainly cost-determined and that the relevant costs were either F.I.F.O.

or average costs, that is, historical costs. (See Dow, 1956, especially pp. 252, 263, 277–81.)[4] The effects of variations in the mark-up, due to changes in demand conditions, are examined later in the note. For the moment it will be assumed that prices are cost-determined and that the percentage mark-up is constant. As F.I.F.O. and average-cost pricing are the most general methods of stock valuation used in the United Kingdom,[5] and if prices are cost-determined, it seems a reasonable inference that most manufacturing companies would use historical-cost pricing policies. If they do, when costs start to rise, real earning rates fall.

3. Consider an economy which uses historical-cost pricing and in which physical sales each stock-turnover period are constant. Suppose also that the purchases of stocks for sale are the only costs of the firms in this economy. If the prices of these stocks rise at a constant percentage rate, real earning rates (in this case, current incomes as proportions of the current values of funds employed in stocks) will fall in the stock-turnover period following the start of the rise in costs and then remain constant at this lower level. If costs rise at an increasing percentage rate, real earning rates will fall continuously. If costs rise at a decreasing percentage rate, real earning rates will be *less* than apparent earning rates, but will themselves rise each stock-turnover period. Apparent earning rates (in this case, accounting profits as proportions of the historical-cost values of funds employed in stocks) will follow the same patterns as those of real earning rates, that is to say, they will fall to a lower level and then remain constant if costs rise at a constant percentage rate; they will fall continuously if costs rise at an increasing percentage rate. However, the apparent earning rate of any period always will be greater than the real earning rate of the same period.[6]

4. If physical sales as well as costs rise, these results still hold. When costs are rising and F.I.F.O.-cost pricing is used, real earning rates can be maintained only if physical sales actually *fall*. If average-cost pricing is used, the falls in real earning rates will not be as great as with F.I.F.O.-cost pricing, but they will still occur. However, if replacement-cost pricing is used and if physical sales are constant each stock-turnover period, real earning rates will be maintained, despite the rises in costs. If physical sales are increasing, real earning rates will fall, but only slightly.[7]

5. Obviously increased mark-ups (even if on F.I.F.O. or average costs) *could* prevent real earning rates falling. The apparent and real earning rates of the manufacturing, chemical and wool companies,[8] estimates of the mark-ups used over this period and of stock appreciation, are shown

in Table 3.1. The apparent earning rates are the accounting profits before depreciation of the companies, divided by the historical-cost values of funds employed in stocks; the real earning rates are their current incomes, also before depreciation, divided by the current values of funds employed in stocks.[9] These ratios approximate (very roughly) to the apparent and real earning rates of the models in paragraphs 3 and 4 and in the Mathematical Appendix. In effect, they are average values of the apparent and real earning rates on stocks for the stock-turnover periods of the years concerned.[10] The estimates of the mark-ups are the annual gross trading profits of *all* companies in the industries concerned, divided by their annual costs.[11] These are annual averages of the mark-ups for the stock-turnover periods of the years concerned. As these figures include figures for non-quoted public companies, they are approximate estimates only of the mark-ups used by the three groups of quoted public companies.

6. If the rates of change of the historical costs of inputs other than purchases differ from those of purchases, accounting profit will reflect these differences. (Further, to the extent that firms do not base their prices on direct costs, these inputs would include factory overheads.) The relationship between the apparent earning rates of stocks shown in Table 3.1, then, will differ from the relationship which would be obtained if purchases were the only costs and mark-ups were applied to them alone. (Clearly, the *absolute* sizes of the two sets of apparent earning rates will always differ.) Similarly, the relationship between the real earning rates shown in Table 3.1 also could differ from that which would be obtained if purchases were the only costs. However, provided that all costs increase, the direction of the changes in earning rates will not be affected.

7. Apparent earning rates on stocks generally rose in the years with greatest stock appreciation, when real earning rates fell. The changes in the mark-ups were moderate only and mark-ups were not always increased in the relevant years. Provided that the increased mark-up was greater than $\frac{(2 + r_i)(2 + g_{i+1})}{4}$. V_O, (F.I.F.O.-cost pricing), and $\frac{2 + g_{i+1}}{2}$. V_O, (average-cost pricing), where r is the rate of increase of costs, g is the rate of increase of physical sales, i is the relevant stock-turnover period and V_O is the original mark-up, the apparent earning rate on stocks of firms using either form of historical-cost pricing would increase. These results could explain the movements in the apparent earning rates in the relevant years. The rate of increase of physical out-

Table 3.1   Apparent and real earning rates on stocks, estimated mark-ups and stock appreciation, 1949-53 (all quoted public companies in the United Kingdom manufacturing, chemical and woollen and worsted industries)

		1949	1950	1951	1952	1953
Manufacturing companies						
Apparent earning rate on stocks [a]	%	49.5	55.8	55.2	*	*
Real earning rate on stocks [b]	%	44.5	32.3	43.0	*	*
Mark-up [c]	%	11.2	12.5	12.7	*	*
Stock appreciation [d]	£m	80	416	216	*	*
Chemical companies						
Apparent earning rate on stocks [a]	%	48.4	58.1	55.0	(39.2)*	52.3
Real earning rate on stocks [b]	%	47.0	48.3	39.0	(34.2)*	49.9
Mark-up [c]	%	10.6	13.6	12.9	(11.1)*	14.4
Stock appreciation [d]	£m	4.0	21.0	45.1	(15.2)*	6.8
Wool companies						
Apparent earning rate on stocks [a]	%	43.3	43.3	(24.8)*	(22.9)*	34.2
Real earning rate on stocks [b]	%	28.9	−25.4	(52.9)*	(35.5)*	26.1
Mark-up [c]	%	12.7	13.5	(8.1)*	(10.4)*	8.8
Stock appreciation	£m	5.9	39.2	(−28.1)*	(−6.7)*	4.4

* Years with negative stock appreciation or recession when the above models do not apply.

[a] Accounting profit before depreciation as per cent of the simple average of the balance sheet values of opening and closing stocks.

[b] Current income before depreciation as per cent of the simple average of opening and closing stocks valued in average prices.

[c] $\dfrac{G/T}{100 - G/T}\%$, where G = Gross trading profit, T = Turnover.

[d] Change in value of stocks less estimated stock accumulation.

Source: *Company Income and Finance 1949-53*, pp. 22, 26, 40. Dow (1956), Table X, p. 280; 95th-99th *Reports of the Commissioners of Inland Revenue.*

put in manufacturing industry each stock-turnover period was relatively modest and levelled off towards the end of 1951. The increase in the mark-ups between 1949 and 1950 could have increased apparent earning rates even though output and physical sales were increasing. Similarly, the nearly constant mark-ups in 1950 and 1951 could have meant a fall in the apparent earning rates. Similar reasoning could explain the rise in the apparent earning rate of chemical companies in 1950. The increase in the mark-up of the wool companies coincided with the boom in their activity, so that their apparent earning rates could have remained unchanged.

8. The cells in Table 3.2 contain the values of the new mark-ups which with constant physical sales and with given original mark-ups and increases in costs, would keep real earning rates constant.[12] It should be remembered that depreciation allowances have to be met out of these increased mark-ups on costs; even if these mark-ups were great enough to cover increases in material costs, increases in capital consumption valued at current replacement cost still could cause falls in real earning rates defined as the ratios of current incomes to current values of *total* funds employed.

Table 3.2 Values of mark-ups needed to keep real earning rates constant, for given original mark-ups and rates of increase in costs

$Vo =$	0.05 F.I.F.O.-C.P.	0.10 F.I.F.O.-C.P.	A.C.P.	0.15 F.I.F.O.-C.P.	A.C.P.	0.20 F.I.F.O.-C.P.	0.25 F.I.F.O.-C.P.
r_1							
0.01	0.061	0.111	0.110	0.162	0.161	0.212	0.263
0.02	0.071	0.122	0.121	0.173	0.171	0.224	0.275
0.03	0.082	0.133	0.131	0.185	0.181	0.236	0.288
0.05	0.103	0.155	0.150	0.208	0.201	0.260	0.313
0.10	0.155	0.210	0.196	0.265	0.248	0.320	0.338

F.I.F.O.-C.P. : F.I.F.O. – cost pricing; A.C.P.: average – cost pricing.
  Values calculated from

$$Vi = Vo\,(1 + r) + r\,(\text{F.I.F.O.-C.P.})$$

$$Vi = \frac{2Vo\,(1 + r)^2 + r\,(2 + r)}{(2 + r)\,(1 + r)} \qquad \text{(A.C.P.)}$$

where Vi = new mark-up, Vo = original mark-up, r = rate of increase of costs, and i is the relevant stock-turnover period. (See Mathematical Appendix.)

9. The rate of increase of the prices of stocks of the manufacturing companies in 1950 averaged 4–5 per cent each stock-turnover period; the corresponding figures for the chemical companies in 1951 and the wool companies in 1950 were 2–3 per cent and 20–30 per cent respectively.[13] The values of the new mark-ups in Table 3.2 corresponding to increases in costs of this order suggest that the actual changes in mark-ups which occurred in these years were not great enough to offset the fall in real earning rates which these increases in costs otherwise would imply.

10. The simple models above and in the Mathematical Appendix ignore wage costs and the fact that funds are invested in fixed assets and

working capital other than stocks. Wage costs may rise less fast than material costs, and the prices of fixed assets and the value of working capital other than stocks may not rise as fast as the prices of stocks. When physical sales are increasing, there may be economies in the use of fixed assets and other working capital, so that the current values of funds employed in these assets may not rise as fast as the current values of funds employed in stocks. Finally, the physical level of stocks may not increase at the same rate as the increase in physical sales. For these reasons, the current values of funds employed may not increase as rapidly as is implied in the simple models above; the falls in real earning rates then would be less. Nevertheless, given the approximations involved in the estimates of the earning rates and mark-ups in Table 3.1 above, historical-cost pricing policies could explain the falls in real earning rates, even if mark-ups were varied. The analysis also shows that firms could maintain their real earning rates by adopting replacement-cost pricing. Furthermore, provided that the mark-ups used by firms in different industries did not contain large (or differential) monopoly elements but were competitively determined and represented the normal profits of each industry, prices generally would reflect current opportunity costs. Purchasers then could choose between different commodities on the basis of a comparison of opportunity costs. This comparison cannot be made when historical-cost pricing is used and it is for this reason that historical-cost pricing leads in the long run to mis-allocation of resources.

Notes

Economic Record, vol. 37, no. 78, June 1961, pp. 217–24. The author is indebted to the members of the Departments of Economics and Commerce, University of Adelaide, for their comments on a draft of this note, and to Mr R. D. Terrell for help with the Mathematical Appendix.

1 The companies are the quoted public companies included in Groups 1–16 of Table B, pp. 22–3 of *Company Income and Finance, 1949–53*, referred to below as the manufacturing companies, and the quoted public companies in Groups 2 (Chemicals) and 9 (Wool), pp. 26–7 and pp. 40–1 of the same publication, referred to below as the chemical and wool companies, respectively.

2 Current income is accounting profit less stock appreciation and a depreciation adjustment which is equal to the difference between depreciation allowances valued at current replacement costs and historical cost depreciation.

3 The historical-cost pricing hypothesis was used originally by Professors Mathews and Grant to explain the low real earning rates of Australian companies over the period of the post-war inflation; see Grant and Mathews (1957; 1958, especially chapter X). In this note, the hypothesis is generalised in order to include the cases of changing physical sales and changing percentage mark-ups.

4 Parkinson has suggested that over the period 1950–2, 'the pricing policies of producers fell somewhere between the historical and current cost method.' (See Parkinson, 1955, p. 181.)

5 See Central Statistical Office, *National Income Statistics: Sources and Methods*, 1956, p. 310.

6 These results and those of paragraphs 4–8 are established in the Mathematical Appendix.

7 The magnitude of these falls and whether they continue or not, depend upon the rates of increase of physical sales each stock-turnover period. For example, with a mark-up of 15 per cent and with physical sales increasing at a constant percentage rate of 10 per cent each stock-turnover period, the real earning rate would be over 14 per cent, whatever the rate of increase of costs.

8 See note 1 above.

9 The historical cost value of funds employed in stocks is the simple average of the balance sheet values of opening and closing stocks each year. The corresponding current value is the simple average of opening and closing stocks expressed in the average prices of the years concerned. The estimates of stock appreciation used to derive the estimates of current income (which are shown in Table 3.1) were calculated as follows. The opening and closing stocks of the companies were divided into three categories – raw materials and fuel, work-in-progress and finished products. Indexes of the prices of each category were prepared, and the opening and closing values of each category were valued in the average prices of the years concerned. The difference between these was stock accumulation, and stock appreciation was the change in the value of each category less stock accumulation. The sources for these calculations were the indexes of wholesale prices (published in the United Kingdom *Board of Trade Journal, The United Kingdom Census of Production for 1951* and *Company Income and Finance, 1949–53*).

10 But see paragraph 6 below. Ideally, the apparent earning rates should be accounting profit after depreciation divided by the historical cost values of net assets, and the real earning rates should be current income net of capital consumption valued at current replacement cost divided by net assets valued in current prices. Because of the difficulties of estimating capital consumption so valued and fixed assets in current prices, and because the analysis above is in terms of simple models which assume investment of funds in stocks only, the latter estimates are not shown here. For what they are worth, they do show the same pattern as those in Table 3.1.

11 The mark-ups of the manufacturing companies are from Dow (1956), Table X, p. 280; those of the chemical and wool companies are from the relevant appendices in 95th–99th *Reports of the United Kingdom Commissioners of Inland Revenue*. These sources show figures of gross trading profits as percentages of turnover. The order of magnitude of the mark-ups used can be obtained by expressing these ratios as proportions of costs, that is, turnovers net of gross trading profits. These estimates contain a downward bias. The figures of costs in the denominator include selling and non-factory administrative costs which, in practice, are excluded from the figures of costs to which mark-ups are applied.

12 If physical sales are increasing, these values should be multiplied by $\dfrac{2 + g_{i+1}}{2}$ where g is the rate of increase of physical sales and i is the relevant stock-turnover period.

13 These figures are obtained from the indexes of prices used in the calculations of stock appreciation.

Mathematical Appendix

1. Let A = apparent earning rate,
   R = real earning rate,
   t = physical sales each stock-turnover period,
   g = rate of increase of physical sales,
   c = costs,
   r = rate of increase of costs,
   $V\%$ = mark-up.

Subscript i refers to the current stock-turnover period.
It is assumed that stocks are purchased at the end of each stock-turnover period.

2. (i) *F.I.F.O.-cost pricing*

$$A_i = \frac{V t_i c_{i-1}}{t_i + t_{i+1} \cdot \frac{c_{i-1} + c_i}{2}} = \frac{4V}{(2 + r_i)(2 + g_{i+1})} \%$$ [1]

$$R_i = \frac{V t_i c_{i-1} - \left\{ (c_i t_{i+1} - c_{i-1} t_i) - \frac{c_{i-1} + c_i}{2}(t_{i+1} - t_i) \right\}}{\frac{t_i + t_{i+1}}{2} c_i}$$

$$= \frac{2V - r_i(2 + g_{i+1})}{(1 + r_i)(2 + g_{i+1})} \%$$ [2]

It can be shown that A_i is always greater than R_i by subtracting [2] from [1] to obtain a positive value.

3. (ii) *Average-cost pricing*

$$A_i = \frac{V t_i \frac{c_{i-1} + c_i}{2}}{\frac{t_i + t_{i+1}}{2} \cdot \frac{c_{i-1} + c_i}{2}} = \frac{2V}{2 + g_{i+1}} \%$$ [3]

$$R_i = \frac{V t_i \frac{c_{i-1} + c_i}{2} - \left[\left(\frac{c_{i-1} + c_i}{2} t_{i+1} - \frac{c_{i-2} + c_{i-1}}{2} t_i \right) - \frac{c_{i-2} + 2c_{i-1} + c_i}{4}(t_{i+1} - t_i) \right]}{\frac{t_i + t_{i+1}}{2} c_i}$$

$$= \frac{2V(1 + r_{i-1})(2 + r_i) - (1 + r_{i-1})(2 + r_i)(2 + g_{i+1}) + (2 + r_{i-1})(2 + g_{i+1})}{2(1 + r_{i-1})(1 + r_i)(2 + g_{i+1})} \%$$ [4]

4. The results of paragraphs 3 and 4 of the note were obtained from equations [1] to [4] by examining the cases of $r_i \geq r_{i-1} > r_0 = 0, g = 0$, and $r_i \geq r_{i-1} > r_0 = 0, g_i \geq g_{i-1} > g_0 = 0$, respectively. If g can be ≥ 0, whether $R_i \geq V\%$ depends upon whether

$$g_{i+1} \gtreqless \frac{-2r_i(1 + V)}{V(1 + r_i) + r_i} \text{ (F.I.F.O.-cost pricing)}$$

and whether

$$g_{i+1} \gtreqless \left[\frac{2V(1 + r_{i-1})(2 + r_i)}{(1 + r_{i-1})\{2V(1 + r_i) + (2 + r_i)\} - (2 + r_{i-1})} - 2 \right]$$

(average-cost pricing)

In both cases, the value of g_{i+1} which makes $R_i = V$ is negative. (See paragraph 4 of the note.)

5. (iii) *Replacement cost pricing*

$$R_i = \frac{V t_i c_i}{\frac{t_i + t_{i+1}}{2} c_i} = \frac{2V}{2 + g_{i+1}} \qquad [5]$$

6. *Increased mark-ups*
   (i) *F.I.F.O.-cost pricing*
       A_i remains equal to $V\%$ if the mark-up in period i is

$$V_i = \frac{(2 + r_i)(2 + g_{i+1})}{4} \cdot V_o\% \qquad [6]$$

where V_o is the original mark-up. The corresponding condition for R_i is

$$V_i = \frac{2 + g_{i+1}}{2} V_o(1 + r_i) + r_i\% \qquad [7]$$

   (ii) *Average-cost pricing*
        The corresponding conditions are for A_i,

$$V_i = \frac{2 + g_{i+1}}{2} V_o\% \qquad [8]$$

and for R_i,

$$V_i = \frac{2V_o(1 + r_{i-1})(1 + r_i)(2 + g_{i+1}) + (1 + r_{i-1})(2 + r_i)(2 + g_{i+1})}{2(2 + r_{i-1})(1 + r_i)} \% \qquad [9]$$

4 The accountant in a Golden Age*

1 In Mrs Robinson's celebrated article, 'The Production Function and the Theory of Capital' (Robinson, 1953-4, reprinted in part in Robinson, 1951-80, vol. ii, pp. 114-31; all subsequent references are to the second source), it is not made clear whether the 'man of words', whose doings are contrasted with those of the 'man of deeds', is an economist or an accountant. It is assumed in this article that he is an accountant; and it is proposed to examine how accurate is the accountant's measure of the rate of profit under 'Golden Age' conditions where uncertainty is absent, expectations are fulfilled, and the rate of profit has an unambiguous meaning.[1] The following question is asked: would the answer obtained by using the accountant's measure of the rate of profit correspond with what is known, under the assumed conditions, to be the right answer, namely, that the *ex post* rate of return equals the *ex ante* one. This does not seem to be an entirely pointless exercise, since a number of 'men of words', economists this time, have used the accountant's measure in their empirical investigations (see, for example, Kuznets, 1952; Phelps Brown and Weber, 1953, especially pp. 272 and 283-8; Barna, 1957, especially pp. 25 and 30; Lutz and Hague, 1961, pp. 82-5; Minhas, 1963, chapter 5; Nevin, 1963, especially, p. 646), and conclusions have been drawn from both the relative and absolute sizes of their estimates. Thus, Minhas used cross-section studies of the rates of return in the same industries in different countries to test his hypothesis about factor-reversals; and Nevin was depressed by the stable, low level of rates of return in British manufacturing in the post-war period. But if it can be shown that the measure is faulty even in the equilibrium conditions of a 'Golden Age', it is unlikely to prove a realistic measure in real world situations.

2 The article is in six sections. In section I the various cases which are examined and the assumptions of the article are outlined; the following sections deal in detail with each case; and a concluding section draws the findings together. The principal conclusion is that the accountant's measure of the rate of profit is extremely misleading, even under

42

'Golden Age' conditions. The measure is shown to be influenced by the pattern of the quasi-rents associated with individual machines in a stock of capital, the method of depreciation used, whether or not the stock of capital is growing, and by what assets are included in the stock of capital. What is more, no easy 'rules of thumb' which would allow adjustments for these factors to be made in the estimates emerge from the analysis.

I

1.1 Four main cases, each of which contains further sub-cases, are considered. The first case is that of the rate of profit, as measured by an accountant, in a business which has a balanced stock of identical machines. The second case concerns the rate of profit in a business, the gross investment in machines of which grows at a constant rate each year. Then, following a suggestion by Mr H. R. Hudson, variants of the two cases are examined: in the balanced stock case, it is assumed that

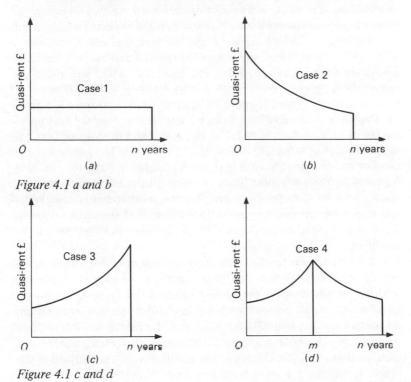

Figure 4.1 a and b

Figure 4.1 c and d

the accumulation of financial assets, which are purchased as a result of allowing for depreciation as the stock of machines builds up but before any replacement expenditure occurs, is included in the capital of the business; in the constant growth case, it is supposed that the accumulation of financial assets, which occurs from the beginning of the firm until the first year of replacement, plus the further accumulation associated with the difference between current depreciation allowances and replacement expenditure of subsequent years (the 'Domar effect'), are included in the capital of the business. The first two cases might be regarded as representative of stationary and growing 'Golden Age' economies respectively, because the capital in them consists entirely of physical assets. The second two cases can be regarded as representative of firms which hold financial assets as well, and which operate in 'Golden Age' economies. (Holdings of financial assets, of course, cancel out for an economy as a whole.)

1.2 For each of the four general cases, four special cases are considered: first, it is assumed that the machines are 'one-hoss shays' and that the expected quasi-rents of each year of operation are equal. This is referred to as the case of the constant q's, where q_i is the expected quasi-rent of year i ($i = 1, \ldots, n, n$ being the life of the machine) and $q_1 = q_2 = \ldots = q_n$. (With the present assumptions, expected and actual quasi-rents always coincide.) Cases 2 and 3 are those of falling and rising q's respectively; for convenience, it is assumed that $q_i = bq_{i-1}$ ($i = 2, \ldots, n$), where $b < 1$ [case 2], and $q_i = aq_{i-1}$ ($i = 2, \ldots, n$) and $a > 1$ [case 3]. Case 4 is a combination of cases 2 and 3; it is assumed that up to q_m ($m < n$), $q_i = aq_{i-1}$ ($i = 2, \ldots, m$), $a > 1$; and from q_m on (but not including q_m), $q_j = bq_{j-1}$ ($j = m + 1, \ldots, n$), $b < 1$. The patterns of the quasi-rents over the life of a machine are shown for the four cases in Figure 4.1. The cases most likely to be met in practice are cases 1, 2, and 4, with $m < \frac{1}{2}n$; perhaps case 2 is the most common case. Prices and wages are assumed to remain constant so that the various patterns show the changes in productive efficiency over the lifetimes of the machines.

1.3 Let r be the expected rate of profit of each machine. The expected rate of profit in a 'Golden Age' is the internal rate of return – the rate of discount which makes the present value of the expected quasi-rents equal to the supply price of each machine. Then, because expectations are always realized in a 'Golden Age', and the rate of profit is uniform throughout the whole economy, it is known that each machine, and each business, is in fact earning r. The question which is analysed in this article is whether the accountant's measure of the rate of profit gives a value of r for each of the four patterns of surpluses for each of the four cases. To answer it, two further sub-cases are introduced, the first assuming that the accountant uses straight-line depreciation when calculating annual accounting profit and the *book* value of capital, the second assuming that he uses reducing-balance depreciation. The accountant's measure of the rate of profit is taken to be the ratio of annual accounting profit to the average of the opening and closing book values of the assets in the business concerned. It is assumed, as is reasonable in a 'Golden Age', that any financial assets owned by a business themselves earn r. Expressions for the accountant's rate of profit for the two sub-cases of the four patterns of surpluses of the four types of businesses are presented in the remaining sections and their values for particular ranges of values of the relevant variables are examined. Where no clear-cut patterns in the accountant's rate of profit were discernible when, for example, the length of life of machines was varied, the numerical values of the rate of profit were found by running a programme on a computer.[2]

1.4 It is not suggested, of course, that an accountant could actually find employment in a 'Golden Age'. Rather, the article is concerned with what would happen if he were to use his customary box of tools in 'Golden Age' conditions. In non-'Golden Age' situations, the only way of finding out whether expectations concerning rates of profit have been realized is to ask accountants – or use their tools.

II

2.1 The first general case considered is that of a business, the capital of which consists of machines only; it is assumed that it owns a balanced stock of machines, which is already established. The accountant calculates depreciation by the straight-line method.[3] The following notation is used:

L number of machines in any age group and purchased in any year;

n length of life of a machine;

q_i expected quasi-rent in year i;

r expected rate of profit;

S supply price of machine: $S = \sum_{i=1}^{n} \dfrac{q_i}{(1+r)^i}$;[4]

$S^* \quad \sum_{i=2}^{n} \dfrac{q_i}{(1+r)^{i-1}}.$

$Q \quad \sum_{i=1}^{n} q_i; \quad Q^* = \sum_{i=2}^{n} q_i;$

K value of capital for the year as a whole;[5]

k book value of capital for the year as a whole (no subscript indicates that straight-line depreciation is used, subscript RB indicates that reducing-balance depreciation is used);

d rate of reducing-balance depreciation; $d = 3/2n$;

A accounting profit (no subscript: straight-line depreciation; subscript RB: reducing-balance depreciation);

$R*$ accountant's measure of the rate of profit; $R* = A/k$.

2.2 *If* the accountant were to value capital as the sum of the discounted values of the expected quasi-rents, using r as the rate of discount, the value of capital for the year as a whole can be shown to be:

$$K = \frac{L}{2r}[(Q+Q*)-(S+S*)].^6$$

The accounting profit for any year is:

$$A = L(Q-S),$$

so that $R*$, *in this instance*, is

$$\frac{2r(Q-S)}{[(Q+Q*)-(S+S*)]}$$

which is approximately equal to r. That is to say, in this particular instance, if the accountant uses the economist's definition of the value of capital (in a 'Golden Age') and his own measure of accounting profit, the resulting expression for the rate of profit gives approximately the right answer. Once growth of the capital stock occurs, though, he would also need to use the economist's measure of depreciation (the decline in the value of capital from year to year), not one of his own, in order for this approach to give approximately the right answer.[7]

2.3 However, the accountant is more likely to use the average *book* value of capital for the year as his measure of the value of capital. This can be shown to be $\frac{1}{2}LnS$;[8] and, it follows,

$$R* = \frac{2(Q-S)}{nS}. \tag{1}$$

In general, this expression is not equal to r. In the 'one-hoss shay' case,

$$R* = \frac{2}{n}\left\{\frac{nr}{1-\{1/(1+r)\}^n}-1\right\}. \tag{1a}$$

As $n \to \infty$, $R* \to 2r$. However, the approach is not monotonic increasing: at $n = 1$, $R* = 2r$; it then falls to a minimum value, which is always greater than r, at values of n which are related to r itself. For example, when $r = 5$ per cent, the minimum value of R^* occurs between the tenth and twentieth year; when $r = 30$ per cent, it occurs between the fifth and tenth year. That is, in the 'one-hoss shay' case, the accountant's measure of the rate of profit will give different answers for two businesses which are alike in every respect except that the machines of one are longer-lived than those of the other. If, for example, the rate of profit is 30 per cent, the accountant's answer for $n = 5$ years is 42.1 per cent and for $n = 30$ years, 53.4 per cent.

2.4 In passing, it could be mentioned that American studies show that some businessmen estimate rates of return as the ratio of accounting profit to the *gross* (that is, undepreciated) value of assets. The book value of capital when straight-line depreciation is used is half the gross value. If the investment projects concerned are 'one-hoss shays' and n is large, the accounting rate of profit would approximately equal r. Expression [1a] may therefore provide a theoretical justification for this business practice.[9]

2.5 The corresponding expressions for cases 2, 3, and 4 – falling; rising; and rising, then falling quasi-rents – are:

$$R^* = \frac{2}{n} \left\{ \frac{(1 - b^n)(1 + r - b)}{(1 - b)[1 - \{b/(1 + r)\}^n]} - 1 \right\};$$ [1b]

for case 3 read $a (> 1)$ for b;   [1c]

$$R^* = \frac{2}{n} \left(\frac{\frac{a^m - 1}{a - 1} + a^{m-1}\left(\frac{b(1 - b^{n-m})}{1 - b}\right)}{\frac{1 - \{a/(1 + r)\}^m}{1 + r - a} + a^{m-1}\left(\frac{b[1 - \{b/(1 + r)\}^{n-m}]}{(1 + r - b)(1 + r)^m}\right)} - \frac{1 - \{a/(1+r)\}^m}{1 + r - a} - a^{m-1}\frac{b[1 - \{b/(1+r)\}^{n-m}]}{(1 + r - b)(1 + r)^m} \right)$$ [1d]

2.6 In case 2, $R^* \to 0$ as $n \to \infty$. There is a value of n where $R^* = r$, as R^* is greater than r for $n = 2$. The rapidity with which this occurs, for certain values of the variables, is shown in Table 4.1.

Table 4.1 Values of R^*, case 2 (balanced stock, physical capital) (percentages)

r	2 years	5 years	10 years	20 years	30 years
	(non-bracketed figures, $b = 0.5$; bracketed figures, $b = 0.9$)				
5	6.7 [7.4]	3.7 [5.7]	2.0 [4.9]	1.0 [3.8]	0.1 [3.0]
10	13.4 [n.a.]	7.4 [n.a.]	4.0 [n.a.]	2.0 [n.a.]	1.3 [n.a.]
20	n.a. [30.3]	n.a. [24.4]	n.a. [21.4]	n.a. [16.4]	n.a. [12.5]
30	40.8 [46.0]	22.5 [37.9]	12.0 [33.5]	6.0 [25.2]	4.0 [18.9]

Would it be too fanciful to suggest that the low levels of rates of profit which Nevin found in British manufacturing may in part be due to a combination of quasi-rent patterns similar to those of case 2 and rather large n's?

2.7 In case 3, the value of $R*$ is greater than r (and the values of $R*$ for cases 1 and 2) at small values of n, falls slightly as n increases, but then quickly increases, approaching ∞ as $n \to \infty$. With $a = 1.1, n = 20$ years, and $r = 30$ per cent, $R*$ is already 108.8 per cent; with $a = 1.5$, the corresponding figure is 796 per cent! ($R*$ is not defined for the case of $1 + r = a$.) Case 4 is a combination of cases 2 and 3. For given values of n, the value of $R*$ lies in between the values of $R*$ of the two previous cases.[10] As $m \to n$, the case 3 result comes to dominate the expression; as $m \to 0$, the case 2 result comes to dominate. This is illustrated in Table 4.2 where certain values of $R*$ for cases 2, 3 and 4 are shown; $r = 10$ per cent, $a = 1.3, b = 0.7$, and $n = 20$ years. Just by a fluke of counterbalancing forces, the accountant's measure could give the right answer in case 4.

Table 4.2 Values of $R*$, cases 2, 3 and 4, varying values of m (balanced stock, physical capital, straight-line depreciation) (percentages)

$R*$	5 years	m 10 years	15 years
Case 2	3.3	3.3	3.3
Case 4	6.3	13.3	24.3
Case 3	36.3	36.3	36.3

2.8 Hudson and Mathews (1963) show that if the quasi-rents decline at a particular linear rate, straight-line depreciation is 'correct'. Substituting this pattern in [1] gives $R* \simeq r$ for moderately large n, say > 10. ($R* = r$, whatever n, if annual accounting profit is averaged as well as the annual book values of capital.)

2.9 If the accountant calculated annual depreciation by the reducing-balance method, the general expression becomes

$$R_{RB}^* = \frac{Q-S}{S\{\frac{1}{2}(2n-1)-e\}},$$ [2]

where

$$e = \frac{d(n-1)(1-d)-d^2(1-d^{n-1})}{(1-d)^2}.$$

Table 4.3   Values of R_{RB}^*, case 1 (balanced stock, physical capital, reducing-balance depreciation) (percentages)

			n			
r	2 years	5 years	10 years	20 years	30 years	50 years
5	10.1	5.2	3.7	3.4	3.4	3.6
10	20.3	10.7	7.9	7.5	7.8	n.a.
30	62.6	35.5	28.1	28.0	28.6	n.a.

The expressions for cases 1 to 4 are not shown but can be easily derived from expression 2. In case 1 at $n = 2$, $R_{RB}^* > r$; it then quickly drops below r, reaches a minimum and, as $n \to \infty$, $R_{RB}^* \to r$. (See Table 4.3.)

The results for cases 2, 3 and 4 are similar, in the sense that they show the same general patterns for variations of n, to those for the corresponding cases using straight-line depreciation. For $n = 2$, $R_{RB}^* > R^*$; otherwise, for all computed values, $R_{RB}^* < R^*$. Again, there is one particular pattern of decline of the quasi-rents which makes reducing-balance the 'correct' depreciation (Hudson and Mathews, 1963, pp. 234–5) and for which $R_{RB}^* \simeq r$.

III

3.1 The next main case to be analysed is that of a business, the gross investment of which grows at a constant rate each year. However, it is convenient, first, to comment briefly on the case of a balanced stock where the financial assets which have accumulated over the years 0 to n and which earn r, are included in the capital of the business. By the year n, the value of financial assets (F), in the straight-line depreciation case, is $\frac{1}{2}LnS$, which is the same as the book value of physical assets. Once the year n is reached, the balanced stock is established. Therefore, for all $n + j$ years afterwards ($j = 0$ in year n, then 1, 2, . . .), the book value of physical and financial assets in the year $n + j$ is: $k_{n+j}^T = LnS$. Accounting profit in year $n + j$ is:

$$A_{n+j}^T = L\{(Q - S) + \tfrac{1}{2}rnS\},$$

so that

$$R_{n+j}^{*T} = \frac{(Q - S) + \tfrac{1}{2}rnS}{nS},$$

which it is convenient to write as

$$R^{*T}_{n+j} = \frac{(Q-S)}{nS} + \tfrac{1}{2}r.$$ [3]

Now,

$$\frac{Q-S}{nS} = \frac{1}{2}\left\{\frac{2(Q-S)}{nS}\right\},$$

which is *half* the general expression for the balanced stock, physical capital case (see expression [1]). The accountant's rate of profit in this case, then, is always equal to half its value for the corresponding physical capital case, plus a constant, $\tfrac{1}{2}r$.

3.2 The corresponding general expression if reducing-balance depreciation is used is:

$$R^{*T}_{RB,n+j} = \frac{Q}{nS} - \frac{1}{n} + \frac{r(\tfrac{1}{2}+e)}{n}.$$ [4]

Again, while the values for particular cases show the same pattern of variation around r as n changes, the disparity between the accountant's measure and r is always less. That is to say, in general the influence of financial assets is to reduce the discrepancy between the accountant's measure and r. The explanation is obvious: the accountant's measure now includes in the numerator and denominator elements, namely, financial assets and the income earned on them, which, if expressed as a ratio, equal r. The influence of the inclusion of financial assets in capital on R^* is illustrated in Table 4.4 where the accountant's values for balanced stocks of machines with lives of 10 years and $r = 10$ per cent are shown.

Table 4.4 Values of R^* for $n = 10$ years, $a = 1.5$, $b = 0.5$, and $r = 10$ per cent (percentages)

	Straight-line depreciation		Reducing-balance depreciation	
Case	Physical capital	Total capital	Physical capital	Total capital
(1)	12.5	11.3	7.9	8.3
(2)	4.0	7.0	2.5	4.0
(3)	22.7	16.4	14.3	13.4
(4)	10.5†	10.3†	6.6†	7.3†

† $m = 5$ years

IV

4.1 The next main case considered is that of a business, the gross investment each year of which is the stream: $LS, cLS, \ldots, c^{n-1} LS, \ldots$ ($c > 1$). It has been argued already (see para. 2.2 above) that, if the capital stock is growing, the use of conventional accounting methods of reckoning depreciation prevents $R^* \simeq r$, even if capital is valued 'correctly'. If straight-line depreciation is used,

$$R^* = \frac{2(1+r-c) \left[\sum\limits_{1}^{n} c^{n-i} q_i - (S/n) \{ (c^n - 1)/(c - 1) \} \right]}{\sum\limits_{1}^{n} c^{n-i} q_i + \sum\limits_{2}^{n} c^{n+1-i} q_i - c^n (S + S^*)};$$

if reducing-balance depreciation is used,

$$R^*_{RB} = \frac{2(1+r-c) \left[\sum\limits_{1}^{n} c^{n-i} q_i - S(x) \right]}{(\alpha)},$$

where

$$x = 1 - \frac{d(1-d^{n-1})}{1-d} + \frac{cd^n \{ 1 - (c/d)^{n-1} \}}{d-c}$$

and

$$\alpha = \sum\limits_{1}^{n} c^{n-i} q_i + \sum\limits_{2}^{n} c^{n+1-i} q_i - c^n (S + S^*).$$

Neither of these expressions, in general, approximately equals r.

4.2 Expression [5] is the general expression for R^* for the constant growth case in the $(n + j)$th year (that is, after replacement expenditure has started) when the *book* value of physical capital and straight-line depreciation are used.

$$R^*_{c,n+j} = \frac{2n(c-1)^2 \left\{ \sum\limits_{1}^{n} c^{n-i} q_i - S(c^n - 1)/n(c-1) \right\}}{S(\beta)} \qquad [5]$$

where

$$\beta = \{ (2n-1) c^{n+1} - (2n+1) c^n + (1+c) \}.$$

This expression is independent of c^j (though the expressions for accounting profit and the book value of capital contain it), but not of c itself. The patterns of behaviour of R^* as n changes appear to be the same, for the four types of machines, as for the balanced-stock cases. However, *in general*, the higher is the rate of growth of the capital

Table 4.5   Values of R^*, for $c = 1.0$, 1.01, and 1.2, $r = 30$ per cent, $a = 1.5, b = 0.5$, and straight-line depreciation (percentages)

Case	c	5 years	n 10 years	20 years
1	1.0	42.1	44.7	50.3
	1.01	41.8	44.0	48.7
	1.20	36.8	34.8	33.5
2	1.0	22.5	12.0	6.0
	1.01	23.1	12.9	7.1
	1.20	31.6	26.9	24.6
3	1.0	60.9	122.4	796.0
	1.01	59.7	116.7	713.4
	1.20	41.5	49.1	88.0
4 †	1.0	34.7	39.6	75.9
	1.01	34.7	39.5	74.5
	1.20	35.2	35.0	50.0

† $m = \frac{1}{2}n$

stock, the closer, for given n, are the values of the accountant's rate of profit to the correct value. This is illustrated in Table 4.5, where values of R^* are shown for rates of growth between 0 and 20 per cent.

The general expression for the constant growth case when reducing-balance depreciation is used is:

$$R^*_{RB,c,n+j} = \frac{2(1-c)(1-d)(c-d)\left\{\sum_{1}^{n} c^{n-i} q_i - S(x)\right\}}{S(y)} \qquad [6]$$

where

$$y = (1-d)(c-d)(1+c-2c^n) - $$
$$d(1+c)\{(1-d^{n-1})(c-d) - c^n(1-d)(1-(d/c)^{n-1})\}.$$

(Expressions for the four types of machines can be easily derived from expressions [5] and [6].) Except for the case of $n = 2$, R^* for the reducing-balance case is usually less than the corresponding value for the straight-line case. For values of n below twenty years, anyway, the effect of growth is usually to make R^* closer to r than in the corresponding balanced stock case.

V

5.1 To complete the analysis, the case of constant growth where the accumulation of financial assets occurs is briefly examined. The accumulation of financial assets consists of two parts:

(i) the accumulation over the first n years before any replacement expenditure occurs;

(ii) the net addition to this fund in subsequent years $(n + j)$ because current depreciation allowances exceed current replacement expenditure. The summation of the two relevant parts gives the financial capital for the year $n + j$, on which r is earned, and these income-capital ratios combined with expressions [5] and [6] respectively, give the general expressions for $R^{*T}_{c,n+j}$ and $R^{*T}_{RB,c,n+j}$:

$$R^{*T}_{c,n+j} = \frac{2n(c-1)^2\left\{c^j\left(\sum_1^n c^{n-i}q_i - (S/n)\{(c^n-1)/(c-1)\}\right) + \tfrac{1}{2}rS(g)\right\}}{S(h)} \quad [7]$$

where

$$g = \frac{2n(c^n-1)}{c-1} + \frac{c(c^j-1)(c^n-1)}{(c-1)^2} - \frac{(\beta)}{(c-1)^2} - n\left(\frac{c^j-1}{c-1}\right)$$

and

$$h = 2n(c^n-1)(c-1) + c(c^j-1)(c^n-1) + (c^j-1)(\beta) - n(c^j-1)(c-1);$$

$$R^{*T}_{RB,c,n+j} = \frac{2\left\{c^j\left(\sum_1^n c^{n-i}q_i - S(x)\right) + \tfrac{1}{2}rS[(p)+(t)\{(c^j-1)/(c-1)\}]\right\}}{S(u)} \quad [8]$$

where

$$u = \frac{c^j}{(1-c)(1-d)(c-d)}(y) + (p) + (t)\left(\frac{c^j-1}{c-1}\right),$$

$$p = 1 + \frac{d(1+c)}{(1-c)}\left[\frac{1-d^{n-1}}{1-d} - \frac{c^n(1-(d/c)^{n-1})}{c-d}\right];$$

and

$$t = d\left(\frac{c^n(1-(d/c)^{n-1})}{c-d}\right) + \frac{c-1}{c} - \frac{d(1-d^{n-1})}{1-d}.$$

5.2 Expressions for the four types of machines can be derived from expressions [7] and [8]. These expressions contain a new term, c^j, so that values were computed for a number of values of c^j (the range was: $j = 1\tfrac{1}{2}n - 3n$). For the range of values of j examined, though, the values of R^* were hardly affected by variations in j. For example, with $a = 1.5$, $b = 0.5$, $c = 1.01$, $n = 20$, and $r = 5$ per cent, the range was 8.6–8.8 per cent, in the straight-line cases, and 6.96–6.98 per cent in the reducing-balance cases. Again, while the patterns of change of R^* with respect to n have the same general shapes as those of the corresponding constant growth, physical capital cases, the discrepancy between the values of R^* and r, for given n, is usually reduced. Moreover, because the influence of growth is also usually to improve the accountant's measure, the discrepancies between R^* and r, for given n, are least of all of the cases examined. This is illustrated in Table 4.6 where values of R^* for the balanced stock, total capital and constant growth, total capital cases for $n = 10$ years, $a = 1.5$, $b = 0.5$, $r = 30$ per cent, and $c = 1.1$ are compared.

Table 4.6   Values of R^* for $n = 10$ years, $a = 1.5$, $b = 0.5$, $c = 1.1$, $r = 30$ per cent (balanced stock, total capital; constant growth, total capital) (percentages)

Case	Straight-line depreciation		Reducing-balance depreciation	
	Balanced stock	Constant growth	Balanced stock	Constant growth
1	44.7	36.0‡	28.1	30.2‡
2	12.0	23.3‡	7.5	18.7‡
3	122.4	62.0‡	77.1	53.8‡
4	39.6†	35.3†‡	24.9†	29.6†‡

† $m = 5$ years   ‡ $j = 30$ years

VI

6.1 The article is concluded by briefly summarizing the variations of R^* with respect to n for the various cases examined. The following diagrams illustrate, schematically, the patterns of variation with respect to n.

(i) *Straight-line depreciation, balanced stock, physical capital*

Case 1:

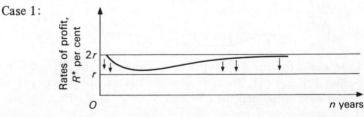

Figure 4.2

(The arrows show the influence of growth and financial capital on R^*.)

Case 2:

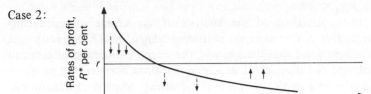

Figure 4.3

(Dotted arrows show the influence of changes in b - the smaller is the value of b, the faster is the approach to zero.)

Case 3:

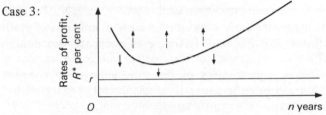

Figure 4.4

(Dotted arrows show the influence of changes in a - the greater is the value of a, the faster is the approach to ∞. The function is not defined at $1 + r = a$.)

Case 4: This case cannot be shown in a general diagram because it depends on the ratio, m/n. Its value approaches that of (2) as $m (<n) \to 0$.

(ii) *Reducing-balance depreciation, balanced stock, physical capital*

Case 1:

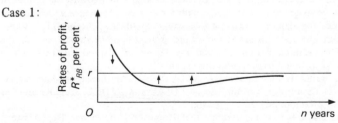

Figure 4.5

Cases 2 and 3 are similar to those for straight-line depreciation but, for $n > 2, R_{RB}^* < R^*$.

6.2 The implications of the analysis of the article are rather disheartening. It had been hoped that some rough 'rules of thumb' might be developed; and that these would allow accounting rates of profit to be adjusted for the lengths of life of machines, the patterns of quasi-rents, rates of growth, and the method of depreciation used. However, it is obvious from the calculations that the relationships involved are too complicated to allow this. A systematic presentation of the values of R^* for the various cases has not been attempted (though they have been computed). Nevertheless, on the basis of the above analysis, it seems safe to add to the already well-known defects of accounting data on profits and capital (see, for example, Mathews, 1962, chapters 5 and 6; Roses, 1965) the main conclusion of this article, namely, that as an indication of the realized rate of return the accountant's rate of profit is greatly influenced by irrelevant factors, even under ideal conditions. Any 'man of words' (or 'deeds' for that matter) who compares rates of profit of different industries, or of the same industry in different countries, and draws inferences from their magnitudes as to the relative profitability of investments in different uses or countries, does so at his own peril.

Notes

* *Oxford Economic Papers*, vol. 17, no. 1, March 1965, pp. 66–80. The writer is especially grateful to Professor H. F. Lydall for suggesting the research project on which this article is based and for his comments and help. He would also like to thank Mr R. D. Terrell, members of the Department of Economics and Commerce, University of Adelaide, and members of the joint DAE-Faculty Seminar, University of Cambridge. Miss J. M. Higgins checked the mathematical results.

1 'To abstract from uncertainty means to postulate that no such (unexpected) events occur, so that the *ex ante* expectations which govern the actions of the man of deeds are never out of gear with the *ex post* experience which governs the actions of the man of words, and to say that equilibrium obtains is to say that no such events have occurred for some time or are thought liable to occur in the future' ('The Production Function and the Theory of Capital', p. 120). These conditions are assumed to prevail in this article.

2 The writer is indebted to Dr M. V. Wilkes, Mathematical Laboratory, University of Cambridge, for the use of EDSAC and to Dr L. J. Slater and her assistants for programming the expressions.

3 This case was first analysed by Joan Robinson in her paper 'Depreciation' (in Robinson, 1951–80, vol. ii, pp. 216–19).

4 In a 'Golden Age', the supply prices of machines are always equal to the

present values of the expected quasi-rents, the uniform rate of profit being the rate of discount. (See 'The Production Function and the Theory of Capital', p. 123.)

5 Capital is valued for the year as a whole rather than at its beginning or end, because this procedure accords with the accounting practice of averaging the opening and closing values of assets when calculating annual rates of profit.

6 Suppose that machines are bought at the beginning of each year and that incomes accrue at the end. The value of a balanced stock of capital at the *beginning* of any year (K^*) is:

$$K^* = L\left(\frac{q_n}{(1+r)}\right) + L\left(\frac{q_{n-1}}{(1+r)} + \frac{q_n}{(1+r)^2}\right) + \ldots + L\left(\frac{q_1}{(1+r)} + \ldots + \frac{q_n}{(1+r)^n}\right).$$

By gathering up terms and forming the appropriate geometric progressions,

$$K^* = \frac{L}{r}(Q - S)$$

is obtained.

Similarly, the value of capital at the *end* of any year (K^{**}) can be shown to be:

$$K^{**} = \frac{L}{r}(Q^* - S^*).$$

For the year as a whole, therefore,

$$K = \frac{L}{2r}[(Q + Q^*) - (S + S^*)].$$

7 H. R. Hudson discussed this point and gave the formula for 'correct' depreciation in an unpublished paper which was read to the Seminar on Economic Growth, held in the University of Adelaide in August 1960. See also, Hudson and Mathews (1963).

8 At the beginning of any year the *book* value of the machines in the business (k^*) is:

$$k^* = LS + L\left(S - \frac{S}{n}\right) + \ldots + L\left(S - \frac{(n-1)S}{n}\right).$$

By gathering up terms and forming the appropriate arithmetic progressions,

$$k^* = \frac{LS(n+1)}{2}$$

is obtained.

Similarly, the *book* value at the end of any year can be shown to be:

$$k^{**} = \frac{LS(n-1)}{2}.$$

For the year as a whole, therefore,

$$k = \frac{LnS}{2}.$$

The remaining expressions in the article may be obtained by following procedures similar to those in this note and note 6 above.

9 The writer is indebted to Mr F. K. Wright for bringing this practice to his notice.

10 There is an exception to this statement when $m = 1$; but this result can be ignored as it has no economic relevance.

5 The measurement of the rate of profit and the bonus scheme for managers in the Soviet Union*

1. In a recent article Mr Merrett discussed some of the implications of linking money bonuses for managers to the rate of profit in Soviet industry (Merrett, 1964). The purpose of this note is to comment on some further implications of the bonus scheme which arise from the measure of the rate of profit used in the Soviet Union. It is shown that managers in charge of enterprises which use particular types of machines are favourably treated by the bonus scheme and that *if* the sizes of expected bonuses influence the choice of investment projects, the measure of the rate of profit has an arbitrary impact on these decisions. The note concludes with a discussion of the relation between the bonus scheme and the criterion of choice of technique put forward by Professor Meek (Meek, 1964).

2. According to Merrett, 'profitability is equal to price less average variable cost multiplied by output, and expressed as a percentage of total fixed and working capital' (Merrett, 1964, pp. 401-2). Working capital and fixed costs are ignored in what follows; depreciation is assumed to be reckoned on the straight-line basis (this is the method used in the Soviet Union) (Levine, 1960); the fact that the lengths of life implied by the depreciation rates allowed in the Soviet Union are too great is ignored; and the under-pricing of capital goods in the Soviet Union is ignored also (but on this, see below, paras 7 and 11). The rate of profit is then seen to be the accountant's measure of the rate of profit: the ratio of annual accounting profit to the book value of the assets in the enterprises concerned. Merrett shows that the bonuses paid to managers can be calculated (approximately) from the following expression:

$$B = 0.075\sqrt{p}.K = 0.075\sqrt{(PK)}, \qquad [1]$$

where

B = bonus; P = accounting profit;
K = book value of capital; $p = P/K$ = the rate of profit

(Merrett, 1964, pp. 401-2).[1]

59

3. It can be shown that the accountant's measure of the rate of profit is a faulty measure of the *ex ante* rate of profit even under 'Golden Age' conditions where uncertainty is absent, expectations are fulfilled, and the rate of profit has an unambiguous meaning (Harcourt, 1965b). In particular, if a balanced stock of 'one-hoss shays' (i.e. constant annual expected quasi-rents associated with each machine) is considered, p approaches a value which is twice the *ex ante* internal rate of return (r), the longer-lived are the machines in the stock; moreover, under any circumstances, p is always greater than r. If the expected quasi-rents decline exponentially from year to year, p approaches a value of zero, the longer-lived are the machines (ibid., pp. 71-2). These results are obviously relevant in the present context, since the size of the bonus is a function of p, not of r, the internal rate of return of the project concerned. It is not assumed that there is anything sacrosanct about the internal rate of return, which is used merely because it is a simple and well-known index of 'equivalence'. The present value of investment projects could just as easily be used and the main points of this note would remain unaffected.

4. In this note, the sizes of bonuses and rates of bonus per unit of capital associated with balanced stocks of machines which have the same supply prices but different expected lives, internal rates of return, and patterns of expected quasi-rents, are examined. Each machine is assumed to have a supply price (S) of £1,000. The lengths of life examined are: $n = 5, 10, 15, 20, 30$ years; the internal rates of return are: $r = 10, 16, 25$ per cent. The first pattern of quasi-rents (q) is that of constant q's, $q'_1 = q'_2 = \ldots = q'_n$; the second is that of declining q's, $q''_i = bq''_{i-1}$ ($i = 2, \ldots, n, b = 0.9$). In the 'one-hoss shay' case,

$$q'_i = \frac{rS}{1 - (1/1 + r)^n}.$$ [2]

In the second case,

$$q''_1 = \frac{(1 + r - b)S}{1 - (b/1 + r)^n}.$$ [3][2]

The values of q'_i and q''_1 for various values of n and r, and for $S =$ £1,000, are shown in Table 5.1.

5. The annual accounting profit associated with a balanced stock of like machines is: $P = Q - S$, where $Q = \sum_{i=1}^{n} q_i$. The book value of capital is $K = \frac{1}{2} nS$ (Harcourt, 1965b, pp. 70-1).[3]

Substituting these expressions in [1],

$$B = \frac{3}{40\sqrt{2}} \sqrt{\{(Q-S)(nS)\}} \qquad [4]$$

is obtained. In the 'one-hoss shay' case,

$$B_1 = \frac{3}{40\sqrt{2}} \sqrt{\{(nq_i' - S)(nS)\}}. \qquad [5]$$

In case 2,

$$B_2 = \frac{3}{40\sqrt{2}} \sqrt{\left\{ \left[q_1'' \left(\frac{1-b^n}{1-b} \right) - S \right] [nS] \right\}} \qquad [6]$$

The values of B_1 and B_2, and B_1/K and B_2/K, are shown in Table 5.1.

Table 5.1 Values of $q_i', q_1''; B_1, B_2; B_1/K$ and B_2/K $(S = £1,000; n = 5,$ 10, 15, 20, 30 years; $r = 10, 16, 25$ per cent; $b = 0.9)$

$n =$	5		10		15		20		30	
r	q_i'	q_1''	q_i'	q_1''	q_i'	q_1''	q_i'	q_1''	q_i'	q_1''
‖					(£)					
10	264	316	163	231	132	210	118	204	106	201
16	305	362	207	282	179	266	169	262	162	260
25	372	434	280	364	259	353	253	351	250	350
r	B_1	B_2	B_1	B_2	B_1	B_2	B_1	B_2	B_1	B_2
‖					(£)					
10	67	64	133	119	203	168	276	211	429	279
16	86	82	168	154	267	217	365	270	570	355
25	110	105	225	196	349	276	478	342	741	445
r	B_1/K	B_2/K	B_1/K	B_2/K	B_1/K	B_2/K	B_1/K	B_2/K	B_1/K	B_2/K
‖					(per cent)					
10	2.7	2.6	2.7	2.4	2.7	2.2	2.8	2.1	2.9	1.9
16	3.4	3.3	3.4	3.1	3.6	2.9	3.7	2.7	3.8	2.4
25	4.4	4.2	4.5	3.9	4.7	3.7	4.8	3.4	4.9	3.0

6. It can be seen that if machines are 'one-hoss shays', managers in charge of longer-lived machines get greater benefits, in relation to the capital invested, from the bonus scheme. Thus, if machines last five years, the value of B_1/K is between 2.7 and 4.4 per cent, depending on the value of r; if they last 30 years, B_1/K is between 2.9 and 4.9 per cent. If, however, machines are of the second type, managers in charge of shorter-lived machines are favoured. With $r = 16$ per cent, $B_2/K = 3.3$ per cent for $n = 5$ years and 2.7 per cent for $n = 20$ years. Moreover, if the values of n and r are the same for two enterprises, managers in charge of case 1 machines are favoured relative to those in charge of case 2 machines. With $r = 16$ per cent and $n = 20$ years, $B_1 = £365$,

$B_2 = £270$, $B_1/K = 3.7$ per cent, and $B_2/K = 2.7$ per cent. Can any welfare theorist, either side of the Iron Curtain, say why this should be so?

7. The prices of capital goods are systematically under-priced in the Soviet Union. Suppose that the 'correct' prices of the machines in Table 5.1 all exceed $S = £1,000$ by the same amount. Then, it can be shown that the longer-lived are 'one-hoss shays' with the same initial r, the higher are their 'correct' r's (though obviously they are always less than the initial value). Furthermore, the 'correct' r of a 'one-hoss shay' is always greater than that of a case 2 machine with the same n and initial r. Therefore, paying greater benefits to managers in charge of long-lived 'one-hoss shays', or 'one-hoss shays' with the same n and initial r as case 2 machines, may be partially justified by these new results. On the other hand, the 'correct' r's of case 2 machines with the same initial r are greater, the longer are their lives; so favouring managers in charge of shorter-lived case 2 machines appears to be even 'worse' than before.

8. Now suppose that the prospective sizes of bonuses to managers influence investment decisions, especially the choice of projects. As major investment decisions in the Soviet Union are taken above the enterprise level, managers cannot directly decide the choice of technique. It is believed, however, that the blueprints eventually sanctioned are often powerfully influenced by proposals originating from the enterprise level. Moreover, managers have considerable say as to the current input-output mix and the way in which existing equipment is used and maintained. These decisions may be influenced by the bonus scheme and they, in their turn, may influence those who are directly responsible for investment decisions. Such considerations no doubt underlie discussions of the link between the Liberman proposals and investment decisions, including that of Merrett, and the following arguments proceed on the basis of them.

9. The first point to notice is that, in general, there is no way in which the present value to managers of bonuses associated with particular projects can be calculated. The value of a bonus is a function of the annual average accounting rate of profit. It is impossible to isolate, as it were, the contribution of marginal investment projects to future annual averages. However, if n, r, and S are assumed to be the same for two projects, and if managers have a high rate of time discount, they may well favour projects with high accounting profits in the early years, i.e. those with the $b^{i-1} q_i''$ streams of Table 5.1 rather than those with constant q_i''s. Capital will be increased by the same amount each year,

but the profits of case 2 projects will be greater in the earlier years than those of case 1 projects. For example, with $n = 15$ years and $r = 16$ per cent, $q_i'' > q_i'$ for the first four years.

10. On the other hand, if managers have either low rates of time discount, or none at all, they will tend to favour 'one-hoss shays', because, for given S, n and r, $Q' > Q''$, i.e. the total undiscounted quasi-rents (and profits) of a 'one-hoss shay' are greater than those of a case 2 project. Moreover, regardless of their rate of time discount, they will tend to favour investment in shorter-lived machines with the same pattern of quasi-rents and r, because, as a glance at Table 5.1 shows, the q_i's of the shorter-lived machines exceed those of the longer-lived ones. Mr Merrett might like to justify these implications of the effect of p on the size of bonuses and investment decisions, because they also follow from his suggested rule that bonus payments be based on the level of profits (Merrett, 1964, p. 407).

11. If, now, account is taken again of the under-pricing of capital goods, and if managers have high rates of time discount, the bonus scheme encourages them to choose 'wrongly', i.e. to choose machines with the lower 'correct' r's. If managers have low rates of time discount or none at all, the bonus scheme tends to make them choose projects with the higher 'correct' r's. Finally, the preference for shorter-lived projects noted in paragraph 10 is seen to be a preference for projects with lower 'correct' r's, regardless of the pattern of quasi-rents of the machines concerned.

12. Professor Meek has argued that if two mutually exclusive ways of producing a commodity are compared, the technique with the lower total annual costs is the socially 'correct' one to choose (Meek, 1964, p.335). Consider two projects A and B, both 'one hoss shays' with the same n and producing the same amount per year of a given commodity. Let the total annual costs of A be greater than those of B, and q_b/q_a $(= Q_b/Q_a) < S_b/S_a$. Then, on the Meek criterion, project B should be chosen. It will now be shown that the bonus scheme will always give a greater rate of bonus per unit of capital to managers in charge of a balanced stock of the 'wrong' machines, i.e. A machines, and that there is a considerable chance that these managers will also receive larger total bonuses as well.

13. Let $Q_b = \alpha Q_a$, where $\alpha > 1$, and $S_b = \beta S_a$, where $\beta > 1$. Then

$$\frac{Q_b}{Q_a} (= \alpha) < \frac{S_b}{S_a} (= \beta), \quad \text{i.e. } \alpha < \beta.$$

Now

$$p_a = \frac{2[Q_a - S_a]}{nS_a} \quad \text{and} \quad p_b = \frac{2[\alpha Q_a - \beta S_a]}{n\beta S_a}.$$

It is clear that $p_a > p_b$, i.e. that the rate of profit on a balanced stock of A machines is greater than that on a balanced stock of B machines. It follows that the rate of bonus per unit of capital is also greater on the stock of A machines.

14. The conditions for $B_a \gtrless B_b$ are now established. From [4],

$$B = \frac{3}{40\sqrt{2}} \sqrt{\{(Q - S)(nS)\}}.$$

Therefore $B_a \gtrless B_b$ if

$$(Q_a - S_a)(nS_a) \gtrless (Q_b - S_b)(nS_b),$$

i.e. if

$$(1 - \beta^2)/(1 - \alpha\beta) \gtrless Q_a/S_a.$$

In general, there is no reason why the top inequality should not be satisfied in some cases, in which cases, $B_a > B_b$.

Notes

* *Oxford Economic Papers*, vol. 18, no. 1, March 1966, pp. 58–63. The writer is grateful to Esra Bennathan, C. J. Bliss, M. H. Dobb, James A. Mirrlees, R. E. Rowthorn, Aubrey Silberston, Ajit Singh, and R. H. Wallace for helpful discussions, to Francis Seton for his comments on an earlier draft and for suggesting the analysis of paras 7 and 11, and to Miss Marion Clarke for carrying out the calculations.

1 The writer is indebted to Mr D. M. Nuti for pointing out the misplacement of the decimal point in Merrett's original formulation, which does not, however, affect the subsequent argument.

2 $S = \sum\limits_{i=1}^{n} \dfrac{q_i}{(1 + r)^i}$. In the 'one-hoss shay' case, $S = q_i' \left[\dfrac{\{1 - (1/1 + r)^n\}}{r} \right]$,

so that

$$q_i' = \frac{rS}{1 - (1/1 + r)^n}.$$

Similarly, it can be shown that

$$q_i'' = \frac{(1 + r - b)S}{1 - (b/1 + r)^n}.$$

3 For simplicity it is assumed that there is only one machine in each age group.

Part II
Post-Keynesian economic theory

6 A critique of Mr Kaldor's model of income distribution and economic growth*

Since 1956 Mr Kaldor has been developing a model of income distribution and economic growth in order to explain the observed constancies in the capital-output ratios, the distribution of income, and the rates of profit on capital of the United Kingdom and United States economies.[1] Whether or not the three ratios are in fact constant is in dispute. For example, the participants in the recent conference on capital theory at Corfu, faced with the same empirical evidence concerning the capital-output ratio of the United States, split into two groups – one arguing that it was stable, the other that it was not (see Lutz and Hague, 1961, pp. x-xi). However, the dispute is irrelevant to the present discussion which is concerned with the technical features of Kaldor's model. Moreover, his views on the forces which determine the distribution of income and the rate of growth of capitalist economies warrant consideration independently of whether their formal expression in a model implies constancy of the above ratios.

There are three novel features of Kaldor's approach. First, he uses the Keynesian savings-investment relationship to determine the distribution of income instead of the level of output and employment. Second, he rejects the traditional idea that it is possible to distinguish between movements on a given production function and movements of the function itself when analysing relationships between growth in productivity, capital accumulation and technical progress. Instead, he uses a technical progress function to describe the relationship between the proportionate rates of growth of output and capital over time. The technical progress function has been modified in the *R.E.S.*(*2*) paper; it now describes the relationship between the proportionate rate of growth of gross investment per operative and the resulting proportionate rate of growth of productivity of that labour which operates the new machines. Third, Kaldor regards scarcity of resources rather than lack of effective demand as the main obstacle to economic growth; this view implies that full employment is the long-run equilibrium position of a *growing* economy. Each of these features is described more fully below.

67

The purposes of this paper are, first, to argue that the distributive mechanism (which Kaldor originally described as operative only in the long run) must work in the short period if it is to be included in the model; second, to set out the conditions which have to be fulfilled if the distributive mechanism is to work in the short period; third, to argue that Kaldor's demonstration that 'it is . . . impossible to conceive of a *moving* equilibrium of growth to be an under-employment equilibrium' (*Economica* paper, p. 220; *Corfu Conference* paper, p. 201) is unsatisfactory. The paper is in four sections. In section I the distributive mechanism, the technical progress function and the investment function are briefly described. In section II the criticisms relating to the distributive mechanism and its operation in the short period are developed. It is shown that when the level of planned investment changes as between short periods, the conditions which allow it to work in the short period may imply pricing, and other, behaviour by the entrepreneurs in the investment-goods sector significantly different from the behaviour of entrepreneurs in the consumption-goods sector. Behaviour patterns may differ not only within the bounds of one short period but as between succeeding short periods as well. Section III contains a discussion of the 'representative firm' model of the *Economica* and *Corfu Conference* papers. The criticism of this device as a means of justifying the assumption of full employment in the main model is set out in section IV. The concept of a 'representative firm' which is a replica of the whole economy is shown to be untenable when the analysis is extended to a two-sector model. The account in the *Economica* and *Corfu Conference* papers of the movement from an under-employment equilibrium position to a full-employment one is shown to violate the assumptions underlying the construction of the 'representative firm' model. Finally, it is shown that there is no position of full-employment equilibrium in the model. Rather, the model implies that over time a capitalist economy will tend either towards a position of under-employment equilibrium, or towards a position of full employment with inflation.[2]

I

The distributive mechanism

Kaldor developed his theory of distribution because he did not consider marginal productivity to be an adequate explanation of the determination of distributive shares in capitalist society. Briefly, he argues that marginal productivity theory has to assume that it is possible to construct an isoproduct curve showing the different proportions of capital and labour which produce a given level of national output. The slope of this curve plays a key part in the determination of the relative prices of capital and labour. However, the curve cannot be constructed and its slope measured until the rates of profit and wages that it is intended to determine are themselves known; for it is only when these rates are known beforehand that capital can be valued. Moreover, the value of the same physical capital and the slope of the iso-product curve vary with the rates chosen – and this makes the construction unacceptable.[3] Kaldor substitutes instead the fruitful idea that the long-run share of profits in national income is likely to be greater, the greater is the enthusiasm, vigour and (therefore) desire to accumulate capital, of the businessmen in the economy concerned.

A closed two-sector economy with a constant workforce is assumed in the analysis below. In Kaldor's argument, if profit margins are flexible, if the savings propensities of profit- and wage-earners are given; if savings out of profits are greater than those out of wages; and if investment expenditure is determined independently of the distribution of income, the share of investment in the national income determines the distribution of income. Initially, investment is taken as given. 'The interpretative value of the model . . . depends on the "Keynesian" hypothesis that investment, or rather, the ratio of investment to output, can be treated as an independent variable, invariant with respect to changes in the two savings propensities . . .' (*R.E.S* (*1*) paper, p. 95). The distribution of income (which is assumed to be *full-employment* income) is found by substituting the value of I/Y in the equation,

$$\frac{P}{Y} = \frac{1}{\beta - \alpha} \cdot \frac{I}{Y} - \frac{\alpha}{\beta - \alpha}$$

(which reduces to $P = I/\beta$ if $\alpha = 0$) where I = investment, Y = output or income, P = profits, β = the average and marginal propensity to save out of profits, and α = the average and marginal propensity to save out of wages. It is assumed that the levels of wages and profits are such that the real wage rate exceeds 'a certain subsistence minimum' and the rate of profit exceeds 'the minimum . . . necessary to induce capitalists to invest their capital' (*R.E.S.* (*1*) paper, pp. 97–8).

The model can be illustrated by a simple diagram (see Figure 6.1). The ratios of long-run planned savings and investment to full-employment national income are measured on the vertical axis, and the

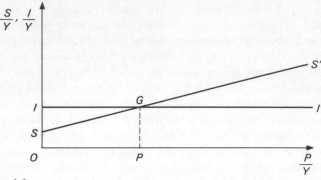

Figure 6.1

share of profits in long-run full-employment national income is measured on the horizontal axis. The I/Y ratio is autonomous, that is, it is drawn as a horizontal straight line, as I/Y is assumed to be independent of P/Y. On the other hand, S/Y is shown as an increasing function of P/Y, which reflects the assumption that the marginal propensity to save out of profits is greater than that out of wages. If profit margins are flexible, prices will so move in relation to money wages that the distribution of income which gives the planned savings required to offset planned investment will be established. In terms of Figure 6.1, if the ratio of investment to income is OI, the share of profits in income will be OP.

The technical progress function

Kaldor rejects the traditional idea that it is possible to distinguish between movements on a given production function and movements of the production function itself. Instead, he assumes that the flow of new ideas over time occurs at a steady rate, but that their impact on productivity per man depends on the rate at which capital is accumulated. This concept gives the technical progress function, TT', in which the proportionate rate of growth of output $(Y_{t+1} - Y_t)/Y_t$ is an increasing function of the proportionate rate of growth of capital $(K_{t+1} - K_t)/K_t$ (see Figure 6.2). With no capital accumulation, productivity per man would still grow over time at the proportionate rate, OT. Faster rates, however, require capital accumulation; hence TT' has a positive slope. At E capital and output are growing at the same proportionate rate. The main purpose of Kaldor's papers (from the *E.J.* paper on) is to show that there are forces at work in a capitalist economy which make

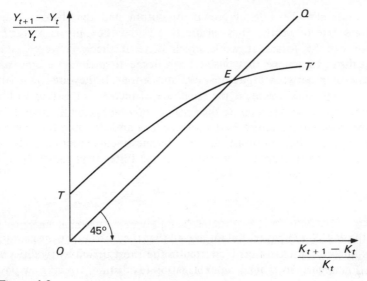

Figure 6.2

E the position of long-run equilibrium. There, the ratio, K/Y, is constant. With capital and output growing at the same proportionate rate, I/Y will be constant also, which implies both constant distributive shares and a constant rate of profit on capital.

The investment function

The technical progress function shows how output will change if certain rates of investment are implemented. The rate of investment is determined by the investment function and the distributive mechanism. The investment function determines the *planned* investment of each period; the distributive mechanism determines whether it becomes *actual* investment. The rate of actual investment determines the position of the economy on the technical progress function in each 'period'. The length of the 'period' is such that by its end, actual capital is brought to the level of capital desired at the beginning of the 'period'. In the investment function in the *E.J.* paper it is assumed that businessmen wish to maintain a constant relationship between capital invested and output; that this relationship is an increasing function of the rate of profit on capital; and that businessmen expect the same rate of growth of output in the current 'period' as occurred in the previous 'period'. These assumptions make current planned investment a function of the previous 'period's' rate of growth of output and the change in the current rate of profit. They ensure that if the economy is not at E, there will be forces at work which drive it there. However, it is unrealistic to assume that businessmen desire to maintain a constant relationship between capital invested and output. If they are to the left of E, they could maintain the same rate of increase of output with a falling capital-output ratio. In the *Corfu Conference* paper this objection is overcome by assuming that investment is an increasing function of the expected rate of profit and that businessmen expect the rate of profit to rise if output is currently growing faster than capital (*Corfu Conference* paper, pp. 212-14).[4]

II

In the *R.E.S.* (*1*) paper, Kaldor argued that the distributive mechanism was long-run in character, frustrated in the short period by rigidities in profit margins, so that as an explanation (as distinct from an *ex post* identity) it was of relevance only in this long-run sense. But in the later papers he requires the mechanism to work within a period of time which is only long enough to allow the investment plans made at the beginning of the period to be carried out, that is, within the gestation period (*E.J.* paper, pp. 604-6). Thus, the intersection of the graph of the functional relationship between S/Y and P/Y with that of the relationship between I/Y and P/Y 'indicates the *short period* equilibrium level of profits and of investment as a proportion of income' (*E.J.* paper, p. 600, italics not in original. '. . . all this is perfectly consistent with Marshallian orthodoxy – looking at it as a *short period* theory of distribution' (*Economica* paper, p. 220). These statements conflict with the position taken in the *R.E.S.* (1) paper and indeed in the *E.J.* paper itself. In the latter paper, he suggests that

> the theory of distribution underlying this model – which makes the share of profits in income entirely dependent on the ratio of investment to output, and the propensity to save out of profits and wages – is only acceptable as a 'long run' theory, since changes in these factors exert only a limited influence in the short period. As was indicated in my earlier paper [*R.E.S.*(*1*), pp. 99-100], in the short period profit margins are likely to be inflexible . . . around their customary level – which means that they are largely historically determined. What is suggested is that the long-term investment requirements and saving propensities are the underlying factors which set the standard around which these customary levels are found . . . . (*E.J.* paper, pp. 621-2.)

For Kaldor's model of economic growth to work, the distributive mechanism must operate in the short period, despite his disclaimer to the contrary. Otherwise, the planned investment of each short period may not become actual investment and the growth of output of each short period then will not be obtained by putting the value of *planned* capital accumulation in the technical progress function. The actual rate of capital accumulation could always be applied to the technical progress function, but there would then be no guarantee that the economy would move towards E.

What patterns of entrepreneurial behaviour with regard to pricing would allow the Kaldor distributive mechanism to work in the short period (which is taken to be the gestation period of investment)? By 'work in the short period' is meant that any change in planned investment at the beginning of a short period is so accompanied by movements of resources, prices and the distribution of income, that the investment planned at the beginning of the period becomes actual investment by the end. In the Kaldor mechanism prices so adjust to changes in demand that the distribution of *full-employment* income changes so as to bring forth the required savings. The purposes of the remainder of this section are, first, to derive the relevant conditions for equilibrium in the short period for a model of a closed two-sector economy, the properties of which are outlined below; second, if planned investment is allowed to change from short period to short period, to analyse the process of adjustment, both within each period and as between periods that allows planned investment to become actual investment in each short period.

Consider the following closed two-sector economy which, initially, is in equilibrium at full employment, that is to say, planned investment equals actual investment, and prices are so related to money-wage costs that the required savings are forthcoming. Suppose that the consumption-goods and investment-goods sectors produce homogeneous commodities, bread and steel respectively. For simplicity, assume that wage-carners spend all their incomes, and profit-carners save all theirs. To avoid the problems associated with the earnings of machines being spread over a number of short periods, assume that the capital stocks of each sector only last for one short period, so that they have to be replaced each period. Assume a constant workforce *which is fully employed each period*; that labour will move immediately from one sector to another in response to a rise in money wages; that the amount of labour which moves is a known function of the rise in money wages; and that a definite relative wage structure is associated with each conceivable distribution of the workforce between the two sectors (a special case of this relationship is that the same relative wage structure applies, whatever the distribution of the workforce). Assume that demands for steel are lodged at the beginning of each short period; that the resulting production plans remain unchanged for each period; and that the final production itself occurs at a point in time, in this case, at the end of the short period concerned.[5] It follows that the production of any short period must be undertaken by labour working with the capital stock in existence at the beginning of the period, and that the steel production of the period concerned cannot itself be used to produce steel and bread until the next period. That is to say, the existing stock of steel in each sector is specific, not 'Swan-type' meccano sets which can be easily dismantled and moved from one sector to another in the short period. Finally, it is assumed that labour rather than physical capacity is the principal bottleneck, especially in the steel sector. This implies that production will change proportionately with changes in the input of labour.[6] The labour inputs per unit of output of bread and steel in each short period will be determined by the size of the capital stocks in their corresponding sectors, but will be unaffected by changes in the employment of labour itself.

Planned investment will become actual investment and the distributive mechanism will work in the short period, if the following four conditions are fulfilled:

1. the investment sector has sufficient labour to produce the desired amount of steel and, once the required amount of labour has been secured, the relative wage structure is such that there is no tendency for labour to move from one sector to the other;
2. the price of bread is such that, if the level of money demand for bread is known (that is to say, the total wages bill), there is neither unsatisfied demand nor unintended changes in stocks;
3. the price of steel is such that the expected rates of profit on the marginal machines in current steel output going to each sector are equal;[7]
4. all members of the workforce are employed.

The following notation is adopted:

n,N: number of men required to produce one unit of bread and steel respectively;
m,M: the stocks of machines in the bread and steel sectors respectively, measured in steel units;[8]
w,W: the money wage rates per man per short period in the bread and steel sectors respectively;
p,P: the prices of bread and steel respectively;
x,X: employment in the bread and steel sectors respectively.

The above conditions can be set out formally as follows:

Condition 1

Suppose that the production of planned investment requires X men working with the existing capital stock in the steel sector. That is to say, planned investment is X/N in physical terms and PX/N in value terms. The employment of X men implies a particular relative wage structure: W/w.

Condition 2

The price of bread, p, can be deduced from the following equation:

$$wx + WX = \frac{px}{n}$$

that is

$$p = wn \left(1 + \frac{WX}{wx}\right) \qquad [1]$$

That is to say, the price of bread is its wages cost per unit marked up by the product of the relative wave structure and the ratio of employment in the two sectors (if $w = W$, the mark-up is the ratio of employment alone).

Condition 3

The price of steel can be deduced as follows: assume that entrepreneurs in both sectors expect the prices, wages, and the employment and output shares, of the current period to recur in the next period, also.[9] One unit of steel in the steel sector produces PX/MN value units of steel, and one unit of steel in the bread sector produces px/mn value units of bread. Condition 3 therefore is that

$$\frac{\dfrac{PX}{MN} - \dfrac{WNX}{MN}}{P} = \frac{\dfrac{px}{mn} - \dfrac{wnx}{mn}}{P}$$

that is

$$P = WN \left(1 + \frac{M}{m}\right) \qquad [2]$$

That is to say, the price of steel is its wages cost per unit marked up by the ratio of the capital stocks of the two sectors in existence at the beginning of the period.[10] With the special assumption concerning the lengths of life of machines, equation 2 can be written as:

$$P = WN \left(\frac{1}{1-\lambda}\right)$$ [2a]

where λ is the proportion of the *previous* period's production of steel which went to the steel sector itself.

Condition 4

All members of the workforce will be employed if

$$x + X = \overline{X}$$ [3]

where $\overline{X}$ is the total workforce.

These conditions must hold in each short period; otherwise, planned investment will not become actual investment by the end of the period, and the Kaldor distributive mechanism will not have worked.[11]

With the conditions of short-period equilibrium established, it is now necessary to ask, first, how must profit margins and prices change, and labour move, *within a period*, given the level of planned investment of this period relative to that of the period before; second, how must profit margins and prices change, and labour move, *as between different periods*, if the pattern of planned investment over time is given? The first question concerns the dynamic process that occurs within a given period. The second question is concerned with comparative statics, the comparison of successive short-period equilibrium situations. Unfortunately, there are no clear-cut answers to either question. They depend upon whether or not technical progress is occurring; on the level of investment of the preceding period (in the case of the first question); and on the pattern of change of investment over time (in the case of the second question).

The simplest case is to assume that there is no technical progress; that planned investment each period has long been constant; that money wages in both sectors are the same; that labour moves simply because new jobs are created; and that full employment is maintained. If the analysis is started in period t, the prices ensuring equilibrium will be

$$p_t = wn_t \left(1 + \frac{X_t}{x_t}\right); P_t = wN_t \left(\frac{1}{1 - \lambda_{t-1}}\right)$$

Suppose that planned investment increases in period $(t + 1)$. This will create additional job opportunities in the steel sector, and as labour moves immediately to this sector, entrepreneurs in the bread sector will realise that they can no longer maintain their present level of production. However, provided that they charge a price of

$$P_{t+1} = wn_{t+1} \left(1 + \frac{X_{t+1}}{x_{t+1}} \right)$$

which is greater than p_t, as X_{t+1}/x_{t+1} is greater than X_t/x_t, the lower production of bread will be sold without there being either queues, or an unintended fall in stocks of bread. The steel sector will have gained the additional labour that it needed; the current steel production will sell at a price of

$$P_{t+1} = wN_{t+1} \left(\frac{1}{1 - \lambda_t} \right)$$

and planned investment will become actual investment. Now $P_{t+1} = P_t$ (because w is unchanged, N_{t+1} is equal to N_t and λ_t is equal to λ_{t-1}), so that profit margins will remain unchanged in the steel sector though they have lengthened in the bread sector. The share of profits in the national income will have risen, reflecting the rise in investment as a proportion of the national income. Full employment will have been maintained.

It may be supposed that the proportion of steel output which goes to the steel sector at the end of $(t + 1)$ is such that the amount of steel going to the bread sector actually falls.[12] This reflects the expected fall in demand for bread and the expected rise in demand for steel. If, in period $(t + 2)$, planned investment drops back to its original level, equilibrium in this short period requires, first, that *more than the additional labour* of the previous period which moves to the steel sector move to the bread sector; second, that profit *margins* on bread fall below their original level; third, that the profit margin in the steel sector lengthen as λ_{t+1} is greater than λ_t. The price of bread may, or may not, rise depending upon whether or not the fall in the profit margin is outweighed by the rise in wages cost per unit due to the lower amount of steel in the sector. Similarly, the price of steel may, or may not, rise because the fall in the wages cost per unit may offset the rise in the profit margin. In period $(t + 3)$, the steel production of $(t + 2)$ having been distributed as in period t, the prices, profit margins, and the compositions of output and employment of period t are all restored. If the rise in planned investment of period $(t + 1)$ is permanent, the story in period $(t + 1)$ is the same, but now the bread profit margin does not fall by as much in period $(t + 2)$ and the price either rises more or falls less. Prices and profit margins take on levels which reflect the fact that the original capital-labour ratio in the steel sector has been restored at the new, higher level of steel production. By period $(t + 3)$ the profit margins and prices of bread and steel will all be at their new, long-period levels. As there is no technical progress the long-period capital-labour ratios of both sectors remain unchanged, and therefore the percentage increases in profit margins in each sector will have been the same. The percentage changes in prices will also have been the same; wage costs per unit in both sectors will have fallen because of the larger amount of steel in both sectors in the new situation. Finally, if investment increases period by period, the story in period $(t + 1)$ is the same, but bread profit margins and prices then rise period by period. Whether after period $(t + 2)$, the profit margins on steel rise by the same percentage amounts as those on bread depends upon the percentage rate of increase of planned investment.[13] Prices will *never* change by the same percentage amounts because of the rises in wages costs per unit in the bread sector and the falls in wages costs of the steel sector.

The above analysis suggests that the characteristics of the dynamic process within each short period are, first, that entrepreneurs in the steel sector are active; actively bidding for labour (or sacking it), and actively raising (or lowering) production in response to changes in demands. Second, and by contrast, the entrepreneurs in the bread sector are passive: passively accepting the loss (or return) of labour and the consequent changes in production. Their only active role is to set the price of bread appropriate to each situation. The analysis also shows that, as between periods, the changes in profit margins and prices over time, and the movement of labour over time, are determined by the corresponding pattern of planned investment. There is no guarantee that the percentage changes in profit margins and prices of the two sectors as between periods will be the same. That is to say, there may be significant differences in the entrepreneurial behaviour of the two sectors *as between the comparative static positions.*

The introduction of technical progress complicates the analysis. Technical progress shows itself by the changes over time in the input coefficients, n and N, the values of these coefficients in any period being determined by the investment of the *previous* period. Consider, first, the case of a once-and-for-all change in the level of planned investment occurring in period $(t + 1)$. Suppose that prior to this change, planned investment each period was constant, so that the labour force in steel fell at a rate determined by the fall in the input coefficient, N. The proportion of steel going to the steel sector each period is assumed to fall also, so that the capital-labour ratios in the two sectors remain constant. Profit margins in the bread and steel sectors would then have been falling (whether at the same percentage rate or not will depend upon the percentage fall in N); prices of bread and steel would also have been falling, first, because of the fall in profit margins, second, because of the fall in wages costs per unit.[14] When planned investment rises in period $(t + 1)$, it is by no means certain that labour will have to move to the steel sector. All that can be said is that the falls in the profit margin and price of bread will now be less than they otherwise would have been. The profit margin and price of steel will be unaffected relative to what they would have been in period $(t + 1)$ in the 'otherwise' situation, though they will be lower than in period t.

Alternatively, it could be assumed that prior to period $(t + 1)$, labour remained constant in the two sectors (so that total steel production each period increased by the same percentage as the increase in productivity per man) and that the proportion of steel going to the steel sector remained constant. Profit margins will have remained constant, and prices will have fallen as between periods by amounts determined by the falls in the input coefficients, n and N. In this case, a rise in planned investment in period $(t + 1)$, which is greater than that which can be accommodated by the increase in productivity, will definitely entail a shift of labour to the steel sector and a corresponding rise in the profit margin on bread, though not necessarily in the price of bread. The profit margin on steel (but not the price of steel) will remain unchanged. In period $(t + 2)$, if planned investment now reverts to increasing at a rate which can be accommodated by the change in N each period, the profit margin on bread will fall to a level determined by the movement back to this sector of the labour which moved to the steel sector in the previous period. The profit margin on steel will lengthen in period $(t + 2)$, but in period $(t + 3)$, and subsequently, it will remain constant; both bread and steel prices will resume patterns similar to those followed before the change in planned investment.

Obviously, there are many more variations on this theme. However, enough cases have been analysed to show that it is very doubtful whether entrepreneurial behaviour in the two sectors would be such as to allow the Kaldor distributive mechanism to work in the short period, or over time. The most likely outcome of an increase in investment demand in the short period when there is full employment is inflation, especially when the increased production of investment goods implies a cut in real wages.[15] In summary, there is no guarantee that planned investment will become actual investment, and whether it does or not depends on entrepreneurs in the bread sector following significantly different pricing policies to those in the steel sector. When the assumption of equal money wages is dropped this conclusion is not altered significantly. Full short-period equilibrium will then require either that the initial relative wage differential be immediately restored, or that a new one be immediately established. Accordingly, when planned investment increases and if, as a result, the steel sector requires additional labour, steel entrepreneurs will raise money wages in order to attract labour. Bread entrepreneurs must accept passively the resulting loss of labour even though they, at the same time, will be faced with an increased money demand for bread due to the higher money wages in the steel sector and the higher money wages that (under the first alternative) they will have to pay to restore the previous relative wage differential. If a period of time (shorter than the gestation period of investment) elapses before money wages in the bread sector are raised so as to restore the previous relative wage structure, two prices of bread will have to be set within the one short period. The increase in the price of bread within this period will be entirely accounted for by the increase in money wage costs per unit as the profit per unit, WX/x, associated with each price will be the same. With these modifications, the 'stories' are the same as before, and what happens to profit margins and prices depends upon the pattern of investment and the rate of technical progress. Furthermore, if the special assumption concerning the lengths of life of machines is dropped once again the analysis is not significantly affected. The profit margin in the steel sector must now be interpreted as $[1 + (M/m)]$; m and M of period t are the capital stocks appropriate for the expected levels of output of period $(t - 1)$.

III

The 'representative firm' model

In its simplest form Keynesian theory assumes that effective demand has no effect on the price level, but only on the level of output. However, if the level of demand affects the relationship between prices and money wages, a given level of autonomous investment will be associated with different levels of income, depending upon the distribution of that income between wages and profits. Furthermore, once more than normal profits are being earned, so that the current stock of capital is being worked at more than the normal level of capacity, businessmen will be encouraged to add to the capital stock, that is, induced investment will occur. From these ideas Kaldor derives a demand curve for output relating different distributions of income to different levels of output. He uses a 'representative firm' which behaves like a small-scale replica of the economy as a whole (so that variations in its output reflect variations in aggregate output). The supply curve, SS', consists of average prime costs, and a minimum margin of profit below which businessmen will not go for fear of spoiling the market (see Figure 6.3). Average prime costs are wages only as raw material costs cancel for the economy as a whole. The constancy of average prime costs up to near full employment reflects the fact that employment rather than physical capacity is the principal limitation on output.

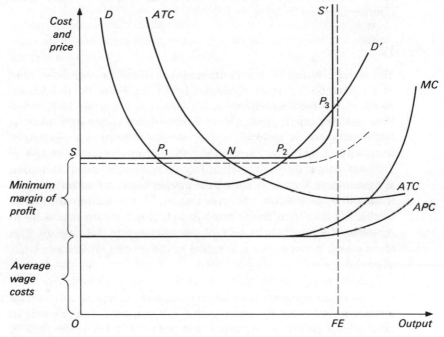

Figure 6.3

The corresponding demand curve, DD', is U-shaped showing, first, that the lower are prices relative to wages, the greater is the level of income associated with any given level of autonomous investment; second, that once normal profits are being earned (at the point N, where the average *total cost* curve, including normal profits, cuts SS') induced investment will occur. However, there must be a shift to profits in order to bring forth the required planned savings, since in this range of output, the marginal propensity to invest at any *given* distribution of income will exceed the corresponding marginal propensity to save (*Economica* paper, p. 219; *Corfu Conference* paper, p. 200). There are three possible equilibrium positions, namely, P_1, an under-employment one with no induced investment, P_2, an unstable one, and P_3, a full-employment one with positive induced investment. As the national incomes of capitalist economies have, in fact, grown over time, Kaldor argues that only P_3 is consistent with these observations, for only at P_3 does induced investment occur and capacity grow. That is to say, 'it . . . is impossible to conceive of a *moving* equilibrium of growth to be an under-employment equilibrium' (*Economica* paper, p. 220; *Corfu Conference* paper, p. 201).

IV

The major criticism of this model is the use of the 'representative firm' as a replica of the whole economy. Is it a replica of the investment-goods sector, the consumption-goods sector, or a mixture of the two? How can its output, presumably a homogeneous commodity, move at the same speed as national output which (at best) is a mixture of consumption and investment goods, the outputs of which change at different rates at different levels of income and employment? Moreover, as is shown in section II above, the pricing behaviour of businessmen must differ as between the two sectors, if the Kaldor distributive mechanism is to work in the short period. It is therefore impossible to represent the pricing behaviour of the economy in one diagram. This alone makes it inadequate as a model of the process of inflation, if not of growth.

Unless the equilibrium point, P_1, is the result of applying the multiplier to an autonomous level of consumption, or unless autonomous investment is completely unproductive, it *is* possible for an economy to exhibit both growth in output per head *and* under-employment, that is, for the economy to be at P_1. The fact that the national incomes of capitalist economies have, in fact, grown therefore does not necessarily imply that the long-run equilibrium position is a full-employment one. Indeed, if autonomous investment does increase productivity, average wage costs will fall, lowering the SS' curve, and a given distribution of income and level of autonomous investment will be associated with a higher national product, so that the downward portion of DD' curve will also move to the right. P_1 therefore will move to the right over time, showing that economic growth and under-employment equilibrium are consistent with one another. It is doubtful whether the section of the demand curve between P_1 and P_2 could exist, since the price level needed to establish the output in this range is below the minimum supply price, that is, the price below which businessmen will not cut for fear of spoiling the market. Unless the economy is at an output greater than that associated with P_2, there is no mechanism in the model by which it could reach P_3. Furthermore, it is doubtful whether P_3 could exist, either. The upward sloping portion of the DD' curve shows that there must be a shift to profits to allow planned investment to be offset by planned savings. The DD' curve must rise faster than the money-wages prime-cost curve, APC, and therefore the supply curve, SS', so that it could never cut SS' from above.[16] That is to say, the 'representative firm' model shows that over time capitalist economies tend either towards a position of under-employment equilibrium or towards a position of full employment with inflation. N indicates the level of output where the existing capital stock is worked at normal capacity. As drawn, N occurs at a level well below full employment which is inconsistent with the assumption that labour is the main bottleneck, and with the constant prime costs associated with it and larger outputs. Finally, it is hard to see the logic of using the distributive mechanism which implicitly assumes full employment to ensure that the economy gets to full employment.

Notes

Australian Economic Papers, Vol. 2, no. 1, June 1963, pp. 20–36. This article is a revised version of a paper read to Section G, *Jubille A.N.Z.A.A.S. Conference*, held in Sydney, August 1962. The writer is greatly indebted to Mr Kaldor for his detailed comments on a draft of section II. He is also indebted to the members of the Department of Economics and Commerce, University of Adelaide; Professor J.E. Isaac, University of Melbourne; Dr J.D. Pitchford, Australian National University; and Mrs Joan Robinson, University of Cambridge; for their comments on drafts of this paper, but is alone responsible for the views expressed.

    1 The latest version of the model is contained in, 'A New Model of Economic Growth', *Review of Economic Studies*, June 1962, pp. 174–92. Other important papers are: 'Capital Accumulation and Economic Growth', in Lutz and Hague (1961); 'Economic Growth and the Problem of Inflation – Parts I and II', *Economica*, August and November 1959, pp. 212–26 and 287–98; 'A Model of Economic Growth', *Economic Journal*, December 1957, pp. 591–624; and 'Alternative Theories of Distribution', *Review of Economic Studies*, March 1956,

pp. 83–100. They are referred to in the text as the *R.E.S.* (*2*), *Corfu Conference*, *Economica*, *E.J.*, and *R.E.S.* (*1*) papers, respectively. The *R.E.S.* (*2*) paper was written jointly with James A. Mirrlees.

2 Sections III and IV are based on an unpublished paper written jointly with Messrs R. Blandy, J. Y. Henderson and N. Sarah.

3 Detailed accounts of Kaldor's objections to marginal productivity will be found in the *R.E.S.* (*1*) paper, pp. 89–91; the *E.J.* paper, pp. 602–3; and the *Economica* paper, p. 224.

4 The criticism of the investment function in the *E.J.* paper was first made by Mr H. R. Hudson and Professor J. E. Meade. Their objections may be said to have been overcome in the *Corfu Conference* paper. However, the criticism in this paper (in section II) concerning the determination of the rate of actual investment applies as much to the later version as to the earlier one.

5 The writer is indebted to Mr Kaldor for suggesting the bread and steel model. The assumptions about the nature of the total production process seem a fair interpretation of the period analysis used in his *E.J.* paper (pp. 600–10).

6 Kaldor explicitly assumes this (see, for example, the *E.J.* paper, p. 593, and the *Economica* paper, pp. 216–17); it reflects his view that the long-run equilibrium position of a growing developed economy is a full-employment one. Formally, it involves short-run production functions of the form: $O = f(L, K^*)$, where O is output per short period, L is labour, K^* is the constant capital stock in the sector concerned and $\delta f / \delta L$ is constant over the relevant range. See also the prime cost curves in Figure 6.3.

7 In correspondence Mr Kaldor has suggested that equality of the overall profit rates as between sectors is the relevant condition. However, this condition seems more appropriate for long-period equilibrium. As it happens, the same price of steel is implied, whichever condition is used.

8 With the special assumptions concerning the lengths of life of machines, m and M are in fact the steel production of the previous period. More generally, they are the stocks of capital in existence at the beginning of each short period in each sector. n and N are functions of m and M respectively such that $\delta n / \delta m$ and $\delta N / \delta M$ are both negative, but they are not related to the employment levels of the two sectors.

9 This assumption is consistent with the assumptions underlying the investment function in the *E.J.* paper (pp. 600–1).

10 If the alternative condition of equality of profits rates is assumed, the same result can be obtained by solving for P in the following equation:

$$\frac{WX}{Pm} = \frac{\dfrac{PX}{N} - WX}{PM}$$

(As wage-earners are assumed to consume all their income and profit-earners to save all theirs, profits in the bread sector are equal to the wages bill in the steel sector.)

11 However, for planned investment to become actual investment, only condition 1 need be satisfied. The entrepreneurs in the bread sector could set a price lower than that implied by equation [1], and allow queues to occur so that actual savings would be greater than planned savings. There would then be a situation of suppressed inflation. This would allow the main model to work, but not because

the distributive mechanism operated in the short period. The writer is indebted to Dr K. J. Hancock for this point.

12 The writer is indebted to Mr J. R. Hubbard for pointing out an error in a previous version of this paragraph.

13 Obviously, this process cannot go on without limit, for there is a level below which real wages cannot be made to fall, so that the transfer of labour to the steel sector will eventually stop.

14 Thus, even if profit margins fall at the same percentage rate in both sectors, prices may not move together because the percentage changes in N may differ from those in n. The actual falls in n and N consist of two elements: the falls in the coefficients associated with given levels of steel, and the changes in the levels of steel itself in the two sectors because of the previous period's investment.

15 This occurs when there is no technical progress, and/or when the rise in planned investment requires such a shift of labour to the steel sector that even with the rise in productivity per man in the bread sector, total bread production falls.

16 The writer is indebted to Mr E.A. Russell for this point.

7 A two-sector model of the distribution of income and the level of employment in the short run*

Many of the models of economic growth which have been developed in the post-war period have been concerned with the implications of the capacity-creating effects of investment expenditure for the level and rate of growth of national income. This was the natural next step to take, once the Keynesian questions about the employment-creating effects of investment expenditure in the short run had been answered. Unfortunately, most of these models either ignore, or do not take sufficient account of, the following features of advanced industrial economies:

    (i) Manufacturing firms are usually price-makers rather than price-takers.

    (ii) Capital goods, once created, are specific, not malleable, so that responses to both technical progress and changes in relative factor prices can only occur as additions, at the margin, to existing capital stocks.

    (iii) Money wages are the outcome of bargaining processes between wage-earners and profit-earners in which the levels of effective demand and employment, and the rate of price inflation, play prominent roles.

    (iv) The economic process can be viewed as a succession of short periods in which the levels of the principal aggregates, prices and the distribution of income are the outcomes of decisions made, short period by short period, which are themselves influenced by the actual happenings of past short periods and the expected happenings of future short periods.

The factors which determine the distribution of income between wage-earners and profit-earners have been much debated in this post-war discussion of economic growth. There have been two main sides to the debate: one side has argued that distributive shares can be explained by the workings of competitive market forces in conjunction with technical conditions which are summed up in the notion of a production function; the other has argued that macroeconomic forces, in particular the savings-investment relationship, are the key ones in the explanation.

The model which is outlined in this paper includes the four features mentioned above; moreover, it shows how both elements of the debate about distribution might be combined in an explanation of short-run distributive shares. It has as predecessors, models of Kaldor (1956, 1959), Joan Robinson (1956; 1951–80, vol. ii, pp. 145–58), Sen (1963) and the present writer (1963); it also includes some ideas which were first developed by Salter (1960, 1965). The paper is an attempt to produce a model in which the short-run distribution of income and the level of employment in an economy which experiences both population growth and technical progress are determined. The model is a short-period one in the sense that it sets out the conditions for equilibrium in the short run, which is defined as the gestation period of investment goods. But, by linking the happenings of one short period to both those preceding it and those following it, it is hoped eventually to say something about longer periods of time as well. The model also allows a discussion of multipliers other than the usual Keynesian income multiplier. In this paper the model is explained and the happenings of *one* short period are discussed.

The model has the usual shortcomings of this branch of aggregative analysis: it assumes that business decisions are made at the same point of time for the same length of time and cannot be revised until the period of time is up; and it has no government or overseas sector. In addition, the assumption concerning the length of life of investment goods is highly artificial; one result is that the influence of the amount of capacity in existence on planned investment expenditures cannot be taken into account. The model does, however, allow population growth and technical progress to influence the values of the variables in it. And it does not assume full employment in order to explain the distribution of income.

The plan of the paper is as follows: in section I, the assumptions are set out. Sections II and III contain the notation that is used and the main equations. Section IV contains the key derived equations, namely, those for the distribution of income, the level of employment, and the level of money expenditure. A multiplier analysis is presented in section V together with some comments on what may happen when the equilibrium values implied in the model are inconsistent with either the amount of labour or capacity available.

I   Assumptions

1. The economy

A closed, two-sector economy is assumed – a consumption goods sector producing a homogeneous commodity, bread, and an investment goods sector producing a homogeneous commodity, steel, both being measured in appropriate physical units.

2. Savings behaviour

Wage-earners spend all their incomes and profit-earners save all theirs.

3. Production conditions

Investment goods last for one period only; that is to say, machines disappear just when either technical progress or changes in relative factor prices first start to make them obsolete. This assumption enables the analysis to avoid the problems associated with the fact that the earnings on particular capital goods are spread over several periods of time, and those associated with the determination of the obsolescence of existing plant; but this is at the expense of not allowing existing capital to influence investment demands. Investment demands are lodged at the beginning of each period and the resulting production plans remain unchanged for the duration of the period, with the production of investment goods being completed by the end of the period. The production of bread, however, is assumed to take less time.

The short-run production functions in the two sectors exhibit constant returns up to their capacity outputs so that, with constant money wage rates, the resulting marginal and average cost curves are L-shaped. The constant inputs of labour per unit of output of the period depend upon:

(i) Technical progress in the sectors concerned, which is assumed to be autonomous and which takes the form of the iso-quant of a given unit of product moving inwards towards the origin.[1]

(ii) The choice of technique, which is determined by the expectation of this period's factor prices – the expected wage rates of the sectors concerned, the expected rate of profit and the price of steel – in the previous period. The choice of technique is described more fully below – see section I, no. 5. Here, it is sufficient to state that technical progress consists of new methods of producing bread and steel; that in any period, there is more than one 'best-practice' technique; that each technique requires a different steel-labour ratio; and that the choice between them is made on the cost-minimizing principle.[2] Capital can be measured in physical units of steel, but each technique is assumed to require a 'machine' made from a different number of units of steel.

Labour inputs per unit of output will be lower, the faster has been the rate of technical progress, and the higher has been the expected wage rate relative to expected unit capital costs. However, their sizes are independent of the current levels of employment of labour in the sectors, up to capacity outputs. Most importantly, machines, once made, are specific to their own sectors: they cannot be dismantled and set up in the other sector – that is, they are not 'Swan-type' meccano sets. Current steel production is non-specific in the sense that a choice can be made as to the types of machines for which it will be used. But the current output of bread and steel can be produced only by labour working with the machines made at the end of the previous period – the production of steel in the current period cannot itself be used to produce bread and steel in the same period.

4. Money wages in the two sectors

A. Bread sector

The money wage in the bread sector is set once a period, at its start, either by a process of collective bargaining or by arbitration. In either case, it is a function of the previous period's money wage, price of bread, changes in productivity (in both sectors) and unemployment. (By making it a function of the previous period's unemployment, population growth can be introduced into the model.) The money wage can fall as between periods, because it is taken to include overtime payments. This function includes the principal factors which influence money wage demands (and the extent to which they are met) in the real world, or at least that part of it to which advanced industrial economies belong.

B. Steel sector

The money wage in the steel sector is also set at the beginning of the period, momentarily after the money wage in the bread sector. It is a function of the current money wage in the bread sector and the current employment requirement in the steel sector. A relative wage structure is thus introduced, with the money wage in the bread sector being the floor and employment requirements – which depend upon the demand for steel and the technical conditions of production, see section I, no. 5 below – determining the height above the floor. It is assumed that labour is homogeneous in the bread sector but not in the steel sector. If the problem of simultaneously determining the two money wage-rates is thought to be a nuisance, the money wage-rate in steel can be regarded as a function of five variables, four of which are the same as those influencing the money wage-rate in the bread sector, with employment requirement in the steel sector as the fifth.

5. Demand for steel

The demand for steel is a function of the previous period's profits, the total demand being the sum of the two separate demands (and functions) of each sector. It is expressed in real terms – as a particular amount of steel – with the money profits of the previous period being deflated by the price of steel of the previous period. This assumption reflects the longer-run dependence of investment demands on retained profits; expressing profits in real terms brings out the investment aspect of business savings, that is, their steel value. (Treating investment demand as a demand for certain quantities of steel is equivalent to deflating money expenditures on machines by a price index of identifiable parts of different sorts of machines.)

The form which the steel is to take (what machine is to be built for each sector) depends upon the current 'best-practice' techniques, the expected rate of profit, the current price of steel (which will be known, see section I, no. 7 below) and the expected money wage rate of the sector concerned. The expected rate of profit is assumed to be a function of the realized gross rate of profit of the preceding period for the economy as a whole. It is shown below (see section III, no. 2N) that this equals one plus the rate of growth of the capital stock – the ratio of investment (the aggregate output of steel) to the inherited stock of capital (the steel equivalent of the stock of machines) in the previous period – *if* the inherited capital stock is revalued in terms of the price of steel of the relevant period. Otherwise, the ratio of steel prices also affects the value of the realized rate of profit and it becomes a ratio of *values* instead of a ratio of *commodities*. It is a gross concept (that is, the rate of profit before amortization). This may be used in a simple model because, having arbitrarily determined the lengths of life of the machines, the problem of determining depreciation is subsumed.[3] The

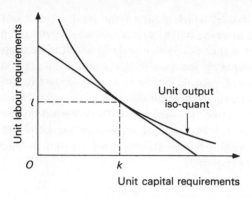

Figure 7.1

expected money wage rates are assumed to be functions of the actual wage rates in the sectors concerned.

Following Salter, the iso-product curve of a unit of bread or steel, using the 'best-practice' techniques, is drawn as in Figure 7.1, with unit capital requirements (the costs of which can be determined once the length of life, the expected rate of profit and the current price of steel are known) plotted on the horizontal axis and unit labour requirements on the vertical axis. The technique which minimizes expected costs is chosen – in this case, that using Ol labour per unit and Ok capital per unit; at this point the iso-product curve is tangential to the iso-cost curve, the slope reflecting expected relative factor prices. This determines, for each sector, how many machines their total demand for steel in physical units will become.[4]

6. Employment in the steel sector

Employment in the steel sector is governed by the demand for steel in real terms and by the inherited capital stock in the steel sector which determines the input of labour per unit of output of steel.

7. Price of steel

The price of steel per unit is assumed to be its money wage cost per unit, plus a mark-up which is assumed to be a function of the real demand for steel in the present period and the existing capacity in the steel sector. (With the present assumption about the length of life of machines, this is simply the proportion of the previous period's production of steel which went to the steel sector itself.) Given the existing level of capacity, the greater is current investment demand in real terms, the higher will be the mark-up which is set; conversely, given the level of demand, the greater the existing capacity, the lower the mark-up. Current demand rather than past expenditures is allowed to influence the mark-up, because demand in the investment goods sector is typically expressed through orders. The assumptions about the mark-up lie between the extremes of a constant mark-up and the flexible margins that Kaldor has to assume if his distributive mechanism is to work in the short period.[5]

8. Price of bread

The mark-up in the bread sector is assumed to be a function of the previous period's money expenditure on bread (which is equal to the previous period's total wages bill) and the existing capacity in the bread sector. As in the steel sector, the mark-up will be higher, the higher is past expenditure on bread; and it will be lower, the greater is existing capacity – in both cases, given the relevant *ceteris paribus* conditions. As consumption goods typically are not ordered, expectations as to the level of current sales are assumed to be based on recent past experience.

9. Employment in the bread sector

Employment in the bread sector is determined as follows: given the real wages in the two sectors, the input of labour per unit of output of bread, employment in the steel sector, and given that wage-earners spend all their incomes, employment in the bread sector must be sufficient to feed both the wage-earners in the steel sector and those in the bread sector itself. The current demand for bread is the total wages bill.

It is assumed that in each period the current productions of bread and steel are bought. If the correct employment is offered in the bread sector and too high a price is set, stocks will start to accumulate; if too low a price is set, queues will start to form. If too much employment is offered but the right price is set, stocks will start to accumulate; if too little, queues will start to form. There appears therefore to be a reasonable chance of reaching short-period equilibrium in the bread sector. As orders are placed in the steel sector at the start of the period, there is no problem there of matching supply and demand (as long as the solutions of the equations of the model are consistent with overall technical considerations).

II   Notation

The following notation is used. Lower-case letters refer to the bread sector, capitals to the steel sector, capital letters with bars are grand totals, subscripts refer to the time period, and starred variables are expected values from the previous period.

$i, I, \bar{I}$:   steel, measured in steel units;

c: bread, measured in bread units;

$x, X, \bar{X}$:   employment;

$\bar{\bar{X}}$:   available workforce;

m, M: capital stocks, measured in steel units;

n, N: labour inputs per unit of output;

w, W: money wage rates per man;[6]

p, P: prices;

S: savings;

$\pi, \Pi, \bar{\Pi}$:   profits;

r: realized gross rate of profit;

$\hat{t}, T$:   technical progress;

Y: national expenditure, product, income.

III   Unknowns and equations

1. Unknowns

There are twenty-two unknowns: n, N; i, I, $\bar{I}$; c; w, W; w*, W*; r, r*; p, P; x, X, $\bar{X}$; π, Π, $\bar{\Pi}$; S; Y.

2. Equations (in period t)

No form is given to the functions and only the signs of the partial derivatives are given. Equations designated (a) or (b) are already implied in other equations of the system.

A. Labour input coefficients

Bread sector:

$$n_t = f(P_{t-1}, r^*_{t-1}, w^*_{t-1}, \hat{t}_{t-1}) \tag{3.1}$$

where $f_{P_{t-1}}, f_{r^*_{t-1}} > 0; f_{w^*_{t-1}}, f_{\hat{t}_{t-1}} < 0$.

Steel sector:

$$N_t = F(P_{t-1}, r^*_{t-1}, W^*_{t-1}, T_{t-1})$$ [3.2]

where $F_{P_{t-1}} > 0, F_{r^*_{t-1}} > 0; F_{W^*_{t-1}} < 0, F_{T_{t-1}} < 0.$

That is, the labour input coefficients are determined by the inherited capital stock, in which is reflected the technique that was installed in the previous period. Both $\dfrac{\delta n_t}{\delta x_t}$ and $\dfrac{\delta N_t}{\delta X_t} = 0$, up to capacity outputs.

B. Demand for steel

$$i_t = g\left(\frac{\pi_{t-1}}{P_{t-1}}\right)$$ [3.3]

where $g' > 0$.

$$I_t = G\left(\frac{\Pi_{t-1}}{P_{t-1}}\right)$$ [3.4]

where $G' > 0$.

$$\bar{I}_t = i_t + I_t$$ [3.5]

C. Choice of machines

$$w^*_t = h(w_t), h' > 0$$ [3.6]

$$W^*_t = H(W_t), H' > 0$$ [3.7]

$$r^*_t = l\left(\frac{\bar{I}_{t-1}}{\bar{I}_{t-2}}\right) \text{ or } l\left(\frac{P_{t-1}\,\bar{I}_{t-1}}{P_{t-2}\,\bar{I}_{t-2}}\right),$$ [3.8]

$$l' > 0.$$

It is shown later (see section III, no. 2N) that the realized gross rate of profit is either one or other of the expressions in brackets; the equations for w_t and W_t are given later (see section III, nos 2E and 2G). $P_t, \hat{t}$ and T are also known, so that the choice of techniques in both sectors can be made (see section I, no. 5 above).

D. Employment and production in the steel sector

$$X_t = N_t \bar{I}_t$$ [3.9]

$$\bar{I}_t = X_t / N_t$$ [3.9a]

E. Money wage in the steel sector

$$W_t = J(w_t; X_t) \qquad\qquad [3.10]$$

where $J_{w_t}, J_{X_t} > 0$.

F. Price of steel

$$P_t = W_t N_t \{1 + [B(\bar{I}_t, I_{t-1})]\} \qquad\qquad [3.11]$$

where $B'_{\bar{I}_t} > 0, B'_{I_{t-1}} < 0$.

G. Money wage in the bread sector

$$w_t = j\left(w_{t-1}; p_{t-1}; \frac{n_{t-2}-n_{t-1}}{n_{t-1}}, \frac{N_{t-2}-N_{t-1}}{N_{t-1}}; \frac{\bar{\bar{X}}_{t-1}-\bar{X}_{t-1}}{\bar{\bar{X}}_{t-1}}\right) \qquad [3.12]$$

where $j_{w_{t-1}} > 0, j_{p_{t-1}} > 0$, and $j\left(\frac{n_{t-2}-n_{t-1}}{n_{t-1}}, \frac{N_{t-2}-N_{t-1}}{N_{t-1}}\right) > 0,$

$$j\left(\frac{\bar{\bar{X}}_{t-1}-\bar{X}_{t-1}}{\bar{\bar{X}}_{t-1}}\right) < 0$$

H. Price of bread

$$p_t = w_t n_t \{1 + [A(p_{t-1} c_{t-1}, i_{t-1})]\} \qquad\qquad [3.13]$$

where $A_{p_{t-1} c_{t-1}} > 0, A_{i_{t-1}} < 0$.

I. Demand for bread

$$p_t c_t = w_t x_t + W_t X_t \qquad\qquad [3.14]$$

J. Employment and production in the bread sector

As has been indicated (see section I, no. 9 above), employment in the bread sector must be sufficient, at the known real wages, to feed the wage-earners in the steel sector and the wage-earners in the bread sector who produce the bread for both groups. That is:

$$x_t = \left[\frac{\dfrac{W_t}{p_t} X_t}{\dfrac{1}{n_t} - \dfrac{W_t}{p_t}}\right]$$

$$= \frac{W_t X_t n_t}{p_t - w_t n_t} \qquad\qquad [3.15]$$

In other words, employment in the bread sector is the real wages bill in the steel sector divided by the difference between bread produced per man and the real wage per man in the bread sector:

$$c_t = \frac{x_t}{n_t}. \qquad\qquad [3.15a]$$

K. Total employment

$$\bar{X}_t = x_t + X_t \qquad\qquad [3.16]$$

L. Profits

$$\pi_t = W_t X_t \qquad\qquad [3.17]$$

$$\Pi_t = \frac{X_t}{N_t} P_t - W_t X_t \qquad\qquad [3.18]$$

$$\bar{\Pi}_t = \pi_t + \Pi_t = P_t \bar{I}_t \qquad\qquad [3.19]$$

M. Savings

$$\bar{\Pi}_t = S_t \qquad\qquad [3.19a]$$

$$S_t = P_t \bar{I}_t \qquad\qquad [3.20]$$

N. Realized gross rate of profit

$$r_t = \frac{P_t I_t}{P_{t-1} \bar{I}_{t-1}} \;\; or, \text{if } \bar{I}_{t-1} \text{ is revalued using } P_t, r_t = \frac{\bar{I}_t}{\bar{I}_{t-1}} \qquad [3.21]$$

O. National expenditure, production and income

$$Y_t = p_t c_t + P_t \bar{I}_t \qquad\qquad [3.22]$$

$$= \frac{x_t}{n_t} p_t + \frac{X_t}{N_t} P_t \qquad\qquad [3.22a]$$

$$= w_t x_t + W_t X_t + \bar{\Pi}_t \qquad\qquad [3.22b]$$

While these are identities, the workings of the model do imply that planned demands and supplies are equal, and that planned investment does offset planned saving.

IV   Derived equations for the distribution of income $\left(\dfrac{\overline{\Pi}_t}{Y_t}\right)$, the level of employment $(\overline{X}_t)$ and the money demand for output (Y_t)

1. Distribution of income

$$\frac{\overline{\Pi}_t}{Y_t} = \frac{\pi_t + \Pi_t}{w_t x_t + W_t X_t + \overline{\Pi}_t}$$

$$= \frac{W_t X_t \{1 + [B(\overline{I}_t, I_{t-1})]\}}{w_t x_t + W_t X_t + W_t X_t \{1 + [B(\overline{I}_t, I_{t-1})]\}}$$

which, with further substitution, becomes:

$$\frac{A[1+B]}{1 + A[2+B]} \tag{4.1}$$

where $A = A(p_{t-1} c_{t-1}, i_{t-1});$

$B = B(\overline{I}_t, I_{t-1});$

and $\dfrac{\delta}{\delta A}\left(\dfrac{\overline{\Pi}_t}{Y_t}\right) > 0, \ \dfrac{\delta}{\delta B}\left(\dfrac{\overline{\Pi}_t}{Y_t}\right) > 0.$ [7]

That is, the share of profits in the national income of any short period depends directly upon the mark-ups in the two sectors. These in turn are related, either directly or indirectly, to happenings in preceding periods. The share of profits will be greater, the greater are the real profits of the preceding period and money expenditure on bread; they will be lower, the greater are the inherited capital stocks of the two sectors. Thus, while demands and the supply of funds play direct parts in influencing the distribution of income, technical conditions only influence it indirectly through the inputs of labour per unit of output, the sizes of which are reflected in wages and prices. Both macro-economic and microeconomic forces are involved, but the influence of the former is predominant.

2. Level of employment

$$\overline{X}_t = x_t + X_t$$

which, by substitution, becomes:

$$CF\left[1 + \frac{J(j, CF)}{jA}\right] \tag{4.2}$$

where $C = g\left(\dfrac{\pi_{t-1}}{P_{t-1}}\right) + G\left(\dfrac{\Pi_{t-1}}{P_{t-1}}\right);$

$F = F(P_{t-1}, r^*_{t-1}, W^*_{t-1}, T_{t-1});$ as in [3.2];

$j = j\left(w_{t-1}; p_{t-1}; \dfrac{n_{t-2} - n_{t-1}}{n_{t-1}}, \dfrac{N_{t-2} - N_{t-1}}{N_{t-1}}, \dfrac{\overline{\overline{X}}_{t-1} - \overline{X}_{t-1}}{\overline{\overline{X}}_{t-1}}\right)$

as in [3.12];

and A is as defined for [4.1].

C is investment demand in real terms, F is the input of labour per unit of output in the steel sector, j is the money wage rate in the bread sector and A is the mark-up in the bread sector. Each of these in turn is a function of variables, the values of which are determined in the previous short period. Employment in any short period will be greater, the greater is the demand for steel in real terms and the greater is the input of labour per unit of output in the steel sector. It will be smaller, the higher is the profit margin on bread, because this reduces real wages and the demand for bread associated with any given level of employment in the steel sector.

The influence of the money wage rate in the bread sector is less clear. On the one hand, because the profit margin on bread is a mark-up on its wages cost per unit, employment will tend to be lower, the higher is the base on which the mark-up is placed; and the base will be higher, for given technical conditions, the higher is the money wage rate in the bread sector. On the other hand, the money wage in the bread sector sets the floor on which the money wage in the steel sector is based. The higher it is, the higher will be the money wage in the steel sector and therefore the money demand for bread associated with any given level of employment in the steel sector. Which effect will be the stronger depends upon the parameters of the functions involved.

The values of each of the above variables are, in turn, the outcome of relationships occurring in previous short periods. Thus, the demand for steel depends upon both the money profits earned in the previous period and the price of steel in that period. The influence of the price of steel is uncertain; the higher it is, the lower is the real value of any given level of money profits, but the more labour-intensive are the 'best-practice' techniques chosen and reflected in the capital stock of the current short period. The influence of the expected rate of profit and wages in the steel sector in the previous period, technical progress in the steel sector, and the previous period's expenditure on bread and investment in the bread sector, in so far as they affect the profit margin in the bread sector, is clear. But the impact of the money wage in the bread sector, the price of bread, the overall increase in productivity, and the level of unemployment in the previous period are uncertain because they influence the current level of employment through the money wage rate in the bread sector, the effect of which has been shown to be uncertain.

3. Demand for output

$$Y_t = p_t c_t + P_t \bar{I}_t$$

which, by substitution, becomes:

$$\{J(j, CF)\} \{CF\} \left(2 + B + \frac{1}{A}\right) \qquad [4.3]$$

where A, B, C, F and j are as defined for [4.1] and [4.2].

This means that the money demand for total output in any short period will be greater, the greater is the money wage-rate in the steel sector, the demand for steel in real terms, the labour input per unit of output and the profit margin in the steel sector; and it will be smaller, the greater is the profit margin in the bread sector. The variables with positive partial derivatives reflect the key role which steel demand and supply conditions have in generating demands and incomes, directly in the steel sector and indirectly in the bread sector through the derived demand for bread. The inverse relationship with the mark-up on bread reflects its impact on the real wage levels associated with any given level of demand and employment in the steel sector. Thus, for a given level of investment demand in steel terms, the demand for bread will be lower, in money and real terms, the greater is the profit margin in the bread sector. The surplus of bread per wage-earner in the bread sector is equal to the profit margin in the bread sector multiplied by productivity per man in the bread sector (A/n); for given n, the demand for bread will be lower, the greater is A.

V Multipliers

The impact on employment, money expenditure and the distribution of income of a lower mark-up in the bread sector and a greater expenditure on steel than are implied in the equations of the model are now examined. This is an extension of the usual Keynesian multiplier analysis to an economy where prices as well as output can change. It is assumed that the basic equations would otherwise imply an under-employment, short-period equilibrium – under-employment of both capital and labour. The case of inflation is then briefly considered. The procedure is to compare the short-period equilibrium levels of employment, and so on, in two different situations: one where the equations of the model apply, the other where they do not in one respect; for example, where there is a different mark-up in the bread sector or a different demand for steel.

Suppose, first, that the mark-up in the bread sector is less than that implied in equation [3.13]. Real wages will be higher in both sectors, which will lead to a higher level of employment, greater output of, and expenditure on, bread, and a shift to wages in the distribution of income (though money profits will be the same in the two situations). It can be shown that if the new mark-up is A^*_t $(< A_t)$ – that is, the initiating cause is a cut of $A_t - A^*_t$ in the mark-up – employment will be greater by a multiplier of $\dfrac{W_t X_t}{w_t A^*_t A_t}$; expenditure by a multiplier of $\dfrac{W_t X_t}{A^*_t A_t}$; the output of bread by a multiplier of $\dfrac{W_t X_t}{w_t n_t A^*_t A_t}$. The change in distribution of income is determined by a multiplier of $\dfrac{\overline{\Pi}_t}{\pi_t} \left\{ \dfrac{1}{[1 + A_t(2 + B_t)] [1 + A^*_t(2 + B_t)]} \right\}$, where $\overline{\Pi}_t$ and π_t are the profits implied by the equations of the model.

Suppose now that expenditure on steel is greater by one unit in real terms and by $N_t(1 + B_t)$ $(\Delta W_t \overline{I}_t + W^*_t)$ in money terms, where ΔW_t is the increase in the money wage rate in the steel sector and W^*_t is the new money wage in the steel sector. It can be shown that this unit increase in steel demand has an employment multiplier of $1 + \dfrac{(\overline{I}_t \Delta W_t + W^*_t)}{w_t A_t}$ and expenditure multiplier of $\dfrac{1 + A_t(2 + B_t)}{A_t(1 + B_t)}$. There is, however, no change in the distribution of income. (It should be stressed that the analysis in this section consists of comparisons of 'otherwise' situations, and not of descriptions of processes.)

If in the period following the fall in the mark-up on bread, the old relationships are restored, the higher mark-ups on bread associated with the higher than otherwise expenditure of the previous period would lead to a shift to profits (relatively) and a lower level of employment and money demand for output. The choice of technique is unaffected by the previous period's happenings (relatively to what it *would* have been), but there is a chance that, in *this* period, lower money wages could rule. This depends upon whether the lower than otherwise price of bread has a greater effect on money wages than the smaller than otherwise level of unemployment. If the bread price effect outweighs the unemployment effect, there is a force tending to raise employment in the following period, by raising the labour-intensiveness of the 'best-practice' techniques chosen. But, obviously, this is a very weak link on which to rely for higher levels of employment, especially if overall technical progress is lowering employment requirements per unit of output anyway.

Suppose now that the employment and money expenditures implied by the equations involve inflationary conditions. First, assume that the bottleneck is labour, that is, that the capacity levels of output of the plants are full employment ones. This is the assumption made by Kaldor (1957, p. 593; 1959, pp. 216–17). Equilibrium could be attained, first, by cutting investment in real terms or, second, by departing from the predetermined mark-up in the bread sector. In the latter case, the mark-up becomes the Kaldor short-period one, as set out in Harcourt (1963, p. 28), namely $\dfrac{W_t X_t}{w_t x_t}$, where $x_t = \overline{X}_t - X_t$, that is, the full employment value of the workforce less employment in the steel sector.

It may be noticed in passing that, given C, the level of real investment demand, there is one A, the profit margin on bread, that is consistent with full employment, and, corresponding to this level, there is a unique, full employment distribution of income $\overline{\Pi}^f/Y^f$. And, given A, there is one level of real demand for steel which will give full employment. There is, however, no unique full employment distribution of income between profits and wages in this case, though there is a unique one between wage-earners in the bread sector and wage-earners in the steel sector. Nor does there seem to be any mechanism which will bring about full employment, except by an accident.

If labour is the bottleneck, it is more likely that the money wage equations will cease to hold, as employers in the bread sector will raise wages in an attempt to attract labour from the steel sector, and those in the steel sector will retaliate in an attempt to keep it. Therefore, unless the profit margin on bread is raised even higher, proportionately, than money wages, so that with the labour force distributed as before the real demand for bread matches its full employment supply, there will be a cost-inflation and no equilibrium in the short period. Moreover, even if a short-period equilibrium were reached, re-establishing the relationships of the model in the next period may start off cost-inflation anew.

Suppose, finally, that the bottleneck is machines in the bread sector, and that capacity there is used up before full employment is reached. Let $\bar{c}_t$ be the capacity output of bread and $\bar{x}_t$ the employment associated with it. Both $\bar{c}_t$ and $\bar{x}_t$ are assumed to be less than the values of c_t and x_t implied by the equations of the model. It follows that $\bar{c}_t [w_t n_t (1 + A)] < (w_t \bar{x}_t + W_t X_t)$, that is, if the price of bread is $w_t n_t (1 + A)$, the wage-earners are not on their consumption function. There is, however, a higher price at which the capacity supply and the demand for bread will be equal. At this price, the share of profits in the national income and money expenditure will be greater, though total employment will be the same. In this case, the existence of unemployment may prevent a cost-inflation occurring.

IV   Concluding remarks

The purpose of this paper has been to examine, for one short period, a model which includes some features of modern industrial economies that have been neglected in recent discussions of economic growth. The features are price-making, the specificity of machines once they are produced, and the forces which determine money wages year by year. The main conclusion of the paper is that the traditional Keynesian analysis of short-period equilibrium can be easily adapted to include decisions concerning price-making and choice of technique, with the result that the distribution of income as well as the level of employment can be determined. If the approach is thought to be useful, the next steps will be, first, to extend the analysis to a period by period discussion, and, second, to introduce more realistic assumptions about consumption and investment expenditures, and the lifetimes of capital goods.

Notes

* *Economic Record*, vol. 41, no. 93, March 1965, pp. 103–17. The writer wishes to thank John Cornwall, Vincent G. Massaro, James A. Mirrlees, Joan Robinson, Aubrey Silberston and Marjorie S. Turner for their helpful comments.

1 The three measures of the technical aspects of this movement – the extent of the movement inwards, the factor biases, and the changes in the degree of substitution between factors – can be found in Salter (1960, chapter III).

2 Even if the 'best-practice' techniques are the same in two or more consecutive short periods, a different one will be chosen if the relative factor prices change as between the periods.

3 Salter used a similar analysis in Salter (1965).

4 If the determination of the expected rate of profit by the realized rate of profit is thought to be unsatisfactory, a forward-looking rate of profit may be

used to determine the choice of technique in the following way. Knowing the present price of steel, expected money wage rates, and the relevant 'best-practice' techniques, businessmen in the relevant sectors may be assumed to choose those techniques which offer the highest expected rate of profit. (As constant returns to scale are assumed, expected levels of output need not be known.) In the steel sector, a further assumption must be made about expected employment levels there; otherwise the expected money wage-rate cannot be determined. There is also no guarantee that the expected rate of profit will be the same in both sectors.

5 The equation for the price of steel in Harcourt (1963, pp. 28–9), in which the mark-up is the ratio of the capital stocks in the two sectors and which is derived from the condition that the expected rates of profit on the marginal machines going to the two sectors are equal, cannot be used when technical progress is occurring. The correspondence between the actual inputs per unit of output and the expected inputs explicitly assumed in this equation breaks down once the choice of new technique is allowed.

If $N^* \neq N$ and $n^* \neq n$, where the starred letters are expected values and N and n are the labour inputs per unit of output in the equation:

$$\frac{\frac{P^* X^*}{M^* N^*} - \frac{W^* N^* X^*}{M^* N^*}}{P^*} = \frac{\frac{p^* x^*}{m^* n^*} - \frac{w^* n^* x^*}{m^* n^*}}{P^*},$$

it cannot be solved for the actual price of steel ($P^* = P$) of the period. See section II for the meaning of the symbols.

6 The numeraire of the system, in which money wages, etc., are measured, can be taken to be the price of bread in some arbitrarily chosen short-period of the past.

7 The equation for the share of wages is therefore:

$$\frac{\overline{W}}{Y} = \frac{1 + A}{1 + A(2 + B)} \tag{4.1a}$$

which has negative partial derivatives.

8 Pricing and the investment decision*

Introduction

Recently there has been a discussion (Eichner, 1973) and series of exchanges (Hazledine, 1974; R. Robinson, 1974; Eichner, 1974, 1975; De Lorme and Rubin, 1975) concerning the determination of the size of margins in industries characterized by 'oligopoly-*cum*-price leadership' (Kaldor, 1970, p. 3). The focus of the discussion has been the demand for and supply of finance for investment purposes obtained as a result of varying the firm's mark-up policy. One element of the investment decision, its finance aspect, has been singled out as a prime determinant of the mark-up under oligopoly. However, in principle, three main decisions with regard to investment expenditure may be distinguished (the decisions, of course, may be made simultaneously): first, the *amount* of extra capacity to be laid down each period; second, the *sort* of investment to be done, that is, the choice between alternative ways of producing the same product; and third, the method and cost of *finance*.[1] The main aim of this article is to incorporate *all* of these aspects of the investment decision into a theory of the determination of the mark-up. It will become obvious as the argument proceeds that we are extending Salter's pioneering analysis of technical progress and the investment decision (Salter, 1960) into a non-perfectly competitive setting.

The link between the pricing decisions of oligopolistic firms and investment plans and levels of expenditure has been a feature of much of the Post-Keynesian literature.[2] However, until the recent exchanges, there has been some ambiguity and lack of detailed analysis concerning the exact nature of the relationship between the firm's pricing and investment decisions.[3] Indeed, Katzner and Weintraub, while postulating a link between pricing and the investment decision at the level of the firm, decided that for their purposes 'this phenomenon may be ignored' (Katzner and Weintraub, 1974, p. 488).

We hope that this article will help further to clarify some of the issues involved. It may be that such a relationship, when properly defined, will help to provide an explanation of the determination of the margin above costs in cost-based theories of pricing in oligopoly. The lack of such an explanation in the past (with the possible exception of Kalecki's work and now, of course, Adrian Wood's important new book, *A Theory of Profits*), provides a clue to the tardiness of many economists in accepting the (many) empirical verifications of cost-based pricing theories.[4]

In *section I* of the article we state the problem that we are examining in general terms and list our assumptions. *Section II* contains an analysis of the pricing and investment decision for a firm where there is only one possible 'best-practice' technique of production available at any moment of time. *Section III* considers the problems involved when the firm does have a choice between different techniques. We end the article by listing our conclusions.

I

The focus of the article is a manufacturing firm which is the price leader operating in an oligopolistic market environment characterized by mutual interdependence. We assume that the firm produces only one product. The means of producing output in the short period are taken to be fixed, as are the input-output coefficients which determine the technique of production for each 'vintage' of plant. Consequently, the firm faces constant costs per unit of output up to the point of (technically determined) full-capacity utilization of each vintage of plant. When the capacity of each vintage of equipment is exhausted, its unit costs curve becomes perfectly inelastic. Furthermore, it is assumed that the firm's *primary* goal is to maximize the growth in the value of its sales subject to a minimum profit constraint.[5] It is also assumed that the firm retains the bulk of its profits and that the greater part of investment is funded from internal sources.[6]

As we assume a market structure of oligopoly, there is no force pushing the firm to full-capacity utilization of plant. The actual rate of capacity utilization will depend on the level of demand; however, it is likely that the firm will *attempt* to operate at less than full capacity, for operating at less than full capacity gives the firm a safety margin with which to accommodate sudden swings in demand. Rothschild's maxim that oligopolistic firms are concerned to a very large extent with security so that they attempt ' "to hold what they hold", – and should an opportunity arise – to launch an offensive into rival territory' (Rothschild, 1947, p. 310), makes plausible the proposition that when firms are engaged in constrained battles over market shares under conditions of uncertainty, they will not want to be caught without extra capacity with which to accommodate sudden increases in orders.

The firm may plan *ex ante* to under-utilize its stock of capital equipment, and so the capital utilization rate becomes an economic decision-variable. Recently it has been shown that under conditions of uncertainty in imperfect competition, the firm will attempt to operate its plant, on average, below the full capacity rate (Smith, 1969, pp. 56–7). The firm may plan *ex ante* to under-utilize its stock of capital equipment, not only because of random demand shifts, but also, for example, where product demand changes rhythmically (and predictably) so that there are peak loads on the plant of the firm, and where input prices also vary rhythmically so that it becomes rational for the firm not to use part of its productive capacity in high cost periods. Of course, there will be unavoidable or unplanned periods of idleness due to maintenance time, unwanted accidents and unanticipated events. For example, idleness would result from deficient short-period effective demand.[7]

The firm has to decide on its price and its desired productive capacity. It is plausible that both of these decisions are related to the investment decision in all its aspects, the amount of extra capacity to be laid down in each period, the choice of techniques (if such a choice be available) and the methods and cost of finance. The trend in the ratio of the *actual* rate of capacity utilization to the *desired* rate of capacity utilization gives the firm an indication of what would be for it a *'proper'* investment policy. A *'proper'* investment policy would provide a more or less constant *average* level of capacity utilization over the cycle at the chosen mark-up and resulting output price. As the firm is assumed to retain the bulk of its profits and as the greater part of investment is financed from internal sources, we argue that the firm attempts to set its margin so that the periodic accrual of retained profits will be sufficient to finance its investment plans. In other words, the firm has a double objective in setting its mark-up. First, the resulting price must be such as to be consistent with its expectations, in very general terms, of demand for its product, and second, the price must be such as to provide sufficient retained profits to finance its investment plans. When firms are successful in setting mark-ups which yield sufficient retained profits with which to expand capacity in the desired manner in step with the growth in market demand, a stable situation is possible where investment keeps capacity growing in step with market demand in a tranquil world of stable market shares.[8]

To recapitulate, then, it is assumed that, first, the firm (which we take to be the price leader for the current pricing period) makes a decision on future investment plans on the basis of the relation between the trend in actual rates of capacity utilization, and some desired rate of plant utilization, given its expectations about the future growth of market demand and the expected profitability of various alternative investment projects. It then chooses a mark-up that will produce the required level of retained profits with which to finance the desired investment expenditure, and persists with the implied price, allowing capacity utilization to vary with the level of demand around some average expected level associated with the chosen mark-up. These decisions are made with reference to the state of demand that experience suggests to the firm as being reasonable. That is to say, the mark-up policy of the firm is influenced by the general state of business confidence and this same state of confidence also determines the firm's investment plans. Investment plans and the size of the mark-up are inexorably linked through the demand for and supply of funds in the form of retained profits with which the firm finances proposed investment projects. The actual price, however, is determined directly far less by current demand than by the mark-up which the firm considers necessary in order to be able to increase its capacity sufficiently to meet the expected future level of demand.

II

Our analysis of the pricing and investment decision under oligopoly begins by dividing time into price-making and investment plan-making units – similar to Hicksian 'weeks' but *much longer*, certainly far longer than the 'weeks' which are appropriate for short-period production decisions. The price-making period may not be of the same length as the investment plan-making period. Although it is plausible that both the price and the investment plan-making decisions will be made on the same 'day' because of the interdependence of the two decisions, it is possible that there will be overlaps between successive pricing and investment plan-making periods. These overlaps are related to the fact that investment plans, and the laying down of new capacity, have a long gestation period, and over that gestation period pricing decisions may have to be revamped in the light of changed business conditions (*e.g.* unexpected changes in the prices of investment goods, changes in government economic policies which affect the state of business confidence, and so on). There is also a possibility that while maintaining the price of its product, the firm may revise its investment plans as conditions alter from those which were expected at the beginning of the relevant decision-making period.[9] For simplicity, however, we abstract from these puzzles and collapse the two periods into one.

We assume that decisions on prices and investment expenditure are taken at the *beginning* of the period and then are held for that length of time. Furthermore, we suppose that the firm at the beginning of the current period has formed expectations about the levels of money wages and raw materials prices, and likely tax rates, as well as about its sales – prices *and* quantities – for this and the next period. It has also formed expectations about the scrap values of existing equipment.[10] Let the firm know now the capacity which will be in operation by the start of the current period. (This newly installed capacity is expected to cope with the expected demand of the current period and is the result of plans made in the past, for simplicity, in the last period.)

These assumptions allow us to draw up the *expected* marginal cost curve (*EMC*) for *existing* vintages for the firm for the next period: see Figure 8.1. It is a step function with each step showing the output to be catered for by different vintages of equipment which were laid down in previous periods. Each step shows the marginal (equals average variable) cost of each segment of output *plus* the scrap value,[11] itself a declining function of age, of each set of vintages. For example, *OA* is the output which will be catered for by the most recently laid down capacity, the result of plans which were made in the previous period.

From the *EMC* curve for existing vintages we can establish, given the

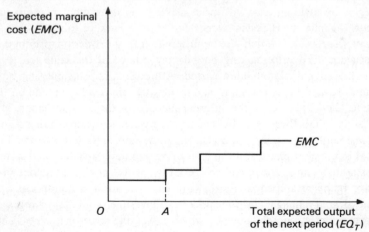

Figure 8.1

expectations of the firm with respect to demand for its product in the next period and the scrapping rule for 'old' vintages, the amount of new capacity which would have to be provided for the next period at various prices.

The expected sales-expected price relationship of the *next* period, *dd*, is now superimposed on the expected marginal cost function. The expected sales-expected price relationship is drawn as a nearly vertical line in order to indicate the relative independence of expected quantities – 'normal' quantities – over at least a *range* of prices: see Figure 8.2. This is the essence of the market situation with which the article is dealing and is consistent with the 'normal' pricing hypothesis associated with Neild, Godley and Nordhaus and others.[12]

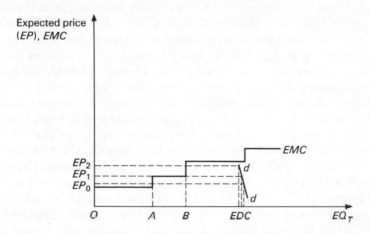

Figure 8.2

We argue that the price of the firm's output moves in relation to the requirements of the firm for internally generated funds with which to maintain its overall growth goals through investment in additional productive capacity *and* in relation to 'normal' prime costs. A 'normal' variable is defined as '*the value that variable would take, other things equal, if output were on its trend path*' (Godley and Nordhaus, 1972, p. 854). Following Neild (and Godley), it is argued that businessmen, whilst not conscious of the trend in output, unconsciously introduce it into their prices as they make new costings whenever new equipment (or new products) are introduced (Neild, 1963, p. 4, and in private correspondence with us). That is, the trend in unit costs reflects the trend in output. Therefore the price is fixed on the basis of the costs implied by this trend, ignoring short-period variations in unit prime costs which stem exclusively from alterations in rates of capacity utilization as demand changes over the course of the trade cycle. That is, neither *temporary* changes in prime costs, nor *temporary* changes in product demand directly influence to any significant extent output price. It is predominantly output and not price which fluctuates with the level of demand in the course of the business cycle.[13] There is ample empirical evidence which serves to justify this pricing assumption.[14]

If the firm were to set its price between EP_0 and EP_1 (strictly speaking, just below EP_1) in Figure 8.2, existing capacity would cater for an output rate of OA, and output rates of between AC and AD would have to be catered for by new capacity which would be the outcome of investment plans made and carried out during the current period. We assume that existing fossils are scrapped, or at least retired to emergency standby, when expected marginal cost is equal to or greater than expected price. Though this seemingly perfectly competitive version of the more general rule that when quasi-rents are zero at marginal revenue equals marginal cost, machines are scrapped, or at least temporarily retired, it is, of course, consistent with a situation in which output is expected to be independent of price, at least over a range.[15] In these situations only price has a meaning and Nuti's argument that in a world of imperfect competition marginal cost will be *less* than the selling price (so that there would be a contradiction in the scrapping rule)[16] will not hold. The traditional demand and marginal revenue curves of imperfect competition are not relevant in this model because of the independence of price and quantities over a range of prices. Therefore the difference between price and marginal revenue is not only irrelevant but, in fact, non-existent.

If the price were to be between EP_1 and EP_2, OB would be produced by what would be the then existing capacity, and BD to BE would have to be catered for by new investment planned and carried out during the current period.[17] The expected price-output to be catered for by new investment relationship is shown as P_1P_1 in Figure 8.3. It is defined by the *expectations* of the firm concerning price and the output to be catered for by new investment for the next period. It has been derived from Figure 8.2 by plotting the respective expected output levels against the corresponding prices.

As has been argued by, for example, Joan Robinson (1971b, chapters 7 and 8, especially pp. 103-7, and Robinson and Eatwell, 1973, p. 143) and Atkinson and Stiglitz (1969), firms, in deciding on

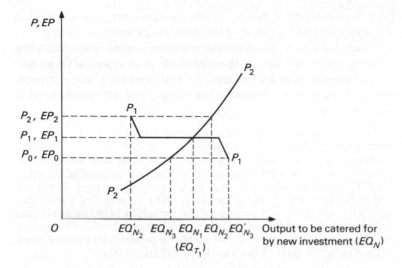

Figure 8.3

the technique of production to be installed in each period, instead of facing a range of superior techniques from which they might choose, may be limited to a single 'best-practice' technique, that is, the *ex ante* production function may be a single point. Joan Robinson and Eatwell write:

> all the controversies that have been going on about the concept of a 'given state of technical knowledge' represented by a book of blueprints belong to the sphere of economic doctrines rather than to the analysis of an actual economy. Obviously, in industry in real life, a great number of alternative blueprints for different techniques do not coexist in time. In real life, techniques are continually being invented, and each is blueprinted only when it seems likely to be used. (Robinson and Eatwell, 1973, p. 143)

The reason why Joan Robinson argues that at any moment of time the *ex ante* production function is restricted to a *point* rather than to a differentiable curve with each point on the curve representing a different production process, or, at least, to a series of points, has as much to do with the nature of the inventive process, as with the nature of the investment decision under conditions of uncertainty. For each point on the Salter iso-quant there will be a different production process, and associated with each process there will be a fund of technical knowledge specific to that technique. In the process of technical progress, as a specific technique is improved, the improvement may have little or no effect on other techniques of producing the same product. This is simply an effect of the nature of the inventive process.

In addition a firm, in considering investment expenditure, will assess as best it can the supplies of labour available to it, as well as taking into account its present stock of plant, its buildings, its physical environment and its fund of technical knowledge. The choice therefore is limited severely.

> The most important influence upon the choice of technique is not the cost of finance or 'factor prices' but the rate of investment relative to the availability of labour . . . .. A large firm whose plants provide an appreciable proportion of the jobs in particular regions has to consider, when planning investment, [*inter alia*] how much more labour it will be able to recruit. It will generally find it necessary to carry out expansion, at least partly, by raising investment per man employed. It is not provided with a predigested 'book of blueprints' of techniques; it must find out what the possibilities are and assess them as best it may. (Joan Robinson, 1971b, p. 106)[18]

According to this view, the whole idea of a 'technical frontier' is blurred in a changing world where expectations play an important role and where knowledge and experience do not just appear independently of the firm's actions, but have to be learnt and gathered by the firm itself. Joan Robinson argues that a move from one technique of production to another *around* the *ex ante* production function, even at the level of the firm 'cannot be represented as adding some capital to a pre-existing stock' (Robinson and Eatwell, 1973, p. 143). She argues that the Salter iso-quant neglects time; time, as it were, runs at right angles from the page at every point on the iso-quant (Joan Robinson, 1971b, p. 104; see also Penrose, 1959, pp. 85–7). Each process has its own past and this past will dominate the future possibilities available to the firm. To move *around* an iso-quant entails a switch *between* time profiles, and, so it is argued, in a world in which time only moves in one direction this is impossible without either redoing the whole capital stock, or embarking on a long future. Hence it is argued that there is only the single point *ex ante* production function.

If there is only one 'best-practice' technique at any moment of time, then given its expectations with respect to marginal costs and demand during the current period, the payout ratio, and the proportion of investment to be financed externally, the firm will have a certain set of expectations concerning the flow over the current period of retained profits for investment expenditure purposes. These expectations will define a unique relationship between the output to be catered for by new investment expenditure and the price that is needed to provide the flow of finance with which to fund that portion of investment expenditure which is to be met by retained profits (assuming that the prices of investment goods are known). This relationship is shown as the upward sloping line, P_2P_2, in Figure 8.3.

In Figure 8.3, the P_2P_2 curve is shown as intersecting the P_1P_1 relationship at a price of P_1 and at an output to be catered for by new investment expenditure level of EQ_{N_1} (which implies total capacity of EQ_{T_1}). It is only at this point that the two expectations sets – the expectations of the firm with respect to price and output to be catered for by new investment *and* its expectations concerning the flow of retained profits for investment expenditure purposes, which define the P_1P_1 and P_2P_2 relationships respectively – are consistent one with the other. For example, if the price were to be P_2, the expectations of the firm concerning the relationship between price and output to be catered for by new investment would suggest to it that capacity be expanded to EQ'_{N_2}. However, at that price, P_2, the expectations of the firm would suggest to it that sufficient funds could be obtained to finance new capacity of EQ_{N_2}. Alternatively, if the price were to be P_0, expectations would suggest an expansion of capacity by an amount EQ'_{N_3} whilst funds to finance new investment at that price can only be expected to cater for an expansion of capacity of EQ_{N_3}. Thus only at the intersection point of the P_1P_1, P_2P_2 relationships are the two expectation sets consistent.

At this stage, it should be pointed out that our analysis leads to the same price being set for both the current and next period and that this might lead to inconsistencies when more than two periods are considered. That is, the price chosen must do two jobs. First, it must provide, during the current period, the funds necessary to lay down the capacity required by the beginning of the next period, but second, it must be consistent with demand conditions in the next period which, together with the scrapping rule, determine the amount of capacity which needs to be laid down. Therefore, as soon as investment plans are formulated in the next period on the basis of demand conditions in the period following, the price so set in the next period may be inconsistent with demand conditions and with the marginal capacity of that period.

However, the apparent inconsistency only arises from the assumption of dividing time into regular discrete periods. In the actual world, demand conditions will change irregularly. Similarly, the firm will not regularly be making investment expenditure plans at the 'beginning' of some arbitrary time period based on a set of demand conditions at a fixed point in the future as periodic analysis implies. Rather a price will be set irregularly on the basis of future demand which the firm considers reasonable. The price will be consistent both with the funds requirements for investment purposes from retained profits and with demand conditions for the foreseeable future.

However, as demand and cost conditions change, the firm will come to realize that its existing capacity is inadequate, and that new investment expenditure is required. At this point, the firm will decide if the flow of funds for investment purposes is adequate at the current price. If it is not, the pricing and investment decision process will begin once again. In other words, decisions will be made at irregular intervals as conditions dictate their necessity, that is to say, as the firm comes to realize that its current price and/or capacity is inadequate for the conditions expected in the near future.[19]

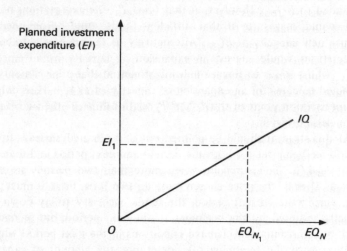

Figure 8.4

The intersection point shows that new capacity of EQ_{N_1}, making possible an output rate of EQ_{T_1} will be installed. With only one 'best-practice' technique there will be a unique level of investment expenditure associated with each expected level of output (which the investment expenditures are to cater for). In Figure 8.4, the relationship between planned investment expenditure and expected rates of output is shown by the IQ curve; with an expected output rate from new capacity of EQ_N, investment expenditure of EI_1 needs to be undertaken.

To arrive at the price P_1 (the actual price which is to be determined for the current period) in Figure 8.3, the payout ratio, the prices of investment goods *and* the proportion of investment to be financed from retained profits *all* need to be known. We assume that the prices of investment goods are known and given. We suppose that the firm is either a price-taker in a competitive market for investment goods, or that the firm possesses some monopsonistic power which enables it to bargain over the prices of investment goods. In either case, the firm would know the prices of investment goods at the time that it makes investment decisions. The payout ratio can be taken as given. It is assumed that in a large oligopolistic manufacturing firm, the dividend payout to shareholders is considered by the management of the firm to be simply another claim on its funds. Shareholders in such firms are assumed to be diffuse, lacking in leadership and unable to give more than a passing thought to the affairs of 'their' companies. They have become passive rentiers whose major concern is the current market price of their shares and the size of their dividends. The management of the firm will set the payout ratio of the firm so that they will pay out only sufficient dividends to forestall take-over bids by other management groups plus whatever additional amounts are necessary to minimize the cost of obtaining funds on the capital market. What remains of the firm's net profits will be used to finance planned investment expenditure.[20]

The question now remains of how the firm will determine the split between external financing of planned investment expenditure by going to the capital market, and financing investment internally through retained profits. This is the crucial question upon which the P_2P_2 relationship depends in Figure 8.3, and has been the focus of recent exchanges concerning the determination of the size of the mark-up under oligopoly. Eichner (1973) has argued that by varying the margin above costs and reinvesting all retentions, the firm can *expect* to alter its flow of retained profits over time in two ways. First, cash flows can be expected to be increased by the increased returns to the investment project thereby being financed, and second, cash flows can be expected to be reduced over the long-period time horizon of the firm by the cumulative effects of substitution away from the firm's product expected as a result of the higher mark-up, from the entry of new firms into the industry and from anti-trust intervention by government. The substitution effect does *not* contradict the pricing hypothesis of this article, for a short-period demand curve is *not* being considered. Every decision which is made, is made in a short-period situation, but it has short-period and long-period consequences. 'Decisions are long period decisions if they bind us into long period commitments [as investment obviously does] and therefore require us to have *expectations* about the long period. [This] is a long period in the *historical* future' (Krimpas, 1974, p. 49; our emphasis). It has been argued that in the (Marshallian) short period, there is a range of prices over which the expected level of output is independent of the price. However, once the price is outside the relevant range, and/or once the time horizon of the firm lengthens, the firm may *expect* that one of the consequences of a decision made in the here and now to raise the mark-up will be for some substitution away from its product to occur, and that this will result in a decline in cash flows over time.[21]

These effects determine the firm's demand and supply functions respectively for funds for investment purposes, although Hazledine has argued that an element of the demand curve for internally generated investment funds will be the ability of firms to obtain a rate of return commensurate with that obtained from new investment projects by lending funds on the money market.[22] An implicit interest rate for internally generated funds can be obtained by expressing as a percentage, the ratio of the funds expected to be lost because of the substitution, entry and anti-trust intervention effects, to the additional funds generated in the meantime from the higher mark-up. (Both the numerator and denominator of this ratio will be suitably discounted if the firm uses time discounting procedures.) The implicit interest rate is a function of the size of the margin and of the firm's time horizon. A comparison of this rate with the relevant market rate of interest at which a *comparable* sum of finance could be obtained from the capital market for planned investment expenditure gives the trade-off between internal and external financing, and so determines the size of the mark-up (and so the price) which the firm needs to set in order to generate over time the funds required for its planned investment expenditure.

This price will be both a minimum *and* a maximum, given the firm's investment plans, when the firm's primary goal is to maximize under constraint the growth of its sales. As the firm increases, in conditions of uncertainty, the amount of investment funds that it wishes to obtain (either by external or internal methods), it will be taking greater and greater risks. In an uncertain world the firm will be a risk minimizer (Kalecki, 1937). Such a firm would not be expected to sacrifice expected future sales by increasing its mark-up over and above that level necessary to accommodate its definite planned investment expenditure for the next period. It is these calculations which determine the shape and position of the P_2P_2 curve and so give the unique price-expected quantity configuration in Figure 8.3.[23]

III

If, however, there *is* more than one 'best-practice' technique at any moment of time, that is, when a Salter iso-quant (or at least a small arc of it around 'neighbouring' techniques – see Harcourt, 1972, p. 56) exists, a problem arises, for there will be a number of ways of producing a unit of output (and therefore level of output if it is assumed that the *ex ante* production function exhibits constant returns to scale). Which technique will be chosen will not, as we shall see below, be independent of the price, regardless of the investment decision rule that is used. In this situation, therefore, P_2P_2 in Figure 8.3 is not a unique relationship but merely one of a *family* of possible relationships, each member of which is defined both by the price *and* by the investment decision rule which is used. There are now three possible relationships between two variables, P and EQ_N. For EQ_N determines the extra capacity required which in turn depends on the investment-decision rule *and* on the price. But EQ_N itself also depends upon planned investment expenditure, given the payout ratio and the proportion of that investment expenditure which is to be financed from external funds. What is to be done?

Suppose it is assumed that the expected level of output is independent of the price, at least over a certain range of prices: see *dd* in Figure 8.2. This assumption is consistent with the cost-based 'normal' pricing hypothesis of this article. Now two relationships can be defined. The first is that between investment expenditure and price, given the investment-decision rule which is used, the current price of investment goods and the level of output which is to be catered for by the new capacity. This relationship is given by the *II* curve in Figure 8.5. There is a different *II* curve for each investment-decision rule. An analysis of the *ordering* of the relative investment intensities of investment projects as a result of the use of different investment-decision rules has been done by Harcourt (1969b). He showed that in a given technological framework, that is, with a given 'book of blueprints', and with given expectations by businessmen concerning future movements in prices and money wage rates, the pay-off period criterion (*POPC*) usually results in the choice of a technique which is more investment-intensive (less labour-intensive) than those resulting from discounted cash-flow procedures (*DCF*). The accounting rate of profit criterion could not be

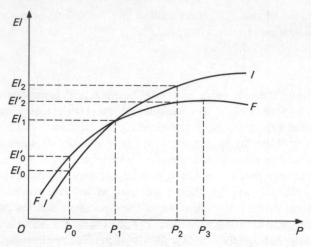

Figure 8.5

graded precisely; it was also shown that among the *DCF* criteria, the present value rule results in a more investment-intensive technique being chosen than when the internal rate of return rule is used.

If we know the level of output to be catered for by new investment, the second relationship that can be defined is that between price and the funds available for investment expenditure, given the expectations of the firm with respect to marginal costs, its sales – prices and quantities – during the current period, the payout ratio and the externally financed proportion of the planned investment expenditure: see *FF* in Figure 8.5. There is a family of *FF* curves, each member of which corresponds to a different level of output to be catered for by new investment.

Although the stability properties of the intersection of the *II* and *FF* curves are not, we argue, relevant for the present analysis, the *shapes* and positions of the curves are of some importance if there is to be a unique price-investment solution for a given level of output to be catered for, such as at P_1, EI_1 in Figure 8.5. The first thing that can be said is that there is no reason why the *II* and *FF* curves should coincide, since the two relationships are completely independent of one another and, as will be seen below, there are positive reasons why the curves will diverge on either side of the intersection point.

It can be shown that when the pay-off period criterion is considered for the choice of techniques, and the price is (conceptually) increased, the investment intensity of the technique chosen increases but at a

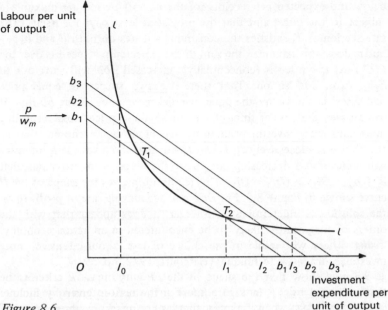

Figure 8.6

decreasing rate. In Figure 8.6, the line, ll, is the Salter iso-quant showing the various configurations of labour and investment expenditure which may be used to produce a unit of output. The line $b_1 b_1$ is the POPC constraint, for the POPC is:

maximize: $b(p - w_m l)$
subject to: $b(p - w_m l) \geq I$
where: b = the pay-off period
             p = the product price
             w_m = the money wage rate
             l = the labour requirements per unit of output
             I = the investment expenditure per unit of output.

The *equality* form of the constraint may be written as

$$l = \frac{p}{w_m} - \frac{1}{bw_m} I$$

which is a straight line with the slope of $1/bw_m$ and an intercept of p/w_m on the vertical axis.

The technique chosen by the POPC is that associated with the second intersection of $b_1 b_1$ with ll (i.e. at T_2) where ll cuts $b_1 b_1$ from below and expected net receipts for the pay-off period are maximized subject to the constraint that the project at least pays for itself. (The intersection at T_1 satisfies the constraint – it lies on both ll and b_1b_1 – but it does not maximize the sum of the expected net receipts over the *POP*.) As the price is (conceptually) 'increased', bb will shift out to b_2b_2, b_3b_3, and so on. That there are two successive equal price 'increases' is shown by the equal parallel movement of the bb line. It can be seen that, other things being equal, these price 'rises' result in a more and more investment-intensive technique being chosen, that is, the choice is successively I_1, I_2 and I_3, but that the investment intensity will increase at a decreasing rate due to the shape of the iso-quant, that is, $(OI_2 - OI_1) > (OI_3 - OI_2)$. This relationship gives the shape of the *II* curve shown in Figure 8.5. For *DCF* and accounting rate of profit rules, the solution is indeterminate. However, it does appear that with the orders of magnitudes likely to be encountered in an actual economy, 'rising' prices will result in the choice of less labour-intensive, more investment-intensive techniques (Harcourt, 1972, pp. 59–60).

We now show that the shape of the *FF* curve may be taken to be that indicated by *FF* in Figure 8.5. For the reasons given by Eichner (1973, pp. 1190–3), we expect that as the mark-up above 'normal' prime costs (and so, the product price) is increased, and as the time horizon of the firm is extended so that the substitution, entry and government anti-trust intervention effects have a greater and greater bearing on the firm's planning and decision-making, the flow of funds generated internally for planned investment expenditure will increase at a decreasing rate (and maybe, eventually, decrease absolutely, if we consider a sufficiently long time horizon). These factors give the *FF* curve the shape shown in Figure 8.5. We note that beyond a price of P_3, the firm *expects* its cash flows to decline absolutely, so that the *FF* curve begins to decline.

That the *FF* curve lies above the *II* curve below the intersection point, and under it thereafter may be inferred from the Salter iso-quant, ll, in Figure 8.6. If the price were to be relatively low, for example at P_0 in Figure 8.5, then given the positive association between price and investment intensity, and the choice of technique decision rule, the *II* relationship indicates that the investment intensity of the technique chosen will be relatively low, for example, EI_0 in Figure 8.5 or I_0 in Figure 8.6. Therefore, it is highly probable that the flow of retained profits for planned investment at that price, EI_0', given the payout ratio, the externally financed proportion of planned investment expenditure and the expected level of output, will be *greater than* the funds *actually* required for intended investment at that price, EI_0. However, if the price were to be relatively high, for example, P_2, the technique chosen according to the II curve will be relatively investment-intensive, for example, EI_2 in Figure 8.5 or I_3 in Figure 8.6. It is plausible to expect that the funds generated for investment at that price, EI'_2 in Figure 8.5, will be *less than* those *actually* required for the planned investment which the firm would want to carry out at that price, EI_2. We saw above that the II curve increases at a decreasing rate. It was also shown that the FF curve may in fact eventually decline, for the flow of retained profits for planned investment expenditure may decrease absolutely given a sufficiently large increase in margins and/or a sufficiently long time horizon. Therefore, for the most part, a *unique* intersection point between the II and FF curves can be expected, giving a unique price-planned investment expenditure solution for a given level of output to be catered for.

Bliss has shown that there is an interesting exception to this conclusion *if* the present value rule is used, and *if* the elasticity of substitution of the Salter iso-quant, ll in Figure 8.6, is 'large' (Bliss, 1968a). We argued above that with the orders of magnitude likely to be encountered in the real world, when the PV choice of technique decision rule is used, a positive relationship between price and investment intensity can be expected. Suppose that the elasticity of substitution of the ll curve in Figure 8.6 is 'large' and that businessmen have the plausible expectation that money wage rates will rise *faster* than the price of their product because money wages are expected to reflect increases in prices *and* overall productivity (that is to say, businessmen expect *real* wages in terms of *their* product to rise over time). Then there will be a positive relationship between the expected economic length of life of investment projects and investment intensity. If the possibilities of substitution of investment for labour are very great, and the price is conceptually increased, small (proportionate) increases in investment expenditure will lead to large savings in labour, and so to considerable (proportionate) increases in expected economic lives. It follows that in these circumstances there may not be a unique choice of technique because there may be more than one point where the present value of investment expenditure is at a maximum. Therefore the II curve *may* not be a smoothly rising concave-to-the-origin curve such as II is in Figure 8.5. Rather it may have bumps in it, which may result in multiple price-investment expenditure solutions, depending on the position of the FF curve. Bardhan has shown that Bliss's result holds *only* if the elasticity of substitution of the *ex ante* production function is greater than unity (Bardhan, 1969). This gives precision to our term, 'large'.

In the 'oligopoly-*cum*-price leadership' world that is under discussion in this article, it is more likely that the firm will use a *POPC* rather than a *PV* rule for the choice of technique so as to reduce the effects of uncertainty, and so there would not be the *possibility* of multiple inter-section points between the *II* and *FF* curves. If, however, a *PV* rule is used, and the elasticity of substitution of the *ex ante* production function is greater than one, such a possibility must be considered, even if it is unlikely. The possibility would become an empirical question.

The question remains, given the shapes and slopes of the *II* and *FF* curves, of whether there will be a price so determined that falls within the range of prices for which output may be regarded as being indepen-dent of price (or whether there will be a positive intersection of the *II* and *FF* curves at all). If the price so determined does *not* fall within the relevant range, then the payout ratio and/or the investment-decision rule will have to give until a price is obtained which will serve both to finance the investment expenditure *and* be consistent with the expected level of output. Or the expected level of output will have to change until a price is found which will do the financing task, given the investment-decision rule, the payout ratio and the externally financed proportion of investment expenditure. That is to say, either *FF* or *II* will have to change in order to give a compatible price. We may conceive of this as an iterative process taking place until all the expec-tation sets of the firm – the price-expected quantity expectations, the price-flow of funds expectations and the price-investment expenditure expectations – are consistent one with another.

Conclusion

The article set out to examine the relationship between the pricing decisions and investment expenditure plans of an oligopolistic firm. The relationship, if it holds, provides, we argued, a theory of the determin-ation of the size of the mark-up in cost-based theories of pricing in oligopoly. It was assumed that over a range of prices in the short period, prices and quantities are independent, an assumption which was based on the empirical work of Neild, Godley and Nordhaus and others. When all aspects of the investment decision are considered – the *amount* of extra capacity to be laid down each period, the choice of technique and the method and cost of finance – it was established by the use of a simple model that, for the most part, a unique solution could be found for the size of the margin above 'normal' prime costs and the level of planned investment expenditure, given the firm's expectations about the future level of demand. A situation under which multiple solutions may be arrived at was also examined briefly.

Notes

* Κμκλος, Vol. 29, 1976, Fasc. 3, pp. 449–77. This article was written in collaboration with Peter Kenyon. We are grateful to Kevin Davis, Al Eichner, Alan Hall, Peter Hammond, John Hatch, Ian McDonald, Neil Laing, Robert Neild, Neville Norman, Brian Parmenter, Joan Robinson, David Vines, Bob Wallace, Adrian Wood and the members of the staff/student seminars in Economics at the Flinders University of South Australia and the University of Adelaide for helpful comments on earlier drafts of this article.

1 There is another aspect to the investment decision which lies behind the three elements indicated in our argument, namely, the choice of product. The firm, in making an investment decision, will design its plans in order to fit its choice of product. However, for simplicity, we abstract from this aspect of the investment decision.

2 We follow Kregel (1973) in the use of the term 'Post-Keynesian' with which to describe the theories and approaches now associated with Cambridge (England) economists and their followers. For examples of Post-Keynesians who have postulated a link between the pricing and investment decisions, see Asimakopulos (1970, 1975a, 1975b, 1977), Eichner (1973, 1976), Harcourt (1972, pp. 210–14), Harris (1974), Kaldor and Mirrlees (1962), Kaldor (1966, 1970), Kalecki (1971, pp. 110–23), Katzner and Weintraub (1974), Kregel (1973, pp. 135–41), Krimpas (1974, p. 39), Joan Robinson (1971b, chapters 2 and 7) and Wood (1975, chapters 1–3). The postulated link between price and planned investment expenditure is not merely a theoretical or 'as if' construct. In a recent article concerning the British National Board for Prices and Incomes (N.B.P.I.), Pickering notes that one of the criteria used by the N.B.P.I. for approving 'a higher price depends . . . upon the effect which a particular level of profit has on the firm's ability to finance future investment, either to expand productive capacity or merely to replace existing capacity' (Pickering, 1971, p. 232).

3 In a recent article, Harris examined the simple model in Harcourt (1972, pp. 210–14) in which a relationship between price and investment expenditure was postulated. He argued that in Harcourt's model '[no] direct causal relationship between investment and price formulation at the micro level is implied' (Harris, 1974, p. 148, n. 10). The aim of the present article is, in fact, to posit such a direct causal relationship at the level of the firm and so provide some microeconomic foundations for the macro model in *Some Cambridge Controversies . . . .* It will also be seen that the model provides a microeconomic argument with which to support the oft-stated claim that Keynes's world is essentially that of quantity rather than price adjustment in the face of variations in the level of demand.

4 See, for example, Eckstein and Fromm (1968), Godley and Nordhaus (1972), Lanzillotti (1958), Means (1972), Neild (1963), Yordon (1961). This is a

small but representative sample of a very large (and increasing) population of studies supporting cost-based pricing theories.

5 We argue that it is not possible empirically to distinguish between profit maximization over time and the maximization of growth over time in a world in which the growth of firms depends in large part on their ability to generate investment funds on the basis of retained profits. See, for example, the uncertain findings of Hall (1967, p. 154), and Mabry and Siders (1967, p. 377). Mabry and Siders state that their results suggest 'that the sales maximization hypothesis is not inconsistent with the profit maximizing hypothesis in the long-run'. See also, the conclusions of Penrose (1959, pp. 26–30) on profit maximization over time.

6 See Anderson (1964, p. 25). He estimates that over 90 per cent of the investment in manufacturing industry in the U.S. is financed internally from retained profits. See, also, Bosworth (1971).

7 For a survey of the theory of capital utilization, see Winston (1974).

8 'Tranquility is a minimum prerequisite for the adjustment of short period disequilibrium to internal long period equilibria. You can define normal profit, from the upward and the lower end, as that rate of profit which, in the relevant sense dependent on the richness of the model, keeps the *relative* position of the firm intact, with respect to the product market, the financial market, and also the "power" market' (Krimpas, 1974, p. 86).

9 See Asimakopulos (1977, pp. 330, 340–2) for a discussion of the possibility of revamping investment decisions in the light of changed conditions due to the long gestation period of investment plans and the laying down of new capacity. Lags between investment decisions and actual investment expenditure play a prominent role in the work of Kalecki (1971, especially p. 110).

10 We suppose expected scrap value to be a declining function of age, first, because the machines themselves are older, and second, because less and less labour-intensive methods of production may have been installed as time goes by.

11 For simplicity, scrap values may be considered to be zero. However, if scrap values are to be included, they must, on Marshallian grounds, be *added* to marginal costs. The firm will be indifferent as between scrapping a vintage and keeping it in operation if the price is greater than marginal cost by the amount of scrap value. A more sophisticated approach for a firm using discounting procedures (e.g. *DCF* rules for the choice of technique) would be to scrap if the discounted cash flows earned in excess of marginal costs, if the vintage were to be kept in operation, were just less than the discounted cash flow that could be earned by using the funds from scrapping in the next-best alternative profit-earning project.

12 See Godley and Nordhaus (1972), Neild (1963), Norman (1973) and Pesaran (1974). The same pricing hypothesis is made by other writers in this area. See, for example, Eichner (1973, pp. 1184–9), Kalecki (1971, pp. 49–61) and Wood (1975, p. 61).

13 The assumption that it is predominantly output and not price that responds to changes in demand in the manufacturing sector of modern capitalist economies is quite common in Post-Keynesian literature. For example, Pasinetti (1974a, p. 33) writes: 'The basic feature remains, by contrast with more primitive societies, that among the factors concurring to determining prices, fluctuations of demand have become *unimportant*. Therefore, the traditional response mechanism of price changes having become inoperative, another response mechanism is

brought into use. *To changes in demand, producers respond by changing production.*' Our emphasis.

14 See notes 4 and 12.

15 See the exchanges between Nuti (1969), Joan Robinson (1969a) and Kaldor (1970).

16 Under imperfect competition price is greater than marginal cost at the relevant level of output. Therefore equipment cannot be scrapped when price is equal to marginal cost *and* when quasi-rents are zero in conditions of imperfect competition. It should be noted, however, that if quasi-fixed costs (for example, overhead labour costs such as wages for maintenance staff and cleaners) are considered, there will always be a gap between price and *short-period* marginal prime costs when quasi-rents are zero: see Joan Robinson (1969a). In such a situation the marginal plant (the oldest vintage) is scrapped when its average prime cost (equal to the *long-period* marginal cost) is equal to price and quasi-rent is zero. For simplicity, we assume that there are no quasi-fixed costs.

17 In passing, we note that our theoretical framework is consistent with the empirical findings of Bitros and Kelejian (1974) that one of the major determinants of the replacement ratio, the ratio of scrappage to the stock of capital (measured in physical units) 'varies systematically with respect to cyclical variables', and thus invalidates the often stated claim that replacement investment may be treated as a constant proportion of the capital stock: see, for example, Jorgenson (1965, p. 51). Their findings lead them to argue that it is *gross* investment (rather than net investment) and scrappage which are the decision variables governing the potential services of the means of production. This viewpoint is also consistent with our model.

18 The expansion of the firm will be limited also by the amount of 'managerial services' available for expansion: see Penrose (1959, pp. 196–212).

19 Wood (1975, pp. 92–7) also confronts this problem when he extends his argument from a static to a dynamic context. He writes: 'the firm's current activities are always based on target policies which cover a period of several years ahead, but at comparatively short intervals, in the light of informational feedback from its current activities, it reviews and, where necessary, alters its long run targets, at the same time as making adjustments towards them in the face of disequilibrium' (p. 95).

20 See Eichner (1976, chapter 2) and Robinson and Eatwell (1973, p. 233). We do not mean to imply that the decision to be made by the firm about the payout ratio is a simple one. As Wood (1975, pp. 40–52) shows, the decision is indeed complex. However, *once the target payout ratio is established* (and once established it tends to remain *fairly* constant: see Wood, 1975, p. 49, n. *), its *strategic* importance to the firm is minimal.

21 For a discussion of the distinction between the 'long' and 'short period' concepts, see Joan Robinson (1971b, pp. 16–18).

22 Hazledine (1974). For an alternative to this essentially neoclassical view, see Wood (1975, pp. 8–9)

23 In order to extend the analysis from the level of the firm to that of the industry, we assume that the prices for price followers be determined in the following manner: let there be n firms, where n is a small number; also let $P_i = \alpha_i P_j$ ($i = 1 \ldots n - 1$) where P_j is the price of the price leader. If $\alpha_i = 1$ then all firms match the movements in the price set by the price leader. If $\alpha \neq 1$ (it may

be >1 or <1), then the proportionality of each firm's price to that of the price leader is preserved. α may be $\neq 1$ due to product differentiation, the geographical position of firms and so on.

Part III
Salter's contributions, investment-decision rules, investment incentives and related econometric issues

9 Review article of W.E.G. Salter, *Productivity and Technical Change**

Dr Salter's book is an important addition to the distinguished series of Monographs of the Department of Applied Economics, Cambridge. He has examined, theoretically and empirically, using British and American data, the relationships between technical progress and movements in productivity, costs and prices at the industry level. The theoretical sections (Part I) contain an elegant application of neoclassical value theory to this problem. They are simply and lucidly written, and while they throw considerable light on some difficult problems at the moment bedevilling the theory of capital, for example, the measurement of capital in the production function, Salter does not allow these asides to distract him long from the main purpose in hand. The result is an original contribution to economic theory. The empirical sections (Part II) consist of a statistical analysis of changes in productivity, costs, prices, output and employment in selected British and American industries over the period 1923–50. The limitations of the statistical data and results, and the relevance of the results to the models developed in Part I, are clearly brought out. Salter uses, in the main, simple statistical techniques, but in a manner which enables the extraction of as many results as the basic data will allow. The book is addressed primarily to professional economists but is in a form that makes it suitable for use in teaching students.

Actual productivity movements are the outcome not only of the continuous discovery and application of new techniques of production, but also of the rate at which these are incorporated through gross investment in a capital stock which still contains the fossils of past techniques. This is the central theme of the book. Traditional static theory is unable to analyse these processes. It shows 'the equilibrium which would be reached if no further changes occurred, [while] in fact change is continuous' (p. 5). Salter therefore adapts the iso-product analysis in order to examine the factors which affect the choice of best-practice techniques over time. These determine the techniques to be embodied in current investment expenditure (at the industry level).

129

The determinants of the amount of investment expenditure, and therefore of the rate at which technical advances are reflected in productivity changes, are found by examining the factors affecting scrapping, replacement and expansion decisions in a competitive situation.

Techniques of production change over time because of improving technical knowledge and changing factor prices. Improving technical knowledge is shown on the iso-product diagram by the iso-product curve of a given level of output moving inward towards the origin with the passage of time. If technical advances lead to savings in one input but not in another, only certain sections of the curve move inward. If there are no economies or diseconomies of scale this movement is representative of all scales of output. The axes show unit labour and capital requirements (the inverse of the productivity of these factors), and the slope of the iso-cost curve reflects the relative factor prices. The factor of production, capital, is regarded as investment and is measured in 'two dimensions: an initial real investment and the life of this investment' (p. 18). This avoids the vexed problem of measuring capital, for only the output to be produced by best-practice techniques is under consideration. In the simple two-factor case, the production function shows output as a function of labour, real investment outlay and the life of the equipment. In turn, capital costs per annum depend upon the initial real investment, the prices of capital goods, the normal rate of profit and the expected life of the equipment. The best-practice technique at any moment of time is that combination of labour, initial real investment and life of equipment which minimizes the total costs of producing the given level of output. This is given by the point of tangency between the iso-product and the iso-cost curves, which satisfies the marginal productivity conditions that the marginal products of labour, real investment and length of life should be proportional to their respective prices.

The analysis covers new ground but is simple and, formally, very familiar. It contrasts strongly with Mrs Robinson's analysis of the role of capital in the production function,[1] which uses a number of trick assumptions in order to measure capital and a (necessarily) cumbersome and unfamiliar technical apparatus. However, there are good reasons for the contrast. Mrs Robinson is concerned with the concept of an aggregate production function, with the capital stock of the economy as a whole as well as with marginal additions to it and with the aggregate distributive shares of broad classes of factors of production. Because she sees a common element in the incomes accruing to all capitalists, she has to value the whole capital stock. Salter, on the other hand, is concerned with investment decisions of businessmen in individual firms and industries. He is quite happy to recognize the wide varieties of techniques and prices associated with different capital goods. While he also deals with aggregate problems and concepts, for example, total investment expenditure and total productivity changes, they differ from those which interest Mrs Robinson.

Four measures are developed to describe the components of the change in the productivity of best-practice techniques between two periods of time (pp. 29–44). These measures are derived from Laspeyres and Paasche index number forms and the measures of income and substitution effects of consumer demand theory. The first three concern the purely technical aspects of the change, *viz*. the rate at which the curves approach the origin, the change in the shapes of the curves, and the change in the steepness of curvature, that is to say, the change in the ease of substitution of one factor for another. The fourth measure relates to the influence of changing relative factor prices. The measures allow a thorough analysis of the influences at work at the margin of the capital stock. An important result which emerges is that neutral technical progress for the economy as a whole (in the Harrodian sense of a constant capital-output ratio) is shown to be consistent with rising capital productivity in industries that experience rapid technical advance and falling capital productivity in those that do not. The general cheapening of capital goods relative to labour which is a feature of overall technical advance allows substitution of capital for labour which, over all, may result in a constant capital-output ratio. Substitution between factors therefore makes possible both a wide variety of biases towards labour or capital saving in the technical advances of particular industries, and neutral technical progress for the whole economy.

Actual productivity movements also depend on the relative importance of additions to the capital stock. A productivity cross-section of an industry using various techniques can be described in terms of the unit labour requirements of the various plants producing the current level of output, the smallest requirements being those of the most up-to-date plants. Productivity at any moment of time is the inverse of the weighted average of these requirements. Investment in new techniques is carried to the point where the expected long-period competitive price of output is such that new plants can expect just to recover their principals and earn normal rates of return. Old plants are scrapped when they fail to earn surpluses over operating costs. In principle, scrapping and replacement are two separate decisions; however, in the simple competitive model, Salter shows that 'a replacement decision is both a scrapping decision and an investment decision' (p. 57). In this context, gross investment rather than net investment is the meaningful economic variable. A model of a continuous process is developed, with technical advances causing operating costs to fall and gross investment occurring until output so increases that the price level eliminates supernormal profits, the media of investment being new firms entering the industry and old ones scrapping, replacing and expanding. The model produces a moving equilibrium, a series of points reflecting the industry's reactions to changing technical advances, demand conditions and relative factor prices. The rate of change of productivity reveals whether or not the range between labour requirements of best-practice and obsolete techniques has increased or decreased. Price movements in turn are determined by changes in the total costs of current best-practice techniques. The analysis implicitly assumes that technical advances in individual industries occur at points of time rather than continuously, and that the length of time between the points is great enough to allow the industries to reach momentary equilibria. Such an assumption is necessary for period analysis to be used, but it must be recognized that in industries where technical advances are rapid there may not be sufficient time for equilibrium to be reached.[2]

An important feature of the model is the role of gross investment as the vehicle of technical change. Potentially higher productivity becomes actual productivity by means of capital accumulation. Relative prices affect the speed of this adjustment process, because while 'the cost of new capital equipment is the barrier to the immediate general use of new capital equipment, . . . higher operating costs are the price paid for retaining outmoded methods' (p. 69). At the economy level, the real wage determines the extent of the fossils retained in today's capital stock. An economy where investment is cheap relative to labour will use more highly mechanized and up-to-date techniques than an economy where labour is relatively cheap.

Salter's book is based on research done at Cambridge between 1953 and 1955. In 1955 he received his doctorate for a dissertation which was an earlier draft of the present book. At the same time, several Cambridge economists were analysing the relationships between technical progress, capital accumulation and productivity. Mrs Robinson, for example, was lecturing on these themes. (The lectures subsequently became *The Accumulation of Capital* which was published in 1956.) The relationship between growth in output per head and the rate of capital accumulation is the basis of Kaldor's technical progress function (Kaldor, 1957, and 1959, Part I). He first used this concept in a paper (later to become 'A Model of Economic Growth') which he read to a seminar at the Department of Applied Economics in the Michaelmas Term of 1957. It is interesting to see the conflict that exists between Kaldor and Salter. In discussing the technical progress function, Kaldor rejected as untenable the traditional distinction between movements on a production function and movements of the function itself. He also discounted the influence of relative factor prices on the rate and form of capital accumulation. By contrast, Salter shows that it is possible to use the idea underlying the technical progress function and, at the same time, to take account of the important distinction between the impact of technical advances, that is, the movement inwards of the iso-product curve, and the impact of changing relative factor prices on the choice of the techniques to be embodied in current investment expenditures.

The remaining sections of Part I discuss, first, how the analysis can be expressed in terms of demand curves, marginal and average cost curves, and industry supply curves; second, the relevance to the analysis of the Marshallian distinction between short-run and long-run equilibrium; and third, the analytical modifications required when certain assumptions, especially that of a competitive market situation, are dropped. The condition for equilibrium after each round of improvement in best-practice techniques is that price = total costs of marginal new capacity = operating costs of marginal existing capacity. The first part of this condition is the Marshallian long-period equilibrium condition; the second is implied in the Marshallian short-period equilibrium condition. Only the output of current investment need meet the first part, while the second determines whether existing plants are scrapped or not. The section to the left of the equilibrium point on the supply curve illustrating this condition consists largely of the output of existing plants, some of which would be closed down if prices were lower. The section to the right shows the expansion of output that would occur by means of installing more best-practice capacity. The supply curve shifts over time as new technical advances are made, and the new intersection of it with the demand curve for the industry's product determines both what plants will be scrapped and what additions to output will be made by laying down additional capacity using the new best-practice techniques. (The analysis assumes L-shaped cost curves but is easily adapted to U-shaped ones.) Finally, Salter shows that the factors which determine scrapping, replacing and the introduction of new methods in a competitive industry are also effective in a monopoly, *provided that the monopolist is attempting to maximize profits*. When this is not so, and when an oligopolistic situation prevails, the penalty for not introducing new techniques, that is, operating losses on existing plants, may be avoided. The oligopolist in particular may be content to be only one step ahead of his competitors in the installation of new techniques, so that any growth in total market demand will accrue to his new capacity.

The empirical data relate to the experiences of twenty-eight British industries over the period 1924–50 and twenty-seven American industries over 1923–50. The British industries were chosen on the basis of the reliability of the output measures (p. 104), but there is little evidence that they were unrepresentative of industry as a whole. In fact, they covered 30 per cent of the industrial sector. The American figures were included as a check on the British figures and also because reliable figures of output per man hour were available. The analysis of British data consisted of estimating the movements between the years 1924, 1930, 1935, 1948 and 1950, of the following quantities:

volume of output	unit labour cost
employment	unit wage cost
output per head and per operative	unit materials cost
operative earnings	unit gross margin cost
gross prices	
net prices (value added per unit)	

The movements were summarized by the following measures – mean, standard deviation and coefficient of variation. Statistical associations between them were measured by fitting regression lines and examining the regression and correlation coefficients.

The main results were, first, the very great differences in productivity changes as between industries. In the U.K. six industries more than doubled output per head, while five recorded increases of less than 25 per cent. The mean increase was 70 per cent with a standard deviation of 61 per cent and a coefficient of variation of 35.7 per cent. The corresponding figures for the U.S.A. were 108 per cent, 64 per cent and 30.8 per cent. (These figures are for output per man hour.) Second, there was little statistical association between changes in productivity and changes in earnings. The correlation coefficient was – 0.09 in the U.K. (this relates to productivity and earnings per operative) and +0.22 in the U.S.A. (output and earnings per hour). Third, there was a close inverse association between productivity and wage costs, an association between productivity and non-wage costs and, therefore, between

Table 9.1 Regression coefficients, correlation coefficients and standard
errors of the main associations

	U.K. Output per head			U.S.A. Output per man hour		
	R.C.	C.C.	S.E.	R.C.	C.C.	S.E.
Earnings per operative	n.a.	−0.09*	n.a.	n.a.	+0.22‡	n.a.
Unit wage and salary cost	−0.82	−0.91	23.0	n.a.	−0.90	n.a.
Unit gross margin cost	−0.78	−0.31†	128.5	n.a.	n.a.	n.a.
Unit materials cost	−0.78	−0.79	36.4	n.a.	n.a.	n.a.
Gross price	−0.84	−0.88	25.9	−0.61§	−0.76§	35.3§
Output	+0.23	+0.81	35.6	n.a.	+0.62	n.a.
Employment	+0.63	+0.61	50.0	n.a.	+0.05	n.a.

R.C. = regression coefficient   C.C. = correlation coefficient
S.E. − standard error   n.a. = not available

* Earnings and output per operative
† Could be 0.37, discrepancy between Table 16 and Figure 16
‡ Hourly earnings
§ Wholesale prices

productivity and prices. Fourth, there were close associations between
productivity and output in both countries, and between output and
employment in the U.K. These results are shown in Table 9.1, which
contains the correlation and regression coefficients, and the standard
errors of the main associations. Fifth, it is noteworthy that the relative
shares of wages, materials and gross margins in the values of output of
the industries remained remarkably constant despite the great differences in changes in productivity (Table 18, p. 121).

Salter shows that the above findings cannot be explained plausibly
either by increased efficiency of labour alone or solely by the substitution of capital for labour. The first hypothesis is hard to reconcile
with the great differences in productivity changes as between industries,
the absence of an association between changes in earnings and changes
in productivity, and the changes in non-wage costs over the period. The
second hypothesis implies that the greatest increases in productivity
would be associated with the greatest increases in capital costs, and vice
versa. Though the data are very imperfect for testing this, the observed
results are the reverse of the implication of the hypothesis (p. 131). An
alternative hypothesis, based on the analysis of Part I, is not inconsistent with the findings. It is that the differential rates of change of productivity as between industries are due to different rates of technical
advance, that technical advances in different industries had no especially

marked biases in them (or at least not so great as to outweigh re-
ductions in inputs per unit of all factors), and that the observed changes
in relative shares are consistent with a great deal of substitution of
capital for labour, since these shares are relatively insensitive to quite
high values of the elasticity of substitution (Table 20, p. 137). A
further important ingredient of the alternative hypothesis is the
realization of economies of scale. Technical advances and economies of
scale are seen as complementary in their effects on productivity, costs
and prices. Salter leaves open the question whether all industries have
the same potential economies of scale, so that their realization is determined by demand conditions, or whether there are differential
potentialities as between industries.

The findings suggest that, generally, productivity changes have been
passed on to consumers either by lower prices, or by prices rising less
fast than otherwise would have occurred. There is little evidence that
they have been appropriated by any particular group. Thus, there is
little association between changes in productivity and earnings, but
strong association between changes in productivity and prices. The
higher association between changes in productivity and earnings in the
U.S.A. may be accounted for partly by the fact that, as compared with
the U.K., wage agreements in the U.S.A are made more at the firm or
industry level than at the national level.

Salter draws three important and topical policy implications from
the findings. The first is that government economic policy should be
directed towards creating a flexible economy which enables an easy
transference of resources from declining, high cost and price industries
to expanding, low cost and price ones. The second is that wages policy
should be national in scope, rather than related to the circumstances of
particular industries. Relating earnings to the 'capacity to pay' of
particular industries tends to bolster declining industries and hamper
expanding, progressive ones. It delays the introduction of new techniques and has a harmful effect on overall economic growth. Third, a
high rate of gross investment is necessary to allow the structure of production to change quickly and, given the structure of demand, to
increase the output and productivity of those industries where technical
advances are most rapid.

In conclusion, *Productivity and Technical Change* sets an example
which other books on applied economies could follow profitably. The
main problems to be tackled are kept clearly before the reader, and the
theory is developed with these ends and the limitations of the empirical
data in mind. The book is commendably brief, the tables and diagrams

are neatly arranged and the specialist statistical theory is confined to appendices. While mathematical reasoning underlies the theoretical sections, the actual 'squiggles' are mercifully few and also are mainly in appendices.

Notes

* *Economic Record*, vol. 38, no. 83, September 1962, pp. 388–94.
  1 See, for example, Robinson (1953–4).
  2 I am indebted to Dr K. J. Hancock and Mr H. R. Hudson for this point.

10 Biases in empirical estimates of the elasticities of substitution of C.E.S. production functions*

1. Already well-born, the C.E.S. production function made its début to a wide audience in an article by Arrow, Chenery, Minhas and Solow (1963). Minhas subsequently renamed the function and used it for further analysis in his book (Minhas, 1963).[1] The particular empirical findings which led to its début were the close association, as confirmed by the appropriate regressions, between the logarithms of labour productivity (value added per unit of labour used) and money wage rates in the *same* industries in *different* countries. (See Arrow *et al.*, 1963, pp. 227–8; Minhas, 1963, chapter 3.) If the values added and labour inputs used in the regression analysis are assumed to be observations from a C.E.S. production function, the regression coefficient, say b, can be shown to be an estimate of the elasticity of substitution between capital and labour. (See Arrow *et al.*, 1963, pp. 228–9; Minhas, 1963, chapter 2.) It was shown in both studies that the value of b was usually less than one and differed as between industries.

2. The elasticity of substitution which the authors seem to have in mind is that of a production function which is characterized by disembodied technical progress and *ex post* variability of factor proportions, so that, at any moment of time, the machines in the capital stock can be treated as if they have been moulded into the form of the latest vintage. But, clearly, the figures for value added relate to the current total production, and those for labour to total employment on machines of *different* vintages in the respective industries of the countries examined, that is, they are observations taken from the *short-run* production functions of the industries in the countries concerned. Moreover, these short-run production functions are likely to be characterized by embodied technical progress and, if not zero, at least extremely limited possibilities of *ex post* substitution. Therefore b can be interpreted either as a statistic which reflects the past economic histories of the industries and embodies the influences of different patterns of changes in wage-rates, different rates of capital accumulation, and so on; in which case it is not of much interest, for it gives no

reliable information about the possibility of *ex post* substitution of capital for labour, let alone the *ex ante* possibilities of substitution associated with the current 'best-practice' techniques facing business-men of different countries today (see Minhas, 1963, p. 3). Or, it can be regarded as an estimate of the *ex ante* elasticity of substitution (or the elasticity of substitution of the 'best-practice' techniques or latest vintages) in the special case where businessmen have very short time horizons, so that *current* factor prices and output levels alone determine their choice of technique. The purpose of this article is to consider the magnitude and sign of biases that may arise through differences between the data used and those ideally desired for an estimate of the *ex ante* relationship.

3. In what follows, it is assumed that the cost-minimizing technique (in the limited sense as defined in para. 2 above) has always been chosen and that there are many 'best-practice' techniques at any moment of time, so that differences in relative factor prices as between countries determined which of them was actually chosen. It is assumed that there is no possibility of *ex post* substitution.

Let V_1^j = value added associated with (the stocks of) the latest vintage machines in country j ($j = 1, \ldots, m$);

V_0^j = total value added associated with the total capital stock in country j;

L_1^j = labour employed on (the stocks of) the latest vintage machines in country j;

L_0^j = total labour employed on the total capital stock in country j;

W^j = wage rate in country j.

Then, the *ex ante* relationship is:

$$\log \frac{V}{L} = \log A + b \log W \tag{1}$$

with observations on the relevant $\log \dfrac{V_1^j}{L_1^j}$ and $\log W^j$. The actual observations are, however,

$$V_0^j = \alpha_1^j V_0^j + \ldots + \alpha_n^j V_0^j \tag{2}$$

where $\alpha_i^j V_0^j$ is the contribution to *total* value added of the production of the stocks of vintage i (where 1 indicates the latest and n the oldest vintage in use) in country j; and

$$L_0^j = \beta_1^j L_0^j + \ldots + \beta_n^j L_0^j \tag{3}$$

where $\beta_i^j L_0^j$ is the contribution to *total* employment of the labour employed on the stocks of vintage i in country j.

4. Although the regression equation being fitted is [1],[2] the true relationship between the variables is:

$$\log \frac{V}{L} = \log A + b \log W - \log \gamma \qquad [4]$$

where γ^j is defined by $\dfrac{V_0^j}{L_0^j} = \gamma^j \dfrac{V_1^j}{L_1^j}$. There are three possibilities: first, if γ^j is the same for all j, the estimate of A will be biased by a factor γ, but no bias will be introduced into the estimate of b. Second, if γ^j varies but is uncorrelated with W^j, neither the estimate of A nor that of b will be biased (from this source) – the effect will be equivalent to greater random errors. But, third, if γ^j is both variable and correlated with W^j, the estimate of b will be biased.

5. Under what conditions will the observed figures be the same proportion of the desired figures in all countries? Five simple cases are considered; it is hoped that they cover all the 'stylized cases' which correspond to the possibilities of technical progress and economic development. The first case is that in which the labour supply in each country is assumed to be constant and productivity is assumed to grow at a constant rate. There are balanced stocks of vintages in the relevant industry of each country, each containing the same number of vintages. Total labour in each country is distributed equally between all vintages, that is, $\beta_i^j = \dfrac{1}{n}$; and $V_i^j = V_{i+1}^j (1 + g)$, that is, the values added in each country grow as a constant rate, g, from vintage to vintage. In this case,

$$\frac{V_0^j}{L_0^j} = \frac{V_n^j[(1 + g)^n - 1]}{nL_i^j g} \qquad [5]$$

and

$$\frac{V_1^j}{L_1^j} = \frac{V_n^j (1 + g)^{n-1}}{L_1^j} \qquad [6]$$

$$\frac{1}{\gamma^j} = \frac{[6]}{[5]} = \frac{ng(1 + g)^{n-1}}{[(1 + g)^n - 1]}. \qquad [7][3]$$

6. Some values of $1/\gamma^j$ for various values of g and n are shown in Table 10.1. The ranges of values chosen were:

Case 1: $n = 4$-15, inclusive;
Case 2: $g = 0.01, 0.03, 0.05, 0.07, 0.10, 0.15$.

For reasons of space only a selection of the resulting values is shown.[4]

Table 10.1 Values of $1/\gamma^j$ for various values of n and g, case 1

		$n =$	
	5	10	15
0.05	1.10	1.23	1.38
$g =$ 0.10	1.20	1.48	1.79
0.15	1.30	1.73	2.23

7. As long as g and n are the same for all countries, γ^j will be the same also and no bias will arise in estimating b. If, however, g is related to the wage level of particular countries at any moment of time, and the wage levels in different years were correlated within the cross-section sample, or if there are fewer vintages in use in some countries than in others, and these numbers are correlated with wage levels within the sample, the values of $1/\gamma^j$ will differ as between countries and a biased estimate of b will be obtained. For example, if g tends to be greater, the greater is the wage rate at any moment of time, $1/\gamma^j$ will be positively correlated with W (see Table 10.1). If three countries had balanced stocks of vintages, of which there were 10, and the rates of growth of their values added were 0.05, 0.10 and 0.15 respectively, the values of their $1/\gamma^j$'s would be 1.23, 1.48 and 1.73 respectively. It follows that the resulting estimate of b will be biased downwards. Similarly, if n, the number of vintages, is likely to be less, the greater is the wage-rate at any moment of time, a bias is introduced such that the estimate of b will be biased upwards (see Table 10.1).

8. Now consider the case of a constant rate of growth of investment (G) so that

$$\frac{V_0^j}{L_0^j} = \frac{V_n^j \left[\frac{\{(1+g)(1+G)\}^n - 1}{(1+g)(1+G) - 1} \right]}{L_n^j \left[\frac{(1+G)^n - 1}{G} \right]} \tag{8}$$

and

$$\frac{V_1^j}{L_1^j} = \frac{V_n^j (1+g)^{n-1}}{L_n^j}. \tag{9}$$

That is to say, the values added of vintages i reflect the increases in both the efficiency and the number of machines, and the labour employed on them reflects the increase in the number of machines. In this case,

Table 10.2 Values of $1/\gamma^j$ for various values of n, G and g, case 2†

		$G = 0.05$ $n =$			$G = 0.10$ $n =$			$G = 0.15$ $n =$		
		5	10	15	5	10	15	5	10	15
	0.05	1.09	1.21	1.32	1.09	1.19	1.27	1.09	1.17	1.23
$g =$	0.10	1.19	1.43	1.65	1.18	1.38	1.54	1.17	1.34	1.45
	0.15	1.28	1.64	1.99	1.26	1.57	1.81	1.25	1.50	1.66

† Values of $1/\gamma^j$ were computed for: $n = 4\text{-}15$, inclusive; g and $G = 0.01, 0.03, 0.05, 0.07, 0.10, 0.15$.

$$\frac{1}{\gamma^j} = \frac{[(1+g)^{n-1}][(1+g)(1+G)-1][(1+G)^n - 1]}{G\{[(1+g)(1+G)]^n - 1\}}.$$ [10]

The values of $1/\gamma^j$ are shown in Table 10.2. Again, if n, G and g are the same for all countries, no bias is introduced in estimating b. Using Table 10.2, the direction of the tilt given to the regression line in relation to that through the desired observations for various relationships between n, g and G and the ordering of W at different points of time can be predicted. For example, if g or G are positively correlated with W, or if n is negatively correlated with W, it can be seen that the estimates of b will be biased downwards, upwards and upwards respectively. If the three sets of influences act together, though, it is not clear in general which way the *overall* bias will go, because there are offsetting factors at work.

9. The third case examined is that of each vintage contributing the same share to total value added, with a constant decline in labour requirements from vintage to vintage, that is, $L_i^j = L_{i-1}^j(1 + h)$, i (in this case) $= 2, \ldots, n$, where h is the rate of decline in the labour employed from vintage to vintage. In this case,

$$\frac{1}{\gamma^j} = \frac{[(1+h)^n - 1]}{nh}$$ [11]

and values of $1/\gamma^j$ are shown in Table 10.3. The same exercise may be carried out by postulating possible relationships between h and n, on the one hand, and the ordering of W, on the other, and then deducing the direction of the bias given to b.

10. For completeness, two further cases are included: fourth, a combination of growing values added from vintage to vintage associated with falling labour requirements (this is an extension of case 1). Fifth, both investment and values added are assumed to grow from vintage to

Table 10.3 Values of $1/\gamma^j$ for various values of n and h, case 3†

		$n =$	
	5	10	15
0.05	1.11	1.26	1.44
$h =$ 0.10	1.22	1.59	2.12
0.15	1.35	2.03	3.17

† Values of $1/\gamma^j$ were computed for: $n = 4\text{-}15$, inclusive; $h = 0.01, 0.03, 0.05,$ 0.07, 0.10, 0.15

vintage, but the labour employed on each set of vintages is assumed to be the same (a combination of cases 2 and 4). The values of $1/\gamma^j$ for these two cases are:

Case 4:
$$\frac{1}{\gamma^j} = \frac{g[(1+h)^n - 1](1+g)^{n-1}}{h[(1+g)^n - 1]} \qquad [12]$$

Case 5:
$$\frac{1}{\gamma^j} = \frac{n[(1+g)^{n-1}][(1+G)^{n-1}][(1+g)(1+G) - 1]}{\{[(1+g)(1+G)]^n - 1\}}. \qquad [13]$$

The values of $1/\gamma^j$ for various values of n, g, G and h are shown in Tables 10.4 and 10.5.

11. Perhaps the most simple, plausible situation is that where the g's and the h's are the *same* for all countries, that is, the growth rates of output and labour requirements are the same from one set of vintages to another, but there is a systematic relationship between W and n, and between W and G. It seems plausible to suppose that scrapping rates will vary from country to country and that they will be related to the level of W. In an open economy, G can be expected to vary from country to country also. If n is smaller and G is greater, the higher

Table 10.4 Values of $1/\gamma^j$ for various values of n, g and h, case 4†

	$h = 0.05$			$h = 0.10$			$h = 0.15$		
	$n =$			$n =$			$n =$		
	5	10	15	5	10	15	5	10	15
0.05	1.22	1.55	1.98	1.34	1.97	2.92	1.48	2.50	4.37
$g =$ 0.10	1.33	1.86	2.58	1.46	2.36	3.80	1.62	3.00	5.69
0.15	1.43	2.18	3.21	1.58	2.76	4.72	1.75	3.52	7.08

† Values of $1/\gamma^j$ were computed for: $n = 4\text{-}15$, inclusive; g and $h = 0.01, 0.03,$ 0.05, 0.07, 0.10, 0.15.

Table 10.5 Values of $1/\gamma^j$ for various values of n, g and G, case 5†

| | | $G = 0.05$ | | | $G = 0.10$ | | | $G = 0.15$ | |
| | | $n =$ | | | $n =$ | | | $n =$ | |
		5	10	15	5	10	15	5	10	15
	0.05	1.20	1.49	1.81	1.31	1.76	2.27	1.41	2.03	2.74
$g =$	0.10	1.31	1.76	2.27	1.41	2.04	2.76	1.52	2.32	3.24
	0.15	1.41	2.03	2.74	1.52	2.32	3.24	1.62	2.60	3.71

† Values of $1/\gamma^j$ were computed for: $n = 4$-15, inclusive; g and $G = 0.01, 0.03,$ 0.05, 0.07, 0.10, 0.15.

is W, then (at least within the range of values examined) the estimates of b are biased *upwards* in all five cases.

12. To put an order of magnitude on this bias, values of b were estimated for the cement industry, using the data on that industry in 12 countries given by Minhas (1963, p. 104).[5] The values of $1/\gamma^j$ were for case 5 and ranged from 2.54 ($n = 15$) to 1.45 ($n = 4$), ($g = 0.15, h = 0.0$ and $G = 0.03$ to 0.15); and for case 2 and ranged from 1.20 ($n = 15$) to 1.04 ($n = 4$), ($g = 0.03, h = 0.0$ and $G = 0.03$ to 0.15). Case 5 is the most 'realistic' case and case 2, the one most likely to minimize the size of the bias in b. In case 5, b was 0.7045; in case 2, b was 0.8591; both compare with Minhas's estimate of b of 0.9198 (Arrow *et al.*, 1963, Table 1, p. 20).

13. The possibility that the relationship between the ordering of W and n was U-shaped, that is, both very poor and very rich countries have a large number of vintages in the capital stocks of their industries, was examined, again using the data on the cement industry and case 5 values of $1/\gamma^j$.[6] For the two examples computed, b was 1.0506 and 1.0128 respectively.

14. Next, the reverse possibility, namely, that very rich countries have few vintages because of high scrapping rates, and that very poor countries have few because of low rates of capital accumulation, so that the relationship between the ordering of W and n was ∩-shaped, was examined, again using the cement industry data and case 5 values of $1/\gamma^j$.[7] The value of b was 1.0188. Finally, the possibility of a positive relationship between the ordering of W and n was examined, still using the cement industry data and case 5. The value of b was 1.3816.

15. It is most unlikely, especially given the assumptions concerning the economic behaviour associated with production on a C.E.S. production function, that the conditions which give constant $1/\gamma^j$'s will be found

in practice. It follows that the estimates of b in the two works referred to at the beginning of the article contain biases, the nature of which have gone largely unexplored. The analysis of this article suggests, first, that the biases may be substantial and, second, that *a priori*, they can on balance be either upwards or downwards. The article is written in the hope that it may persuade the authors either to explore the biases in further detail, or to make direct estimates, perhaps by means of sample surveys, of the elasticities of substitution (and other aspects) of current 'best-practice' techniques (see Salter, 1962).

Notes

* *Review of Economic Studies*, vol. xxxiii (3), no. 95, July 1966, pp. 227–33. The writer is grateful to P. K. Bardhan, Esra Bennathan, C. J. Bliss, John Cornwall, C. S. Leicester, R. E. Rowthorn, David W. Slater, Ajit Singh and G. Whittington for helpful discussions.

1 The new name is the homohypallagic production function (see Minhas, 1963, p. 32).

2 The actual regressions in Arrow *et al.* (1963) and in Minhas (1963) are of $\log L/V$ on $\log W$; these give negative values of the b's but in no way affect the subsequent arguments.

3 The reciprocal of γ^j was estimated because it is the actual observations which are known; therefore, by applying the $1/\gamma^j$'s to them, the corresponding implied desired observations can be obtained. An alternative approach would be to postulate desired values of b and see what observed values would correspond in each of the cases by multiplying the various $\dfrac{V^j}{L^j_1}$ values by the implied γ^j's.

4 The writer is indebted to Miss Marion Clarke and her assistants for doing the preliminary calculations and to Mr H. T. Burley for programming the main calculations.

5 The cement industry was chosen because there were twelve observations to match the values of $1/\gamma^j$ for $n = 4$–15 inclusive.

6 Values of $1/\gamma^j$ for $G = 0.03$–$0.15, g = 0.15, h = 0.0$ and $n = 15, 13, 11, 9, 7, 5, 4, 7, 9, 11, 13, 15$, and then $n = 15, 13, 11, 9, 7, 5, 4, 6, 8, 10, 12, 14$ were used.

7 Values of $1/\gamma^j$ for $G = 0.03$–$0.15, g = 0.15, h = 0.0$ and $n = 4, 6, 8, 10, 12, 14, 15, 13, 11, 9, 7, 5$, were used.

11 Investment-decision criteria, investment incentives and the choice of technique*

Introduction

Post-war economic policy in the United Kingdom and other advanced capitalist economies has been increasingly concerned with the level and rate of increase of labour productivity, both at the national level and at industry and firm levels. One aspect of this concern has been successive attempts by governments to encourage investment expenditure through fiscal incentives; for example, initial allowances were introduced in the United Kingdom in 1946, investment allowances were introduced in 1954, they were combined in 1959 and they were replaced by cash investment grants in 1966. Over the same period there have been various attempts to encourage the finance of investment by internal funds, the latest of which is the corporation tax (1966), an avowed object of which is to lower dividend payout ratios and so, it is hoped, encourage internally financed investment expenditure.

The United Kingdom Government has also attempted to 'educate' businessmen by encouraging them to adopt certain 'correct' rules of investment appraisal. In particular, the use of *Discounted Cash Flow (D.C.F.) procedures* of investment appraisal has been advocated strongly, and the widespread use of 'rules of thumb', such as the pay-off period criterion, or variants of the accounting rate of profit, have been criticised.[1]

The link between the level and rate of increase of productivity, on the one hand, and investment expenditure in an economy, an industry or a firm, on the other, is obviously a complicated one,[2] and only one small part of the process is discussed in this article, namely, the choice from the current 'best-practice' techniques available of the technique with which to produce a *given* level of output per year. It is clear that the *more* capital-intensive (as measured both by the investment-labour ratio and by the investment-output ratio) is the technique chosen, the greater, *other things being equal*, will be the ensuing rise in labour productivity. Presumably, therefore, the various fiscal devices introduced in the post-war period and the recent encouragement of the use of

D.C.F. procedures were meant, as one of their aims, to result in the choice of *more* capital-intensive techniques than otherwise would have been the case, that is to say, to result in 'deepening' investment expenditure.

The aims of this article are three: first, to attempt to order the *relative* capital intensities which result from the use of various investment-decision rules in a situation characterised by a common technology, given expectations about changes in product prices and money wages, and no taxation or investment incentives;[3] second, to analyse the impact of the introduction of taxation and, then, two alternative investment incentive schemes on the choice of technique. The object here is to see whether taxation changes either the capital intensities or the ordering of the techniques chosen by the rules and whether investment incentives, when associated with particular rules, do in fact lead to more 'deepening' investment than otherwise would have occurred. The third aim is to discuss the implications of past and present United Kingdom tax systems for the choice of technique, as these systems have special features which are not included in the simple systems.

The three investment-decision rules discussed are *the present-value rule* - choose the technique with the highest present value; *the pay-off period criterion* - here defined as choosing the technique which gives the highest expected net receipts over the pay-off period, subject to the constraint that the expected net receipts are at least equal to the investment expenditure associated with the technique (this is *not* the same as choosing the technique with the shortest pay-off period); *the accounting rate of profit rule* - choose the project with the highest expected accounting rate of profit. The three fiscal systems are: a proportional tax; this tax combined with a simple initial allowance scheme; and this tax combined with a simple investment allowance scheme. The United Kingdom tax systems considered are: the old profits tax and standard rate of income tax combined with investment and initial allowances; and the new corporation tax and cash investment grants.[4]

The article is in five sections. In section I the technology, expectations and basic assumptions are set out, the various tax systems are briefly described, and the concepts and notation used are defined. In section II the analysis of the relative capital intensities resulting from the application of the three rules in the *pre-tax* situation is set out. In section III the impact of the three simple tax systems on the choice of technique is analysed. In section IV the results which arise from the special features of the two United Kingdom systems are presented. The main conclusions of the article are gathered together in section V.

I

The basic technology

1.1 Suppose that there are a number of ways of producing a given stream of output per year, characterised by decreasing labour requirements per year as current investment expenditures increase. As the techniques become more capital-intensive, however, the saving in labour is assumed to become less. The labour requirements per year of each technique and the level of output per year are assumed to remain the same for the entire *engineering* life of the equipment associated with each technique (which is assumed to be *considerably* greater than its economic life). Maintenance and raw material costs are ignored.[5] If investment expenditure (K) is plotted on the horizontal axis, and labour requirements per year (l) on the vertical axis, the curve, ll (the *ex ante* production function) is obtained (see Figure 11.1). K_1, K_2 and K_3 are the investment expenditures associated with three 'best-practice' techniques of producing a given level of output (x) and l_1, l_2 and l_3 are their respective labour requirements.

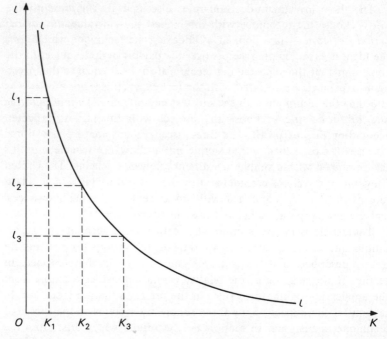

Figure 11.1

Expectations

1.2 Perhaps the most simple, plausible expectations are that the price of the product will rise (for simplicity, at a constant rate per year, g) and that costs will rise at a faster rate than price, mainly because money wages, on average, can be expected to rise at a rate per year (G) which reflects both the rise in the general level of prices *and* the rise in overall productivity. The expected economic life of the equipment associated with a given technique is assumed to be given by the point where the expected net receipts (in this instance sales receipts *less* wage costs) first become zero (but on this, see para. 5.1 below).

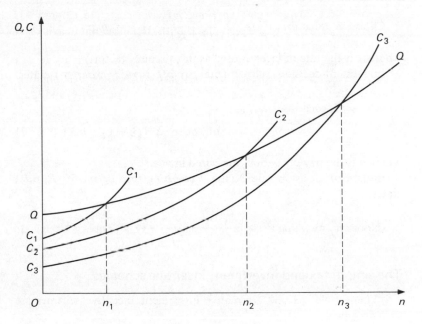

Figure 11.2

1.3 The expected annual sales receipts and the expected labour costs of techniques 1, 2 and 3 of Figure 11.1 are shown in Figure 11.2, together with their expected economic lives, n_1, n_2 and n_3. Length of life in years (n) is measured on the horizontal axis, annual sales receipts (Q) and labour costs (C) on the vertical axis. The curve QQ shows annual sales receipts, and the curves $C_1 C_1$, $C_2 C_2$ and $C_3 C_3$ show the annual labour costs of techniques 1, 2 and 3 respectively. The level of sales receipts at the end of year i $(i = 1, \ldots n)$ are: $Q_i = p_0 x (1 + g)^i$, where $p_0 =$ the price of the product at the beginning of year 1, and x = output per year. Labour costs of technique j ($j = 1, \ldots m$) at the end of year i are: $C_i^j = w_0 l_j (1 + G)^i$, where w_0 = money wage at the beginning of year 1, and l_j = annual labour requirement of technique j. The totals of the expected annual net receipts (q) are the areas between QQ and the respective CC curves. It can be seen that with the present assumptions, capital intensity and economic length of life are positively related.

Investment-decision rules (in their pre-tax form)

1.4 Investment-decision rule 1 (the *present value* (V) *rule*) states:

$$\text{Choose } K_j \text{ such that } V^j = \sum_{i=1}^{n} \frac{(Q_i - C_i^j)}{(1 + R)^i} - K_j = max. \qquad [1.1]$$

where R is the rate of interest used as the discount factor.[6]

Investment-decision rule 2 (the *pay-off period criterion*) states:

$$\text{Choose } K_j \text{ such that } \sum_{i=1}^{b} (Q_i - C_i^j) = max.$$
$$\text{subject to } \sum_{i=1}^{b} (Q_i - C_i^j) \geqslant K_j. \qquad [1.2]$$

where b is the pay-off period, measured in years.

Investment-decision rule 3 (the *accounting rate of profit* (P) *rule*) states:

$$\text{Choose } K_j \text{ such that } P^j = \frac{\sum_{i=1}^{n} (Q_i - C_i^j) - K_j}{nK_j} = max. \qquad [1.3]^{[7]}$$

The simple tax and investment incentive schemes

1.5 The simple tax and alternative investment incentive schemes are now described.[8]

The tax system (Tax system A.1)

Annual company profits, net of 'wear and tear' allowances, are assumed to be taxed at a rate of t per cent. The rate of 'wear and tear' allowance is $\left(d = \dfrac{3}{2\bar{n}}\right)$, where $\bar{n}$ is the length of life of equipment for tax purposes and is assumed to be the *same* for all the machines associated with the current 'best-practice' techniques for producing a particular product.

The accelerated depreciation allowance scheme (Tax system A.2)

An initial allowance of i per cent is given in the year of purchase, together with the 'wear and tear' allowance, so that $K(1 - i - d)$ is left to be written off at a rate of d per year for the remaining $(\tilde{n} - 1)$ years. Taxation is again at a rate of t per cent.

The investment allowance scheme (Tax system A.3)

An investment allowance of I per cent is given in the year of purchase, as well as the 'wear and tear' allowance. $K(1 + I)$ is therefore written off for tax purposes over $\tilde{n}$ years. The rate of taxation is t per cent.

1.6 The three investment-decision rules can all be restated to include the impact of the tax and other provisions on the expected net receipts. For example, under tax system A.1 rule 1 becomes:

choose K_j such that

$$V_j = \left\{ \sum_{i=1}^{n} \frac{(1-t)(Q_i - C_i^j)}{(1 + r_t)^i} \right\} + \left\{ \sum_{i=1}^{n} \frac{tdK_j(1 - d)^{i-1}}{(1 + r_t)^i} \right\} - K_j = max.$$

where $r_t = R(1 - t)$.

The first term is the present value of the expected net receipts adjusted for tax payable on them; the second term is the present value of the tax saved by the receipt of 'wear and tear' allowances. The rate of interest used as a discount factor is measured *net* of tax. (As *post-tax* amounts are being discounted, it seems reasonable to use a *post-tax* rate of interest as the discount factor.) The expressions corresponding to the other rules can be similarly adjusted, both for taxation and for the appropriate investment incentives.

The two United Kingdom tax systems

The old profits tax and standard rate of income tax combined with investment and initial allowances (Tax system B.1)

1.7 Prior to 1966, expenditure on new plant and machinery by manufacturing firms outside the development districts (the discussion will be confined to these firms) carried with it for tax purposes an investment allowance (I) of 30 per cent and an initial allowance (i) of 10 per cent. These two allowances, together with the normal statutory 'wear and tear' allowances (d), were deductible from taxable income (supposing sufficient profits to be earned by the business as a whole, but not necessarily by the new investment itself), though the actual tax remissions were not received until, on average, 18 months later. The total 'wear and tear' allowances of subsequent years were reduced by the amount of the initial (but not the investment) allowance. Taxable profits of companies bore a profits tax ($\bar{p}$) of 15 per cent and the standard rate of income tax (s) of 8s. 3d. in the £. This system is a combination of tax systems A.2 and A.3 above.

The new corporation tax combined with cash investment grants (Tax system B.2)

1.8 Under the new system a cash grant (G_2) of 20 per cent (temporarily raised to 25 per cent for the fiscal year 1967–8) of the purchase price is given, and the investment and initial allowances, but not the 'wear and tear' allowances, are withdrawn. The latter, however, apply only to the *balance* of the purchase price after subtracting the cash investment grant. The cash grant eventually will be received six months after the date of purchase and is not dependent upon a profit being earned. Taxable profits now bear a corporation tax at a rate (c) of 40 per cent, and income tax payable by shareholders depends upon the proportion of post-tax profits (net of depreciation) which is distributed, that is, on the payout ratio (α).

1.9 Again, the three rules can be restated to take account of the tax and other provisions. For reasons of space, they are not shown here (the expressions for the present-value rule are in paras 1.4 to 1.8 of 'Cash Investment Grants, Corporation Tax and Pay-out Ratios'). Finally, it could be noted that it is sometimes claimed that rule 3 is applied in its *pre-tax* form, in which case expression [1.3] is applicable. (See *Report of the Committee on Turnover Taxation*, 1964, para. 282.)

1.10 Now suppose that a businessman decides the technique in which to invest on the basis of one of the rules described in this section. The questions dealt with in the next sections are: can the resulting techniques be ordered according to their *relative* capital intensities? And does the introduction of taxation and investment incentives into the analysis change the capital intensities and their ordering?[9]

II

Investment-decision rules and relative capital intensities in the pre-tax situation

2.1 Essentially, the questions asked in this section are: what are the values of the slope of the *ex ante* production function at the points corresponding to the techniques chosen by each rule, and can they be unambiguously ordered? These values are found, for rules 1 and 3, by obtaining the first-order conditions for a maximum present value and a maximum accounting rate of profit respectively, and expressing them in terms of the slope of the production function, $\frac{\delta l}{\delta K}$. The corresponding value for the pay-off period criterion is obtained by a different method (see para. 2.3 below).

Rule 1

2.2 This rule may be written as:

$$V_j = p_0 x B - w_0 l_j A - K_j = max.$$ [2.1]

where

$$A = \frac{(1+G)\left\{\left(\frac{1+G}{1+R}\right)^n - 1\right\}}{G-R}, \ B = \frac{(1+g)\left\{\left(\frac{1+g}{1+R}\right)^n - 1\right\}}{g-R},$$

and $R > G > g$, by assumption. (For moderate rates of increase of prices and money.wages, this seems a reasonable assumption.)

To find the first-order condition for [2.1] to be a maximum, partially differentiate [2.1] with respect to K and put the resulting expression equal to zero to obtain:

$$-\frac{\delta l}{\delta K} = \frac{1}{w_0 A - \frac{\delta n}{\delta l}\left(p_0 x \frac{\delta B}{\delta n} - w_0 l \frac{\delta A}{\delta n}\right)}$$ [2.2]

Rule 2

2.3 This criterion requires that:

$$p_0 x B' - w_0 l_j A' = max, \text{ subject to } p_0 x B' - w_0 l_j A' \geqslant K_j,$$

where

$$A' = \frac{(1+G)\{(1+G)^b - 1\}}{G} \text{ and } B' = \frac{(1+g)\{(1+g)^b - 1\}}{g}.$$

Write the constraint as the equality:

$$l = \frac{p_0 x B'}{w_0 A'} - \frac{K}{w_0 A'}$$ [2.3]

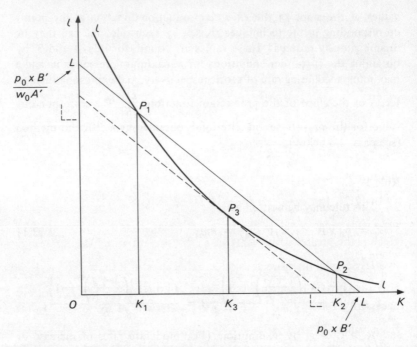

Figure 11.3

[2.3] is a straight line (LL in Figure 11.3) with a slope of $\left(-\dfrac{1}{w_0 A'}\right)$ and an intercept on the vertical axis of $\dfrac{p_0 x B'}{w_0 A}$. The curve, ll, of Figure 11.1 is also shown in Figure 11.3. Provided some labour and some investment expenditure are needed to produce a given level of output, LL will either intersect ll at points such as P_1 and P_2 (where the constraint is satisfied) or will be tangential to ll at a point such as P_3 (or will not cut ll at all, in which case no technique will satisfy the criterion). At P_2 the pay-off period criterion is satisfied (because net receipts for the pay-off period are the highest possible, given that the constraint must be met) and the technique associated with an investment expenditure of K_2 is chosen.

At P_2, $-\dfrac{\delta l}{\delta K} < \dfrac{1}{w_0 A'}$, because ll cuts LL from below. $\bigg($The other possibility is the tangency solution at P_3 and there, $-\dfrac{\delta l}{\delta K} = \dfrac{1}{w_0 A'}.\bigg)$
Therefore

$$-\frac{\delta l}{\delta K} \leqslant \frac{1}{w_0 A'} \qquad\qquad [2.4]^{10}$$

2.4 Now compare [2.2] with [2.4] and suppose, initially, that $n = b$ for all techniques. [2.2] therefore becomes:

$$-\frac{\delta l}{\delta K} = \frac{1}{w_0 A''} \qquad [2.5]$$

where

$$A'' = \frac{(1 + G)\left\{\left(\frac{1+G}{1+R}\right)^b - 1\right\}}{G - R}$$

Because $A'' < A'$, it is obvious that [2.5] > [2.4].

In [2.2], $\left(p_0 x \dfrac{\delta B}{\delta n} - w_0 l \dfrac{\delta A}{\delta n}\right)$ may be $\gtrless 0$. If it $\leqslant 0$, [2.2] > [2.4], for a wide range of values of n;[11] that is to say, over this range, which is greater, the greater is the value of R, the present-value criterion results in a *less* capital-intensive technique being chosen. If $\left(p_0 x \dfrac{\delta B}{\delta n} - w_0 l \dfrac{\delta A}{\delta n}\right)$ > 0 (which is more likely to happen at *low* values of n) it does not necessarily follow that [2.2] < [2.4], especially as $w_0 A < w_0 A'$, for given values of n, and $\dfrac{1}{w_0 A'}$ is the upper value of the inequality, $-\dfrac{\delta l}{\delta K} \leqslant \dfrac{1}{w_0 A'}$. Thus, it seems reasonable to conclude that, given the present assumptions, the pay-off period criterion often results in the choice of a *more* capital-intensive technique than does the present-value rule, and that this is more likely to occur, given the value of the pay-off period, the higher is the rate of interest used as the discount factor and the shorter is the economic length of life of the equipment concerned. If $b = 4$–5 years, $R = 15$–20 per cent, $G = 4$–6 per cent, and $n = 10$–15 years are taken as realistic orders of magnitude, 'back-of-an-envelope' calculations show that the result is widely applicable.

Rule 3

2.5 This rule may be written as:

$$P^j = \frac{1}{nK}\{p_0 x B''' - w_0 l \,_j A''' - K_j\} = max. \qquad [2.6]$$

where

$$A''' = \frac{(1 + G)\{(1 + G)^n - 1\}}{G} \quad \text{and} \quad B''' = \frac{(1 + g)\{(1 + g)^n - 1\}}{g}$$

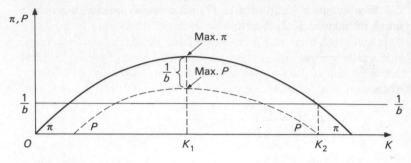

Figure 11.4

A rough idea of the relative capital intensity which results from this rule, as compared, first, with the pay-off period criterion can be obtained as follows. In Figure 11.4

$$\pi_j \left\{ = \frac{\sum\limits_{i=1}^{b} (Q_i - C_i{}^j)}{bK_j} \right\}$$

is plotted on the vertical axis and K on the horizontal axis. The values of π_j are the average expected gross rates of profit for the pay-off period of each technique – the *inverses* of the number of years that it takes to 'repay' the respective investment outlays. Because the undiscounted net receipts of the techniques are bounded by the pay-off period and because labour requirements decline at a decreasing rate as K increases, π will rise to a maximum and then decline as K increases, giving the curve $\pi\pi$ in Figure 11.4. If rule 2 were an instruction to choose the technique with the *lowest* pay-off period the technique associated with an expenditure of K_1 would be chosen. However, it is possible both to increase expected gross profits *and* to satisfy the pay-off period criterion by choosing the technique associated with an expenditure of K_2; at which value $\pi = \dfrac{1}{b}$, the inverse of the pay-off period. With this technique, $\sum\limits_{i=1}^{b} (Q_i - C_i{}^j) = K_j$, and is also maximised.

2.6 Now suppose that annual *net* profits (P) are averaged for a period equal to the pay-off period, and that depreciation is reckoned as $\dfrac{K}{b}$ per year. If P^j is plotted against K (see the curve PP in Figure 11.4) it will reach a maximum at the *same* investment expenditure (K_1) as π. Therefore, with these assumptions, rule 3 results in a *less* capital-intensive technique being chosen than that resulting from rule 2.

2.7 If, now, the assumption that $n = b$ is dropped the maximum of the curve PP may well occur at a value of K which is closer to K_2; but it does seem that there will be a considerable number of cases where this rule results in a *less* capital-intensive technique being chosen.

2.8 What can be said of the ordering of rule 3 in relation to rule 1? To answer this, consider the first-order condition for a maximum P^j. It is:

$$-\frac{\delta l}{\delta K} = \left\{\frac{p_0 \, x \, B'' \, ' - w_0 \, lA'' \, '}{K}\right\}\left\{\frac{1}{w_0 A'' \, ' - \dfrac{K}{n}\dfrac{\delta n}{\delta l} - \dfrac{\delta n}{\delta l}\left\{p_0 \, x\left(\dfrac{\delta B'' \, '}{\delta n} - \dfrac{B'' \, '}{n}\right)\right. \atop \left. - w_0 l\left(\dfrac{\delta A'' \, '}{\delta n} - \dfrac{A'' \, '}{n}\right)\right\}}\right\} \qquad [2.7]$$

Comparing [2.7] with [2.2], and ignoring the last two terms of the denominator of [2.7] and the last term of the denominator of [2.2], the ordering turns on whether the effect of $\left\{\dfrac{p_0 \, x \, B'' \, ' - w_0 \, lA'' \, '}{K}\right\} > 1$, which tends to make [2.7] > [2.2], outweighs, or is outweighed, by the effect of $w_0 A'' \, ' > w_0 A$, which tends to make [2.7] < [2.2]. Therefore, while both rule 1 and rule 3 often result in *less* capital-intensive techniques being chosen than those resulting from rule 2, the techniques corresponding to rules 1 and 3 cannot themselves be ordered.[12]

2.9 The results of this section are summarised in Figure 11.5. $-\dfrac{\delta l}{\delta K}$ is plotted on the vertical axis and n is plotted on the horizontal axis. Because n increases, and $-\dfrac{\delta l}{\delta K}$ decreases, as K increases, a downward-sloping curve such as DD (shown as a straight line for simplicity) is obtained. $-\dfrac{\delta l}{\delta K}$ is also a function of n in the expressions for the first-order conditions for a maximum of rules 1 and 3 (see [2.2] and [2.7]), and of b in the inequality condition of rule 2 (see [2.4]). These expressions are shown in Figure 11.5 by the curves EE (rule 1), FF (which is a horizontal straight line, the height of which is determined by the values of b, w_0 and G) (rule 2) and GG (rule 3). The economic lengths of life of the techniques chosen by the rules are those associated with the points where EE, FF and GG cut DD.

2.10 The positive relationship between K and n is the line HH, in the bottom half of Figure 11.5, and the investment expenditures associated

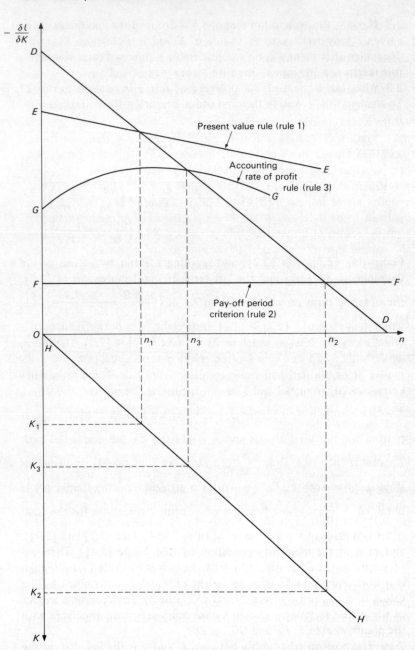

Figure 11.5

with the choices which result from each rule are shown on the vertical axis. (As shown in Figure 11.5, rule 1 results in the choice of a less capital-intensive technique than rule 3; but this ordering need not occur.) The significant result at this stage is that the pay-off period criterion often results in the choice of the *most* capital-intensive technique of the three rules examined (of four rules, if the internal rate of return is also considered, see note 6).

2.11 The next section discusses whether taxation and investment incentives change the relative orderings resulting from the three rules, and whether investment incentives do, in fact, lead to 'deepening' investment expenditure. It could be noticed in passing that if factor and product prices and the inputs per unit of output of each technique are assumed to be independent of the scale of operation of the individual firm the results of this and the following sections relate to the choice of the capital intensity of a *unit* of output. In this case $x = 1$ in the expressions and l and k should be interpreted as the labour requirements and investment expenditure, respectively, of a unit of output.

III

3.1 The expressions for $-\dfrac{\delta l}{\delta K}$ in the *post-tax* situations (which, for reasons of space, are not shown here) are basically similar to those of the *pre-tax* situation, except they have additional terms which contain the rates of taxation, investment incentives and other allowances. In some instances the direction of the change in capital intensity when taxation and investment incentives are taken into account is clear from the expressions themselves. But in others it was necessary, first, to place orders of magnitude on the values of the appropriate variables. The values were: $t = 0.25, 0.50; i, I = 0.10, 0.20, 0.30; d = 0.25, 0.20, 0.15$ (implying $n = 6$, 8 and 10 years, respectively); $G = 0.03, 0.06, 0.09, 0.12; R = 0.10, 0.25, 0.50; b = 2, 3, 4$ and 5 years; and $n = 6, 8, 10, 12, 15$ and 20 years.

3.2 The main results of the analysis of the new expressions are:

3.2.1 The orderings of the capital intensities resulting from each rule in the pre-tax situation probably still hold in the *post-tax* situation, though, in some instances, the range of values of n within which rule 1 results in the choice of a *less* capital-intensive technique than rule 2 is narrowed.

3.2.2 Taxation *by itself* results in the choice of *less* capital-intensive techniques if rules 1 and 2 are used, but has no impact if rule 3 is used.

These results reflect the fact that, relatively, the tax savings associated with the receipt of 'wear and tear' allowances are greater, the *less* capital-intensive is the technique concerned (either because their discounted value is relatively greater (rule 1) or because a greater proportion of their total is included in the pay-off period (rule 2)). The technique chosen by rule 3 is not affected by a proportional tax, as it affects the sizes but not the order of the rates of profit.

3.2.3 Investment incentives do result in more 'deepening' than otherwise would have occurred if rules 1 and 2 are used. Their impact more than offsets the counteracting effect of taxation on the choice of techniques, if rule 1 is used, but not if rule 2 is used. However, if rule 3 is used, accelerated depreciation has no effect, and investment allowances have a 'perverse' effect in the sense that *less* capital-intensive techniques than otherwise would be the case are chosen. This reflects the fact that, relatively, the impact of the tax-saving associated with a given rate of investment allowance on the rate of profit is greater, the *less* capital-intensive is the technique concerned. As the accounting rate of profit rule is said to be widely used in the United Kingdom, this 'perverse' effect of its use in association with investment allowances is not without interest.

3.2.4 For *given* values of I and i, and with the use of rules 1 and 2, investment allowances result in more deepening than do initial allowances. However, there are values of i greater than I which reverse the orderings associated with $I \geqslant i$.

IV

4.1 In this section, the choice of technique under the two United Kingdom tax systems is briefly considered. Tax system B.1 is, in effect, a combination of tax systems A.2 and A.3. Tax system B.2 includes the additional complication that the amount of income tax payable by shareholders, and thus the *post-tax* net receipts of given investment projects, depend upon the size of the payout ratio adopted.

4.2 The expressions for $-\dfrac{\delta l}{\delta K}$ for these tax systems are again not shown; they are similar to those of the *pre-tax* situation, but include extra terms which are analogous to those of the simple tax systems. The following orders of magnitude were placed on the rates of taxation and investment incentives, etc. For reasons explained elsewhere, the values of the fiscal rates were: $\tilde{p} = 0.15; s = 0.4125; c = 0.40; I = 0.30; i = 0.10; G_2 = 0.20;$ and $d = 0.25, 0.20, 0.15$ (implying $\tilde{n} = 6, 8$ and

10 years respectively).[13] $G = 0.03, 0.06, 0.09, 0.12; R = 0.10, 0.25,$ 0.50; $b = 2, 3, 4$ and 5 years, and $\alpha = 0, \frac{2}{5}, \frac{3}{5}, \frac{2}{3}$[14] and 1 were used also.

Comparisons with the pre-tax situation

4.3 Comparing the techniques which result from the use of each rule under the two tax systems with those of the *pre-tax* situation, it is found that the use of rule 1 results in a 'natural' outcome under both tax systems, rule 2 probably results in a 'natural' outcome under tax system B.1 but not under tax system B.2, and rule 3 results in a 'perverse' outcome under both systems. ('Natural' and 'perverse' mean that more (less) 'deepening' than otherwise would be the case occurs.)

'Orderings' under the two tax systems

4.4 Under the old tax system there seems to be no reason to change the finding that the most capital-intensive technique is likely to be associated with rule 2; but there now seems a greater chance that rule 1 may result in the choice of a *more* capital-intensive technique than rule 3. Under the present tax system, it appears that, except in the case of a *small pre-tax* rate of interest ($< 5\%$) or the *combination* of a high payout ratio with higher *pre-tax* rates of interest, the pay-off period criterion still results in the choice of the *most* capital-intensive technique of those chosen by the three rules.

Comparison between the tax systems for common rules

4.5 The final set of comparison relates to the relative orderings, as between the two tax systems, of the capital intensities chosen by a given rule. This is the most interesting set of comparisons, because it throws some light on the impact of the recent (1966) changes to a corporation tax and cash investment grants on the choice of techniques. Too much should not be made of the results, however, because they are the outcome of a 'partial' analysis. While the values of the tax rates used are appropriate for an 'otherwise situation' comparison, it may well be that the prices of capital goods and the rates of increase of product prices and money wages would have been different as between the two situations.

4.6 If the techniques resulting from use of the present-value rule are compared it is found that the technique chosen under tax system B.2 is *less* capital-intensive than that chosen under tax system B.1. Similarly, the use of the pay-off period criterion almost certainly results in a *less* capital-intensive technique being chosen under tax system B.2. (The use of rule 2 under tax system B.1 usually resulted in the choice of a more capital-intensive technique relative to the *pre-tax* situation (depending upon the value of b in relation to $\tilde{n}$, namely, that $b \leqslant \tilde{n}/2$), while the opposite result occurred under tax system B.2).[15]

4.7 Finally, if the capital intensities resulting from the use of rule 3 are compared it is found that, except for very low payout ratios (for the orders of magnitude examined, less than approximately 23 per cent), *more* capital-intensive techniques are chosen under the present tax system (B.2). Therefore there arises the possibility of a paradoxical result, if the corporation tax results in the adoption of very low α's, or if firms already have low α's, or if the income tax payable by shareholders is ignored by managers when investment decisions are made (which is formally equivalent to assuming a payout ratio of zero).

V

5.1 Before setting out the main conclusions of this article, some of the limitations of the analysis are discussed. The first limitation is that the analysis consists, essentially, of comparisons between different situations, where only the variables associated with the particular fiscal system in force are allowed to change. It may well be, though, that the changes in factor and product prices as between the 'otherwise situations' would be so important in practice that the results of the comparisons in this article could not be applied to situations of actual change. The second limitation is that *higher* investment expenditures may not in fact be associated with *lower* labour inputs over the entire life of the equipment involved. The greater is the investment expenditure, the more complex is the equipment likely to be, and therefore the greater may be its maintenance costs (and, thus, indirect labour input) in its later years. This point has been guarded against to some extent by supposing that economic lives are considerably shorter than engineering lives. Third, the expected economic length of life *may* be less than that determined by the point where expected quasi-rents first become zero, if the expected rate of technical progress is taken into account by businessmen in a more sophisticated way than is assumed in this article, or if they operate in an imperfectly competitive situation. However, these considerations do not affect the *ordering* of techniques by length of life, which is the relevant factor for the present analysis. Moreover, this effect increases the possibility that the pay-off period criterion will result in the choice of the *most* capital-intensive technique of three rules considered. Fourth, the comparisons between the tax systems are not applicable if businessmen ignore taxation provisions when making investment decisions.

5.2 The fifth limitation is that the relative capital intensities which result from the use of the various rules have been discussed in the context of a situation in which the *level of expected output* is assumed to be given. If, instead, the level of *investment expenditure* is assumed to be given it can be shown that the pay-off period criterion and, perhaps, the present-value rule result in the choice of *less* capital-intensive techniques than those indicated by the present analysis. Therefore, if businessmen are in the latter situation, or if they see the problem of the choice of techniques as one of allocating a given amount of investment funds rather than as one of deciding the capital intensity to be used to produce a given level (or unit) of output, the orderings associated with the three rules *may* differ from those suggested here.[16]

5.3 Bearing in mind the above limitations, the conclusions of the article are:

Conclusions which apply to all tax systems and to the pre-tax situation

5.3.1 In both the *pre-tax* and *post-tax* situations it appears that the use of the *pay-off period criterion* often results in the choice of a *more* capital-intensive technique than does the *present-value rule*, or the *accounting rate of profit rule*.

5.3.2 Taxation *by itself* results in the choice of *less* capital-intensive techniques than in the *pre-tax* situation if the *present-value rule* or the *pay-off period criterion* is used, but has no impact if the *accounting rate of profit rule* is used.

5.3.3 Investment incentives result in more deepening than otherwise would have occurred if the *present-value rule* or *pay-off period criterion* is used. Moreover, if the former rule is used their effect more than offsets the impact of taxation on the choice of techniques. However, if the *accounting rate of profit rule* is used either they have no effect (accelerated depreciation) or a 'perverse' effect (investment allowances) in the sense that *less* capital-intensive techniques than otherwise would be the case are chosen.

5.3.4 For *given* values of the rates of investment incentives, investment allowances result in more deepening than initial allowances if the *present-value rule* or the *pay-off period criterion* is used.

5.3.5 In general, it is not possible to order the *relative* capital intensities which result from the use of the *present-value rule* and the *accounting rate of profit rule*. However, under all tax systems that include investment incentives there is a greater chance than in the *pre-tax* situation that the *present-value rule* will result in the choice of a *more* capital-intensive technique than that which results from the *accounting rate of profit rule*.

Conclusions which apply specifically to the United Kingdom tax systems

5.4.1 The use of the *accounting rate of profit rule* under both United Kingdom tax systems results in 'perverse' movement in the sense that *less* capital-intensive techniques are chosen than would have been in the *pre-tax* situation. This is also true of the use of the *pay-off period criterion* under the present tax system of a corporation tax and cash investment grants, but probably not of its use under the previous tax system, or of the use of the *present-value rule* under either tax system.

5.4.2 If the *present-value rule* is used the change from the old tax system of profits tax and the standard rate of income tax combined with investment and initial allowances to the present tax system results in the choice of *less* capital-intensive techniques than otherwise would have occurred.

5.4.3 If the *pay-off period criterion* is used the change from the old tax system to the present tax system will almost certainly result in the choice of *less* capital-intensive techniques than otherwise would have occurred.

5.4.4 The *accounting rate of profit rule* will result in the choice of *more* capital-intensive techniques under the present tax system than would have occurred under the old tax system, *unless* payout ratios are very low, or are reduced to very low levels, or the income tax payable by shareholders is ignored by businessmen when making investment decisions.

5.4.5 If at the time when the corporation tax and cash investment grants were introduced a firm changed from using the *pay-off period criterion* to using a *D.C.F.* procedure it may well choose *less* capital-intensive techniques than otherwise would have been the case. A change from the *accounting rate of profit rule* to the *present-value rule* under the same circumstances, however, *may* result in more 'deepening' investment than otherwise would have occurred.

Appendix

Simplifying assumptions about the operation of the British tax systems

1. The cash investment grants are received immediately, initial and investment allowances at the end of the first year of operation.

2. Reducing-balance 'wear and tear' allowances are used, at the three official rates of 25, 20 and 15 per cent, implying lives for tax purposes $(\bar{n})$ of 6, 8 and 10 years respectively $\left(d = \dfrac{3}{2\bar{n}}\right)$.

3. Sufficient profits are assumed to be made in the business to allow the investment and initial allowances to be claimed immediately.

4. Profits tax and income tax apply to the *same* year's taxable income.

5. The rates of interest (r) used as the discount factors for the present-value calculations are assumed to be *net* of tax (see para. 1.6 in the text). Under tax system B.1 $(p + s$ with I and $i)$, $r_1 = R(1 - p - s)$, under tax system B.2 $(c$ with $G_2)$, $r_2 = R(1 - c - \alpha s(1 - c))$, where the subscripts refer to the tax systems concerned.

Notation

Q_i = expected annual sales receipts in year i $(i = 1, \ldots n)$;

C_i^j = expected annual labour costs in year i of technique j, $(j = 1, \ldots m)$;

q_i = expected annual net receipts in year i;

p = product price;

w = money wage;

g = rate of increase of product price;

G = rate of increase of money wage;

x = annual output;

l_j = annual labour requirement of technique j;

K_j = investment expenditure associated with technique j;

r_t, r_i = *post-tax* rate of interest $(i = 1, 2)$,

R = *pre-tax* rate of interest;

ρ = internal rate of return;

V^j = present value of investment project using technique j;

P^j = accounting rate of profit of investment project using technique j;

n = economic length of life in years;

$\bar{n}$ = length of life for tax purposes in years;

b = length of pay-off period in years;

t = rate of tax in simple tax systems;

$\bar{p}$ = rate of profits tax;

s = standard rate of income tax;

c = rate of corporation tax;

I = rate of investment allowance;

i = rate of initial allowance;

G_2 = rate of cash investment grant;

d = rate of reducing-balance 'wear and tear' allowance $\left(d = \dfrac{3}{2\tilde{n}}\right)$;

α = payout ratio;

subscripts 1, 2 refer to the respective United Kingdom tax systems.

Notes

* *Economic Journal*, vol. 78, no. 309, March 1968, pp. 77–95. I am grateful to D. M. Nuti, Graham Pyatt, W. B. Reddaway, R. E. Rowthorn and G. Whittington for helpful comments, to M. Panić and Marion Clarke and her assistants for carrying out the preliminary calculations, to H. T. Burley for programming the main calculations for TITAN and to Professor M. V. Wilkes, Mathematical Laboratory, University of Cambridge, for the use of TITAN. The methods and results of this article are summaries of those of a more detailed paper which is mimeographed and which may be obtained from the Faculty Office, Faculty of Economics and Politics, University of Cambridge, Sidgwick Avenue, Cambridge.

1 See, for example, National Economic Development Council, *Investment Appraisal*, London, 1965.

2 The best analysis of this link at the industry and firm levels is the late W. E. G. Salter's pioneering work, *Productivity and Technical Change* (1960).

3 This topic has been analysed more fully by the writer in Harcourt (1969b).

4 The impact of the change to the corporation tax and cash investment grants from the previous system, and from one which included corporation tax and retained investment and initial allowances, on the present values of given investment projects has been analysed by the writer in Harcourt (1966a and 1967).

5 The significance of these assumptions is discussed further in para. 5.1. Sometimes it is convenient to assume that the inputs per unit of output associated with each technique are *independent* of the scale of operations (see para. 2.11). The influence of raw-material costs on the choice of technique is discussed in Harcourt (1969b, pp. 211–12). With the exception of the accounting rate of profit rule, where their effect is indeterminate, they result in the choice of *less* capital-intensive techniques than otherwise would be the case.

6 Another *D.C.F.* procedure which is often recommended is the *internal rate of return rule*: Choose K_j such that ρ in the expression

$$\sum_{i=1}^{n} \frac{(Q_i - C_i{}^j)}{(1 + \rho)^i} - K_j = 0$$

is a *maximum*, where ρ is the internal rate of return.

It is shown in Harcourt (1969b, pp. 201–2) that (with the present assumptions) this rule *always* results in the choice of a *less* capital-intensive technique than that resulting from the *present value rule*, which is used as the representative of *D.C.F.* procedures in the present analysis.

7 This is one of many possible variants of the accounting rate of profit, see note 12.

8 A number of simplifying assumptions concerning the operation of the two tax systems are in the Appendix to this article; they are discussed in detail in para. 1.1 of Harcourt (1966a).

9 The notation used in the article is in the Appendix.

10 The writer is indebted to R. E. Rowthorn for this proof.

11 If $\left(p_0 x \dfrac{\delta B}{\delta n} - w_0 l \dfrac{\delta A}{\delta n}\right) < 0$ (which is more likely, the *greater* is the value

of n), and because $\dfrac{\delta n}{\delta l} < 0,\ -\dfrac{\delta n}{\delta l}\left(p_0 x \dfrac{\delta B}{\delta n} - w_0 l \dfrac{\delta A}{\delta n}\right) < 0$. It therefore is an offset

(or, at least, not an addition) to $w_0 A$, which, however, becomes greater as n

increases, so that the value of $-\dfrac{\delta l}{\delta K}$ which satisfies [2.2] *decreases* with n.

12 Two other measures of the accounting rate of profit which are widely used in practice are: (i) expected net profit of the *first* year as a proportion of the initial outlay, and (ii) expected net profit as a proportion of the average amount

of capital employed, itself arbitrarily measured as, say, $\dfrac{K}{2}$ (see note 7). The first-

order condition for (i) to be a maximum is:

$$-\frac{\delta l}{\delta K} = \left[\frac{p_0 x - w_0 l}{K}\right]\left[\frac{1}{w_0 - \dfrac{K}{n}\dfrac{\delta n}{\delta l}}\right] \qquad [2.6a]$$

[2.7] is the corresponding condition for (ii) to be a maximum. [2.6] > [2.7] and, for a wide range of values of n, [2.2] and [2.4] also. It follows that this variant of the accounting rate of profit rule *certainly* results in the choice of a *less* capital-intensive technique than those resulting from the other two variants and, often, from the other two rules as well.

13 See para. 2.1 of Harcourt (1966a). They are believed to be the appropriate rates for comparison of 'otherwise situations'.

14 If $\alpha \approx \frac{2}{3}, r_2 (= R(1 - c - \alpha s (1 - c)) = r_1 = R(1 - \bar{p} - s))$.

15 If the values of b relative to $\tilde{n}$ are such that *more* capital-intensive techniques are chosen by rule 2 under B.1 than in the *pre-tax* situation (namely, $b \geqslant \tilde{n}/2$) the use of rule 2 still results in the choice of a *less* capital-intensive technique under the present tax system than under the old, if the payout ratio is greater than the following values:

$\tilde{n}$	6	8	10
b			
4	$\frac{2}{5}$	$\frac{2}{5}$	0
5	$\frac{2}{3}$	$\frac{3}{5}$	$\frac{2}{5}$

16 For a detailed discussion of this limitation see Harcourt (1969b, p. 215, n. 31).

Part IV
Sraffa's *Production of Commodities* and Marxian economics

12 A note on Mr Sraffa's sub-systems*

1. If the whole of the national income is absorbed by wage payments, 'the relative values of commodities [in the economic systems of Mr Sraffa's *Production of Commodities by Means of Commodities*] are in proportion to their labour cost, that is to say the quantity of labour which directly and indirectly has gone to produce them' (Sraffa, 1960, p. 12). To establish this proposition Sraffa refers the reader to Appendix A, 'On Sub-Systems'. We propose in this note to show, both diagrammatically and algebraically, how these sub-systems may be derived from the main economic system, in order to describe their general properties and, in particular, to illustrate the proposition quoted above. We proceed by defining the simple economic system of Sraffa's book and the sub-systems implied in it. We then derive the latter from the former. Finally, we establish the above proposition and mention some possible implications of the analysis.

2. The economic system contains commodities which enter into the production of both themselves and other commodities. Such commodities are called basic commodities, and they are distinguished from non-basics, commodities which do not enter into the production of other commodities. The system consists of industries which produce one commodity. The production cycle is one year. The gross product (or total output) of any industry in a self-replacing economic system may be either greater than or equal to the total amount of the commodity which is used to produce both itself and other commodities. Such an economic system is in a 'self-replacing' state in the sense that it is *capable of*, but need not in fact be, replacing itself.[1] Commodities viewed from their aspect as inputs are called means of production. The excess of the total output of any commodity over that part of it which is equal to its use as a means of production is a component of the net product of the system. The sum of these components, when valued, is equal to the national income of the economy, which, in turn, is equal to the sum of the values of the total outputs less the value of the means of production. It can now be seen that an economy which has a positive

171

or zero national income and in which the production of any basic commodity is at least equal to the amount of it used as a means of production, is in a 'self-replacing' state.

3. Each industry employs labour which is paid a uniform wage at the end of the period. The relative prices of commodities are such that, given the wage-rate and the technical conditions of production, each industry earns the same rate of profits on its means of production.[2] The rate of profits is the ratio of the excess of the value of the total output of the economy over the value of the wages and the means of production to the value of the means of production. The units in which values are measured need not concern us here, as most of the results below can be derived in terms of physical amounts of the same commodity (or, sometimes, of labour). However, it can be taken that there is a standard commodity which is independent of the rate of profits and the wage-rate, which can serve as the unit of measurement for the system as a whole (Sraffa, 1960, chapters IV and V). Finally, the inputs of commodities and labour per unit of output of commodities are constants (but this must not be taken to imply that an assumption of constant returns to scale is made).

4. It must be stressed that the relationships in the economic system described here relate to one year only. They occur within the bounds of that year, and there is no necessary connection between them and the relationships that exist in other years, either past or present. In particular, it is *not* implied that the means of production come from the immediately preceding year, nor that those parts of the gross product which are *equal to* the means of production will be used as means of production in following years. The relationships apply to a particular period of time *and to no other.*

5. We shall consider a three-industry system producing three commodities, *a, b* and *c*, in amounts such that each commodity is a component of the net product. This assumption is dropped in para. 11, and it is shown that it does not affect the propositions derived. We write the system as follows:

$$(1 + r)(x_{aa}Ap_a + x_{ab}Ap_b + x_{ac}Ap_c) + l_a Aw \equiv Ap_a$$
$$(1 + r)(x_{ba}Bp_a + x_{bb}Bp_b + x_{bc}Bp_c) + l_b Bw \equiv Bp_b$$
$$(1 + r)(x_{ca}Cp_a + x_{cb}Cp_b + x_{cc}Cp_c) + l_b Cw \equiv Cp_c$$

where r = rate of profits;

w = wage-rate;

p_i = price of commodity i ($i = a, b, c$);

x_{ij} = input of commodity j per unit of output of i (both i and $j =$ a, b, c);

l_i = input of labour per unit of output of i ($i = a, b, c$);

and A, B, C are the gross products of a, b, c respectively.

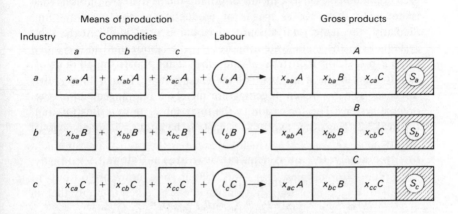

Figure 12.1

Note: No significance should be attached to the sizes of each box or circle.

6. The physical conditions of production are shown in Figure 12.1. 'The commodities forming the gross product . . . can be unambiguously distinguished as those which go to replace the means of production and those which together form the net product of the system' (Sraffa, 1960, p. 89). This is shown by the shaded areas (the components of the net product of the system) and the clear areas (the means of production) of the gross products column of Figure 12.1. The components of the net product in physical terms are

$$S_a \equiv A - \alpha$$
$$S_b \equiv B - \beta$$
$$S_c \equiv C - \gamma$$

where $\alpha \equiv x_{aa}A + x_{ba}B + x_{ca}C;$
$\beta \equiv x_{ab}A + x_{bb}B + x_{cb}C;$
$\gamma \equiv x_{ac}A + x_{bc}B + x_{cc}C.$

7. We now obtain the sub-systems from the main system. The main system can be divided into as many parts as there are commodities

which are components of the *net* product, in such a way that each part is in a self-replacing state with a net product of one commodity only. Each part is called a sub-system – in our example there are three. The net product of each sub-system is equal to the amount of that commodity in the net product of the main system. The total amount of each commodity used as a means of production in the *three* sub-systems is equal to their use as means of production in the main system. Similarly, the same total amount of labour is used in the three sub-systems as in the main system; moreover, the labour used in (say) the three *a* producing industries of the sub-systems equals the amount of labour used in the *a* industry of the main system. That is to say, the three sub-systems taken together are merely a rearrangement of the original system. The formation of the three sub-systems is illustrated in Figure 12.2. The other two sub-systems can be built up in an analogous manner.

8. Algebraically, the sub-systems can be written as follows:

Sub-system 1

$$(1 + r)(x_{aa} A'p_a + x_{ab} A'p_b + x_{ac} A'p_c) + l_a A'w \equiv A'p_a$$
$$(1 + r)(x_{ba} B'p_a + x_{bb} B'p_b + x_{bc} B'p_c) + l_b B'w \equiv B'p_b$$
$$(1 + r)(x_{ca} C'p_a + x_{cb} C'p_b + x_{cc} C'p_c) + l_c C'w \equiv C'p_c$$

where

$$x_{aa} A' + x_{ba} B' + x_{ca} C' \equiv \alpha';$$
$$x_{ab} A' + x_{bb} B' + x_{cb} C' \equiv \beta';$$
$$x_{ac} A' + x_{bc} B' + x_{cc} C' \equiv \gamma'.$$

A', B' and C' are the gross products of the sub-system, which has a net product of a equal to S_q; α', β' and γ' are the means of production of the sub-system; $(S_a + \alpha') = A' > \alpha'$; $B' = \beta'$ and $C' = \gamma'$. Sub-systems 2 and 3 can be similarly written, using A'', B'' and C'' and α'', β'' and γ'' for the gross products and the means of production, respectively, of sub-system 2, A''', B''' and C''' and α''', β''' and γ''' for the corresponding amounts for sub-system 3. There are twenty-seven unknowns in the three sub-systems: the nine gross outputs of the three sub-systems, the nine means of production and the nine labour inputs. That there are also twenty-seven independent equations can be illustrated by setting out the nine equations for sub-system 1, namely, the three gross output equations, the three means of production equations and the three labour equations.

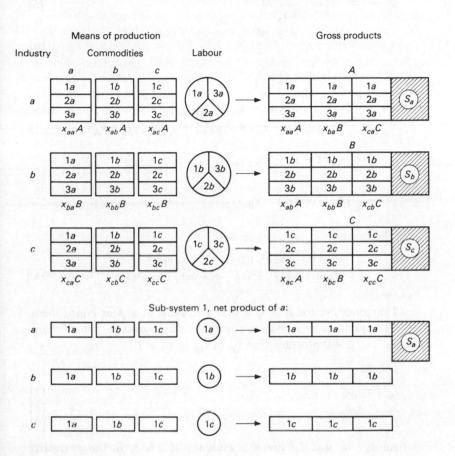

Figure 12.2

Gross outputs

$$A' = S_a + \alpha'$$ [1]
$$B' = \beta'$$ [2]
$$C' = \gamma'$$ [3]

Means of production

$$\alpha' = \frac{x_{aa}S_a + x_{ba}\beta' + x_{ca}\gamma'}{1 - x_{aa}}$$ [4]

$$\beta' = \frac{x_{ab}(S_a + \alpha') + x_{cb}\gamma'}{1 - x_{bb}} \qquad [5]$$

$$\gamma' = \frac{x_{ac}(S_a + \alpha') + x_{bc}\beta'}{1 - x_{cc}} \qquad [6]$$

These can be solved to give:[3]

$$\alpha' = \frac{S_a}{\Delta}\{x_{aa}[(1 - x_{bb})(1 - x_{cc}) - x_{cb}x_{bc}] + \\ x_{ba}[x_{ab}(1 - x_{cc}) + x_{cb}x_{ac}] + x_{ca}[x_{ab}x_{bc} + x_{ac}(1 - x_{bb})]\}$$

$$\beta' = \frac{S_a}{\Delta}\{x_{ab}(1 - x_{cc}) + x_{cb}x_{ac}\}$$

$$\gamma' = \frac{S_a}{\Delta}\{x_{ac}(1 - x_{bb}) + x_{ab}x_{bc}\}$$

where

$$\Delta = (1 - x_{aa})[(1 - x_{bb})(1 - x_{cc}) - x_{cb}x_{bc}] + \\ x_{ba}[-x_{ab}(1 - x_{cc}) - x_{cb}x_{ac}] - x_{ca}[x_{ab}x_{bc} + x_{ac}(1 - x_{bb})]$$

and $\neq 0$.

The condition for $\Delta \neq 0$ is that the inputs of a, b or c into themselves should not be such as to absorb the whole gross outputs of themselves, *i.e.*, $\Delta \neq 0$ provided that x_{aa} or x_{bb} or $x_{cc} \neq 1$.

Labour

$$L_a' = l_a A' \qquad [7]$$
$$L_b' = l_b B' \qquad [8]$$
$$L_c' = l_c C' \qquad [9]$$

where L_a', L_b' and L_c' are the amounts of labour in the respective industries of the sub-system.

9. We now show that the national incomes of both the main system and the sub-systems are equal to wages plus profits. This can be seen by deducting the means of production of each industry from the left-hand and right-hand sides of the appropriate equations. In the main system we are left with:

$$r(x_{aa}Ap_a + x_{ab}Ap_b + x_{ac}Ap_c) + l_a Aw \\ \equiv Ap_a - (x_{aa}Ap_a + x_{ab}Ap_b + x_{ac}Ap_c)$$

$$r(x_{ba}Bp_a + x_{bb}Bp_b + x_{bc}Bp_c) + l_b Bw \\ \equiv Bp_b - (x_{ba}Bp_a + x_{bb}Bp_b + x_{bc}Bp_c)$$

$$r(x_{ca}Cp_a + x_{cb}Cp_b + x_{cc}Cp_c) + l_c Cw \\ \equiv Cp_c - (x_{ca}Cp_a + x_{cb}Cp_b + x_{cc}Cp_c)$$

and in sub-system 1,

$$r(x_{aa}A'p_a + x_{ab}A'p_b + x_{ac}A'p_c) + l_aA'w$$
$$\equiv A'p_a - (x_{aa}A'p_a + x_{ab}A'p_b + x_{ac}A'p_c)$$
$$r(x_{ba}B'p_a + x_{bb}B'p_b + x_{bc}B'p_c) + l_bB'w$$
$$\equiv B'p_b - (x_{ba}B'p_a + x_{bb}B'p_b + x_{bc}B'p_c)$$
$$r(x_{ca}C'p_a + x_{cb}C'p_b + x_{cc}C'p_c) + l_cC'w$$
$$\equiv C'p_c - (x_{ca}C'p_a + x_{cb}C'p_b + x_{cc}C'p_c)$$

When $r = 0$ the whole of the national income is accounted for by wages, that is to say, the values added of the industries in both the main system and the sub-systems are equal to their respective wages bills. If we rearrange the commodities in the sub-systems so that from each gross product is subtracted those parts which equal the means of production we are left with net products of one commodity only, in sub-system 1, commodity a. Thus,

$$l_aA'w + l_bB'w + l_cC'w \equiv (A'p_a - \alpha'p_a) + (B'p_b - \beta'p_b) + (C'p_c - \gamma'p_c) \equiv S_ap_a$$

These net products, however, are each equal in value to the wages bills of the three industries in their respective sub-systems, that is, to the national incomes of each. In sub-system 1 *the net product is equal to the value of the labour which, directly in industry* a *and indirectly in industries* b *and* c, *produced it.* Moreover, the value per unit of the net product equals the direct and indirect labour cost per unit, *i.e.* $p_a = w(l_aA' + l_bB' + l_cC')/S_a$. A similar rearrangement of the main system would show that the value of the total net product was equal to the value of the labour in the three industries.

10. The rearrangements, which essentially consist of adding down the columns of the systems instead of across the rows, reveal four results. First, they show how it is possible for (say) industries b and c in sub-system 1 to pay their wages bills (and profits if $r \neq 0$), even though in total, that is, from the point of view of the sub-system, their gross products are equal to the means of production in the current year. Second, they show that the values of the components of the net product are not in general equal to the values added of the industries which produce them, even though, in total, the values of both are equal.[4] Third, they show that the wages bill of any industry in the main system (say, industry a) is equal to the wages bill of the three industries in the sub-system in which the commodity is the net product, *i.e.* $l_aAw \equiv l_aA'w + l_bB'w + l_cC'w$. Fourth – and this is the principal proposition – the

relative values of the commodities (here interpreted as the net products, S_a, S_b and S_c) are proportional to their direct and indirect labour costs *when the rate of profits is zero*. Sub-system 1 was chosen for illustrative purposes only, and since it also could be shown that the net products of sub-systems 2 and 3 are equal in value to their total wages bills, and therefore that their prices are equal to their direct and indirect labour costs per unit, this main proposition immediately follows.

11. To complete the analysis we show that these propositions still hold when not all the basic commodities exceed their use as means of production. Suppose that only two commodities are in surplus, even though there are three basics in the main system, that is, suppose that S_c (say) $= 0$ in our example. Then we have two sub-systems, but since they are merely a rearrangement of the main system, all the labour and means of production will be shared between them, such that each has a net product equal to its counterpart in the main system. The national incomes will still equal the corresponding wages bills when $r = 0$; and so on. It may be asked: since c is not a component of the net product, what can be said of its value? This question can be answered in at least two ways. The sub-system is a conceptual notion, derived from, but not separate from, the main system. The same relationships therefore apply as much in it as in the main system. In particular, the relative prices and the rate of profits (if $r \neq 0$) which are the solutions of the equations implied in the main system are also the solutions of those in any sub-system. Therefore we may employ the concept of the sub-system to construct a self-replacing system which has a net product of one unit of c; or a set of self-replacing systems which have as their net products the amounts of the commodities which form the means of production in the c industry of the main system. Either of these constructions can then be used to show that when $r = 0$ the price of c is equal to its direct and indirect labour cost per unit. We conclude that the results derived from our three-basic-commodity example are quite general.

12. In conclusion, we note some further implications of the analysis. As we have seen, the total value added and the value of the net product of the system are equal, as both equal the incomes created by the year's production. However, the *commodities* associated with value added (value added does not consist of commodities but is the *value* of the difference between the value of gross output and the value of the means of production) are not in general the same commodities as those which make up the net product of the system. This is clearly seen in a sub-system where, for example, the values of B' and C' exceed those of their corresponding means of production, even though a is the only

commodity in the net product. Amounts of commodities which are components of the net product can be calculated without the need to value commodities, but values added cannot be. Moreover, values added are associated with current production and the means of production employed in the year, while the net product is associated with current production and those parts of the gross product which are equal to the means of production.

13. The last point illustrates a general proposition, that the surpluses of commodities which may be of interest to the economy as a whole for, say, capital accumulation, in general differ in amount and kind from the surpluses which are of interest to businessmen, namely, values added, especially the profits contained therein. Businessmen are interested in values and incomes (values added), while governments and planners may be interested in real goods and services (net product). Finally, we may note that, once the technical conditions of production are given, the net product is determined independently of its division between wages and profits.

Notes

* *Economic Journal*, vol. lxxiv, no. 215, September 1964, pp. 715–22. With Vincent G. Massaro. The writers are grateful to Mr Sraffa for his helpful comments on a draft of this note.

1 While the economic systems of this paper are in fact in 'self-replacing' states, it should be stressed that self-replacement is a property of the basic equations of the economic systems concerned and not necessarily of the economic systems themselves. This implies that there is at least one set of proportions in which the equations can be combined such that they are in a 'self-replacing' state. (See Sraffa, 1960, p. 5, n. 2.)

2 The relative prices and the rate of profits are the solutions of a set of simultaneous equations.

3 We are indebted to Mrs J. D. Frost for obtaining these solutions for us.

4 The equality of totals does not imply that (say)

$$(x_{aa}Ap_a + x_{ba}Bp_a + x_{ca}Cp_a) = (x_{aa}Ap_a + x_{ab}Ap_b + x_{ac}Ap_c)$$

13 Mr Sraffa's *Production of Commodities by Means of Commodities**

Sraffa's *Production of Commodities by Means of Commodities* discusses a number of traditional issues of economic theory. It is concisely written but enough information is given to allow the reader to obtain the results which are presented. The main purpose of the book is to present the foundation for a critique of the marginal theory of value and distribution. Though the relevance of Sraffa's results for this purpose is not made explicit, keeping it in mind helps in understanding the degrees of abstraction adopted and the propositions developed by him. His earlier writings, in particular his well-known 1926 article and his Introduction to Ricardo's *Principles* (1951-5) (written in collaboration with M. H. Dobb) also provide some helpful hints to his method of analysis and main propositions.

The reviews of Sraffa's classic varied from banal to insightful (with one, the author of which shall be nameless, completely incomprehensible). In the former category must be placed the reviews by Quandt (1961) and Reder (1961); one reviewer did not get his sums right and both missed the point (Harrod got *his* sums right but read too much into them: see Harrod (1961) and Sraffa's reply (1962).) In the latter category we may place Joan Robinson's two reviews (Robinson, 1961; reprinted in Robinson, 1951-80, vol. iii, pp. 7-14; and Robinson, 1951-80, vol. iii, pp. 173-81), Meek's (1967, pp. 161-78), and Bharadwaj's (1963). We should also mention, in this context, Nell (1967). Nell's article is not a review; nevertheless it spells out with insight what I and Massaro (1964b) were groping for in our review article.

In this essay we outline the basic structure of Sraffa's arguments. Few reviewers got past Part I - the circulating capital model - and certainly the importance of Part III in which double-switching and capital-reversing are discussed did not get the prominence which we can now see it merited. Nevertheless, the foundations for his critique of economic theory were securely laid in Part I, a point which was emphasized by the perceptive reviewers (and missed by the others).

Sraffa begins with a warning that he is 'concerned exclusively with such properties of an economic system as do not depend on changes in the scale of production or in the proportions of "factors"' (Preface, p. v). The author writes 'factors' because he wishes to contrast the view that regards 'the system of production and consumption as a circular process' with what he regards as the view of modern theory – that it is 'a one-way avenue . . . from "Factors of production" to "Consumption goods"' (p. 93).

It is true that the emphasis on circularity in modern theory is found more in discussions of the expenditure, income-creation process than in the theory of price-formation. Nevertheless, some modern theories, for example, those associated with the work of von Neumann, Leontief and Morishima, are more akin to the first view. But, as Nell (1967, p. 25, n. 8), rightly says, Leontief's system 'must be sharply distinguished from Sraffa's' because the former never deals 'with a uniform rate of profits nor with the effects of changes in distribution upon prices'.

Sraffa's analysis starts at a level of abstraction which excludes the continuous changes characteristic of actual economic systems. Or, we may regard the analysis as concerned with any actual economic system during one 'year', a 'year' being defined as the time taken to produce commodities and distribute them. The economic relationships examined, therefore, occur within, *and are only true of*, the period of time contained within Sraffa's 'year'. (Nevertheless, the author is not prevented from examining, for this period, many questions which are analysed within the context of the theory of economic growth – for example, the distribution of income, the value of capital and the choice of techniques.) Thus Sraffa does not find it necessary to assume constant returns, and the apparent 'changes' examined in the text (the varying proportions of basic equations, the sub-system analysis) are merely different ways of viewing the given, non-changing, basic data.

The author's point of view has the important consequence that by ruling out variations in scale and in 'factors', marginal product is ruled out as well – 'it just would not be there to be found' (Preface, p. v). This is true. However, it should be noted that prices in the marginal theory of value are related to notional instantaneous rates of change which can be thought of as occurring at the margins of the levels of production of the actual economic systems examined here. In other words, there need not be an actual marginal product in order to have a determinate system of prices which is based on marginalist notions.

Sraffa may be hinting that the assumption of mathematical continuity is inappropriate for the analysis of price-formation in an economic system; that is to say, it is impossible to use the device of notional movements along a schedule which shows a relationship between two economic variables and which assumes that everything else remains constant. This is because the very fact of change necessarily implies that the changes in these other things are such that it just cannot be assumed that they remain constant. (Such is the basis of his criticism of supply and demand analysis in Sraffa, 1926.) Alternatively, he might be interpreted as meaning that there is not enough information in any actual economic system to tell us what the marginal (as opposed to the average) product is. Even if it is a valid procedure to derive a system of prices from notional changes, it might still be that the prices associated with the technical conditions of production and with self-replacement are more fundamental than those associated with notional changes.

Meek (1967, pp. 161–78), whose review article is entitled 'Mr Sraffa's Rehabilitation of Classical Economics', provides an interesting explanation of the rationale of Sraffa's approach. Thus,

> Mr Sraffa's important book . . . can be looked at from various points of view. It can be regarded, if one pleases, simply as an unorthodox theoretical model of a particular type of economy, designed to solve the traditional problem of value in a new way. It can be regarded as an implicit attack on modern marginal analysis: the sub-title of the book is *Prelude to a Critique of Economic Theory*, and Sraffa in his preface expresses the hope that someone will eventually attempt the job of basing a critique of the marginal analysis on his foundations. Or, finally, it can be regarded as a sort of magnificent rehabilitation of the Classical (and up to a point Marxian) approach to certain crucial problems relating to value and distribution. It is upon this third aspect of the book that I wish to concentrate. . . . In doing so, I do not of course want to suggest that the *essence* of Sraffa's book lies in this rehabilitation of the Classical approach: Sraffa's primary aim is to build a twentieth-century model to deal with twentieth-century problems. I am approaching his book in this particular way largely because I think it affords the best method of understanding his basic argument. (p. 161)

Meek begins by making three general points, about the relation between Sraffa's model and the old classical models, only the first of which need concern us here.

> Both Sraffa's model and the Classical models are concerned with the investigation of one and the same set of properties of an economic system – those properties as Sraffa puts it, which 'do not depend on changes in the scale of production or in the proportions of "factors"'. The Classical economists, at any rate in their basic

analysis of the economy as such, were usually *in effect* concerned with these properties alone, since they often tended to assume that under given technological conditions returns to scale for the industry as a whole would be constant, and that the proportions in which the different means of production were used in an industry would be technically fixed. Sraffa, by way of distinction, makes no assumption whatever about the variability or constancy of returns. Rather, he simply selects for analysis a particular kind of economic system in which the question of whether returns are variable or constant is irrelevant. This system is one in which production goes on from day to day and from year to year in exactly the same way, without any changes in scale or factor proportions at all. By this means Sraffa is able *deliberately* to concern himself with the investigation of the same properties of an economic system which the Classical economists *objectively* concerned themselves with, while at the same time avoiding the necessity of making any (possibly objectionable) assumptions about the nature of returns. (p. 162)

'Prices' or 'values' in an economy which is merely *capable of* reproducing itself reflect the exchange ratios which would restore the original distribution of the means of production and such prices 'spring directly from the methods of production' (p. 3). For instance, assuming the means of subsistence to be included among the means of production, we may express the conditions of production of k industries producing k products (each industry producing a separate product a, . . ., k) as follows:

$$A_a p_a + \ldots + K_a p_k = A p_a = [A_a + \ldots + A_k] p_a$$
$$\cdots\cdots\cdots\cdots\cdots\cdots\cdots\cdots\cdots\cdots\cdots\cdots\cdots\cdots\cdots \quad [A.1]$$
$$A_k p_a + \ldots + K_k p_k = K p_k = [K_a + \ldots + K_k] p_k$$

where $A_a, \ldots, K_a$ represent the quantities of $a, \ldots, k$ employed in the production of quantity A of a; $A_k, \ldots, K_k$ represent the quantities of $a, \ldots, k$ employed in the production of quantity K of k; and where $p_a, \ldots, p_k$ represent prices.

Since we are able to infer any one equation from the sum of the remaining equations, setting the price of one commodity as unity leaves us with $k - 1$ independent linear equations and $k - 1$ prices. It should be noted that in this case each commodity enters either directly or indirectly into the production of itself and every other commodity. Such commodities are defined as 'basic commodities' and are distinguished from 'non-basics' (commodities which enter neither directly nor indirectly into the production of all commodities) which appear with the production of a surplus.

An economic system with a surplus is one whose equations have the property of *permitting* repetition of the productive process for each industry with the gross product exceeding the means of production. That is, it is possible to replace, item by item, the means of production employed and still have some products remaining. As we can no longer infer any one equation from the sum of those remaining, we are now left with k equations and $k - 1$ unknowns.

At this point, Sraffa introduces the notion of a uniform rate of profits and notes that, since the surplus and the means of production consist of different goods, we cannot determine the rate of profits without prices. Nor, however, can we have prices without having a rate of profits. Thus, Sraffa concludes, prices and the rate of profits must be determined *simultaneously* and through the same mechanism. We may regard the uniform rate of profits, r, as a simplifying assumption or we may view it as the result towards which an actual economic system tends through the operation of long-run competitive forces, which push r to a level determined by the underlying rate of growth and the saving (and borrowing) propensities of its capitalist class.

Assuming a surplus of commodity a (designated by A_s) and introducing r as another unknown, we again have a determinate system which may be expressed as follows:

$$(1 + r)(A_a p_a + \ldots + K_a p_k) = (A_a + \ldots + A_k)p_a + A_s p_a$$
$$\ldots\ldots\ldots\ldots\ldots\ldots\ldots\ldots\ldots\ldots\ldots\ldots\ldots\ldots\ldots\ldots\ldots \qquad [A.2]$$
$$(1 + r)(A_k p_a + \ldots + K_k p_k) = (K_a + \ldots + K_k)p_k$$

Non-basics play no active role in the determination of the prices and the rate of profits. Their 'prices' merely reflect the rate of profits and the 'prices' of the various means of production used to produce them. Basics, on the other hand, play an active role since they enter (directly or indirectly) into the production of one another and hence their 'prices' influence (and are simultaneously determined with) the 'prices' of their means of production. This is one of the key distinctions of Sraffa's book.

Rather than regarding part of the wages as necessities and another part as surplus, Sraffa regards the whole as variable. Also, wages are no longer viewed as 'advanced', and the means of subsistence are now 'replaced' by the quantities of homogeneous labour appropriate for each industry. Our system is therefore altered as follows:

$$(1 + r)(A_a p_a + \ldots + K_a p_k) + L_a w = A p_a$$
$$\ldots\ldots\ldots\ldots\ldots\ldots\ldots\ldots\ldots\ldots\ldots\ldots\ldots\ldots\ldots\ldots \qquad [A.3]$$
$$(1 + r)(A_k p_a + \ldots + K_k p_k) + L_k w = K p_k$$

where $L_a, \ldots, L_k$ represent the appropriate quantities of labour employed in the production of $a, \ldots, k$; w equals total wages; $L_a + \ldots + L_k = 1$; and where $A \geqslant A_a + \ldots + A_k$; $K \geqslant K_a + \ldots + K_k$. The national income (equals the net product) of the system consists of $[A - (A_a + \ldots + A_k)] + \ldots + [K - (K_a + \ldots + K_k)]$. Sraffa sets the value of the national income equal to unity, that is, $[A - (A_a + \ldots + A_k)]p_a + \ldots + [K - (K_a + \ldots + K_k)]p_k = 1$, and adopts this as the new standard in which to express the k prices and w (r is a pure number). We now have $k + 1$ equations and $k + 2$ unknowns.

He then examines the effect on r and relative prices of letting w vary from 1 to 0. At first glance, permitting w to vary without altering the composition of output may not seem permissible. This objection vanishes, however, when it is realized that Sraffa is examining, in a situation of unchanged technical conditions, the effects of changes in the distribution of income on relative prices. He wishes to isolate those changes in relative prices which are due to changes in income distribution from those associated with changing technical conditions.

Under the given assumptions, when $w = 1$, the commodities exchange in proportion to their direct and indirect labour requirements. The device of sub-systems - rearrangements of the equations of the actual system such that only one commodity is contained in the net product of each sub-system - is used to show this proposition. We discuss this device in detail in Harcourt and Massaro (1964a). Here the important point to note is that it is the *equations* of the conditions of production in each industry, and not the *proportions* in which the product of each industry appears in the actual system, which are relevant to the determination of relative prices and r; from which it follows that the given w, relative prices and r of the main economic system and each sub-system are identical.

When w is given a value less than unity, the entire national income no longer goes to wages, and exchange ratios are now influenced by a uniform rate of profits. Prices then vary according to the different ratios of labour to the means of production, with the modification that we must take into account the different ratios producing the means of production at each remove. For instance, in comparing the relative price movements of commodities a and b, where a is apparently more labour-intensive than b, we cannot immediately conclude that the price of a will increase relative to that of b (following a rise in w) since the means of production producing commodity a (and the means of production producing those means of production, and so on) may be highly commodity-intensive; whereas the means of production producing commodity *b* (and again the various means of production producing those means of production, and so on) may be of such a labour-intensive nature as to offset or reverse the price movements initially expected.

We may imagine a commodity produced by an industry employing labour and means of production in a 'balancing' ratio such that, were *w* to rise by a total of $50, total profits (paid at the uniform rate) would decrease by exactly the same amount. We may suppose further that the means of production employed by this industry were produced by the same balancing ratio of labour to means of production and likewise those means of production, and so on. Then, under the given assumptions, we would have found a commodity whose 'price' would not vary in relation to its own means of production when wages rise. Any variation in the prices of other commodities relative to its own would therefore originate in the conditions of production of these other commodities. A commodity with this property would be an ideal standard of value.

In order to discover the 'balancing' ratio, Sraffa adopts the ratio of the value of the net product to the value of the means of production and finds that, when $w = 0$, this ratio is the same for each industry and coincides with the 'maximum rate of profits', R. This is the ratio which, if found, would not vary with changes in w and it is also the 'balancing' ratio.

We now come to the standard commodity, the commodity which is to serve as the standard of value of the system. From an economic system containing only basics, Sraffa constructs a standard system, multiplying each equation of the actual system by unique, positive multipliers such that the commodities of the derived standard system enter and are produced in the same proportion. And a collection of commodities in these proportions *is* the standard commodity. The 'standard national income', the amount of standard commodity which would form the net product of a standard system if it employed the same total labour as the actual system, becomes the new unit in which to measure the prices and wages of the actual economic system. It should be noted that the quantity-ratio of the net product to the means of production of the standard system, that is, the standard ratio, R', would not be affected by changes in distribution, since both numerator and denominator are quantities of the same standard commodity. (It is also equal to R, the maximum rate of profits of the system.) We have thus found a ratio which would not be affected by variations in w (or by the corresponding changes in the rate of profits and prices).[1] Given the share of wages in the standard net product, the ratio of the rate of profits to the standard ratio, R, equals the ratio of the share of profits to the standard net product, that is

$$\frac{r}{R} = \frac{1-w}{1} \quad \text{or} \quad r = R(1-w) \qquad [A.4]$$

This is, of course, Sraffa's version of the wage-rate/rate-of-profits trade-off relation. Notice that Sraffa's straight-line w-r relationship depends upon all values being measured in terms of the standard commodity of *one* technique (or economy). There is, therefore, no *common* unit whereby an envelope consisting of segments of each straight-line w-r relationship could be formed.[2] Since the actual system differs from the standard system only in the proportions in which the same equations enter, the above relation extends to the actual economic system as well. Provided that the wage is measured in terms of standard product, the rate of profits of the actual system, which is a ratio of values, will then be the same as the rate of profits of the standard system, which is a ratio of quantities.

Sraffa shows that if w and r of the actual economic system vary according to the relation $r = R'(1 - w)$, relative prices and w are expressed in terms of a standard net product whose composition is unknown. We can then find R' by calculating the maximum rate of profits of the actual system. But, given r, we can replace the standard net product by a quantity of labour which will serve equally well as a standard of value which is independent of price movements. The quantity of labour which becomes the new absolute measure of value is the labour that can be purchased by the standard net product at any given level of r.

Wages were previously taken as given because they were regarded as subsistence, determined exogenously to that part of the system being examined. This view becomes less satisfactory once we discuss the division of the net product between wage-earners and profit-receivers. Sraffa therefore takes the rate of profits as exogenous to the system, because it is a ratio independent of prices and may be determined by, say, 'the level of the money rates of interest' (p. 33).

Sraffa concludes Part I by examining reduction to 'dated' labour. This operation consists of reducing a given quantity of a commodity into the direct and indirect labour necessary for its production. The commodity is first split into its direct labour and means of production components; the means of production are themselves similarly split into their two components; and so on. This process can, of course, continue without limit. But (provided that $r \neq R$) we may approximate the total labour components of the commodity by making the residue of commodities[3] as small as we like and summing the labour components, each one of which has been accumulated at the appropriate rate of profits up to the 'present' period. Reduction does not occur in historical time (see Harcourt, 1972, pp. 152–4). Rather, it shows the labour component of a commodity, given the current technical conditions, wage-rate and rate of profits.

This technique is used to compare the 'dated' labour components of the same commodity at different rates of profits; and the labour components of different commodities at the same rates of profits. This allows Sraffa to dismiss once and for all the notion of a quantity of capital which is independent of distribution and prices (p. 38).[4]

(The reduction to dated labour terms has some bearing on the attempts that have been made to find in the 'period of production' an independent measure of the quantity of capital which could be used, without arguing in a circle, for the determination of prices and of the shares in distribution. But the case just considered seems conclusive in showing the impossibility of aggregating the 'periods' belonging to the several quantities of labour into a single magnitude which could be regarded as representing the quantity of capital. The reversals in the direction of the movement of relative prices, in the face of unchanged methods of production, cannot be reconciled with *any* notion of capital as a measurable quantity independent of distribution and prices.)

It follows that it is a fruitless task to construct a theory of distribution for the economy as a whole which depends upon the concept of an aggregate production function in which the quantity of capital is one of the factors of production, and the returns to labour and capital are related to the slope of the production function.

In Parts II and III Sraffa adapts the analysis of Part I to include further important characteristics of actual economic systems. He discusses in Part II the implications of joint production for the construction of the standard system and commodity, the definitions of basics and non-basics, and the determination of relative prices and wages for given rates of profits. The main purpose of the discussion is to enable the prices of fixed assets (durable instruments of production) and the rent of land to be included among the unknowns of the main economic system. Thus fixed assets are regarded as joint products, one of the components of total outputs now being fixed assets one year older than those included in the means of production at the beginning of the year. Land is regarded as a non-produced commodity, a non-basic which is included in the means of production of the actual system but not in its products. Part III contains a discussion of different methods of producing single commodities, and the principles underlying switches from one to the other as the rate of profits changes.

The introduction of joint production requires that the concept of an industry which produces one commodity, and for which there is one equation of production, be replaced by the concept of processes in which *all* commodities may be included both as means of production and as products. One process is distinguished from another by the proportions in which the different commodities appear in the means of production and the total outputs. (Of course, the amount of a commodity in any process may be zero, and single-commodity systems are those in which all but one commodity are zero in the total outputs of each process.)

The inclusion of joint production in the analysis explains why Sraffa did not use the more familiar input per unit of output notation in the single-commodity system. This notation has no meaning once there is joint production; on the other hand, joint production is easily accommodated by Sraffa's notation. We write

$$A_1 + \ldots + K_1 + L_1 \to A_{(1)} + \ldots + K_{(1)}$$
$$\cdots\cdots\cdots\cdots\cdots\cdots\cdots\cdots\cdots\cdots\cdots\cdots\cdots\cdots\cdots \quad [A.5]$$
$$A_k + \ldots + K_k + L_k \to A_{(k)} + \ldots + K_{(k)}$$

Quantities of commodities in the means of production of each process have unbracketed subscripts, those in the total outputs have subscripts in parentheses.

The standard system is again defined in terms of the equality of the ratios of the output of each basic commodity to its use as a means of production. The standard commodity, however, becomes an abstract concept instead of one which has a clear economic meaning. With joint production, negative multipliers may be needed to transform the actual system into the standard system. There is a limit to the proportions in which individual commodities can be produced *vis-à-vis* other commodities; for any two commodities and processes, the possible proportions lie between the proportion of one process and that of the other. If the two commodities are used as a means of production in proportions which lie outside this range, negative multipliers must be used in the transformation process. Furthermore, because non-basics may be produced jointly with basics but may not enter the standard system or commodity, negative multipliers are needed to remove them. The inclusion of negative as well as positive commodities in the standard system is likened by Sraffa to an individual share in a company which contains a fraction of each asset and liability.

With joint production, the intuitively satisfying definition of non-basics as those commodities which do not enter directly or indirectly the production of all commodities disappears. Basics and non-basics can now enter the means of production and emerge as products side by side in the same processes. However, the key distinction between basics and non-basics is that the former are *price-determining*. Sraffa now defines non-basics (for a system of k processes and k commodities) as 'a group of n linked commodities' $(n < k)$ where 'of the k rows (formed by the $2n$ quantities in which they appear in each process) not more than n rows are independent, the others being linear combinations of these' (p. 51). It is a property of this definition that a set of multipliers (some positive, some negative) can always be found which when applied to the k equations allows a new system of equations to be formed, equal to the number of basics, and from which non-basics have been eliminated. These equations are called 'basic' equations. They have the property that the maximum rate of profits and the relative prices at each rate of profits derivable from them are the same as those derivable from the actual system.

The basic equations are changed into the standard system by applying the appropriate set of multipliers. If there are j basic commodities there will be j R's and j sets of multipliers. However, as with the single-commodity system, it can be shown that only the smallest of these R's is meaningful – meaningful in the sense that only the standard commodity with which it is associated will give finite prices of commodities as r passes from R to 0 (and w from 0 to 1) in terms of the standard commodity.

The device of sub-systems can again be used to show that, when $r = 0$, the value of any commodity is equal to the value of the labour which directly and indirectly produced it. If we compare two systems, one of which contains in its *net product* more of one commodity than the other does, and the same amount of all other commodities, the extra labour of the first system is naturally associated with the extra amount of the commodity. This is so even if the quantities of the means of production also differ, because indirect labour is as relevant as direct labour. It is as if we were to add to the second system a sub-system which contains all these commodities in its means of production and total outputs, but only the additional amount of the relevant commodity in its net product. It follows that, when $r = 0$, the value of the commodity will equal its direct and indirect labour components.

While the sub-system approach may be used to show the above proposition, the alternative approach used in the single-products system – the reduction to 'dated' labour – cannot be used. To attempt reduction means introducing negative quantities of labour, which have no meaning; moreover, there is no guarantee that the series will converge towards a zero residue of commodities. There are two further modifications of propositions derived from the single-products system. First, it is now possible to have negative prices. With joint production, the prices of some commodities may be raised sufficiently to offset negative prices of other commodities and allow the uniform rate of profits to be earned in the process as a whole. Second, and again because of offsetting movements in other prices, the price of any one jointly produced commodity may fall faster than the wage rate. (This was not possible in the single-products system.) The second modification implies that more than one rate of profits may correspond to one level of wages measured in terms of a commodity, the price of which, measured in terms of the standard commodity, falls faster than the wage, similarly measured.

As we noted above, the interest in joint production lies 'in its being the genus of which Fixed Capital is the leading species' (p. 63). Treating fixed assets as joint products one year older than when they are counted in the means of production introduces as many extra unknowns (that is, prices of fixed assets) as there are years in the economic lifetimes of the fixed assets concerned. (Sraffa does not make clear what determines these lifetimes.) Each industry is therefore divided into processes which are distinguished one from another by the ages of the fixed assets in their means of production and total outputs. The equations of these processes provide the additional equations needed to solve for the prices of the fixed assets.

The fixed assets do not have to be sold for their prices to be effective; the imputed prices of the fixed assets to the process must be such that they correctly allocate profits and allow for depreciation. 'Correctly' means that the annual charge for the use of fixed capital is such that replacement of the means of production is possible, together with payment of the uniform rate of profits on the value of the fixed assets.

Sraffa shows that in the case of 'one-hoss shays', that is, machines of equal productive efficiency over their lifetimes, the annual charge for the use of fixed capital obtained by solving this system of equations equals the expression obtained by using the annuity method to calculate equal annual payments of depreciation and interest combined. The expression is

$$Pm_0 \frac{r(1+r)^n}{(1+r)^n - 1} \qquad\qquad [A.6]$$

where Pm_0 = the original price of the machine;
         r = the rate of profits;
and n = the life of the machine.

The Sraffa formulation, unlike the annuity method, is quite general; regardless of the pattern of productive efficiency over the life of the machine, the prices which emerge allow the correct depreciation to be calculated year by year (depreciation is defined as the decline in the value of the machine over the course of the year). Depreciation plus profit, reckoned as the uniform rate of profits on the value of the machine at the start of the year, give the annual charge for capital, that is, the capital component of the price of the commodity which it helps to produce.

Reverting to the example of machines of constant productive efficiency, it is clear that the price of the commodity which they produce must be the same, irrespective of their ages. It follows that, because the annual charge for capital is the same each year but the prices of machines fall as they age, the profit component of the charge must fall and the depreciation component must rise as they age. Hudson and Mathews (1963) have shown that straight-line depreciation is 'correct' only when the expected net services associated with a machine decline at a particular rate. Sraffa's formulation brings out clearly why this should be so. Suppose that the prices of the commodities which the machine produces are expected to remain constant for its lifetime. The profit component of the annual net service must decline from year to year for the reason given above. Therefore, the depreciation components will rise unless the net services decline at just that rate which will keep them constant.

The proposition that, when $r = 0$, the value of commodities equals the value of the labour which directly and indirectly is used to produce them, can be extended, Sraffa argues, to the cases of new and ageing machines. In the case of a new machine, it is the amount of direct and indirect labour which produces it; in the case of an older machine, it is this quantity less such quantities as have passed in previous 'years' into its product.

Sraffa gives an example on pp. 68-9 which illustrates the proposition. Assume that four units of labour, indirect and direct, are needed to make a tractor of constant productive efficiency which lasts for four years. Suppose that we compare two systems which use the same techniques and which are in self-replacing states; one has 1,000 units of wheat in its *net product*, while the other has two two-year-old tractors as well. When $r = 0$, the total labour of the first system is equal in value to 1,000 units of wheat, so that the labour value of wheat in *both* systems can be calculated. The aim of the comparison is to show that the second system has four extra units of labour in it, from which it follows that each two-year-old tractor in the net product embodies two units of labour.

In the first system, twenty tractors are spread evenly, according to age, among four processes which jointly produce wheat and tractors. There are five new tractors in the means of production of the first process, five one-year-old tractors in those of the second, and so on. (The total outputs similarly contain five tractors, one year older.) In a further process five new tractors are produced each year. In the second system, six new tractors are produced each year. Twenty tractors are again employed in the wheat processes, and are distributed among the means of production as follows: six brand-new ones, six one-year-old ones, four two-year-old ones and four three-year-old ones. Sraffa argues that, when the total means of production are subtracted from the gross product of the second system, two two-year-old tractors appear in the net product, as well as 1,000 units of wheat, and that the two tractors are found to be associated with four extra units of labour.

This example is wrong as it stands unless it is assumed, first, that tractors are made from labour alone; in which case, the result is trivial and, moreover, introduces a process in which, when $r \neq 0$, the uniform rate of profits cannot be earned. Second, it could be assumed that wheat is a non-basic which may be used to make itself but not tractors or other commodities. The example could then be interpreted as what we would see if a spotlight were to light up only those processes, of a much larger economic system, in which the components of the net product, one of which is a non-basic, were produced. But, to regard wheat, a wage good, as a non-basic is most unsatisfactory, as Sraffa himself says on p. 10, where he discusses treating the whole wage, including the 'necessaries of consumption' as part of the surplus, i.e. the net product, to be distributed.

However, the example can be easily adapted to handle the case of two basic commodities, wheat and tractors. There are still only twenty tractors at work in the wheat processes, so that the total output of wheat in the two systems is the same. But there is one more new tractor produced in the tractor process of the second system. It follows either that the tractor process of the second system is at the moment short of the wheat needed to make one tractor; or, alternatively, that the wheat component of the net product as it stands at the moment is this amount short of 1,000 units of wheat. We therefore have to introduce, as it were, a further system which is in a self-replacing state and which has, as its net product, the present short-fall of wheat. This system is easily obtained by scaling down (or up) all the processes of the first system by the ratio of the short-fall of wheat to 1,000 units of wheat. When $r = 0$, the labour value of the short-fall of wheat plus the direct labour content of one tractor is four units of labour. And the labour of the second system, when the two parts are combined, exceeds that of the first system by exactly this amount. We have therefore the desired components in the net product and the desired increase in labour, so the proposition concerning the labour content of the two two-year-old tractors can be established.

Sraffa next discusses depreciation and the value of capital within the context of a balanced stock of machines. He shows that the value of a balanced stock rises as r increases, the limit to the rise being the aggregate value of all the machines in the stock when new. This is, of course, the Kahn–Champernowne formula (see Robinson, 1953–4). In view of the prominence given to this formula in recent years, it is an intriguing question to ask just when among the thirty-to-forty-year gestation period of the present work this proposition was established and in what condition capital theory and economic theory generally would be today if this and other propositions had been published twenty years earlier.

The proposition that the value of capital increases when r *increases is regarded by Sraffa as a 'remarkable' result, because it appears to imply that it is impossible to have a measure of the quantity of capital which is invariant to changes in distribution.* The proposition here must be seen within the context of given technical conditions, equilibrium prices of commodities and machines, and the appropriate wage-rate for each given rate of profits, that is, within the context of the economic system as a whole which is, of course, the relevant context for this proposition.

Durable instruments are easily fitted into the standard system. Machines in the means of production are given such multipliers that machines *of the same age* in the total output of the standard system exceed them by R', the standard ratio. Thus, if m machines are $(n - 1)$ years old (where n is the length of life of the machine) in the means of production of the actual system, there will be $m(n - 1)$-year-old machines, $m(1 + R')(n - 2)$-year-old machines, up to $m(1 + R')^{n-1}$ new machines in the means of production of the standard system. However, reduction to 'dated' labour is impossible with durable instruments which are, as we have seen, joint products.

Part II closes with a discussion of the implications of treating land as a non-basic and includes an account of rent's role in the system. Part III[5] discusses the implication for single-products systems of different ways of producing one commodity. It is concerned with the question: which method will be the most profitable at different levels of the rate of profits? If the commodities are basics, a common unit of value in which prices can be measured must be found; this is a difficulty because each method implies a different economic system and maximum rate of profits. The problem is solved by supposing that, while the commodity can be regarded as identical for all basic uses, so that the choice between methods is entirely on the grounds of cheapness, in its use in the production of non-basics, some uses require one method rather than another. Any system therefore will contain all methods.

In conclusion we may distinguish at least two essential points which constitute the foundation for Sraffa's proposed critique of marginal theory. In an economy in which commodities are mainly produced by other commodities:

1. prices are determined by the methods of production, given the constraints of a uniform rate of profits and the possibility of self-replacement,
2. commodities can be classified into basics and non-basics, with the former playing a vital role in the determination of prices for the system as a whole.

Sraffa prices are therefore based on a labour theory of value. When $r = 0$, the position of the price of any commodity on a scale of relative prices is determined simply by its direct and indirect labour components. Once $r > 0$, the simple relationship no longer holds. Nevertheless, it is always possible *in principle*, provided only that we know r and the direct and indirect labour components of the commodity, to say what its new position will be (even though, in practice, this may be a difficult task). Moreover, by concentrating on technical conditions and *industries* it is unnecessary, in order to explain prices, to make *any* assumptions about the motives and behaviour of individual economic units, in particular, whether they are maximizers or not and, if they are, *what* it is that they maximize.

Meek makes this point very strongly. Thus he postulates: as Marx himself did, an industry in which the ratio of used-up means of production to wages is equal to the ratio of these quantities when they are aggregated over the economy as a whole, . . . an industry in which, to use Marx's terminology, the 'organic composition of capital' is equal to the 'social average'. In such an industry, . . . the ratio of surplus value to means of production . . . is equal to the ratio of these quantities over the economy as a whole . . . We can thus say, as Marx did, that the average rate of profits over the economy as a whole is determined by the ratio of surplus value to means of production *in this industry*, whose conditions of production represent a sort of 'social average'. Or, to put the same proposition in another way, the average rate of profits over the economy as a whole is given by the following expression:

$$\frac{\text{labour embodied in net product of [this] industry}}{\text{labour embodied in its means of production}} \left(1 - \begin{array}{l}\text{proportion of net} \\ \text{product of [this]} \\ \text{industry going to} \\ \text{wages}\end{array} \right)$$

The similarity between this Marxian relation and that expressed in Sraffa's $r = R(1 - w)$ is surely very striking. For, in the first place, let us note that Sraffa's R, although usually expressed as the ratio of the *value* of the net product of the 'standard' industry to the *value* of its means of production, is in fact equal to the ratio of the *labour embodied* in the net product of the 'standard' industry to the *labour embodied* in its means of production. In other words, Sraffa is postulating precisely the same relation between the average rate of profits *and the conditions of production in his 'standard' industry* as Marx was postulating between the average rate of profits *and the conditions of production in his industry of 'average organic composition of capital'*. What both economists are trying to show, in effect, is that (when wages are given) the average rate of profits, and therefore the deviations of price ratios from embodied labour ratios, are governed by the ratio of direct to indirect labour in the industry whose conditions of production represent a sort of 'average' of those prevailing over the economy as a whole. Marx reached this result by postulating as his 'average' industry one whose 'organic composition of capital' was equal to the 'social average'. But his result could only be a provisional and approximate one, since in reaching it he had abstracted from the effect which a change in the wage would have on the prices of the means of production employed in the 'average' industry. Sraffa shows that the same result can be achieved, without abstracting from this effect at all, if we substitute his 'standard' industry for Marx's industry of 'average organic composition of capital'. (Meek, 1967, pp. 176–8)

Finally, it remains to be shown that Sraffa prices are more fundamental than any other system of prices which can be deduced in a 'period' of time. The answer may be found in the view that the distribution of income can, within wide ranges, be regarded as independent of the technical conditions of production. These technical conditions may in turn be influenced by prices and the distribution of incomes through their impact on the choice of technique – Sraffa analyses this aspect in Part III – and resource allocation generally, but this influence may be tenuous and, anyway, is of a long-run nature. Therefore, as a first approximation, it may be reasonable to assume that technical conditions are unrelated to, or at least unaffected by, the distribution of income; and to have relative prices determined by an historically given rate of profits (itself related to the rate of interest, an exogeneous monetary phenomenon, or to the other factors analysed in the Post-Keynesian literature) and existing technical conditions. Such an answer would in turn imply that the elements of the actual economic system which Sraffa has included in his analysis are more important (as far as price-formation is concerned) than those left out, in particular, demand and change. The exclusion of change is crucial. In an actual economic system in which change is occurring, it would not be possible in the absence of constant returns to scale, to determine prices independently of the level and composition of output.

By way of contrast with our assessment, we quote in full Blaug's (1968, pp. 143–4), whose view that theory has a life of its own is cogently argued in *Economic Theory in Retrospect*.

> P. Sraffa, the editor of Ricardo's works, has recently published a puzzling book, entitled *Production of Commodities by Means of Commodities. Prelude to a Critique of Economic Theory* (1960). It is a kind of 'Ricardo in modern dress', containing all the characteristic Ricardian touches: the search for a standard of value independent of demand and unaffected by changes in the distribution of the total product between wages and profits; the neglect of factor substitution and changes in the scale of operations; the division of commodities into two classes – 'basic' commodities that do and 'non-basic' commodities that do not enter into the production of all commodities including themselves; the emphasis on a 'standard commodity' as the yardstick of value, defined as a commodity produced only by basic commodities in a 'standard ratio', that is, in the same proportion as they enter into the production of total output, culminating, of course, in the demonstration that relative prices depend only on the technical conditions of producing the 'standard commodity' and on nothing else. The argument is intimately related to some 20th-century linear-programming models of the economy, and yet no reference is made to any work more recent than Marx. It is the sort of book Ricardo might have written if only he had gone straight to the point without ifs and buts: the reasoning is terse and condensed, no concessions are made to the reader, and it is not clear, even when we reach the end, just how this could constitute a Prelude to a Critique of Economic Theory. Without first struggling through

Ricardo, one might find Sraffa incomprehensible; but after Ricardo, he is plain sailing, and we can almost see on the first page where we are going.

Notes

* This is a slightly amended version of the review article of Sraffa's book which I wrote with Vincent G. Massaro, published in *Economic Record*, vol. xl, no. 91, September 1964, pp. 442–54. The present version is part of the appendix to ch. 4 of Harcourt (1972).

1 Formally, there are k sets of multipliers which would transform the actual system into k standard systems, each with different values of R and different sets of prices. Sraffa shows, however, that there is only one set which will give all positive prices, namely, that associated with the minimum value of R. This is the only solution which has economic relevance.

2 I am indebted to Nobuo Okishio for this point.

3 In Appendix D, Sraffa speaks of Marx's attack on Smith's assertion that the price of a commodity resolves itself entirely into wages, profits and rent, without a commodity residue. Sraffa's view of the economic system, as expressed in this book, reminds us that while macroeconomic theory concentrates on the consolidated national accounts where final expenditures equal total values added and incomes, and intermediate goods cancel, price theory cannot ignore the large stock of commodities which is in existence before the year's production starts.

4 Readers of the first printing should note that the two expressions on p. 37 should read:

$$n = \frac{1 + r}{R - r} \quad \text{and} \quad r = \frac{nR - 1}{1 + n}$$

5 I have left the account of Part III substantially as it was written in 1964 in order to show how completely we missed its significance.

14 Can Marx survive Cambridge?*

Piero Sraffa had to leave Italy in the 1920s because his articles on reconstruction in Europe in the *Manchester Guardian* and the Italian banking crisis in the *Economic Journal* offended Mussolini. Sraffa was already a critic of orthodox economics, then represented by Marshall in England and Walras and Wicksell on the continent, and a Marxist in theory and action. He was a close friend of Gramsci; it was a typical Sraffa gesture, original and helpful, that he opened an unlimited credit account for Gramsci at a Milan bookshop when Mussolini imprisoned Gramsci.

Sraffa was befriended by Keynes, settled at Cambridge, being first a lecturer in the faculty of economics and politics, then the Marshall librarian, and he acted in the post-war years as a guide and mentor of those Cambridge cinderellas, the research students. Initially associated with King's through Keynes, he was elected to a fellowship at Trinity in 1939, where he developed his fruitful collaboration with Maurice Dobb.

Keynes dubbed Sraffa the one 'from whom nothing is hid', a reference to Sraffa's superb detective work in his preparation of the definitive edition of Ricardo's works and correspondence. But the phrase had general application. Keynes, Joan Robinson, Kahn and Kaldor always valued and, I suspect, feared, Sraffa's criticisms of their work more than anyone else's. Along with Frank Ramsey and the author, Sraffa was also responsible for Wittgenstein II. In the Preface to Wittgenstein's *Philosophical Investigations* we read: 'Even more than to [Frank Ramsey's] criticism I am indebted to that which a teacher of this university, Mr P. Sraffa, for many years increasingly practised on my thoughts . . . indebted to *this* stimulus for the most consequential ideas of this book.'

For our present purposes Sraffa's 1960 classic *Production of Commodities by Means of Commodities*, his famous 1925 Italian paper and 1926 *Economic Journal* article, and his introduction to volume I of Ricardo's '*Works*', are of central importance.

Sraffa's 1960 book, which led Samuelson to christen our age the age of Leontief and Sraffa, is subtitled *Prelude to a Critique of Economic Theory*, by which is meant the orthodox neoclassical theory of value, production and distribution. Sraffa wrote in the Preface:

> It is . . . a peculiar feature of the set of propositions now published that, although they do not enter into any discussion of the marginal theory of value and distribution, they have nevertheless been designed to serve as the basis for a critique of that theory. If the foundation holds, the critique may be attempted later, either by the writer or by someone younger and better equipped for the task.

Several younger men and women have seen this mantle descending on their own shoulders. I have no doubt that Sraffa's favorite for the role is Pierangelo Garegnani, whose 1959 Ph.D. dissertation at Cambridge, *A Problem in the Theory of Distribution from Ricardo to Wicksell*, in many ways anticipated what was contained in Sraffa's book, itself written partially in the 1920s!

Garegnani has had an extraordinary influence on a number of very bright young radical scholars, the foremost of whom in the U.K. are John Eatwell, now at Trinity and also a lecturer in the Cambridge faculty itself, and Ian Steedman, the author of the book under review. Under Garegnani's influence and through his own acute understanding of Sraffa's work, Steedman (with Stan Metcalfe) has carried out the critique of orthodox international trade theory implied by Sraffa's propositions. Again under Garegnani's influence, Steedman has revealed the ideological content and the logical flaws in Jevons's theory of capital. Most importantly though, for our present purposes, Steedman, himself a Marxist in theory and practice, has been at the forefront of the battle in the United Kingdom to rid the modern revival of Marxism of its Billy Graham aspects, of its dogmatic devotion to what the master said as being holy writ, of the obscurantism which makes it impossible to concede the possibility of error in the master's analysis and of luddism which rejects the use of modern mathematical reasoning as bourgeois, indeed as vulgar economy at its worst, for which there can be no place in proper Marxist analysis.

Associated with this particular strand of Marxism has been a sustained attack on the Post-Keynesian school, the three major strands of which are that which is associated with Joan Robinson and her followers; that associated with Nicholas Kaldor; and that associated with Piero Sraffa himself and the Italian wing of the Anglo-Italian school. All three overlap and interrelate and Joan Robinson is most explicitly conscious of Sraffa's role and contributions. Nevertheless, for reasons only marginally connected with the present issues, the distinction must be made.

Steedman's most formidable opponent in this regard is Bob Rowthorn; his most vocal, vulgar and extreme opponent is David Yaffe. Both have set out their cases in the *New Left Review*. Rowthorn presents the proper case that may be discerned in Yaffe's rantings and ravings. Rowthorn himself is a brilliant mathematical economist and Marxist scholar who, while he accepts the validity of the critique of the Post-Keynesian school of the vulgar and/or textbook versions of orthodoxy, feels that they miss their mark as far as the most refined form of orthodoxy is concerned – modern general equilibrium theory – and that, moreover, the positive aspects of the Post-Keynesian contributions, just because they are, or can be interpreted as independent and/or ignorant of Marxist categories, risk entering the category of vulgar economy themselves.

Rowthorn's specific allegations are that Sraffa does not use properly the Marxist category of the mode of production, that Post-Keynesians neglect the social relations that are founded in the sphere of production and are the clue to the origin of the category, profits (more generally, non-labor incomes) in the capitalist mode of production, and that Sraffa's book is in the line of the vulgar economists because it concentrates on the sphere of distribution and exchange, i.e. on the surface phenomena, so missing the more fundamental essences which lie beneath the surface, crying out to be revealed by the observing social scientist.

It is to the detailed implications of this general vision that Steedman's book is especially addressed. What Steedman attempts to show is that Sraffa's propositions are not only the foundation for the destruction of orthodoxy – 'a criticism which has now been carried out successfully' (p. 13) – but also for the positive task of carrying Marxist analysis scientifically and rigorously forward into the last quarter of the twentieth century. This is to be done, even though it may involve jettisoning some of Marx's most famous tenets in the process, the most important being the Marxist category of value as a necessary operational concept: 'The irrelevance of Marx's value magnitudes to the understanding of certain fundamental issues has been conclusively demonstrated' (p. 201). Marx, then, would have to be content with having provided us with a rich and fruitful method of approach in the social sciences and the most profound analysis yet of early to mid capitalism. He would not be able to claim to be omniscient, but would have to rest content with being 'just another genius', as Ronald Meek argued years ago.

Steedman is particularly severe on Marx's approach to the 'transformation problem', together with many modern Marxists' discussions of it, and on his analysis of the tendency of the rate of profits in capitalist society to fall. Steedman is too good a Marxist ever to argue that truth comes only in the guise of a mathematical model. He recognises, thoroughly, that in trying to capture aspects of reality within the rigorous confines of a model, we must of necessity leave out much that is important, just because both truth *and* reality are multi-dimensional by nature, never able completely to be so captured.

There is, therefore, a gap between the reality that is to be interpreted and the model and its inner logic which does that interpreting – so much so, at times, that if we have modelled badly, no matter how correct our subsequent logic is, the conclusions of the model nevertheless may fail to illuminate, or may illuminate only very sparingly and unimportantly, actual reality. I say that Steedman knows all this, but I also feel that at times he forgets it.

He argues that we must *start* our analysis, as Sraffa does, with given technical coefficients of production and a given value of the real wage-rate in order to get a theory of the prices of production and of the rate of profits; the two go indisputably, indissolubly together. Formally this is correct and Steedman does include the vital qualification 'proximate'. Nevertheless, this way of starting has the unfortunate effect of pushing into the background the question – a question which is *not* relevant for Sraffa's purposes of critizing orthodoxy but *is* relevant for Marx's purpose of explaining the origin of profits in the capitalist mode of production: why does the economy have the technical coefficients of production, the real wage and level of activity that it does at the point in time when we start the analysis?

Here Marx's interpretation of history as a process of creation and expropriation of surplus is immediately relevant and illuminating. It was with *this* story that Marx associated his fundamental concept of values as logically prior to prices (and profits), for he wished to show that the form which surplus labor took in the capitalist mode of production was the clue to the existence of profits (and prices) in the sphere of distribution and exchange.

Steedman acknowledges this when he argues that the necessary and sufficient condition for observing a positive rate of profits in the prices of production *is* positive surplus labor and/or value in the sphere of production. So qualitatively, he maintains Marx's insight while, quantitatively, he dismisses Marx's solution of the transformation problem as illogical, unsatisfying and, ultimately, unnecessary, a drag on progress towards better things.

Significantly, Steedman ignores Anwar Shaikh's rigorously presented defence of Marx's approach (in *A Subtle Anatomy of Capitalism*, ed. Jesse Schwartz, Goodyear, 1977). Shaikh argues that it was the first term of an iteration procedure which, not only quantitatively but also qualitatively, established the link between total surplus value and total profits.

Steedman claims that no one can logically defend Marx's own solution and that no one can make, or has made, any direct logical criticism of other solutions, such as those offered by von Bortkiewicz, Seton, Sraffa and others, because 'so far as they go, these solutions *are* logically sound'.

If Shaikh is right, we have a rigorous back-up to William Baumol's chapter and verse destruction of Paul Samuelson's interpretation and evaluation of the whole 'transformation problem' literature (Samuelson's article appeared in the *Journal of Economic Literature* in 1971, Baumol's in 1974).

Samuelson, looking at the problem through staunchly orthodox, neoclassical eyes, saw the labor theory of value as a theory of relative prices and not, primarily, as a theory of the origin of profits, to which relative prices were a necessary, but nevertheless minor, appendage.

Shaikh's paper, which is mathematically identical to Morishima's solution, rigorously supports Baumol's characterization of Marx's approach by using the parable of a storehouse. Baumol wrote:

> The substance of Marx's analysis can be summarised in a simple parable, in which the economy is described as an aggregation of industries each of which contributes to a storehouse containing total surplus value. The contribution of each industry is its total output minus the consumption of its labor force. . . . Each industry's contribution is proportionate to the quantity of labor it uses. . . . This is how society's surplus value is *produced*.
> The *distribution* of surplus value from the . . . storehouse . . . takes place via the competitive process which assigns to each industry for profit . . . an amount strictly proportionate to its capital investment . . . the heart of the transformation process – the conversion of surplus value into profit. . . . It takes from each according to its workforce and returns to each according to its total investment.

Another point where I take issue with Steedman is his view that joint production, when interpreted by Sraffa's analysis, allows the construction of a counter example to the proposition that positive surplus labor and value in the sphere of production are necessary and sufficient conditions for observing a positive rate of profits in the sphere of distribution and exchange.

As Steedman himself says, the necessary and sufficient condition may be sustained and Marx's qualitative insight into *why* profits are observed may be retained. This was done by Morishima (and by myself, in company of Cheok, Davis and Madden) by making some simple but plausible economic assumptions. What goes, in the case of joint production, is Marx's conjecture that values – the abstract labor amounts embodied in individual commodities – are necessarily additive in all technically possible production systems.

I started by saying that Piero Sraffa is a Marxist, so that it is ludicrous for him to be critized as non-Marxist by the Billy Graham Marxists and, even more so, by those who both know their Marx *and* modern economic theory and methods and who, therefore, should know better.

We are indebted to Ian Steedman for the much good sense and clear analysis in this book and not least, for showing *why* it is silly for some Marxists and socialists to try to keep Sraffa at arm's length. Instead, they should ponder anew Meek's brilliant review article of Sraffa's book of well over a decade ago and read Eatwell's work on Sraffa, Marx and Garegnani together with Steedman's book. They should note especially Steedman's wise remarks on *proximate* determination. Then, I hope, they will realize that Sraffa's analysis was crucial in smashing orthodoxy and that it is even more valuable as a rigorous foundation for modern progressive thought.

Note

* *Nation Review*, 8–15 March 1978, p. 15. A review of Ian Steedman's book, *Marx after Sraffa* (1977).

15 Marshall, Sraffa and Keynes Incompatible bedfellows?*

I

I want to talk today about three great economists and I want to make my principal theme the role of the (classical) concept of centres of gravity in their work. There are a number of obvious connections between the three - they are (were) all Cambridge economists and both Sraffa and Keynes spent much of their professional life either using, amending, criticising, overthrowing and/or evaluating Marshall's work. Thus Sraffa's 1925 paper and, especially, his 1926 paper specifically were directed to a critique - a devastating one, I would say - of Marshall's contributions to value theory. Sraffa makes this perfectly clear in his reply to D. H. Robertson in the 1930 *Economic Journal* symposium on Increasing Returns and the Representative Firm.

> We seem to be agreed that [Marshall's] theory cannot be interpreted in a way which makes it logically self-consistent and, at the same time, reconciles it with the facts it sets out to explain. Mr. Robertson's remedy is to discard mathematics, and he suggests that my remedy is to discard the facts; perhaps I ought to have explained that . . . I think it is Marshall's theory that should be discarded. (p. 93)

Keynes used, developed and ultimately moved away from, or even rejected (or thought he did), much of Marshall's theory of money and interest. He attempted to absorb Marshallian value theory - the 'homely but intelligible concepts . . . of marginal cost and the elasticity of short period supply' (Keynes, 1936, p. 292) - into his theory of the general level of prices in *The General Theory* in which his purpose was to integrate value, production and monetary theory into one system. He abandoned the specifically Marshallian aspects in 1939 (unless we adopt the Cambridge maxim that it is all in Marshall - it probably was, see the *Principles*, 1890, pp. 374-7) when in reply to Dunlop and Tarshis, he outlined in rudimentary form the normal cost-pricing hypothesis. Keynes wrote a superb biographical essay on Marshall before he was fully into his own revolutionary stride and so was more accepting of

Marshall's monetary theory than he subsequently was to be (Keynes, 1971–9, vol. x, pp. 161–231). Finally, Marshall belonged to, or at least thought or presented himself as belonging to, the classical tradition which Sraffa inherited (and for which in his 1960 book, *Production of Commodities*, he provided the foundations both for a revival and an updating).

One of Sraffa's purposes, though, was to attack the inner logic of Marshall's system of thought because, whether Marshall really believed he was fulfilling what the Old Masters had sensed but not got quite right or had not fully developed – Joan Robinson for one thinks that Marshall was foxing on this[1] – certainly, in Sraffa's view, his *effect* was both to subvert and to emasculate the robust classical tradition on which he drew. When I say in Sraffa's view, I think that there is direct evidence for this in Sraffa's own writings and that it can be read indirectly into them as well from the hints and asides which he gives. Even more, there is another source of indirect evidence which is provided in the writings of Pierangelo Garegnani and Krishna Bharadwaj, who of Sraffa's colleagues and friends are among the most in accord with Sraffa's own views. In Krishna Bharadwaj's fine 1976 R.C. Dutt Lectures, *Classical Political Economy and Rise to Dominance of Supply and Demand Theories*, she explicitly acknowledges that the themes developed there owe much to discussions over the years with Sraffa.[2] She refers in many places, especially in the second lecture, to the 1925 and 1926 papers. Sraffa gave her access to Marshall's copy of Pigou's *Wealth and Welfare* in which Marshall's misgivings about Pigou's extension of his – Marshall's – mode of analysis are only too plainly expressed (Bharadwaj, 1972). There is also her paper on Marshall's early work on value, edited by John Whitacker (Bharadwaj, 1978b).[3]

I have chosen to make centres of gravity the main theme because not only do they feature extensively and centrally in Marshall's and Sraffa's own work (also, I shall argue, in Keynes's work though, of course, in a different context) but also because they have become a major point of disputation in current developments of Post-Keynesian theory by Joan Robinson and her followers, on the one hand, and Pierangelo Garegnani and *his* followers, on the other. (I had better own up immediately to belonging to, I think, the former team!) This is both with regard to the fundamental nature of the critique of orthodoxy which arises out of Sraffa's work (and takes in Marshall's contributions as well as Walras's and Wicksell's and their modern offshoots) and also with regard to the methodology which ought to be followed in the new developments, what the late Ronald Meek called the rehabilitation of classical political economy. If we might summarise briefly the general nature of the disputes, Garegnani is inclined to say that the orthodox theory is wrong but its methodology (in so far as it consists of comparisons of long-period positions) is sound, while Joan Robinson says it is the methodology which is wrong. (The theory *within* this context, she argues, is not too good either, but that is *not* the principal or most fundamental criticism.)

I now outline what I think is entailed in the notion(s) of centre of gravity. (Discussions with John Eatwell, Pierangelo Garegnani, Bertram Schefold and Ian Steedman, together with a run along the Cam towpath greatly helped me to sort these out.) The first three are analogies drawn from physics, the fourth, an analogy drawn from meteorology. The first relates to a frictionless pendulum which always swings but always passes the same minimum point on its path to and fro. The second is a pendulum, the motion of which ends eventually *because* of friction, and so actually settles at the minimum point of its path i.e. *at* the centre of gravity of the first notion. (As we shall see, this notion is most closely related to Marshall's concept of a long-period position or at least to the end point of the process.) The third is, I think, David Champernowne's example of a dog always running towards its master who is riding a bike. The bike is the centre of gravity which itself is moving but the dog's direction of movement at any point in time can be predicted by knowledge of where the bike (and its master) is, at that point in time. The fourth analogy is, in many ways, I think, the most illuminating. We all know that various places and seasons may be characterised (in part) by the concept of their average temperature, even though, on any one day, because of the influence of special or temporary factors, the actual temperature may not coincide with the average. Yet the average is a good, sustained predictor and description over the years, from year to year, and as between places. Similarly, the average temperature itself is explicable in terms of relationships between the *average* values of the factors which determine temperature, even though the actual value of each one of these factors in turn may depart from *its* average value on any particular day. The average temperature thus is a centre of gravity in the sense of a central tendency to which actual temperatures will tend, the outcome of sustained and fundamental forces, that is to say, the average serves to explain most of the orders of magnitude of the values actually observed from day to day.

What of Marshall's work have I reread in order to write this paper? I suppose that I have concentrated on the Prefaces and Book V of the

Principles and, within that, on normal values; the famous (or infamous) Appendix H on increasing returns and long-run normal supply price; and Appendix I on Ricardo's theory of value, on how Marshall came not to bury Ricardo but to fulfil him. In addition, I have looked at Marshall's early essays on international and domestic values, noting, as I think Keynes did, that he worked back from the demand and supply schedules to what he thought underlay them – ultimately utility and disutility – rather than, as the Austrians did, and Wicksteed also, starting from subjective introspection and working outwards to the market phenomena. I also reread the symposium on increasing returns in the 1930 *Economic Journal* (and I thought again how remarkably acute Gerald Shove was – I suspect that Keynes asked him to contribute in order to prise out of him a substantial chunk of that 'unpublished study of the relations between cost and output on which [Shove] had been engaged for some years', which formed part of the Cambridge oral tradition at that time). In addition to the work of Krishna Bharadwaj, I read Keynes on Marshall, Mary Marshall (I liked *it* – or perhaps her – best) and Jevons, and I have had access to a number of unpublished papers by Garegnani and Joan Robinson in which some of the issues discussed are relevant for the present theme. Part of what Garegnani has to say may be found in his comment on Samuelson in the Brown, Sato and Zarembka volume (Garegnani, 1976), and in his 1970 *Review of Economic Studies* paper; the last part of the latter paper is concerned to attack the sort of demand and supply theory that Marshall would have needed to build up *if* he wanted to tell a value and distribution story which gave answers to classical questions concerning the determination of natural rates of profits and wages. Marshall approaches and retreats from such stories in a tantalising way all through the chapters on distribution in the *Principles*. He wants to tell them because they illustrate his faith in the principle of substitution, but he does not want to be nailed down by the inconsistencies which he also senses.

Why do I think criticisms of natural or normal prices, or prices of production (I stress that they are *not* necessarily synonyms) are important? Because there is currently a debate going on concerning whether they should or should not be maintained in a Marxist and/or Post-Keynesian analysis of a modern capitalist economy moving through time. I think that their natural place probably is in the theory of the pricing which characterises important sectors of such economies, in the normal cost-pricing hypothesis and the connection of pricing to the investment decision. In particular, I think that there may be a role for the concepts of the natural rates of profits and of wages, that they are macro concepts associated with the working of the system as a whole, which impose themselves as norms on group behaviour within the system. The centre of gravity concept also may have a part to play in the Keynesian context of short-run rest states (and, possibly, even longer, sustained rest states), a view which I think can be supported by Keynes's own writings and by Jan Kregel's interpretation of them in his 1976 *Economic Journal* article (Kregel, 1976b). This is not an interpretation with which Joan Robinson would agree, nor, I should add, David Levine, who recently gave two stimulating and challenging lectures on cyclical growth in capitalism, in which he denied, in effect, that the prices of production had any operational significance in the development of the analysis of the processes involved (see also Levine, 1980a, 1980b).

II

I return now to Marshall himself. It is clear, I believe, that he wanted to make the concept of normal values, and especially long-run normal values, the centre-pieces of his theory of value (and distribution). The long-run equilibrium positions and the prices associated with them were the partial equilibrium, firm and industry, versions of the long-run positions of the economy as a whole which are found in the classical scheme (and, of course, in Marx). Marshall realised that he would need eventually to have a theory of the levels of the normal profits and normal wages to fit into his theory of the composition of the individual prices of the commodities of individual industries – otherwise there would not be an explanation of a *general* level to which the prices, etc., of each industry would have to measure up – but he kept backing away from going the whole way in supplying them because he sensed the logical difficulties contained therein. Where Marshall differed from the classicals was that his long-run prices were the outcome of the symmetrical and opposing forces of supply and demand.[4] The forces which affected prices conveniently could be placed in one or other of these categories; at the level of a firm or an industry, one set reasonably could be regarded as independent of the other; the prices would settle or tend to settle at levels which the two blades of the scissors (or balls in the bowl) dictated; and in normal conditions the forces were sustained and fundamental enough to make it reasonable to talk of an equilibrium being struck, or being potentially there to be struck, providing the *ceteris paribus* clauses held long enough in practice. A normal price is a price 'which any one set of conditions tends to produce'

(Marshall, 1890, p. 372). (If we were to insert 'ultimately' before 'tends', we would have our second analogy, the pendulum the motion of which is subject to friction.)

Marshall wanted to use the concept of equilibrium (and considerations of its stability) because, despite his many asides and protestations about biology being the Mecca of economists, in his actual analysis (which he was very reluctant directly to apply to actual situations) he really did want to use mechanical analogies – pendulums, etc. He wanted to argue that the state of rest which ultimately would be reached had an effect on what was happening at any moment even if in fact that movement itself was *away* from the equilibrium position. It is true that he tried to be careful, or rather he knew that he should be careful, to keep his statements confined to what would happen near or at an equilibrium, i.e. that any displacements considered were from an already achieved equilibrium – hence his starting point of analysis of a stationary state – but, nevertheless, many of his applications had to occur well away from the intersections and take in the curves (and the areas under them) associated with those positions away from them. There is no doubt that as wily a bird as Marshall knew that there was the world of difference between starting an analysis at an arbitrary point and seeing whether there were any forces that would take the economy, industry, firm, towards any equilibrium that might be implied by forces present at that moment of time; and starting the analysis at an equilibrium from which a chance notional or conceptual displacement has occurred. But with typical Marshallian fuzziness (foxiness), this is never brought out as clearly or as starkly as it should have been.[5]

It was on these very points that Sraffa went after Marshall in his 1926 article – trying to find those situations where the assumptions of partial equilibrium analysis were actually met so that the dependence of supply factors on demand, and vice versa, really was 'of the second order of smalls' and thus could be ignored: '[To] what extent the supply curves based on the laws of returns satisfy the conditions necessary to enable them to be employed in the study of single commodities under competitive conditions' (Marshall, 1890, p. 538). The answer was, as we know, dispiriting – only in those cases where economies were external to the firm but internal to the industry, 'precisely the class which is most seldom to be met with' (p. 540), were the conditions likely to be met.

Marshall also wanted to introduce the concept of substitution, 'the dynamical principle of "substitution" . . . seen ever at work' (p. xv); the universality of the theory of value, distribution and production (instead of their separation as in classical political economy), i.e. that all could be embraced in effect within the theory of exchange; and his adaptations of what he took to be the essential truths of the laws of diminishing and increasing returns in his supply and demand analysis. He wanted, as Joan Robinson has stressed, to analyse an economy moving through time with accumulation going on, yet still use the supply and demand apparatus as the principal illuminator of the process. (This illustrates another characteristic of Marshall's thought and approach: he was at one and the same time the master of empirical generalisations and also a superb user of deductive reasoning.) His attempt to centralise the principle of substitution and his equal stress on continuity led him to develop marginal analysis ('In economics, as in physics, changes are generally continuous', p. 409, n.1), choice and change at the margin, drawing, he argued, on classical uses to justify this, as it first arose in the theory of rent. However, as Krishna Bharadwaj shows, he slurred over the essentially different concepts of the margin in classical political economy – those associated with different *qualities* of land, where there is no change of a neoclassical sort occurring, no counterfactuals as Sen characterises what Sraffa is doing in *Production of Commodities* . . .,[6] as opposed to the typical marginal procedure – in Wicksteed's view, the only non-spurious one – derived from changing the intensity of production on a given piece of land. Marshall attempts to encompass within one framework the essentially different historical tendency to diminishing returns in agriculture and the increasing returns phenomena of manufacturing and the accumulation process generally. The latter was sensed and first developed by Smith and understood and completed by Ricardo and, especially, Marx, but only kept alive, really, in modern times, by Schumpeter, Allyn Young, Kalecki, and Kaldor – and also Arthur Smithies, many years ago, in a perceptive comment on one of Solow's papers.[7] Apart from the mixing of the essentially different processes involved, it was the difficulties of obtaining a *functional* relationship between cost and output levels and changes in the latter which especially concerned Sraffa and which he felt undermined the partial equilibrium method.

Marshall vitally breaks with classical methodology also when he attempts to derive a uniform framework – a common set of principles – with which to deal with value, distribution and production (with the latter not separated from the former, as in Marx's analysis). Classical theory did not look for universality and uniformity but for specificity[8] – for separate explanations of the different incomes of the different classes, with the explanation of value being different from and logically subsequent to the explanation of distribution. Thus, distribution preceded value in a logical sense – a view that is in Ricardo and in Marx as much as it is in Sraffa, with his construction of the Standard system and Standard commodity in order to 'give transparency to a system and render visible what was hidden'.[9] Such an approach contrasts with the symmetry that Marshall found in diminishing marginal utility and decreasing returns, despite their different roots 'in the quality of human nature . . . [and] the technical conditions of industry'. Sraffa's response to this, as Krishna Bharadwaj noted (p. 51), was to wonder why 'two such heterogeneous elements as human nature and industrial technology should bring about results so similar'. His answer was that there was an underlying behavioural premise which implied an ordering between alternatives but also destroyed the neat dichotomy of the facts of nature, psychology and engineering, on the one hand, and economic choice and valuation, on the other, so common in the usual presentation of orthodox theory. (See Bharadwaj, 1978a, pp. 51–4.)

Nevertheless, as we have seen, Marshall wished to have a theory of long-period normal prices which included as ingredients normal profits and normal wages. He thus distinguished, as we all know, a number of time periods, though he argued that they merged imperceptibly one into another, and could be short or long according to the purpose in hand, and actual or potential, according to the realism of the factors caught in the *ceteris paribus* pound in any particular case. He himself seemed to vacillate between whether they are actual or potential, sometimes naming periods of calendar time as illustrative of what he had in mind, wishing, I suspect, to have it both ways. That is to say, he wished his long-period normal prices, etc., to be real centres of gravity – to help make sense of *actual* observations in *actual* time, yet he knew that if he simultaneously had in mind an economy which was moving forward through time with accumulation and technical advances occurring, there were puzzles in setting them up as being revealed by the averages of observations on actual prices. Indeed, he himself says that only in the stationary state can the normal and the average coincide, be 'convertible terms' (Marshall, 1890, p. 372). It was, of course, Salter (1960) who first applied the traditional notions in a more general framework – and went as far as it is possible to solve the puzzles in a neoclassical framework – by having the equilibrium prices determined by intersections of supply and demand curves but at the same time insisting that it is only the latest vintages – the 'best-practice' technique actually embodied in the stock of capital goods by investment expenditure – which *have* to earn the normal rate of profits. (Of course, as Tom

Rymes reminds me, the prices of the earlier vintages, *ceteris paribus*, will stand below the prices of the latest vintages, so that all 'earn' – receive – the same money rate of return.) This procedure gives any one industry a chance for its process of accumulation to reach this point, with output at the appropriate level, before the next wave of innovations occurs and changes the centres of gravity involved. Marshall, I am sure, sensed this solution but he never spelt it out as neatly or as fully as Salter did. A similar concept of the centres of gravity that are associated with the latest techniques (or, rather, in their view, the *dominant* technique) and the prices of the products which they help to produce is to be found in Marx and the modern classical writers, e.g. Garegnani, Eatwell.[10]

Because Marshall was wedded to demand and supply analysis, and to having his long-period equilibrium positions determined at the intersections of supply and demand curves, he had to concern himself with problems of uniqueness and stability in a manner which the classical economists could avoid. This had the further implication, as Krishna Bharadwaj argues, that neoclassical analysis only applies in situations where the conditions for stability are met – there is not the freedom of action in this framework which exists in classical analysis and its modern counterparts, and also in the 'horses for courses' approach of Joan Robinson and Kalecki, for example.

> [The] classical theory [of value] is not constrained to permit only some specific changes of the many possible ones as alone consistent with the theory[;] . . . does not have to presume more than is necessary for the limited objective of determining relative values at one 'observed' position of the economic system. . . . [The] supply and demand theories sought to explain a single observed position in terms of potential changes . . . as brought about by the balancing of marginal quantities operating through the principle of substitution . . . [;] to be consistent with these explanations, the changes had to be in a direction . . . of the type postulated by theory. (Bharadwaj, 1978a, p. 67)

Moreover, once Marshall had committed himself to a long-period position which is the outcome of the forces of supply and demand, and to having schedules, he was committed to not allowing the *approach* to equilibrium to affect the equilibrium position itself. More, he was committed to an assumption of reversibility, if the supply curves were to mean what he said they meant, which, as he knew, and Sraffa made *very* plain in his 1926 *Economic Journal* article, makes the concept of the long-run supply curve a very fuzzy one indeed. (That was why Marshall was so worried about Pigou using a long-run supply curve in

Wealth and Welfare.) Marshall discusses these issues in Appendix H and wants to dodge the conclusion that the long-run supply curve is irreversible, that it can only be an historical statement as opposed to a conditional one. But certainly Sraffa does not let him get away with this, either by use of the device of the representative firm or by other means.

I do not wish to imply that Sraffa himself does not believe in the value of what he calls the statical method, the use of the concepts of long-period positions and their comparisons. When he introduced the downward-sloping demand curve analysis in 1926, with each firm its own little monopoly and so on, he said that he was dealing with situations where the determining events stay steady enough for long enough, are sufficiently sustained (or may be treated theoretically as if they are) to allow the statical method to be used.

> Many of the obstacles which break up that unity of the market which is the essential condition of competition are not of the nature of 'frictions', but are themselves active forces which produce permanent and even cumulative effects . . . frequently . . . endowed with sufficient stability to enable them to be made the subject of analysis based on statical assumptions. (Sraffa, 1926, p. 542)

It was Marshall's use of the method *in conjunction with supply and demand curves* which he found objectionable. That is to say, Sraffa is *not* attacking the centres of gravity concept as such and, indeed, his entire book (1960) *is* about them – he determines the pattern of the prices of production (which are associated with the uniform rate of profits), given the levels of activity, the techniques of production in an economy at a given instant of time, and either the wage-rate or the rate of profits. Some, usually orthodox economists, have argued that Sraffa's systems are already in, or are necessarily in, balanced or appropriate states, with the input-output arrangements and the prices of production being consistent with reproduction (and/or expansion). This, for example, was, until very recently anyway, even Joan Robinson's interpretation of Sraffa's system (see, for example, Robinson, 1951–80, vol. v, pp. 285–7); it is *as if* we had *already* reached the end of Marshall's long period, with long-run values established (but *not* by the forces of supply and demand) and all fossils from previous epochs removed, and all production processes in their most appropriate form. But the fact that Sraffa stresses that there is no implication that what happened in this period need *necessarily* happen again, or had happened before, or that the means of production used this period *necessarily* came from the last period, or that those produced this period will *necessarily* be used to replace those used up this period, nor that there is any historical significance to be attached to his procedure of reduction to dated quantities of labour, suggests that this interpretation, though not unreasonable, is not necessarily what he had in mind.[11] Rather, he takes the economy just as it is and asks: What pattern of prices of production is implied if we know (say) the wage-rate and assume that a uniform rate of profit is to be received in each activity? And how do they alter when *we* alter the value of the wage rate? Of course, it can be argued, what *is* the point of such a procedure if there is *not* an implication of stability, that is to say, that our temperature analogy can be said to apply, so that those positions can serve to underlie the patterns of actual prices. These, of course, are influenced by temporary factors as well, yet we *have* isolated the effects of sustained and fundamental forces by our procedures – this certainly is Garegnani's argument and it is at this point that Joan Robinson (and Levine) part company with him.[12]

III

The same problems arise during consideration of Keynes's system of thought in *The General Theory*, and as it has been adopted and developed in the Post-Keynesian macro theories of distribution. If his theories are to have operational content, it is argued, and, in particular, if they are to be a guide to model-builders and policy-makers, we need to be able to say that the actual observations on national production, expenditure and income, and their components, are pretty good approximations to their theoretical counterparts. The latter themselves are the values that would be associated with the short-run rest states of the system that are implied in actual situations at any moment of time.[13]

We all know how we make this point in our first-year classes: we draw the aggregate planned expenditures schedule (*not* Keynes's aggregate demand schedule, which shows, rather, the total of what business people expect their receipts will be, for any given level of employment) and the 45° line (which, given certain, not unreasonable, assumptions about expectations and business people's behaviour, may be interpreted as a functional relationship between the total of sales expected at any moment of time, including desired stock accumulation and the total of the production and, therefore, employment that they will call forth from the existing short-run utilisation functions). We argue that if the economy is not at the point of intersection of the two when we start the analysis, so that unintended changes in stocks occur, what changes is *not* either of our two schedules but the business people's perceptions of what their expected sales are. They change their production and employment levels accordingly, collectively taking the economy closer to the point where what is expected and what actually happens coincide. In other words, the initial non-fulfilment of investment plans leads not to *their* change but to a change in the perceptions of what sales are. In this way, there is a reasonable chance that the economy will not be too far away from its implied rest states at any moment of time, unless, of course, it has been buffeted by a large shock or shocks.[14] The point I want to make is that Keynes, and we, are using the concept of centres of gravity to tell this story, a procedure which Joan Robinson would regard as illegitimate, at least in some instances. Thus, she criticises *IS/LM* analysis because unless the economy is actually at the intersection of the *IS* and *LM* curves, its actual movement will disturb the *ceteris paribus* factors underlying their construction; or to return to the textbook model, she argues that by the time income has moved to a level where planned saving is equal to a previous level of planned investment, the level of planned investment may well have changed. We then are required to scrap the short cut of using the statical method and tell a much more sophisticated story of the initial failure to reach an implied rest state changing the rest state itself, by, for example, changing the rate of planned investment, especially in stocks. That is to say, we let expectations have their way and so work with a theory which, as Garegnani said of Hick's temporary equilibrium method in *Value and Capital*, is barren of 'definite results' *because* it had scrapped the notion of long-run positions determined by sustained and fundamental forces (and comparisons of them) in favour of a method of short-period equilibrium and a sequence of them. (We have gone even further, of course.)

Keynes himself moved back and forth between both views, for there are many stories in *The General Theory* where a process is traced out over 'time', while at other places Keynes concentrates on the characteristics of a *sustained* rest state. His principal purpose was, of course, to show that a capitalist economy left to itself could get stuck in a prolonged slump, that it would not give out signals that would lead it from there to a position of full employment. Moreover, by the time he had published *The General Theory*, he had all but despaired of finding a determinate unit of time into which all the various interrelated processes and decisions he was analysing could be fitted – so he decided never to push any particular piece of analysis very far past its starting point, preferring to get across the central message only. Even then, as he says in his 1937 lectures, as Kregel (1976b, p. 213) has documented, were he to write the book again, he would start with the simplest model in which (in textbook terms) the economy is already at the total planned expenditures, 45° line intersection, because short-run expectations are assumed to be correct and fulfilled, so as 'to distinguish the forces determining the position of equilibrium from the technique of trial and error by means of which the entrepreur[s] [discover] where the position is' (Keynes, 1971-9, vol. XIV, p. 182, quoted by Kregel, 1976b, p. 213).

That Keynes himself at times used the classical concept of a sustained rest state, a long-period position around which the actual positions fluctuated, may be inferred from, for example, the passages at the end of Book IV of *The General Theory* (Chapter 18, Part III, pp. 249-54). There, he states that

> it is an outstanding characteristic of the economic system in which we live that, whilst it is subject to severe fluctuations in respect of output and employment, it is not violently unstable . . . seems capable of remaining in a chronic condition of subnormal activity for a considerable period without any marked tendency either towards recovery or towards complete collapse. (p. 249)

Keynes discusses four conditions (relating to the characteristics of the consumption function, the marginal efficiency of capital schedule, the money wage rate and the impact of achieved investment rates on the marginal efficiency of capital schedule) which

> together are adequate to explain [why] . . . we oscillate, avoiding the gravest extremes of fluctuation in employment and in prices in both directions, around an intermediate position appreciably below full employment and appreciably above the minimum employment a decline below which would endanger life . . . a mean position . . . determined by 'natural' tendencies . . . which are likely to persist. (p. 254)

Sadly, we see today the consequences of his views about the upward stability of money wages (and therefore prices) *not* being borne out.[15]

The same trouble with handling time, which as we have seen troubled Marshall too, also may be illustrated by Keynes's discussion of the marginal efficiency of capital and the reasons why it is a declining schedule. You will remember that he argued that the shorter is the time period involved, the stronger will be the influence of rising supply prices of capital goods in reducing the marginal efficiencies of particular assets; while the longer is the time period that we have in view, the

greater will be the influence of expected? actual? falls in the prices of
the products which the assets are to help to produce, as larger and
larger supplies of the products come onto markets to be sold. Obviously,
Marshall's influence is of major importance here. Equally obviously, the
analysis will not do because we are trying to determine *now* what the
rate of planned investment expenditure will be – there is not the time
to wait for these processes to work themselves out, which they never
would in fact, because of the factors that would escape from the *ceteris
paribus* pound in the meantime.

IV

Exactly the same puzzles hound the concept of prices of production,
especially when we try to incorporate them as operational concepts in
an analysis of modern oligopolistic economies. It is not, as orthodox
economists would argue, that the existence of a tendency to equality of
rates of profit in all activities may be questioned because of oligopolistic structures, barriers to entry and all the other paraphernalia of
modern I.O. It is, rather, that the dynamic nature of capitalist development with the embodiment of technical advances through investment
expenditures is so rapid in most periods as not to allow sufficient
historical time for centres of gravity of a lasting nature to be formed.
There is not the time, as Joan Robinson puts it, for the traders to
become familiar, through actual experience, with what is the norm, so
that when their bearings are cut loose, they – and the economists, too
– literally are all at sea, rudderless, not knowing *where* they are heading,
either back or to. The factors that we need theoretically to take as
constant in order to allow the centres of gravity which they imply to be
struck (for example, by the forces making for the formation of normal
prices) are changing as fast as, or even faster than, the outcomes that
the relationships between them are intended to determine. In making
this point, though, we should notice Eatwell's comment (Eatwell,
1979, p. 2) that the forces which determine the centres of gravity are
the more dominant, systematic and persistent and that '[whether] this
centre of gravity is a temporal constant, or takes different values through
time, does not affect the essence of the method'.

   And yet: there must be a grain of truth – or more than – in the concept of centres of gravity. It is true that Solow is sceptical of the
validity of the great ratios, the stylised facts which it was his and
Kaldor's, Joan Robinson's and Henry Phelps Brown's purposes to
explain, i.e. he asks: Does what is to be explained exist or not? But we

do know that well-established rules of thumb exist in the business world, that pay-off periods, or desired or target rates of return, for example, fall within definite ranges, where exactly depending on expectations, confidence and the extent and intensity of uncertainty at any moment of time. We know that wage-earners have concepts of what is fair in relative wage structures, and in the overall share of wages, too, and that conservative politicians remind us, as they attempt to cut real wages, that they are trying to re-establish the historical share of profits without which it is not possible to expect the accumulators to accumulate. (As an aside, we might argue that one of the reasons for the instability in modern industrial economies is that people have lost their 'feel' for what is a reasonable, 'normal', 'natural', rate of increase of, say, money wages or prices. Figures which 10–15 years ago were way outside the range of credibility crop up all the time now.) All of these notions derive from the macroeconomic characteristics of the system, are imposed by its total workings on the individual decision-makers and therefore have a macroeconomic basis, as Pasinetti, for example, often has stressed. Hence, we have had in the Keynesian–Kaleckian tradition the development of macro theories of distribution, the Post-Keynesian theories of the rate of profits, where $r = \dfrac{g}{s_c}$, with g (sometimes) assumed to be independently given, mistakenly in my view, and corrected, of course, in von Neumann's model and in Joan Robinson's model.[16] It is suggested that these factors feed through, in a very general way, to the determination of individual prices, and so on, and that it is when there are wide departures from them that instability and crises are most in evidence, because microeconomic behaviour is not in accord with the macroeconomic constaints imposed by the structure of the system.[17] Moreover, if we ally some of these notions with Sraffa's contribution of production interrelations, we get close to the normal cost-pricing hypotheses where the expected trend values of costs are married to profit margins, sometimes constant, sometimes variable in order to take in investment expenditures and their finance. All of this grows out of Sraffa's and then Keynes's criticisms of the original and simplest form of Marshall's explanation of pricing.

Notes

* *Eastern Economic Journal*, vol. 7, no. 1, January 1981, pp. 39–50. This paper was originally given at the session on Marshall and his *Principles* at the Eastern Economic Association Meeting in Montreal, 8–10 May 1980. I have left the style

and overall content of the paper much as it was, though the details of the argument have been influenced by comments from Tom Asimakopulos, Melanie Beresford, Krishna Bharadwaj, Jon Cohen, John Eatwell, Pierangelo Garegnani, Peter Groenewegen, Prue Kerr, Bruce McFarlane, Murray Milgate, Dušan Pokorný, Alessandro Roncaglia, Tom Rymes, Claudio Sardoni, Bertram Schefold and Ian Steedman. As ever, I thank them all but implicate none. The paper itself should be seen principally as speculative and exploratory.

1 Joan Robinson is but one amongst many, for example, Cannan, Schumpeter, Ashley, Dobb, Meek, Sraffa himself.

2 'I have drawn liberally upon the writings of Piero Sraffa and on the innumerable and stimulating discussions we have had over a long period.'

3 The subversion referred to in the title (Bharadwaj, 'The Subversion of Classical Analysis: Alfred Marshall's Early Writing on Value'), consisted essentially of moving away from the objective facts of production to a psychological, subjective view of consumption, etc., in value, distribution and production theory, and in scrapping the central concept of the surplus – its creation, extraction and allocation – in favour of a theory of the allocation of *given* resources, arbitrarily given initial endowments, in which the role of substitution in consumption and production could have full play. (Walsh and Gram (1980) provide a most comprehensive statement of this general theme in their splendid *Classical and Neoclassical Theories of General Equilibrium.*) Even though Marshall presented himself as attempting to be a half-way house, he in fact got trapped nearer the end of the subjective theory of value: witness the real costs which lie behind the supply curve and the almost tautological relationships implied in his demand and supply schedules – the inducements needed to call forth efforts, demands and so on. 'What is actually paid out is what is *necessary* to be paid out in order to induce the sacrifices: or else, the services would not be forthcoming' (Bharadwaj, 1978a, p. 35).

4 Peter Groenewegen reminds me that 'the Classical concept of natural price was not necessarily independent of supply and demand'. But I think it is fair to say that, as a generalisation, their role was minor to non-existent relative to the central role that they play in Marshall's analysis.

5 In saying that Marshall wanted to use mechanical analogies, I am aware, of course, that he had in common with Marx a view of economies as structurally changing organisms though he would have objected to the thesis anti-thesis, inherent contradictions, seeds of its own destruction, aspects of Marx's analysis.

6 '[Sraffa's methodology] can be seen as exploring how much can be said about the *inter-relations* between prices, distribution and quantitative magnitudes using only directly observed data, without making any use of *counter-factuals*, [the use of which] is an essential part of any "marginalist" analysis (what *would have* happened had the facts been different, e.g., if one more unit of labour had been applied?)' (Sen, 1978, pp. 180–1). What, though, are we to call Sraffa's procedure when he considers different values of (say) the wage, while holding the methods of production constant?

7 'Perhaps the whole problem is too complicated for adequate reflection in a formal model. In that event, we could do worse than reread Adam Smith . . . . In Book I, he said that the division of labour was the mainspring of economic progress, and in Book II, that accumulation was a necessary condition for increased division of labour. How far have we gone beyond that?' (Smithies, 1962, p. 92).

8 It is ironic that Marshall, who was so keen ultimately to adopt biological methods, nevertheless should have adopted in practice the very method which distinguishes the method of modern physics from that of modern biology.

9 Of course, production – and human labour – logically precede both, as Marx explicitly stresses, and Sraffa, to some extent only implicitly, too. (See Harcourt, 1981.)

10 'At any one time a given commodity may be produced by means of a variety of techniques: some "fossils" embodying out of date methods, . . . not being reproduced since at existing prices they would yield a rate of return on their supply price lower than the general rate of profit, but which . . . do yield positive quasi-rents; some "superior" techniques . . . used only by a limited number of producers . . . yield super-profits. . . . [Theories] of value and distribution are not concerned with these, but with "the conditions of production normal for a given society" (Marx, 1976, p. 129), the "normality" being defined by dominance throughout the competitive market' (Eatwell, 1979, p. 4).

11 Indeed, I know from personal experience that it is not: it was at Sraffa's insistence that Vincent Massaro and I put the following paragraph in our 1964 *Economic Journal* note on Sraffian sub-systems: 'It must be stressed that the relationships in the economic system described here relate to one year only. They occur within the bounds of that year, and there is no necessary connection between them and the relationships that exist in other years . . . *not* implied that the means of production come from the immediately preceding year . . . that those parts of the gross product which are *equal* to the means of production will be used as means of production in the following year' (Harcourt and Massaro, 1964a, p. 716).

12 As Peter Groenewegen again reminds me, 'this is the crux of the problem of the interpretation and use of natural prices in economics, at least as Ricardo saw it'.

13 But see pp. 215–17 for a discussion of whether they are *short-run* states.

14 The same story may be told in terms of Keynes's aggregate demand and supply schedules, and the three cases of possible relations between short-run and long-run expectations and their feedbacks or lack thereof, which Kregel outlines in his 1976 *Economic Journal* article.

15 I am especially indebted to Murray Milgate for bringing this point of view to my notice and making me reread *The General Theory* with it in mind. John Eatwell (1979, pp. 5–6) interprets Keynes in this context as abstracting in his analysis from the effects of accumulation (other than on employment), i.e. from changes in the dominant and persistent forces which lead to secular movements in the rest states and the other centres of gravity, e.g. normal prices. If we accept *this* interpretation, what I have called a short-run rest state, he calls a long-period position 'where by long-period is meant not that which occurs in a long period of time, but rather that which is determined by the dominant forces of the system within a period in which those forces are constant or changing but slowly' (p. 4).

16 Thus, in Joan Robinson's version, $g = g(r), g' > 0; g = s_c r$. Then $g(r) = s_c r$ and r may be solved for.

17 Sadly, we now seem to have entered a stage in the history of industrialised economies where both the centres of gravity themselves change rather rapidly *and* departures from them into the range of values where instabilities result are more often the rule than the exception. I am indebted to Dušan Pokorný for some very perceptive comments on this baldly stated theme.

Part V
The capital theory controversies

16 Capital theory
Much ado about something*

Introduction

I suppose that to most people economists are very dull dogs and the thought of them being cross within or without the confines of their discipline is a surprising one. Yet there are several areas of economic theory in which controversy has been rampant and no more so than in the realm of the theory of capital. Indeed, a feature of the trade has been virulent outbreaks from time to time of really vitriolic exchanges between opposing schools of capital theorists, the latest of which has been happening over the last twenty years or so. It is associated especially with the brawls between the two Cambridges – Cambridge, England, and Cambridge, Mass. Several of the world's leading economists are involved – Joan Robinson (it was her celebrated paper, 'The Production Function and the Theory of Capital' (1953-4), which started it all off), Nicholas Kaldor, Maurice Dobb, Piero Sraffa, Luigi Pasinetti, Frank Hahn and James Meade, of Cambridge, England; the indissoluble duo, Paul Samuelson and Robert Solow, and also Franco Modigliani, all of M.I.T., Cambridge, Mass. (Geography is not a good classifier of rival groups, however, because some of the Cambridge, England, group have their spiritual home in Cambridge, Mass.)

The discussions themselves are about fundamentals, but the arguments tend to be highly technical and abstract, so much so that, in places, one side will accuse the other, often with some justice, of not knowing what is in fact being discussed. There are communication problems, both between the participants and for the spectators, partly because of the revolution in analytical techniques that has occurred, especially in the U.S.A., over the last twenty-five years and partly because of ideological differences, which are often unconscious (and personality clashes, which are not).

In August 1968 I was asked by the American Economic Association to write a poet for poets survey of these areas for the assocation's *Journal of Economic Literature*. I completed it in early 1969 (see Harcourt, 1969a), and so was able to emerge from behind a door which

225

usually I like to keep open but which for that time had been closed with a forbidding notice saying 'Man at Work' (which someone thoughtfully amended to 'Maniac at Work').[1] I suspect that I was chosen because I had been closely associated with the Cambridge, England, school but also had friendly relations with the other lot, including some of the (then!) younger M.I.T. products and Cambridge, England, men who take an M.I.T. stance on the issues. For convenience of reference, I refer to the first group as Post-Keynesians[2] and to the second as Neoneoclassicals.

The paper is in four sections. First, we set out the historical background and context. Second, we consider the specific capital theory issues – the search for a unit in which to measure 'capital' which is independent of distribution and prices, the role of the concept of the rate of return on investment in the present controversies and the reswitching debates. The third section deals briefly with alternative explanations of the rate of profits in capitalist economies. We close with a short concluding section.

Historical background[3]

While a most complicated subject, the theory of capital is associated with the very fundamentals of the discipline, in particular, with the roles of 'capital' and profits in capitalist societies. Historically, political economy as a discipline developed as an analysis of the 'rules of the game' of capitalist economies, reaching its zenith in this regard with the great classical school of political economists, the leading lights of which were Adam Smith, David Ricardo (aided and abetted by Thomas Malthus) and Karl Marx. I include Marx because he inherited the classical tradition though, of course, he both radically added to and altered it.

Marx, in particular (but drawing on Smith and Ricardo, champions in their own right, not hired prize-fighters), made an especially acute analysis of the workings of capitalism. He gave star-billing to its classes and institutions, respectively, the property-owners and workers, and the competitive market mechanism wherein property-less workers sold their labour power at a (natural) price determined like that of any other commodity by direct and indirect labour components. Profits emerged as a surplus which the property-owners received, not because of their contributions (or those of the means of production, the productivity of which was taken for granted as a technological fact of life) but because of their monopoly of the means of production, especially of the man-made instruments of production (which neoclassical economists, misleadingly in Marx's view, refer to as 'capital'), and their ability to impose the conditions of work, particularly the number of hours worked, on the working class. Marx admired capitalism as a productive machine and recognized that profits were needed for the further accumulation of 'capital' and the ensuing growth of productive power. He believed, of course, that capitalism was but one stage of the historical development of societies, a stage that would eventually give way to a higher stage, nudged bloodily on its way by the workers' revolution.

The so-called marginal or neoclassical revolution, which was associated with Jevons, Marshall and Wicksteed in the United Kingdom, Menger, Walras, Böhm-Bawerk and Wicksell on the Continent of Europe (they weren't all Europeans then) and J. B. Clark in the U.S.A., was in one aspect the non-Marxist backlash. Their answer consisted, essentially, of changing the question. The classical political economists' questions and answers were proving too embarrassing, based, as they were, on the labour theory of value with the further implication that labour was the only socially relevant factor of production, so that wages alone of the distributive shares were not a surplus. Furthermore, they were concerned with the historical processes of growth, accumulation and distribution over time and they stressed conflicting class and political, that is to say, social, relationships and interests. The marginalists skewed the subject round to preoccupation with the formation of equilibrium relative prices in situations of *given stocks* of productive resources, eventually neutrally to be known as inputs $a, b, c,$ . . . rather than as labour, 'capital' and land. The determination of the prices (not rewards) of the services of these inputs was divorced from the institutions and historical processes of society. Classes as a tool of economic analysis went out, the individual, together with his subjective preferences, and algebra came in, and economists, no longer political, started to be concerned with one aspect of life, the theory of rational choice in situations of scarcity – and certainty. Elegance and rigour became (and remain) the rage, but, as we all know, these characteristics are often associated with barrenness and sterility.

The great truths associated with Adam Smith's concept of the invisible hand, which was really concerned with the beneficial effects of competition in a dynamic setting of growth, became formalised beyond recognition into the virtues of the perfectly competitive general equilibrium model as the begetter of a social optimum in a stationary state in which economic power is diffused equally between all individuals. This, though a great intellectual feat in its own right, was not really fertile ground for further developments of practical relevance. The Keynesian revolution of the 1930s was an oasis of realism in a desert of formalism, but generally, economic theory fell on hard times in the interwar years. This has now been admitted by the modern exponents of general equilibrium theory who argue that in attempting rigorously to show why the claims made for the invisible hand might be true, good reasons emerge as to why they are not (see Arrow and Hahn, 1971). Moreover, general equilibrium theory is not descriptive, principally because it cannot handle historical time, being very strong on equilibrium and very weak on how it comes about, i.e. on actual processes. It is able to model time only in so far as time takes on the characteristics of space.

The post-war revival of interest in the problems of growth and accumulation, heralded by Sir Roy Harrod's classics (1939, 1948), and followed up by Joan Robinson's *magnum opus, The Accumulation of Capital* (1956), brought the old issues to the fore again. They were principally preoccupied with the capacity-creating effects of the accumulation of capital goods and the accompanying problem of maintaining full-employment of labour and the stock of capital goods over long periods of time. Modern neoclassical theorists entered the lists in order to tackle, using concepts from the land of the margin, unfinished business and other puzzles thrown up by Harrod and Joan Robinson's work. Empirically, they have used aggregate neoclassical models that stress the principle of substitution and marginal productivity relations (of which more below) in order to attempt to sort out the relative contributions to growth in output per head of the accumulation of capital goods and improvements in technical knowledge.[4] Much of the theory is set in the context of advanced capitalist societies (sometimes treated as socialist ones), with the Neo-neoclassicals playing down the relevance of institutions and social groupings and the Post-Keynesians (and Neo-Marxists, as Joan Robinson and Piero Sraffa made some of Marx's views respectable) playing them up. Add to this, by and large, conflicting political views as between the two groups, as well as a struggle for the 'hearts and minds' of the profession, and it is not surprising that the old flames of controversy flared anew.

Capital theory issues

As far as the capital theory aspects are concerned, there are three main *technical* areas which have been worked over. First, is it possible to find a technical unit in which 'capital' may be measured, a unit which is independent of distribution and prices, so that 'capital' may be used in neo-neoclassical aggregate production function analysis to help to explain the distribution of the national product between wage-earners and profit-receivers?

Second, what is, or should be, the key concept of capital theory – 'capital' itself, together with 'its' marginal product, or, following Irving Fisher and, later, Solow, the rate of interest and the rate of return on investment? (Under conditions of certainty the rate of interest is indistinguishable, as far as orders of magnitude are concerned, anyway, from the rate of profits.)

Third, what determines the level and the rate of profits in capitalist society? The attempted answers to this question have produced, if not the most light, then certainly the most heat, as may be seen by examining the choicer passages in the exchanges between Pasinetti, Kaldor, Meade, Hahn, Joan Robinson and Samuelson and Modigliani in the 1962–6 issues of the *Review of Economic Studies* and the *Economic Journal*, two of the trade's most prestigious journals. (See Pasinetti, 1962; Meade, 1963; Pasinetti, 1964; Meade and Hahn, 1965; Pasinetti, 1966b; Meade, 1966; Samuelson and Modigliani, 1966a; Pasinetti, 1966c; Kaldor, 1966; Robinson, 1966a; Samuelson and Modigliani, 1966b.)

A unit independent of distribution and prices

'Capital' measured in a unit which is independent of distribution and prices has long plagued those economists who have tried to explain processes in capitalist society, because of the dual role which capital goods play. First, they are an aid to production, a role that is common to all societies; second, collectively, they are the owned property of a particular class, enabling capitalists to share in the distribution of the national product. The search for the unit founders on the impossibility of reconciling these two separate roles, a point which the Post-Keynesians have pressed home *ad nauseam*, but which the Neo-neoclassicals have been most reluctant to admit (and, finally, when they have been forced to, as in the reswitching debates of the mid 1960s, have tended to damn as being a non-question in the first place). It should be stressed that it is the *meaning*, not the *measurement* of 'capital' which is at issue.

Why should one want such a unit, anyway? The answer is contained in the neoclassical view (associated, historically, with Wicksell, J. B. Clark (1891, 1889) and Hicks (1932) and given its latest expression by Ferguson (1969)), that the relative supplies of 'capital' and labour, and their accompanying marginal products are *determinants* of the returns to and shares of 'capital' and labour *in the national income*. (These concepts and relationships may make much more sense at the micro level of the individual firm or industry (see Boulding, 1971, p. 338), a view which many Neo-neoclassical economists would heartily endorse.) In order for this to be so, the amount of 'capital' must be measured *prior* to the start of the analysis (as labour may be, making certain approximations, in terms of, say, man hours), even though the prices of the products and of the services of the factors themselves may be determined simultaneously as the equilibrium solutions of a general equilibrium analysis. That is to say, the technical conditions of production, whereby total output is regarded as a function of 'capital' and labour, formally expressed in terms of an aggregate production function,[5] must exist *before* the equilibrium solutions are derived, in the same way as the subjective preferences of individual consumers, the other set of determinants in a general equilibrium analysis and the focal point of the neoclassical marginalist revolution, exist prior to and independently of, the ultimate equilibrium solutions. Only in this way can the relative supplies of 'capital' and labour be regarded as *ultimate* determinants of the shares of profits and wages as capital goods are accumulated over time. But aggregate 'capital' on which the capitalist class earns a uniform rate of profits in competitive conditions must be valued in terms of prices that, themselves, contain the rate of profits as an element. The fact that the prices *and* the rate of profits, and, therefore, the value of 'capital', can be obtained as the *end* results of analysis at each point in 'time' is thus beside the point, as, in this context, is 'the major contribution of the marginal productivity school' whereby is pointed out 'that the theory of factor prices and distribution of income is only one aspect of the general theory of prices and one aspect of general equilibrium theory' (Johnson, 1973, p. 2).

The rate of return on investment

Solow published an important book in 1963, *Capital Theory and the Rate of Return*,[6] in which he attempted to get round 'capital' measurement problems by concentrating, instead, on the rate of return on investment, a view that is in the Wicksell, Fisher tradition. His attempt was not completely successful, even within his own terms of reference, as 'capital' (and 'its' marginal product) had a habit of reappearing, especially in the specification of models for the econometric exercises that were the subjects of the third lecture. The book does serve to highlight some of the basic differences between the Post-Keynesians and the Neo-neoclassicals. Especially did it bring out the relevance of Keynesian *short-run* effective demand puzzles for the longer-run questions of accumulation and distribution over time.

Solow draws on the Fisherian tradition whereby rates of interest are regarded as intertemporal prices. Their determinants are, on the one hand, the preferences of individuals concerning the subjective rates at which they are willing to swap present goods for future goods, and, on the other, the technical possibilities available where, by postponing the consumption of present goods, they may be transformed through the process of saving (*equals* – is – investing) into future goods. (The theory may be interpreted, in one aspect, as a rationalisation for the existence of rentier income.) Solow was principally concerned with the latter set of determinants at the economy level, which he defined in a number of ways as rates of return on investment for society as a whole. He investigated a number of widely different situations in order to establish the equality (or, at least, a close relationship) between the rate of return on investment and the rate of profits under competitive conditions. In those situations where substitution of 'capital' for labour at the margin was possible, the above equality had added to it a further equality with the marginal product of 'capital'. This theoretical background set the stage for empirical estimates of the rates of return on investment in the U.S.A. and West Germany, practical answers to the question: 'What is the (potential) pay-off to society in the future of a little more saving now?'

In a review article of his book by Joan Robinson in the *Economic Journal* in 1964, these matters were thrashed out, Joan Robinson interpreted Solow's purpose as partly to provide a theory of the rate of profits in capitalist society, first, in terms of marginal productivity theory and, second, in terms of the rate of return on investment. As to the former approach, Joan Robinson produced some telling blows that derived from short-run Keynesian theory and the respective 'visions' of the economy that each writer had in mind. As to the latter, she thought at least a variant of the rate of return a superb concept for a Kibbutz, in the sense of being a guide to its members as to the size and differing uses of the annual surplus, but wondered what it had to do with the rate of profits on 'capital' in capitalist society. In my survey article I awarded a victory on points[7] to Joan Robinson, whose fundamental hard-hitting carried the day against Solow's elegent footwork and fancy boxing style. (Solow partially conceded this when in a later paper with Stiglitz, he developed aspects of the basic Keynesian criticisms made by

Joan Robinson of his approach. It then seemed that he had retired altogether but he recently made brief comebacks in the *Times Literary Supplement* (1975a), and *Quarterly Journal of Economics* (1975b).

The reswitching debates

The issues that have received the most prominence in the Cambridge controversies are the related (but separate) phenomena of reswitching and capital-reversing. Technically, *reswitching* (or *double-switching*) is the possibility that the same technique of production may be the most profitable of all possible techniques at two or more *separated* values of the rate of profits even though other techniques are the most profitable ones at rates of profits in between. *Capital-reversing* is the possibility of a positive relationship between the value of 'capital' and the rate of profits when the switch from one technique to another is considered.

In a sense this prominence is misplaced, especially in so far as it related to the papers which were published in 1965-7, principally in the *Quarterly Journal of Economics* and which have received most attention (see Levhari, 1965; Pasinetti, 1966a; Levhari and Samuelson, 1966; Morishima, 1966; Bruno, Burmeister and Sheshinski, 1966; Garegnani, 1966; Samuelson, 1966; Robinson and Naqvi, 1967). First, the phenomena themselves were discovered long before by Joan Robinson (1953-4), Champernowne (1953-4) and, especially, by Sraffa (1960).[8] Indeed, Joan Robinson recently wrote a paper entitled 'The Unimportance of Reswitching' (Robinson, 1975a), which was published in the *Quarterly Journal of Economics*, together with comments by Samuelson (1975) and Solow (1975b) and a reply by Joan Robinson (1975b). Rather, what is involved is the internal logic, and the methodological approach and the 'vision' associated with Neo-neoclassical economics. Underlying those versions of neoclassical economics that are intended to tackle the problems which interested the classical political economists are four propositions (known, now, as the neoclassical parables). Prior to the 1965-7 debates they were regarded as virtually axiomatic. They are (i), (ii) and (iii) negative associations between the rate of profits and the value of 'capital' per man, value of 'capital' to output ratio and sustainable steady-state levels of consumption per head, respectively; (iv) that, in competitive conditions, the distribution of income between wage-earners and profit-receivers may be explained by a knowledge of the 'capital'-labour ratios and the accompanying marginal products of 'capital' and labour which equal the rate of profits and the wage-rate respectively. They express perfectly the notion of price - in this case, the rate of profits - as an index of scarcity, ideal vehicles for 'the apologist for capital and for thrift' (Samuelson, 1966, p. 577).

The fourth parable can be established most easily in a simple one all-purpose commodity world in which 'capital' is assumed to be a primary factor treated as if it were a malleable quantity measurable in its own technical unit, so that the 'capital' to labour ratio may be changed marginally and/or costlessly and timelessly, to any value desired. (This is the notorious assumption of malleability of 'capital' that has received much attention in the literature: see Swan (1956), Johnson (1971, p. 16) and Joan Robinson - anywhere.) The problems associated with the heterogeneity and durability of capital goods, uncertainty and disappointed expectations are abstracted from and accumulation therefore may be analysed as a marginal process. If perfect competition is assumed and profit-maximising businessmen are considered, it follows as a logical inference that, in equilibrium, the wage-rate equals (measures) the marginal product of labour and the rate of profits equals the marginal product of 'capital'. This in turn implies that there is a negative relationship between (the equilibrium values of) the wage-rate and rate of profits, each pair of which is associated with a particular equilibrium position of the economy and 'capital' to labour ratio. The slope of this relationship at each point can be shown to be equal to the 'capital' to labour ratio, and its Marshallian elasticity, to be equal to the ratio of profits to wages in the national income, that is to say, to measure the distribution of income.[9]

In the real world, of course, capital goods are hard objects that take time to construct and to wear out. The expectations of profits entertained for them prior to their installation may not therefore be realised in fact. The value of 'capital' is relevant for the construction of 'capital' to labour ratios and determination of the rate of profits in the economy as a whole. Let us consider worlds in which capital goods *are* hard objects, but from which we banish uncertainty by assuming that each possible world is in long-run competitive equilibrium. Suppose that we can show that the wage-rate-rate of profits relationships associated with these worlds have properties that are identical with those of the corresponding relationship of the simple one-commodity worlds above; in particular, that the slopes measure the (value of) 'capital'-to labour ratios, and the elasticities, the distribution of income, so that the wage-rates and rates of profits may be viewed 'as if' they were marginal products. Then, we would have grounds for believing that behaviour which was true of the simple worlds could also serve to illuminate the behaviour of the more complex ones of heterogeneous capital goods. This was the problem to which Samuelson addressed himself in 1962 in his famous surrogate production function article (Samuelson, 1962a), one object of which was a partial justification of the Neo-neoclassical contribution to growth theory and econometric exercises: see note 4.

There is one special case[10] in which the wage-rate–rate of profits relationship has the desired properties. We consider the wage-rate–rate of profits relationship that is formed by the envelope of the corresponding relationships for each of a number of possible stationary states. Each stationary state is characterized by the conditions of production in each of the industries that comprise it. The wage-rate–rate of profits relationship is obtained by finding the rates of profits that correspond to the range of values of the wage-rate that the economy technically could pay. These are superimposed on one another and the outer envelope so formed shows the stationary states, techniques, and rates of profits that will be associated with particular values of the wage-rate (in long-run competitive equilibrium): see Figure 16.1. If the individual relationships are straight lines, the desired results follow. But a straight line is only obtained when there are identical value of 'capital' to labour ratios in all industries of each economy. This is, of course, the implicit assumption of uniform organic compositions of 'capital' of vol. 1 of *Das Kapital*. It implies that labour values rule, being proportional to the (competitive) prices of production.[11] Once we depart from this assumption, which Böhm-Bawerk used to ridicule and reject (his version of) Marx's labour theory of value, the wage-rate–rate of profits relationship no longer has the desired properties. In particular, reswitching and capital-reversing may occur, so that parables (i) to (iii) no longer necessarily hold true of the heterogeneous capital goods world, and the wage-rate and rate of profits may no longer be viewed 'as if' they were equal to their respective marginal products.[12]

The Post-Keynesian critics of the Neo-neoclassicals fastened onto these results with great glee. Partly, this was because in 1965, Levhari claimed to have shown that reswitching and capital-reversing could not occur in an economy, even if they could in an industry, and partly it was because Samuelson's 1962 article had been interpreted as claiming more for this surrogate ('as if') production function as a justification for neoclassical analysis than was in fact the case. Now that the tumult and shouting have died down, we can see that the real significance lay not in the particular results themselves – no one is going to storm the barricades with a reswitching diagram on his banner, not even one of mine – but because the debate serves to reveal again the inadequacy, for

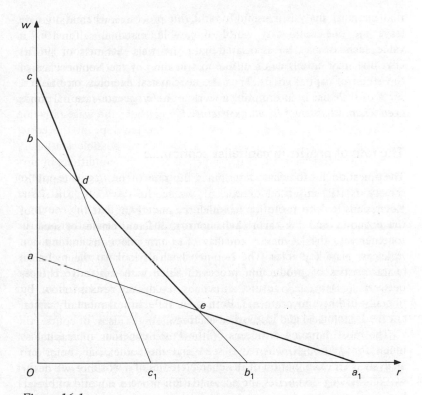

Figure 16.1

Note: aa_1, bb_1 and cc_1 are the (straight-line) $w - r$ relationships corresponding to three stationary states, they form an envelope of $u_1 e d c$, with u being operative for the ranges of w, r corresponding to $a_1 e$, b for those corresponding to ed, and c for those corresponding to dc.

the particular purposes in hand, of a particular methodology. Especially is this Joan Robinson's point. In her 1953–4 paper (and n times since), she has pointed out that comparisons of long-run equilibrium positions one with another are extraordinarily poor guides to what would happen during a process of accumulation of capital goods over actual historical time. All of the reswitching results are either comparisons of stationary states or steadily growing ones in long-run equilibrium, yet all the interesting questions relate to out-of-equilibrium processes. An unfortunate by-product of the analysis has been the belief that at least the ultimate outcomes of processes are inevitably indicated by points on the wage-rate–rate of profits envelope. Moreover, it has been suggested that marginal analysis is useful for studying processes, whereas once we leave the one-commodity world of parable, marginal differences in value such as may be associated with the wage-rate–rate of profits envelope may entail major differences in the physical composition of the stock of capital goods. Thus the neoclassical parables, on balance, seem of little use in interpreting a world of heterogeneous capital goods *even when we abstract from uncertainty.* [13]

The rate of profits in capitalist economies

The question as to what determines the rate of profits in capitalist society is still unsettled except, of course, for Marxists. The Post-Keynesians look to a solution in which the underlying rate of growth of the economy and the saving behaviour of different classes of society, together with the Keynesian equality of *ex ante* injections and induced leakages, play key roles. The Neo-neoclassicals look to the technical characteristics of production processes allied with subjective choices between present and future, either by atomistic consumers or by liberally inclined governments. Both views reflect fundamentally different methodological and ideological leanings.

The most damning criticisms of the Post-Keynesian approach lose much force, though, when it is seen that the context of the critic's analysis is an examination of the characteristics of a world in which the workers' saving dominates the accumulation process, a world of bloodless revolution in which socialism in the guise of a workers' state has been painlessly ushered in and the characteristics of which, though fascinating in their own right, have little to do with a debate about what determines the rate of profits in capitalist society. By the same token, the Post-Keynesian analysis is usually confined to a world of long-run equilibrium in which expectations are realised, so that the expected and realised rate of profits coincide. While it is true that only in this context may we speak rigorously of a rate of profits, it is also true that the expected rate of profits in a world of uncertainty and disappointed expectations is much more relevant to analysis of the distribution of income between classes as capital goods are accumulated over time.

Conclusion

The interpretation that I have given is obviously personal and controversial, a stance akin in some ways to spitting into the wind (with all its accompanying unpleasant consequences). After all, the great bulk of the trade live in the U.S.A. and practise neoclassical economics, so that as a betting man I would put my money on Neo-neoclassical views prevailing, at least in the short run and to the detriment of the discipline's relevance to real problems. Furthermore, it is up to the critics to come up with substantial positive alternatives and this, at last, they seem to be doing, inspired by the re-awakening of interest in the most neglected of all great modern economists, Michal Kalecki, and his mentor, Marx. But that is another story.

Notes

* This paper is a slightly revised version of a paper which was published in *Economic Papers*, no. 49, March 1975, pp. 36–49. It was published in this form by the *Thames Papers in Political Economy*, 1975.

1 I followed the survey with a book of readings (Harcourt and Laing, 1971); *Some Cambridge Controversies in the Theory of Capital* which was published in 1972, and a sequel paper, subtitled 'The Afterglow', in 1973: see Harcourt (1972, 1975a).

2 A misleading title, nevertheless, for a heterogeneous group containing at least three sub-groups – Neo-Keynesians, Neo-Ricardians and Neo-Marxists. While united against a common enemy, they are often as cross with, and in as much disagreement amongst themselves. I have listed the 'heavies' of the two main schools in the text. There are, of course, m and n (where m is considerably less than n) lightweight Post-Keynesians and Neo-neoclassicals respectively scattered throughout the discipline.

3 For a masterly account of the theoretical issues that concern us here, set in an historical context, see Dobb (1973).

4 The seminal neoclassical works are Solow (1956, 1957, 1970a); Swan (1956); Meade (1961); and Arrow, Chenery, Minhas and Solow (1961).

5 Usually, constant returns to scale are assumed, which implies that the production function is linear and homogeneous. It may then be written as $q = f(k)$, where q = output per man and k = 'capital' per man, with $f'(k) > 0, f''(k) < 0$. ($f'(k)$ is the marginal product of 'capital'.)

6 Solow (1963) was originally presented at the prestigious Dr F. de Vries Lectures for 1963.

7 In my book, it was a t.k.o. in the third and final round.

8 Sraffa's 1960 classic, *The Production of Commodities by Means of Commodities*, which is subtitled *Prelude to a Critique of Economic Theory*, had an incredibly long gestation period dating back at least to the mid-1920s (see Sraffa, 1960, p. vi).

9 Refer to the properties of the production function in note 5. Clearly, $f'(k)$ ($= r$, the rate of profits), is smaller, the larger is k. Now $w = f(k) - f'(k)k$ and $\frac{dw}{dk} = -f''(k)k > 0$, so that w is larger, the larger is k. The slope of the $w - r$

relationship, $\dfrac{dw}{dr} = \dfrac{dw}{dk} / \dfrac{dr}{dk} = -k$ and the Marshallian elasticity, $E_, = -\dfrac{dw}{dr} \cdot \dfrac{r}{w} = \dfrac{rk}{w}$.

10 If we confine ourselves to stationary states. There is another special case if we consider steadily growing economies: see Harcourt (1972, p. 149).

11 Consider a two-sector economy that produces a consumption good and a capital good under conditions of constant returns to scale. Ignore depreciation, use the consumption good as *numeraire* and write the 'prices of production' equations of the economy as

$$wl_c + rp_k k_c = 1$$
$$wl_k + rp_k k_k = p_k$$

where l_c, l_k, k_c, k_k are labour and capital good inputs per unit of output in the two sectors and p_k is the price of the capital good in terms of the consumption good. Solving for w in terms of r, we obtain:

$$w = \frac{1 - rk_k}{r(k_c l_k - k_k l_c) + l_c}$$

and solving for p_k in terms of r, we obtain:

$$p_k = \frac{l_k}{r(k_c l_k - k_k l_c) + l_c}$$

If $\dfrac{k_c}{l_c} = \dfrac{k_k}{l_k}$ $(= \lambda)$, $w = \dfrac{1}{l_c} - \dfrac{k_k}{l_c} r$, which is a straight line. Now in this case, $p_k = \dfrac{l_k}{l_c}$ (relative prices are Marxian labour values, independent of r) so that $l_c = \dfrac{l_k}{p_k}$. Therefore, $w = \dfrac{1}{l_c} - \dfrac{p_k k_k}{l_k} r = \dfrac{1}{l_c} - \lambda p_k r$, which is a straight line with a slope of $p_k \lambda$, the value of 'capital' to labour ratio for the economy as a whole.

12 Write $q = rk + w$, so that $k = \dfrac{q - w}{r}$.

Then $dq = rdk + kdr + dw$ and $\dfrac{dq}{dk} = r$ only if $k = -\dfrac{dw}{dr}$. But $k = -\dfrac{dw}{dr}$ only if each wage-rate–rate of profits relationship is a straight line. For only then does $k = \dfrac{q - w}{r} = -\dfrac{dw}{dr}$ (see Garegnani, 1970; Harcourt, 1972, p. 148).

13 The relevance of the results, to the literature on the rate of return on investment, is discussed in a series of exchanges: Nuti (1974), Pasinetti (1969, 1970, 1972, 1974b), Solow (1967, 1970b) and Dougherty (1972).

17 The Cambridge controversies
Old ways and new horizons — or dead end?*

> The established critics of a theory have nearly as much interest in the survival of the theory they criticize as its supporters; for when it is abandoned they are transported from the exciting forefront of current scientific debate to a dignified but unexciting position in the museum of the history of the subject. (Nuti, 1974, p. 364)

> If anything explains the heat of debates in growth [and capital] theory, it is the difficulty thinkers in the scholastic tradition have in appreciating that, for workers in the scientific tradition, it makes sense to entertain a model and use it without being committed to it, while the scientists cannot imagine why mere models should be the object of passion. (Mirrlees, 1973, p. xxi)

I

1. I subtitled an earlier paper on related themes 'The Afterglow', because what have become known as the Cambridge controversies (in capital theory)[1] reached their climax in the reswitching and capital-reversing debates of the mid 1960s and what has come after has been the afterglow, albeit a stormy one at times. The climax itself was not very satisfying because it occurred in the wrong, or at least not in the most important or fundamental areas. In this article I outline the background to the controversies (section I), attempt to sort out some misunderstandings and confusions which have bedevilled the debates, often to the extent that the two sides communicate as little as trains that pass in the night (section II), sketch in the main results and their implications (sections III to VI), and generally try to evaluate and suggest where we are and where we go from here (section VII). We may note immediately the irony that the Cambridge (England) school now appears to be under attack from both ends of the ideological and analytical spectrum. On the one hand, the champions of mainstream orthodox neo-neoclassical analysis are fighting back vigorously. We may cite Hahn's introduction to his now published Ph.D. thesis; Stiglitz's 1974 'view from New Haven', ostensibly a review article of my 1972 *Some Cambridge Controversies*, but in fact his critique of what he takes

239

to be the Cambridge (England) approaches to what he also takes to be the main issues; Blaug's 1974 I.E.A. paperback, *The Cambridge Revolution: Success or Failure?*, a fine surface performance played under ground rules of his own making; Ng's 'non-Cambridge' surveys of the issues as seen by him; and a number of papers in American journals, the objects of which are either to remove entirely or play down the significance of some of the more disturbing results (Hahn, 1972a; Stiglitz, 1974; Blaug, 1974; Ng, 1974a, 1974b; Burmeister and Turnovsky, 1972; Gallaway and Shukla, 1974; Sato, 1974).

2. On the other hand, those members of the Cambridge (England) School who explicitly draw their inspiration from Sraffa's classic *Production of Commodities by Means of Commodities*, have been identified as Neo-Ricardians by some Marxist and Socialist writers (Rowthorn, 1974; Medio, 1972; and in defence, Eatwell, 1974) – and certainly not in a flattering way. The (so-called) Neo-Ricardians' contributions in attacking the inner logic of certain branches of neoclassical economic theory have been recognized and generally applauded; nevertheless their overall approach and influence have been criticized as inimical to a proper understanding of Marxist and/or Socialist economic analysis and practice. For example, Rowthorn (1974) criticizes the concentration on the sphere of circulation and exchange to the (alleged) virtual exclusion of the sphere of production and the role of social relationships within it, which is seen as one of the characteristics of the Neo-Ricardians' approach. Finally, Nuti (1974) now seems to stand apart from *both* the Neo-neoclassicals *and* the Cambridge (England) school. He defends the former against some of the attacks of the latter, but only the better to clear the ground for his own knockdown blow of modern neoclassical analysis (in its general equilibrium form) as an unsuitable and irrelevant vehicle for an analysis of a capitalist economy.

3. The starting point is the proposition that, like all good differentiated products, the neoclassical theory of value, production and distribution comes in at least three handy sizes. Not taking this into account has been the source of confusion and misunderstanding in the literature. A good example is the exchange between Joan Robinson (1971a) and Franklin Fisher (1971). Fisher is pictured as having 'sawn off the bough that he was sitting on [while expecting] . . . to remain in the air all the same' – a reference to his attempt, in Joan Robinson's view, to evade the conclusion that the marginal productivity theory of distribution is rendered meaningless by his demonstration that, in general, aggregate production functions do not exist. While agreeing that 'if aggregate capital does not exist . . . one cannot believe in the marginal product of

aggregate capital', Fisher adds that it does not stop the consideration of the marginal products of well-defined *individual* capital goods – a reflection of his view that the marginal productivity theory of distribution is a microeconomic one. Moreover, the wages in the simulation experiments which confirmed his view that 'aggregate production functions are not generally even good approximate descriptions of the technical conditions of a diverse economy' were generated as marginal products at the micro level.[2]

4. The aggregate production function version, which is associated historically with J. B. Clark (1889, 1891), Ramsey (1928) and Hicks (1932), is the simplest and most persuasive version at both the pedagogic and apologetic levels, even if it is not the most respectable or rigorous one intellectually. Moreover, it links most satisfactorily, on the surface anyway, on to the preoccupation of the great classical political economists with the distribution of income between broad social classes as capital goods accumulate over time. Joan Robinson clearly had it in mind when she wrote her famous paper, 'The Production Function and the Theory of Capital', which was the initial play in the present debates. The charm of the aggregate production function, especially Cobb–Douglas, as a teaching device is self-evident. In its one all-purpose commodity form – Solow (1956, 1970b), Swan (1956) – it is also useful apologetics for reactionaries and revolutionaries alike. For if the distribution of income under competitive conditions is a simple matter of technology allied with relative 'factor' supplies (or of technology and relative 'factor' supplies allied with individual tastes, as Johnson (1971, 1973) reminds us), the unions may be bashed with a clear conscience, while revolutionaries may point out anew the fruitlessness of working within the existing system, so that the only alternative that remains is to smash it completely.

5. The above and other related themes are elaborated by Rowthorn and, also, by Hahn.[3] Hahn (1972a, p. 2) deplores the overlay of ideological claptrap and argues that the 'thing to do is to get the purely technical argument right'. Johnson (1973, p. 37) agrees:

> the positive theory that factors derive their incomes from their contributions to the productive process should be sharply distinguished from the question of whether the owners of the factors are ethically entitled to own them, or whether their returns would be different if ownership or preferences were different.

He does add, though: 'The focal point of social criticism should be the justice of ownership of capital by those who own it or of the processes by which they have acquired and retain it' (p. 117). So perhaps he would agree that, in a social science, ideology and analysis cannot be separated easily, if at all, and that we should be explicit about the presence of both elements.[4] Moreover, it is surely not only for the love of analysis that Samuelson, for example, has returned again to a critical appraisal of Marxian economics. (See, for example, Samuelson, 1971, 1972, 1973; Samuelson and Weizsäcker 1971.) Johnson (1973, p. 117), while asserting the positive purity of his own brand of analysis by maximization and minimization under constraints, suggests that

> economists of socialist persuasion from Marx down to the leaders of the contemporary Cambridge (England) school have attempted to provide apparently scientific underpinnings for their social convictions by efforts to develop theories of distribution in which the returns on capital are not explainable *economically* by its contribution to production but are somehow determined arbitrarily. (Emphasis added)

6. The other versions are, first, the development of Irving Fisher's theories of the rate of interest in an aggregate, economy-wide setting and, second, the modern model of general equilibrium. Solow (1963, 1967, 1970a) is especially associated with Fisher's theories - 'a seminal breakthrough' (Ferguson, 1972, p. 175) - as, in a disaggregated, general equilibrium framework, is Hirshleifer (1958, 1970). Arrow and Hahn (1971) have set out the general equilibrium model and marginal productivity theory in their most general form. Johnson (1971, 1973) set them out in forms which, just because they are more suitable for teaching purposes, have had to draw on some of the characteristics of the aggregate production function model.

7. The implications of the results of the reswitching and capital-reversing debates of 1965-7 bear directly only on the first two versions of neoclassical theory, i.e. the aggregate versions. (That they sometimes have been regarded as all-embracing has been a cause of confusion and misunderstanding: witness the Robinson–Fisher exchange in para. 3 above). I use the term 'aggregate' because this is how these versions are usually described in the literature. It would be unfortunate, though, if it were to be deduced from this term that only aggregation and an index number problem are involved because this is not so. As Joan Robinson (1975a, p. vi) has pointed out, the problem is not the *measurement* of 'capital' but its *meaning* - and that means specifying what sort of economy the writer has in mind - its institutional framework, 'rules of the game', and social relationships. Moreover, if we are dealing with a capitalist economy in which we sharply distinguish between the different classes, there *is* a difference between the

aggregation of, say, 'capital', on the one hand, and labour (and output) on the other. The owners of capital goods have to be paid a uniform rate of profits on their value (in long-run equilibrium).[5] What is involved is the relevant 'vision' of the economic system and the historical processes associated with its development. In particular, stress is laid by the Cambridge (England) school on production and distribution as involving underlying social relations, especially their implications for production and distribution, accumulation and growth, that the capitalists own the means of production (a necessary condition for undertaking production) and the wage-earning classes can only sell their labour services to the capitalists. Capital hires labour but labour does not hire capital. Technically, it refers to those models in which are embedded natural or normal prices – central tendencies – and a long-run normal or natural rate of profits, as opposed to those that are concerned with short-run supply and demand prices which momentarily clear markets and quasi-rents on existing capital equipment.

8. Analytically, *reswitching* (or *double-switching*) is the possibility that the same technique may be the most profitable of all possible techniques at two or more *separated* values of the rate of profits even though other techniques are the most profitable ones at rates of profits in between. *Capital-reversing* is the possibility of a positive relationship between the value of 'capital' and the rate of profits when the switch from one technique to another is considered. The 1965–7 debates were a direct result of the implications of the earlier examples of these phenomena in the literature – Sraffa (1960),[6] Robinson (1953–4, 1956), Champernowne (1953–4) – beginning to sink in and of Levhari's attempt in 1965 (Levhari, 1965) to expunge them, or, at least, to reduce them to the status of curiosa, one a Ruth Cohen curiosum (Robinson, 1956, pp. 109–10).

9. The two aggregate versions of neoclassical theory underlie a significant proportion of the literature of the post-war period, in particular, that part of the modern theory of growth which is couched in terms of aggregate – one all-purpose commodity – neoclassical growth models and the specification of models in econometric studies which attempt to estimate the relative contributions of capital accumulation and technical progress to the growth of productivity in advanced industrial countries. The seminal works in the former area are Solow (1956), Swan (1956) and Meade (1961); the most succinct exposition is Solow (1970b). In the latter area, they are Solow (1957) and Arrow, Chenery, Minhas and Solow (1961). Mention should also be made of Solow's work on theoretical and empirical estimates of the social rate of return

on investment which draws on both aggregate versions of neoclassical theory. There are now literally hundreds of surrogates of these particular 'heavies' in these two branches of the literature.

10. Yet one might be forgiven for thinking, if we may judge from some of the more recent statements of neo-neoclassical economists, that the neoclassical theory of value, production, and distribution is inter-temporal general equilibrium theory, *and no other*, that the other versions are good old Cambridge strawmen rather than good old theory. Thus, von Weizsäcker (1971, p. 97) defines modern orthodox (neo-classical) theory as the general equilibrium theory of Arrow–Debreu. He adds that the 'debates and polemics on capital theory of the last few years make use of models, the assumptions of which are consistent with those of the general equilibrium theory *à la* Arrow–Debreu'. Moreover, 'essentially all the models from Joan Robinson and her direct scholars are to be understood as special cases of the Arrow–Debreu set of assumptions' (p. 97). Within this framework, von Weizsäcker argues, interest rates are but inter-temporal prices and the appropriateness and meaning of the marginal productivity theory of distribution has nothing to do with reswitching, saving behaviour or aggregate 'capital'. It relates, rather, to the propositions that, first, in equilibrium, marginal products of labour equate with, and are measured by, wage-rates; second, in equilibrium, market rates of interest – no uniform rate of profits here – equal 'the private rates of transformation between quantities of consumables at different dates' and 'reflect the social marginal rates of return of savings' (p. 98); and third, that 'income distribution depends on the initial distribution of resources, on preferences and on technology' – 'an interdependent relation' (p. 98). (As he is also happy to live with the possibility of multiple equilibria, he needs not explain what *is* the missing link that would give a *unique* distribution.) Del Punta (1970) quotes with approval the narrow microeconomic bounds within which Schumpeter (1954) confined the rightful use of the concept of a production function and marginal productivity theory proper. (Blaug, 1974, would also approve.) He admits that some degenerate neoclassical practitioners have provided a 'wrong target' which 'Mrs. Robinson's criticisms . . . hit' but adds that *'she has not really criticized the marginal productivity theory as she and her followers seem to think, but only the very questionable way in which some people have thought to be able to use it'* (p. 25, emphasis in original). Yet Ferguson's book (1969) is not the invention of the Cambridge (England) school. And we have no less an authority than Hahn (1972a, p. 8) stating: 'It is extremely unfortunate, and to some

extent the fault of its practitioners, that neo-classical theory has come to be identified with this aggregate version.'

11. Moreover, suppose that we accept that general equilibrium (in its Arrow–Hahn but not its Johnson form) *is* the only intellectually respectable and viable form of neoclassical theory, that it cannot be 'criticized . . . on logical grounds where . . . it is particularly robust' (Hahn, 1972a, p. 2). Are we, then, closer to satisfactory answers to the sorts of questions that the classical political economists were attempting to answer, in particular, the determination of the relative shares of profits and wages[7] as capital goods accumulate over time, and what happens to the living standards of broad class groupings, to the rate of profits (the uniform, long-run, natural or normal rate of profits, that is) and to the techniques of production in the process – broad, aggregative, sociological questions associated with the 'laws of motion' of capitalist societies? The answer is, of course, a resounding 'no', as Hahn for one pointed out over twenty years ago, and for a number of reasons. Consider also Joan Robinson's comment (1951–80, vol. iv, p. 247):

> the concept of the rate of profit[s] on capital is essentially the same in Ricardo, Marx, Marshall, and Keynes, . . . the essential difference between these, on one side, and Walras, Pigou and the latter-day textbooks on the other, is that the Ricardians are describing an historical process of accumulation in a changing world, while the Walrasians dwelt in timeless equilibrium where there is no distinction between the future and the past.

Moreover, all of these questions are as relevant and as in need of answers today as are the other questions which were posed by the classicals, on which the general equilibrium theorists have concentrated and to which they have attempted to provide refined and rigorous answers. Thus Stiglitz's strictures (1974, pp. 898 9) that neoclassical 'distribution theory nowhere requires the use of aggregates' and that basic qualitative statements require 'only convexity of the technology' are beside the point once we ask what is the economy that is being modelled. If it is not a Walrasian world – and it is not – then aggregates are required in order to deal with the social relations in production and distribution. In 'long-run equilibrium theory, capital goods have to be aggregated, in value terms, since the [rate of profits][8] on their value is uniform' (Steedman, 1975b, p. i).

12. It is only by a study of 'disequilibrium adjustments' that we will get adequate answers to the questions posed above.[9] The general equilibrium model is neither designed for, nor adequate to answer such questions, being 'strong on equilibrium and very weak on how it comes

about . . . far less helpful in studying processes' (Hahn, 1973b, p. 327). Tobin (1973, p. 109) concurs. In discussing the treatment of expectations and the problems which they introduce into economic theory 'which Mrs. Robinson rightly and repeatedly stresses', he adds: 'I believe she is right to object that Walrasian general equilibrium, even when enlarged to postulate markets in all commodities in all contingencies at all future dates, is no real solution.' Discussions of sociological factors and of their relationship to economic factors, and of power relationships, are deliberately excluded from general equilibrium. Instead, there is a concentration on the behaviour of self-seeking individuals between whom power is diffused *equally*. The production system is analysed formally in remarkably similar terms to those used in the sphere of circulation and exchange – 'the analogy between the maximization of utility and the minimization of cost (or maximization of profit) may be drawn quite exactly' (Johnson, 1973, p. 3). Technical not social relationships are stressed (see Rowthorn, 1974; Hahn, 1972a, p. 2). Thus we have another paradox: that what to its proponents is its greatest strength – 'the major contribution of the marginal productivity school [was] to point out that the theory of factor prices and distribution of income is only one aspect of the general theory of pricing and one aspect of general equilibrium theory' (Johnson, 1973, p. 2) – is to its opponents its very weakness.[10]

13. General equilibrium theory is not an explanatory (except in the very special sense cited from Debreu, 1959, by Kaldor, 1972, p. 1237) nor a descriptive[11] hypothesis, principally because it cannot handle historical time. The Post-Keynesian criticis, especially Joan Robinson and also, now, Pasinetti (1974a), emphasize the importance of developing economic theory that employs causal models and treats of historical time (the present stands between a past that cannot be changed and a future that cannot be known) rather than of logical time, at any moment of which 'the past is determined just as much as the future' (Robinson, 1962b, p. 26). The use of logical time (until very recently) has been characteristic of general equilibrium models, so that time could be modelled only in so far as it had the features of space.[12] Pasinetti (1974a, pp. 43-4) refers to the approach of Keynes (also Ricardo) which continues to inspire the Cambridge (England) school, whereby an economic theorist has a duty to single out the most important variables and freeze out the others by simple assumptions. There is a directness with which assumptions are stated because 'he is always looking for fundamentals'. 'The characteristic consequence of this methodological procedure is the emergence . . . of a system of

equations of the "causal type" . . . as opposed to a completely inter-dependent system of simultaneous equations . . . the attitude – so common to marginal economic theorists – that "everything depends on everything else".' Furthermore,

> one of the tasks of the economic theorist [is] to specify which variables are sufficiently interdependent as to be best represented by simultaneous relations, and which . . . exhibit such an overwhelming dependence in one direction (and such a small dependence in the opposite direction) as to be best represented by one-way-direction relations.

14. General equilibrium theory is, therefore, a set of consistent equilibrium relations and rigorous statements of what *cannot* be said. The general equilibrium theorists 'show what the world would have to look like if the claim [that a myriad of self-seeking agents left to themselves will lead to a coherent and efficient disposition of economic resources] is to be true. In doing this they provide the most potent avenue of falsification of the claims' (Hahn, 1973b, p. 324). 'In attempting to answer the question "Could it be true?", we learn a good deal about why it might not be true' (Arrow and Hahn, 1971, p. vii). Arrow and Hahn show that it is not possible, except under very unrealistic and special conditions, to prove either uniqueness – 'GE would note at once not only that there may be no equilibrium level, but also that if there is one such level there may be very many' (Hahn, 1973b, p. 324) – or local and/or global stability. The latter is a lack of robustness that neither Arrow nor Hahn thought would emerge when they started on their mammoth task in 1963.[13]

15. Finally, in their more pessimistic moments, anyway, Arrow and Hahn suggest that general equilibrium analysis has now come to the end of a road which started in the last century. We must, therefore, try other tasks – 'If one takes the view . . . a reasonable one . . . that . . . processes must be understood if any actual economy is to be understood, then without denying the great merit of GE in settling a particular intellectual debate one may well wish to argue that the time has come to start from scratch' (Hahn, 1973b, p. 327). Indeed, we need to go back to square one, to wit, the Keynesian short period, from which many of us were reluctant to stray in the first place.[14]

16. The modest claims of Arrow and Hahn contradict Johnson's 'escape by general equilibrium' assertions, as illustrated by his answer to the question

> whether or not it is possible to construct an aggregate production function including capital as an argument and according it a marginal

product? [Thus] . . . it is not always possible mathematically to perform the feat, though it is possible in a large number of cases to do it with enough general equilibrium mathematics. [In any event] . . . no important issue in economics depends on this conclusion, since if one can define the problem one can find the answer with enough mathematical labour. (Johnson, 1973, pp. 36–7)

And, again, on p. 118: 'This appears to pose an insuperable circularity, but it can be handled with sufficient mathematical general equilibrium analysis.' And, yet again, on p. 123:

it is the classical and neo-classical framework of analysis in terms of an aggregate production function . . ., combined with the notion that capital is augmented by saving, that makes the differences between real capital and value of capital a source of difficulty. The value of capital is not necessarily a relevant concept for analysis, and resort to it can be avoided by constructing appropriately disaggregated models.

So sure is Johnson of these views that he is on record recently as follows:

One of the most confident predictions that can be made about the future development of economics is that eventually economic analysis will come to be taught, and research into theoretical and applied problems in particular specialized fields approached, from the beginning in terms of a general equilibrium framework, . . . one including money as a specific element . . .. (Johnson, 1974, p. 7)

Perhaps this statement will come to rival Mill's on the state of the theory of value.

17. Garegnani (1959, 1960, 1970, 1973), while a stern and rigorous – also vigorous – critic of *any* supply and demand approach to the theory of distribution such as is contained in Marshall, Walras and Wicksell,[15] is also critical of the way out suggested above. He is loath to scrap the lengthy tradition in which economic theory is concerned with the determination of natural or normal prices, including a uniform long-run natural or normal rate of profits, and a methodology which employs the comparison of long-run equilibrium positions, such as underlie Ricardo's 'strong cases' and ultimate consequences. To do so would be to confine 'the theory to short-run equilibria and a dynamics made of a sequence of them . . . to a theory which becomes barren of definite results'.[16] Garegnani himself would prefer us to return to classical modes of thought in which the theory of distribution was largely separated *in context* (though not in time) from the theory of value:

distribution is governed by social forces, the investigation of which falls largely outside the domain of the pure theory of value. The proper object of value theory was [and is] . . . the study of the *relations* between the wage, the rate of profits and the system of relative prices. [While] the theory of value will lose the all-embracing quality it assumed with the marginal method[, it will gain] in consistency and . . . in fruitfulness. (Garegnani, 1970, pp. 427–8)[17]

Dobb's new book (1973) may be seen in part as a persuasive argument for this point of view, though with characteristic modesty he refrains from predicting the outcome.

Whatever the particular outcome, one can say that the discussion of the 1960s was manifestly a turning-point. If only because what has been widely accepted as an orthodoxy of the textbooks has been shaken, and an older, discarded tradition revived, nothing can ever be quite the same again as it was before. (p. 266)

II

18. Before we review briefly the relevance of the results of the Cambridge controversies for the first two branches of neoclassical theory, there are a number of further misconceptions that merit discussion. The first is the argument that the Cambridge (England) school do not (or will not or cannot) understand the nature of the solutions to a set of simultaneous equations; they have the choice of being either fools or knaves.[18] It is argued that the Cambridge (England) school confuses equilibrium relationships with causal relationships, in that they believe that marginal products determine (cause, explain) the wage-rate and the rate of profits. The criticism that the use of the concept of aggregate 'capital' involves circular reasoning because it is impossible to conceive of a unit in which to measure 'social' capital that is independent of distribution and prices, is said to be another example of this fallacy. We may quote von Weizsäcker (1971, pp. 97–8) as a typical example of the neo-neoclassical argument:

I really fear that Joan Robinson . . . has not really understood the basic principle of a system of simultaneously solvable equations and therefore worries about the derivation of the rate of interest from the capital stock, while the definition of the capital stock presumes the knowledge of the interest rate. Where does the puzzle come in all this if one has really understood what a system of interdependent variables is about?

Stiglitz (1974), on a similar theme, suggests that the Cambridge (England) school confuses causality in a temporal sense with it 'in the

formal analysis of the structure of a set of equilibrium conditions . . .
only in the temporal sense . . . has [it] any economic significance'
(p. 894). But Pasinetti's discussion of Keynes's (and Ricardo's)
methodology,[19] whereby there is 'an asymmetrical relation among
certain variables, namely as indicating a one-way direction in which, in
a formal sense, the variables of the system are determined', suggests
that it *is* Stiglitz who is confused, especially as he goes on to outline the
conditions under which the marginal productivity of different capital
goods and the rate of interest are *determined* by given endowments of
capital goods and labour. Joan Robinson also has consistently stressed
the difference between logical and historical time and their relation to
equilibrium and causal models, so it is hard to see why she should be
regarded as confused on this point.

19. Anyone familiar with the works of Joan Robinson, Kaldor and
Sraffa really could not argue that they do not understand the nature of
the solutions to sets of simultaneous equations. It is sufficient to cite
the analysis in Joan Robinson's 1953–4 paper and in Sraffa's 1960
book to make this point. When marginal products are spoken of as key
determinants of equilibrium values, what is meant is that the relationships which are being partially differentiated in order to obtain the
marginal products need to be technical relationships, formally akin to
psychological ones like utility functions, so that they exist *before*, and
are *independent* of, the equilibrium values which are the solutions of
the sets of simultaneous equations. (The equalities (or inequalities)
themselves between (say) marginal products and equilibrium prices are
characteristics of the equilibrium solutions. They are therefore the
consequences of the ultimate causes – preferences, technical endowments, and maximizing behaviour. Yet even though there has been
looseness of expression, the thrust of the argument is perfectly clear.)[20]
Clearly, the marginal product of 'social' or aggregate 'capital' cannot be
fitted into this mould because it cannot be measured in a unit which is
independent of distribution and prices. This is what the argument is all
about, and why it is so important to make clear *which* version of the
neoclassical theory is being discussed.[21]

20. In putting forward the above interpretation, I find myself with
some good, if unusual, bedfellows. For, though Hahn (1972a, pp. 2–3)
(also Blaug, 1974, p. 7) quotes with approval D. H. Robertson's statement that the wage *measures* the marginal product rather than the
marginal product determining the wage, in the company of Arrow
(Arrow and Hahn, 1971, p. 4), we have their statement that 'the
marginal productivity conditions help . . . to determine the prices of

resources'. Similarly, we have Pasinetti's reference (1969, p. 511) to Irving Fisher's view that the ' "*marginal* rate of return over cost" . . . an element in our account of the conditions determining the rate of interest . . . supplies, on the . . . productivity side of the analysis, what the marginal rate of time preference supplies on the psychical side' (Fisher, 1930, p. 176). But it should be stressed that Fisher has in mind *annual* rates of interest which clear the loan market. In principle, those of any year do not have to equal those of other years and they certainly are *not* the same concept as the long-run natural or normal rate of profits which J. B. Clark (and indeed the classical political economists themselves) had in mind (see Dougherty, 1972, pp. 1325–6, 1334). Nevertheless, it was this view of Fisher's, together with Solow's work on the rate of return on investment, that led Pasinetti to investigate the conditions under which the rate of return on investment for the economy as a whole could be calculated independently, in all relevant senses, of the equilibrium value of the rate of profits in a 'closed' system. It then could be regarded as a determinant of it. As soon as we consider aggregative shares, broad classes with similar income receipts and spending and saving behaviour, and the rate of profits in the economy as a whole,[22] a valuation problem emerges. We are in a situation where general equilibrium *à la* Arrow–Hahn does not apply. Therefore, it is the aggregative versions of neoclassical theory which must provide the insights if neoclassical theory is to make a contribution. It is therefore beside the point for Stiglitz to accuse the Cambridge (England) school of not understanding what modern general equilibrium theory is about. They are not discussing it but another set of questions to which neoclassical theory was to provide the answers. Hence, also, the amount of time (and space) Joan Robinson has spent showing what the answers would have to be *within their neoclassical contexts*, only to be accused of being a neoclassical economist herself!

21. Garegnani (1959, 1960, 1970, 1973) would have us go further. He argues (see Garegnani, 1959, part II, chapters II and III; 1960, part II, chapters II and III) that Walras was unable to explain the long-run equilibrium rate of profits (unless capital goods are malleable, in which case we would be no longer within the context of Walras's system), principally because the (supply and demand) prices which clear the market for the services of existing capital goods are not in general consistent with the prices of newly produced capital goods within which a uniform rate of profits is included. Later developments in general equilibrium theory, as we saw in para. 20 above, while logically intact, seem to have changed both the questions being tackled and the concepts of equilibrium and prices that are used.

The equality between the interest rate at which a commodity is lent and borrowed, and the rate of *time preference* for the same commodity is solely the preoccupation of general equilibrium theory, while the 'classical' approach focusing on the wage–profit relations says nothing on this. (Nuti, 1974, pp. 357–8)

Garegnani argues that *any* theory based on supply and demand which wishes to provide an explanation of normal prices cannot overcome the problem associated with 'capital' *as a factor of production*, which nevertheless *is* essential to such a theory. If there are fixed specific inputs, the analysis is short run and no uniform rate of profits emerges. Whereas, if there are broad factors, no *independent* quantitative meaning may be given to 'capital', the amount of which is to remain constant. (On this, see also Dobb, 1973, pp. 182, 196.)

22. These views contrast strongly with the alternative explanation offered by Johnson. The corollary of his statement (Johnson, 1973, p. 4), that 'although there are different versions of the [Cambridge, England] approach, . . . all interpret the marginal productivity theory as saying that shares are determined through knowledge of the production function and amounts of the available factors without reference to individual preferences' is that 'the Cambridge (England) school, bluntly speaking, has misinterpreted "orthodox" theory (in their terms) because it has misunderstood it' (p. 37).

23. Another source of confusion is the failure always to distinguish between the critical and the positive tasks that the Cambridge (England) school have set themselves. Too often, the apparatus which has been used for a destruction job within the enemy's frame of reference has been interpreted as the tool with which an alternative paradigm to the currently received neoclassical one is to be constructed. It is inevitable that, sometimes, there will be such a coincidence; nevertheless, the two tasks should be distinguished in principle. Thus, the modes of thought in Sraffa's 1960 book have been so used by some authors, for example, Nell (1967). Just because Sraffa chooses to examine those properties of an economic system which are independent of change does *not* imply, for example, that demand is an unimportant factor in an explanation of price formation in reality, as has sometimes been argued. Of course, it *could* be a sign that Sraffa himself thinks it unimportant.[23] Dougherty (1972) sometimes appears to be confused about the particular objects of particular exercises. In the conclusion to his comment on Pasinetti's 1969 article, he writes: 'The Sraffa/Pasinetti approach seems to favour the analysis of equilibrium in a stationary state' (p. 1348). 'The crucial difference between the two systems [Sraffa/Pasinetti and Irving Fisher]

concerns their scope' (p. 1349). But it is only fair to add that Pasinetti (1969) provides some justification for Dougherty's interpretation. Thus: 'But we possess nowadays much more powerful analytical tools than those which Irving Fisher had at his disposal, and in the following pages we shall be able to analyse, directly with reference to a complete economic system, whether this theoretical framework of Irving Fisher's is consistent . . .' (p. 511). 'The theoretical features of such an economic system have been extensively investigated in recent economic literature [the best single reference is perhaps Sraffa, 1960] and there is no need to go into details here' (pp. 511–12).

24. Nevertheless, Sraffa provided little justification for such a confusion to arise. He explicitly described his work as a prelude to a critique of economic theory, an attempt to provide propositions on the base of which, if they held, the critique itself might be erected.[24] However, the fact that he solved in the process some unsettled questions of political economy, for example, the transformation problem, an invariable or absolute measure of value,[25] both shows that the distinction is often hard to make in practice and provides a hint that he would not be unhappy if the alternative paradigm were to draw on classical, especially Ricardian and Marxian, offshoots. This, in fact, it does appear to be doing, along with the insights of Keynes and Kalecki.[26] Thus, Pasinetti (1974a) has published a book of essays which 'have in common the same basic conception of the working of the economic system' and which explore

> the deep Classical and particularly Ricardian, foundations of Keynesian and post-Keynesian economic theory. . . . Keynes' theory of effective demand . . . so impervious to reconciliation with marginal economic theory, raises almost no problem when directly inserted into the earlier discussions of the Classical economists. . . . [The] post-Keynesian theories of economic growth and income distribution, which have required so many artificial assumptions in the efforts to reconcile them with marginal productivity theory, encounter almost no difficulty when directly grafted on to Classical economic dynamics. (p. ix)

25. It is, therefore, a *non sequitur* to suppose that acceptance of the logic of the critics of neoclassicism inevitably implies either acceptance of the positive alternatives or that the alternatives themselves are free of shortcomings and errors. Nevertheless, real advances have been made, especially in those areas which draw explicitly on the insights of Marx, Keynes and Kalecki.[27] These insights are certainly more than 'the concomitant reliance upon accounting identities rather than behavioural relations' which Ferguson (1972, p. 164) argues that the stress on the

importance of aggregation implies in Post-Keynesian theory. Indeed, it is a fundamental misunderstanding to suppose that identities alone are involved. After all, the essence of Keynes's contribution was to work out the implications of autonomous injections being independent of induced leakages, an extraordinary powerful insight, the value of which should not need restating in this day and age. It is a healthy contrast to Blaug's view that economic theory should be based on a general equilibrium analysis that has no institutional framework, that does not deal with historical time and yet apparently can be used to explain anything (see Blaug, 1974, pp. 84-6). Sometimes, of course, the emphasis in Post-Keynesian theory has been misplaced or misdirected. The exercises in economic growth implied in Golden Age analysis have had too much read into them by their users and their critics, though not by their inventors. The last group have made very modest claims for them and usually, with the exception of Kaldor, have stressed their limitations. (See, for example, Kahn, 1954; Pasinetti, 1962; Dobb, 1973, pp. 233-4.)[28]

III

26. Before the implications of the reswitching debate were given wide circulation, there were a number of propositions which most economists would have regarded as virtually axiomatic. These have become known as the neoclassical parables. They are a negative association between the rate of profits and 'capital' per man (parable 1); a negative association between the rate of profits and the 'capital'-output ratio (parable 2); and a negative association between the rate of profits and sustainable steady-state levels of consumption per head (parable 3).[29] The fourth parable is the marginal productivity theory of distribution, namely, that in competitive conditions the distribution of income between wage-earners and profit-receivers[30] may be explained by a knowledge of 'capital'-labour ratios and the accompanying marginal products of 'capital' and labour which equal the rate of profits and the wage-rate respectively.[31] A corollary of the fourth parable which is of central importance in what follows is that the slope of the wage-rate-rate-of-profits trade-off relationship equals the 'capital'-labour ratio and the Marshallian elasticity at each point measures the distribution of income. I have used the term 'capital' rather vaguely in order to fit in with the existing tradition.

27. The parables may be established most simply within the confines of the J. B. Clark-Ramsey malleable one-commodity or jelly world.

(See Swan, 1956; Samuelson, 1962a; Ferguson, 1969.) In this world the future is collapsed or telescoped, as Joan Robinson has it, into the present and the past into the present, because any disappointed expectations may be overcome immediately. The 'capital'-labour ratio may always be made appropriate by instantaneously and costlessly changing its form and by adding marginally to the 'capital' stock relative to the labour supply. It is, therefore, 'as if' we always have perfect foresight. The parables thus purport to tell us what we may expect from a process of 'capital' accumulation-deepening – whereby the 'capital'-labour and 'capital'-output ratios rise over time. They are the perfect vehicles 'for the apologist for capital and for thrift' (Samuelson, 1966, p. 577). The parables underlie the two important branches of the modern literature of economics that we itemized in para. 9 above and, of course, most of the modern literature on international trade theory.

28. To illustrate the parables, write the constant-returns-to-scale production function as

$$q = f(k) \tag{1}$$

where $f'(k) > 0$, $f''(k) < 0$ and q = output per man, k = 'capital'-labour ratio, all measured in terms of the malleable all-purpose commodity. Each point on the production function is a sustainable stationary state which may be reached by saving (equals investing) the appropriate amount of the commodity. With perfect competition, static expectations, and constant returns to scale, $r = f'(k)$ and $w = f(k) - f'(k)k$, where r = rate of profits and w = wage-rate.

29. From parable 4 we derive a trade-off relationship between w and r which is called the factor price frontier by neo-neoclassicals. The slope of the w-r trade-off relationship equals $-k$, the 'capital'-labour ratio, and the Marshallian elasticity at each point, E, measures the distribution of income, rk/w.[32] These results depend vitally on the equality of equilibrium factor prices with marginal products. We shall draw on them again when we come to Samuelson's surrogate ('as if') production function below.

IV

30. Two things should be noted about the J. B. Clark-Ramsey model. First, the production function allied with perfect competition allows us simultaneously to solve the twin problems of production and distribution in terms of our knowledge of the technical characteristics of the production function and relative factor supplies. Second, we may use

marginal concepts in order to analyse the process of accumulation through the substitution of 'capital' for labour over time because always the appropriate 'capital'-labour ratio may be established. But in order to do this we have to abstract from the following characteristics of real capitalist economies. First, 'capital' has at least two separate meanings - finance seeking investment opportunities and hard objects that often take long periods to construct and have long lives, so that the hopes entailed when the finance was first committed may well turn out to be dashed by actual events. This reflects the essential nature of investment as a commitment of finance and resources in the face of uncertainty. When expectations are not realized, the calculations of the man of words and of the man of deeds part company for ever (Robinson, 1953-4, p. 81, n. 1).

31. Second, when we look outside the one-commodity world for a unit in which to measure 'social' capital as the counterpart to land and labour in the classical triad, we are forced inevitably to use a price measure which, itself, contains the rate of profits. That is to say, the marginal product of 'social' capital, even if it could be given a meaning, is not independent of the value which it itself is trying to help determine (unlike the marginal products of land and labour, the intensive and extensive margins of the Malthusian–Ricardian theory of rent from which the marginal productivity theory of distribution originally derived, see Garegnani, 1970). Unlike 'capital', aggregate labour and land may be measured in terms of their own physical units.[33]

32. Nevertheless, Samuelson (1962a) wished to argue that for some purposes, in particular, aggregate neoclassical growth models and econometric specification of the aggregate production function, it certainly would be useful and possibly would be justifiable to abstract from the puzzles outlined above. He wished to view both theoretical concepts and actual statistics 'as if' they came from the J. B. Clark–Ramsey jelly world, even though we know in fact that the world contains heterogeneous capital goods of all manner of sizes, shapes and durability. He proposed to show that under certain conditions a marriage could be arranged, through the good offices of the surrogate production function, between the world of jelly and the heterogeneous capital goods world of 'reality' in which *ex post* substitution of capital goods for labour within a technique was ruled out.

33. He proceeded as follows: suppose that there are known a number of different constant-returns-to-scale techniques for producing, by means of a capital good and labour, a consumption good and the capital good itself. Each technique contains a consumption good sector and a

capital good sector and constitutes a stationary state in which the consumption good alone features in the net product of the system. The capital goods differ from system to system. Corresponding to any arbitrarily given value of either w or r, there will be either one technique which is the most profitable or pays the highest wage-rate (or two which are equi-profitable or pay the *same* wage-rate). Moreover, if we assume perfect competition, and that expectations are always realized, this, in fact, will be the stationary state in existence. It will be in long-run competitive equilibrium with a uniform wage-rate and rate of profits and, so, 'normal' prices ruling.

34. If we use the consumption good as *numeraire* (and ignore depreciation), we may obtain from the price equations in Samuelson's example the following expressions for the w–r trade-off relationship (or factor price frontier, in Samuelson's terminology) in the heterogeneous capital goods world and relative prices respectively:

$$w = \frac{1 - rk_k}{r(k_c l_k - k_k l_c) + l_c} \tag{2}$$

$$p_k = \frac{l_k}{r(k_c l_k - k_k l_c) + l_c} \tag{3}$$

where l_c, l_k, k_c, k_k are labour and capital good inputs per unit of output in the consumption and capital goods sectors respectively and p_k is the price of the capital good in terms of the consumption good.

35. Now assume that $k_c/l_c = k_k/l_k = \lambda$, where λ is a constant, i.e. there are identical capital good–labour ratios in both sectors. (A special case of this assumption is $k_c = k_k = k^*$, $l_c = l_k = l$, i.e. we have effectively, from the point of view of production, a one-commodity world, which Garegnani (1970) argued that Samuelson's special case essentially is.) We obtain:

$$w = \frac{1}{l_c} - \frac{k_k}{l_c} r \tag{4}$$

$$p_k = \frac{l_k}{l_c} \quad (= 1 \text{ when } l_c = l_k = l) \tag{5}$$

Expression [4] is a straight line. Moreover, it is easy to show that the slope of the straight line, k_k/l_c, is, in fact, the value of 'capital' to labour ratio for the system as a whole.

36. From [5],

$$l_c = \frac{l_k}{p_k} \tag{6}$$

Substituting expression [6] in expression [4], we obtain

$$w = \frac{1}{l_c} - \frac{p_k k_k}{l_k} r = \frac{1}{l_c} - p_k \lambda r \qquad [7]$$

where $p_k \lambda$ is the value of 'capital' to labour ratio for the system as a whole.[34]

37. Now examine the three possible w–r trade-offs in the top half of Figure 17.1. In the bottom half are shown the values of k (in terms of the consumption good) corresponding to each trade-off. The unbroken

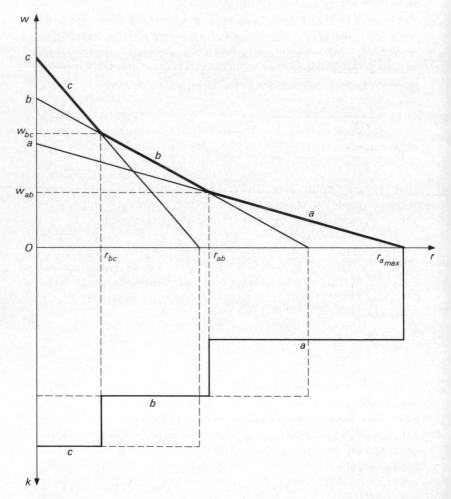

Figure 17.1

lines indicate which value of k is associated with the outer envelope made by the w–r trade-offs (shown as thicker lines). With competition ruling, only points on the envelope are possibilities. It is easy to show – see the Appendix at the end of the article – that if w–r trade-offs are straight lines, the value of k for each relationship is invariant to changes in r. (If they are concave to the origin, $dk/dr > 0$, and if they are convex to the origin, $dk/dr < 0$.) The economic reason for the invariance of k with respect to r in the straight-line case is that p_k is then independent of the level, and changes in the level, of r. Thus, in expression [5], p_k equals the ratio of the direct labour inputs in the two sectors, l_k/l_c. Marxian labour values thus rule, p_k is independent of r.
38. From Figure 17.1 we may see, for example, that lower rates of profits are associated with higher values of k. These associations are akin to parable 1. It is also easy to show that there are inverse relationships between k/q and r (parable 2) and sustainable steady states of consumption per man - q - and r (parable 3).[35] Moreover, the slope at *each* point on the envelope is equal to the appropriate value of 'capital'-labour ratio so that the Marshallian elasticity at each point, E, is a measure of the distribution of income, rk/w (parable 4). That is to say, there is a seeming correspondence between the four parables of the jelly world and those of the completely different world of heterogeneous capital goods. Therefore, we may interpret r and w 'as if' they were marginal products of (jelly) capital and labour respectively and we may use the slope of the envelope as a simple one-number measure of 'capital' per man. Moreover, as expression [4] is but a special case of expression [2], it was hoped that this interpretation might survive the relaxation of the special assumptions which transformed expression [2] into expression [4].

V

39. There are, however, at least two serious flaws in the justification (to the first of which Samuelson at Garegnani's behest drew attention in his 1962 paper and which he analysed in his 'summing up' paper, Samuelson, 1966). First, suppose that in the heterogeneous capital goods world we have curved instead of straight-line w–r trade-offs within each technique. Consider Figure 17.2 in which both capital-reversing and reswitching occur. It can be seen immediately that, in general, parables 1–3 need no longer hold. For example, as we consider values of r just below r_{ba}, the value of 'capital' per man moves in the *same* direction as r.

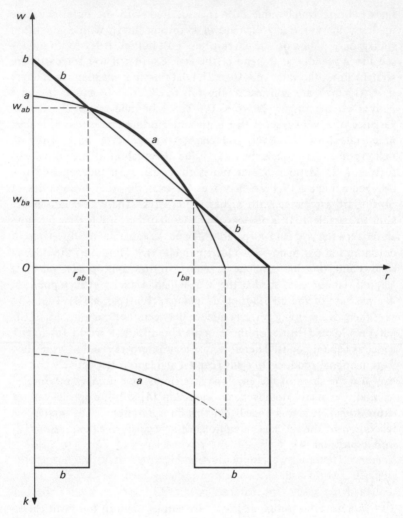

Figure 17.2

40. Now consider the curved w–r trade-offs for *one* technique shown in Figure 17.3. We know that, always, $q = rk + w$ so that $k = (q - w)/r$ by definition. The tangent of the angle θ in Figure 17.3 equals $(q - w)/r$ for the point P on the w–r trade-off curve. $-dw/dr$ is the slope of the tangent to the curve at P. Clearly the two measures are not equal. But $k = (q - w)/r$ is always true by definition so that, in general, $-dw/dr \neq k$ for non-straight w–r relationships[36] and the elasticities at

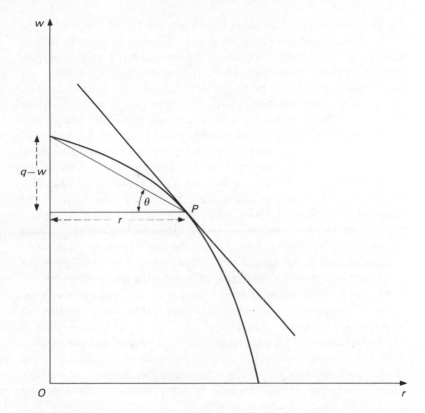

Figure 17.3

the points on the envelope are *not* measures of the distribution of income. Therefore we cannot view observations 'as if' they came from the jelly world – in particular *r* and *w* may not be viewed 'as if' they equalled the respective marginal products of 'capital' and labour and $-dw/dk$ is not a simple, one-number measure of *k*. With straight-line *w–r* trade-offs they may be so viewed. However, as we shall see, in one sense the straight-line world of Samuelson is really a one-commodity (or, at least one-sector) world,[37] within the confines of which no one ever doubted the truth of the parables anyway. In another sense, it leads only to a pseudo-production function. So that the 'logical soundness of J. B. Clark-type models of production does not imply that the operation of an actual economy can be investigated *as if* the productive transformations of the economy were summarized by a production function' (Nuti, 1974, pp. 350–1).

41. One interpretation of Samuelson's assumption of proportionality of the capital good–labour ratios is that the outputs of both sectors must be the *same* good physically – the 'corn as input, corn as output' case of Ricardo, if you like. Then, as between techniques, there are only changes (which may be marginal) in the seed corn to labour ratios. We are in a one-commodity world. This, however, is an uncharitable view. If we view Samuelson's example as a special case of Sraffa's production systems in which 'commodities are produced by means of commodities', there *are* different capital goods as between the systems.

42. Now consider the example of 'production of commodities by means of commodities' in Robinson and Naqvi (1967, p. 585 *passim*). In one of their examples, (B), *when* $r = 0$, the *labour* value of the means of production to labour ratios are the same in all industries of a given economy, *even though there are different proportions of each commodity in the various means of production*. (Samuelson's example is a special case of this special case.) This implies that the values of the means of production, i.e. the value of 'capital' to labour ratios for the systems as a whole, are invariant to changes in r and that the w–r trade-off relationships will be straight lines. But it does not imply that we have returned to the jelly world.

43. From these results we may move on to our second and more fundamental criticism that in general the marriage between the heterogeneous capital goods and jelly worlds has only seemingly achieved a satisfactory union, *even in the straight-line case*. It is true that in the jelly world we are able to have a *marginal* process of substitution of 'capital' for labour. In the other world, however, we may only have a series of comparisons, one with another, of alternative equilibrium stationary states, each with its *own* past and expected future. That is to say, moving up the factor price frontier envelope consists of us passing from one state to the other, not of a process of substitution of 'capital' for labour in historical time. Only a pseudo-production function has been created (see Robinson, 1970a and Harris, 1973). An attempt to *change* from one stationary state to the other by, for example, changing the rate of accumulation, would rupture the economy's long sustained equilibrium state and usher in a transition-out-of-equilibrium process. Comparisons of long-run equilibrium states are very poor guides as to what may either initially or even ultimately happen during such a process[38] – as Joan Robinson pointed out ages ago (see Robinson, 1953-4, 1975d). Hence her cryptic injunction to Gallaway and Shukla (1974, p. 348 n.*): 'Do not bother. Neoclassical theory is no better off even when there is no reswitching.'[39] Samuelson (1974c, p. 18)

concurs: 'steady-state relations . . . cannot correctly be used to describe time-phased input–output relations that hold in *un*balanced dynamic paths.'

44. Moreover, even with straight-line *w–r* relationships, marginal changes, even if they could occur, may not be sufficient to take the economy from one equilibrium position to another. Even if only small differences in the value of 'capital' are involved, yet nevertheless, wholesale differences in the composition of the means of production also may be involved; indeed, in general, they will be. In any event, as Pasinetti (1972, p. 1352) stated succinctly, 'continuity in the scale of variation of the rate of profits *does not* imply continuity in the change of amounts of capital per man'. Concentration on the absolute equality of the inputs in the two sectors as happened in Garegnani's criticism of Samuelson's analysis fortuitously excluded this more fundamental point.[40]

45. A divorce between the two worlds would seem to be in order.

VI

46. We now come to the modern work on Irving Fisher's concepts in *aggregative form*. Solow has been the most prominent writer in this area and Ferguson, his most enthusiastic proponent:

> The situation appeared almost hopeless for *aggregate* neoclassical theory until a seminal breakthrough by Solow, 1963, 1967, established the grounds for resurrecting *aggregate* capital theory. He proved that under certain weak assumptions the rate of interest, however defined, must equal the social rate of return on investment.[41]

The essence of Solow's argument (in Ferguson's hands) is that 'arbitrage . . . a fact of life . . . in a capitalistic system . . . guarantees that the rate of interest must equal the social rate of return. All of the *essential* inferences of neoclassical theory follow . . ., including inferences concerning distribution' (Ferguson, 1972, p. 175, emphasis in original), and all without any *necessary* need (as opposed to practical and/or empirical expediency) to resort to a 'capital' aggregate or value or marginal product *of any sort*. Hahn, in referring to Bliss's 'splendid paper (Bliss, 1968b) and Solow's fine book', makes a more cautious assessment: 'Sometimes this [the measurement by the rate of interest of the social rate of return to the economy as a whole] can be demonstrated' (Hahn, 1972a, p. 1). Solow, too, is more cautious, he wished only to demonstrate 'the much weaker proposition [than the *necessary* equality of the rate of interest and the social rate of return] that if the private and social marginal products of capital coincide, then the private and social rates of return will coincide' (Solow, 1963, p. 65).

47. The social rate of return on investment in all of its variants, from one period to perpetuity, is a measure of the pay-off to society in the future of a little more saving now.[42] In order empirically to estimate it, Solow used a vintage model (so as to include embodied technical progress) with a one-number measure of the capital stock, a model in which, under conditions of perfect competition and certainty, certain simple relationships between the social rate of return on investment, the marginal product of 'capital', and the rate of profits could be shown to exist (see Solow, 1963, lectures 2 and 3; Harcourt, 1972, chapter 3). Either an 'as if' one-commodity world was assumed or certain assumptions had to be made about the price levels associated with the initial, final and 'otherwise' situations, namely, that they were common to all situations and unaffected by the transition. Technocratic comparisons between the situations were held to describe the actual process of accumulation that implementing the schemes would imply. These themes were examined further in his 1967 paper. Switch-point comparisons (which imply given and common prices in the two situations) were used to establish the equality of the social rate of return with externally given values of the rate of interest and to indicate the nature of the transition processes that were involved. Solow confined himself to models of centrally planned economies and talked only of the rate of interest being 'an accurate measure of the social rate of return to saving' (p. 30). At the end of his 1963 lectures, Solow hinted at the presence of a *full* Irving Fisher model underlying his work by referring to discrepancies between his estimated rates of return on investment in the U.S.A. and the indications given of the orders of magnitude of marginal time preference in the U.S.A. by the rates of interest on riskless assets (Solow, 1963, p. 96). But that is the only hint given. Principally he concerns himself with an aggregate, economy-wide version of Fisher's investment-opportunity curve, and 'is ambiguous on whether or not he operates with a general equilibrium system' (Nuti, 1974, p. 361).

48. It was these constructions which lay behind Pasinetti's reconsideration of Fisher's analysis and its extension to the modern context (Pasinetti, 1969, 1972), as Dougherty (1972) is careful to point out. Thus:

> a careful reading of Dr. Pasinetti's article reveals that . . . he is not
> . . . attacking the Fisherian theory of the rate of profit [;] . . . his

objective is to demolish any suggestion that a 'Fisherian' concept of the rate of return could be used to resurrect John Bates Clark's parable of the determination of the rate of profit . . .. (p. 1324)

But, as the development of Pasinetti's article, in Dougherty's view, was such that it *could* be interpreted as an attack on Fisher's logic *within Fisher's own context*,[43] Dougherty came steadfastly to his hero's defence.

49. Pasinetti wished to show at least three things. First, that Fisher's constructions were meant to provide the productivity side of his theory of the rate of interest (profits?) in the economy as a whole. The quote in para. 20 above concerning the purposes which the 'marginal rate of return over cost' came to fulfil is his evidence for this proposition. It should be clear by now, though, that, if we accept the interpretation of the modern general equilibrium theorists, Fisher's rate of interest and the rate of profits for the economy as a whole are not the same thing. Thus, as we change from one to the other, so we change from Fisher's context to the specification of the models in Solow's theoretical and empirical work, and also to a consideration of neoclassical answers, either actual or what logically would be required, to classical questions.

50. Second, Pasinetti wanted to derive the conditions whereby the rate of return on investment, as well as being *a* determinant of the rate of profits, would also act as a well-behaved index of scarcity of 'capital' in a general equilibrium system of prices. Then, in so far as the rate of profits was equal to the rate of return, the rate of profits would also be a well-behaved scarcity price.[44] That Fisher (as well as Solow) had in mind the overall system is at least suggested by Dougherty's quote from Fisher (1972, p. 1348, n. 2), to the effect that it was only for simplification that prices were taken as given while the rate of interest was investigated. But, again, it may have been a different concept that Fisher had in mind; in particular, in Dougherty's view, there is *no* suggestion that in the *Fisherian model* the rate of profits would clear a market for 'capital' or act as a scarcity index of 'capital'. Third, Pasinetti wished to show that the argument has been confused by two different concepts having the same name, to wit, the marginal product of 'capital'.

51. Dougherty (1972), when defending Fisher, considers these aims of Pasinetti redundant and irrelevant, first, because neoclassical capital theory can do without the concepts of 'capital' and the rate of profits, so that this generalization of Fisher's work is in *physical* (completely disaggregated real) terms, not in value terms. Second, because Fisher sacrificed rigour only in order to communicate with businessmen and

politicians, so that 'the purely didactic concept of the rate of return' which allowed this dialogue to take place nevertheless was not strictly needed for his theory. So again Dougherty has taken himself back to the general equilibrium domain of momentary or temporary equilibrium and annual rates of interest while Pasinetti wishes to discuss applications outside it. We may notice also Blaug's criticism of Pasinetti, to the effect that he ignored 'Fisher's well-known objections to the view that interest is a distributive share . . . [because for] Fisher, interest was a way of looking at income of every kind' (Blaug, 1974, p. 50, n. 1). This, too, supports the view that it was Solow's work and the traditional marginal productivity theory, set in a classical context, that Pasinetti had in his sights.

52. Pasinetti's argument contains essentially two steps. The first is to show that if the rate of return on investment in an aggregate or economy-wide sense can be defined independently of prices as a ratio of physical quantities, then Irving Fisher's marginal rate of return over cost, a marginal concept in the full sense of the word, including its traditional association with continuity, emerges with the corollary that there is a downward sloping relationship between the quantity of 'capital' per man, on the one hand, and the size of the rate of return, on the other hand. Pasinetti illustrates this proposition with a 'corn as seed corn, corn as output' example within the context of a Ricardo–Sraffa circulating capital goods model. As the measure is independent of prices and the rate of profits, it could form the basis for the construction of an investment-opportunity curve with the 'right' shape.

53. The social rate of return on investment is essentially a consumption foregone, consumption thus gained, concept. At an aggregate level, the consumption foregone – saving – has to be invested: new capital goods have to be constructed in an out-of-equilibrium transition process – and the impact of this on the overall price level cannot be ignored.[45] Moreover, more than a marginal change in the composition of the means of production before and after the transition may be involved, as we saw in another context in paras 42–4 above. Pasinetti shows that if we assume malleability (no redundancy of commodities in the means of production because of the transition), infinite possibilities of substitution and the 'unobtrusive postulate' of no capital-reversing, then, even though the calculations of the rate of return at every level depend on arbitrarily chosen sets of prices yet, in all *essential* respects, the rate of return so calculated is akin to the corn rate of return above. It may be given a marginal interpretation, it is 'well-behaved', and it can act as a determinant of the rate of profits in the economy as a whole.

54. Once we remove the 'unobtrusive postulate', i.e. allow for the possibilities of capital-reversing and reswitching, however, the (physical and value) marginal interpretations are no longer possible: 'continuity in the scale of variation of the rate of profits *does not* imply continuity in the change of amounts of capital per man' (Pasinetti, 1972, p. 1352). The social rate of return on investment ceases to have the relevant properties of the corn rate of return. In this context, Pasinetti's argument seems unassailable though it is, of course, Solow's rather than Fisher's arguments and applications that he ultimately has in mind. Dougherty, however, was not concerned to discuss Solow's applications in his actual defence of Fisher and this is one source of the disagreement between Dougherty and Pasinetti. When Dougherty and Pasinetti clash over the implications of the rate of return making no sense unless one assumes 'that there exists an infinite number of techniques and that the transition from [one to the next] requires a very small amount of investment ("a marginal change")' (Pasinetti, 1972, p. 1351; Dougherty, 1972, pp. 1345–6), it is because Dougherty is arguing that Fisher does not *need* the concept for a full and rigorous general equilibrium analysis of inter-temporal prices in which the production sets and consumer preferences are defined in completely disaggregated, real terms and in which there need be no uniform rate of profits for the economy as a whole. Pasinetti, by contrast, is arguing that the concept of the rate of return on investment *must* survive in order that the theoretical and econometric specifications that Solow was attempting may survive as well. Moreover, in Pasinetti's view the latter *are* an application of Fisher-type analysis to the traditional classical political economists' problem. Presumably, Pasinetti would argue (as Garegnani and Dobb do, see para. 21 above) that the general equilibrium framework of supply and demand cannot provide a theory of a long-run normal rate of profits because a concept of 'capital' *is* necessary for this and cannot be defined prior to the start of the analysis,[46] at least in the present context. Pasinetti is examining the logical underpins of Solow's 'cheap vehicles [one capital good models] for interpreting data (which seem to behave that way)' (Solow, 1970b, p. 424) – and finding them wanting. It could also be pointed out that the cheap vehicles work *because* the data seem to behave that way – and not the other way round (Fisher, 1970).

55. Finally, one should mention the subtle change in the meaning of the marginal product of 'capital' that has taken place in these discussions. The traditional meaning, according to Pasinetti (1969, pp. 529–31), is the incremental change in output in relation to the

incremental change in 'capital' when the rate of profits is changing infinitesimally. One technique ceases to be the most profitable and another takes its place, but only a marginal change is involved – hence the need to measure 'capital' independently of the rate of profits and, so, unaffected by Wicksell effects, yet in a homogeneous unit. In general equilibrium theory proper and in the aggregate analysis of the rate of return on investment, the marginal product of 'capital' has been measured in terms of constant (equilibrium) prices with only 'quantities' allowed to change. In the aggregate analysis, a switch-point comparison is made and the price level is common to both the initial and final situations. The marginal change is obtained by considering only an infinitesimal change in the proportions in which two equiprofitable techniques are combined. In the general equilibrium example, we consider sets of inputs and sets of outputs, all of which are 'close' to their respective counterparts. They are then valued at the one *set* of equilibrium prices, namely, those associated with the equilibrium point around which a notional change is being considered. The unit of measurement is Swan's equilibrium dollar's worth.[47]

56. In aggregate analysis of the distribution of income, 'capital' has two dimensions, prices as well as quantities, and so it seems wrong to take a partial as opposed to a total derivative. When the latter is done, price and real Wicksell effects occur and rupture the equality between the rate of profits and the marginal product of 'capital'.[48] The definition used by Malinvaud (1953) (and, of course, by many other economists by the time that he wrote) was designed to overcome the puzzle, namely, that what individuals in a competitive situation may take as parameters become variables for the system as a whole when individuals act simultaneously. He preferred his definition, whereby he related 'the gain in consumption . . . to the corresponding increase in social capital . . ., both . . . evaluated [at a common set of prices]' (Malinvaud, 1953, p. 261), to that used by 'a long line of economists', including Wicksell. They defined the marginal product of 'capital' 'as a ratio between the increase in value of commodities . . . to the increase in value of real capital' in which both prices and quantities changed. The virtues that Malinvaud saw in his definition included the equality ('just') of his concept with the rate of interest, its suitability for welfare analysis, and that it was '*directly* related to the physical conditions of production, like other substitution ratios in an efficient position' (p. 261). But this is achieved only by considering marginal changes and individual capital goods and proceeding

as though relative prices in the two states [of the economy being compared] were identical. As a device for micro, partial, or efficiency analysis, this approach is acceptable. In the study of income distribution, however, it is not, and differences in relative prices between the two states must be taken into account. (Rowthorn, 1974, pp. 72-3, n. 7)

It is the inability to escape from these limitations which prevents the extension of the Malthusian–Ricardian theory of rent to all 'factors', i.e. to including 'social' or 'aggregate' 'capital' on all fours with labour and land.

VII

57. We now conclude: if the arguments of this article are accepted, while general equilibrium *may* emerge logically intact as 'the theory of inter-temporarily efficient paths and their price duals' (Hahn, 1972a, p. 3), it is *not* the theory which is relevant for the issues raised in the Cambridge controversies. The attempts to use the other versions of neoclassical theory flounder both on the results of the reswitching and capital-reversing debates, with which is allied the problem of the measurement of 'capital',[49] and the (more fundamental) criticisms that stem from the distinction between comparisons and changes.

The problem of the 'measurement of capital' is a minor element in the criticism of the neo-classical doctrines. The major point is that what they pretend to offer as an alternative or rival to the post-Keynesian theory of accumulation is nothing but an error in methodology – a confusion between comparisons of imagined equilibrium positions and a process of accumulation going on through history.[50]

The latter unfortunately have been overshadowed by the extent of the literature that has grown up around reswitching and the misconceptions that have accompanied it.

58. We therefore have to start on a different tack. One possibility is the 'here and now' of the Keynesian–Kaleckian short period and its developments which have been neglected in the literature on the theory of growth (though the hints are certainly there in *The Accumulation of Capital*, Robinson, 1956). 'The Keynesian method is to describe a set of relationships (intended to correspond . . . to the relevant features of the economic system) and to trace the effects in the immediate and further future of a change taking place as an event at the moment of time' (Robinson, 1975f, p. 92). There is *some* common ground *between*, but not necessarily *within*, both sides on this one. Thus, we noted earlier

(see para. 17 above) that some critics of neoclassical analysis, for example, Garegnani and Dobb, are not only reluctant to give up classical preoccupations and methods of long-run analysis, but, also, view the alternative paradigm itself as growing, in some respects, out of a return *to* classical modes of analysis. Thus, though they may accept Joan Robinson's argument that equilibrium comparisons can rarely analyse changes in the context of an analysis of the process of the accumulation of capital goods, they would not accept it as a general critique of the methodology of traditional economic analysis. Other critics of neoclassical analysis *are* more inclined to accept it and so do look to the Keynesian–Kaleckian short period, to expectations and to the linking together of short periods in dynamic sequences as an alternative method of approach. In this, of course, they are joined by many more orthodox economists, for example, Bliss, Hahn, Samuelson and Stiglitz. A related approach is also taken by Hicks in *Capital and Time* (Hicks 1973), in which out-of-equilibrium processes are analysed in a sequential fashion, with emphasis placed, however, on the time patterns of production.

59. The other avenue of analysis by which a satisfactory theory of the 'laws of motion' of capitalist society might be developed has been suggested by the Marxist economists (see, for example, Meek, 1967, p. 112, Rowthorn, 1974, pp. 75–87). It is the attempt to develop a theory of *endogenous* technical progress by reasserting Marx's own emphasis (which is associated with his theory of the origin of profits) on the importance of the sphere of *production* as opposed to the sphere of circulation and distribution, in particular, the conditions of work and production themselves and the modes of extraction of the surplus. It has been the neglect of these elements and of the concept of the mode of production which is the main basis for the dissatisfaction of many Marxist and Socialist economists with the approach and contributions of the so-called Neo-Ricardian school. The suggested approach itself involves detailed studies of working hours and conditions, of worker attitudes, of hierarchical structures in modern industry, and of the reactions of businessmen to competitive pressures as far as the accumulation of new capital goods and reorganization of existing layouts are concerned. In these ways, as well as by the more traditional stress on pricing and distribution and financing, macro and micro theory could be fruitfully integrated.[51] In doing so, moreover, we may not only take up again the classical and Marxian traditions but may also return, as Victoria Chick has it, to the 'Cambridge [England] tradition of economics as a moral science, with its acknowledgement that a

changing universe is its subject, [to] acute observation, sense of relevance and social purpose, [and to a] willingness to use . . . intuition at the same level as . . . intellect'. Thus we may escape from a tradition whereby 'today's economists [are] trained to use pure logic to extend and refine existing theory, on the implicit premiss that immutable laws can explain economic events. Unfortunately new theory is not created, nor old theory understood, by the exercise of logic alone' (Chick, 1975, p. ii).

Appendix[52]

$$k = \frac{q - w}{r}.$$ [A.1]

Differentiate k with respect to r to obtain

$$\frac{dk}{dr} = \frac{1}{r}\left[-\frac{dw}{dr} - \frac{q-w}{r}\right].$$ [A.2]

Thus,

$$\frac{dk}{dr} \gtrless 0, \quad \text{if} -\frac{dw}{dr} \gtrless \frac{q-w}{r}.$$ [A.3]

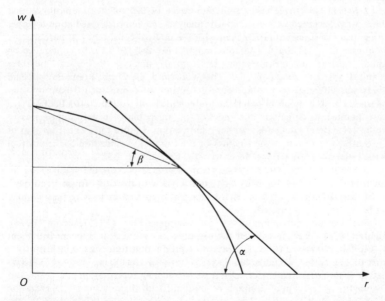

Figure 17.4

Now $-\dfrac{dw}{dr}$ is represented by tan α, and $\dfrac{q-w}{r}$ by tan β in Figure 17.4, which illustrates the case of a concave to the origin w-r relationship.

Notes

* This article is a revised and updated version of a paper that I gave at the Association of University Teachers Conference at the University of Warwick in March 1973 (which was published in the volume of the papers of the conference, Parkin and Nobay, 1975). Earlier versions were given as a Special University Lecture at Birkbeck College, University of London, and at seminars at other places too numerous to mention during a year's study leave from the University of Adelaide at the Faculty of Economics and Politics and Clare Hall, Cambridge. In preparing this article, in addition to comments at the seminars, I have benefitted greatly from comments by Tom Asimakopulos, Christopher Bliss, Christopher Dougherty, John Eatwell, Keith Frearson, Pierangelo Garegnani, Frank Hahn, Jan Kregel, Alfredo Medio, Mario Nuti, Joan Robinson, Bob Rowthorn, Eric Russell, Ian Steedman, Peter Wagstaff and John Wright. I thank them all but implicate none.

1 See Ferguson (1972, pp. 162–3) for a complete list of descriptions and Harcourt (1972) for a detailed survey of the debates. They are designated 'Cambridge' controversies because of the permanent or temporary associations of the principal participants with one or both of Cambridge, England, and Cambridge, Mass.

2 Sen (1974) suggests, as a further cause of lack of communication, that Fisher was concerned with econometric analysis and empirical prediction together with actual measurement rather than with the internal consistency of pure theory. He quotes (p. 331) Sraffa's famous remarks (at the 1958 Corfu conference on capital theory) on measurement in (capital) theory: 'theoretical measures [require] absolute precision . . .. The work of J. B. Clark, Böhm-Bawerk and others was intended to produce pure definitions of capital, as required by their theories, not as a guide to actual measurement. If we found contradictions, . . . these pointed to defects in the theory . . . an inability to define measures of capital accurately'. Sen adds: 'Fisher's motivation is quite different from that of . . . Sraffa, and to quote the findings of the former as vindication of the position of the latter does not get one closer to enlightenment' (p. 332).

3 See Rowthorn (1972, 1974); Hahn (1972a, especially the preface; 1972b) Rowthorn's paper was originally written in 1972 with the title 'Vulgar Economy'.

4 See Dobb (1973, pp. 4–7) for a cogent argument as to why the two may not be legitimately separated.

5 Yet many commentators – for example, Bliss (1975), Blaug (1974), Stiglitz (1974) – have intepreted the disputes so, as though it is the measurement of 'capital', rather than the aggregation of production functions, which is at the heart of the matter. (I shall argue that it is *neither*.) Thus Blaug (1974, p. 17) says that 'it is the measurement of capital to which they return again and again. But meaningful aggregation of capital is no more difficult than meaningful aggregation of labour . . . just as difficult'. He quotes with approval, Bliss (1975, p. 162): 'the widespread belief that there is a notable, particular and distinct problem posed by

capital aggregation is at best an ill-formulated idea, and at worst is based simply on ignorance'.

6 Sraffa (1960) is placed first because of 'the disproportionate length of time over which so short a work [was] . . . in preparation'. When exactly these particular parts of the embryo took shape is not known but, as they are 'central propositions', we may hazard a guess that it was the late 1920s (see Sraffa, 1960, p. vi). Dobb (1973, p. 252) evaluates Sraffa's 'rigorous demonstration of the possibility of . . . the "double-switching of techniques" . . . as . . ., perhaps, [his] most important single contribution to "a Critique of Economic Theory" '.

7 We leave aside for the moment the distinction between the distribution between classes, on the one hand, and income categories, on the other.

8 Steedman errs in using the phrase 'interest rate' at this point.

9 Strangely enough, this proposition is agreed to by both the modern general equilibrium theorists – see, for example, Hahn (1973a) and the Robinsonians – but not by Garegnani, Pasinetti and Dobb. One of the causes of disagreement may be that an approach which is suitable for analysing the accumulation of capital goods and the distribution of income over *actual* time may not be appropriate for an explanation of the long-run natural rate of profits: on this, see Robinson (1975e).

10 Dobb (1973, p. 11) comments wryly: 'If this progress in analytical techniques involved some restrictions on the boundaries of the subject as compared with those more generously drawn by the classical pioneers, this was something to be applauded [:] . . . a cost well compensated for by the resulting gain in scientific rigour.'

11 'the most obvious explanation why one studies [general equilibrium] theory, which is known to conflict with the facts, is that one is not engaged in description at all' (Hahn, 1973b, p. 323).

12 'Without wishing to suggest that [steady-state, long-run equilibrium models] . . . and . . . the "essentially timeless" Arrow–Debreu model . . . [are] useless and provide no insights, it must be said that [they are] severely limited in application . . . can treat of time only where time is much like space in its effects' (Bliss, 1974, p. 1).

13 Nuti (1974) attacks modern general equilibrium theory from a different tack, namely, that it is unable satisfactorily to model capitalist society. In a capitalist world investment decisions are taken on the basis of expected prices, not prices ruling in perfect future markets. This implies that there is no necessary equality between the money rate of interest and the *social* rate of return on investment, even if an equilibrium were to be attained. Moreover, there can be no forward (or conditional) market for labour for 'it is one of the distinctive features of capitalism that labour is wage–labour and no command can be acquired over the labourer himself – a command implicit in a hypothetical purchase of forward labour' (p. 366).

14 See, for example, Robinson (1964b), Harcourt (1965a; 1972, chapter 5), Asimakopulos (1969, 1970), Kregel (1973) – and also Hahn (1972a, 1973a). By Keynesian I mean Keynesian without quotes, i.e. Keynes, the people who originally worked with him and his and *their* followers, not the general equilibrium theorists as represented by, say, Bliss. The latter wish to confront directly the problems of short-run equilibrium in a world in which the future is uncertain, 'by using the method of *temporary equilibrium*', that is to say, 'a situation in

which current markets and a restricted set of forward markets are clearing'. This approach maintains the essentials of the general equilibrium framework and virtually ignores the sphere of production, social relationships, broad classes, institutions and the 'rules of the game' of particular economies. With, for example, Bliss's approach, it is isolated individual agents operating on competitive markets that face the uncertain future, while for the Post-Keynesian, it is groups locked together in social relationships who do so – and, moreover, the market structures are not necessarily competitive.

15 A succinct statement of his position is the following: 'In Wicksell profits appear as a uniform rate over the value of capital. . . . As a result he had to refer to supply and demand for capital considered as a single homogenous factor – a value substance which could take any physical form . . . because the structure of the capital stock had to adapt itself to the conditions of long-run equilibrium. Wicksell needed then to exclude reverse capital deepening to have a well-shaped demand function for capital and thus ensure the existence and stability of equilibrium in the factor markets' (Garegnani, 1973, p. 365). This criticism does *not* extend to modern general equilibrium theory which, as Rowthorn (1974, p. 74, n. 9) reminds us, 'allows for the possibility of aggregate capital being a discontinuous function of the rate of profit'.

16 Garegnani (1973, p. 365). We are irresistibly reminded of another dispute. 'It appears to me that one great cause of our difference of opinion . . . is that you have always in your mind the immediate and temporary effects of particular changes – whereas I put these . . . quite aside, and fix my whole attention on the permanent state of things which will result from them' (Ricardo to Malthus, 24 January 1817, in Sraffa with Dobb, 1952, p. 120).

17 While the gist of what Garegnani is proposing is clear, his critique of the neoclassical approach at this juncture does not attain the otherwise admirable clarity of the arguments of his 1970 paper.

18 Stiglitz (1974, p. 901) not only provides the reason why but also casts his net even wider. 'There is a well-known propensity of individuals to dislike what they don't or can't understand. This book (Harcourt, 1972), as well as the writings of the other Cambridge economists, makes perfectly clear that they do not understand neoclassical capital theory.'

19 See Pasinetti (1974a, pp. 42–5, especially p. 44, n. 27). Stiglitz (1974, p. 894) criticizes the Cambridge (England) economists for, in effect, adopting Keynes's method in arguing that the rate of profits is determined by the rate of growth and the saving propensity of the capitalist class which in turn (in a neoclassical model) determine the marginal product of capital (or own marginal productivity of capital goods). Stiglitz wrote these comments before Pasinetti's Essay VI, 'The rate of profit in an expanding economy', was published.

20 Walras certainly understood this general principle (see Dobb, 1973, pp. 103–4). Dobb adds: 'once a system like the Walrasian has been given an economic interpretation – and *a fortiori* economic application – a determination of some factors by others necessarily emerges' (p. 210). Modern general equilibrium theorists have tried to escape from this implication, with the result that their work seems to many to have become increasingly barren and irrelevant (see, for example, Kaldor, 1972).

21 Sraffa (1960, p. 38) is crystal clear on both these points: '(The reduction to dated labour terms has some bearing on the attempts that have been made to

find in the "period of production" an independent measure of the quantity of capital which could be used, without arguing in a circle, for the determination of prices and of the shares in distribution. . . . . The reversals in the direction of the movement of relative prices, in the face of unchanged methods of production, cannot be reconciled with *any* notion of capital as a measurable quantity independent of distribution and prices.)' (Emphasis in original.)

22 While it *is* understood by the Cambridge (England) critics that, in general equilibrium theory, rates of interest are inter-temporal prices, it sometimes appears that neo-neoclassical economists forget that it is a completely different animal, the (classical) rate of profits in capitalist society, that is being discussed in the present contexts. (On this and related topics, see Kregel, 1971; Harcourt, 1973.) Blaug (1974) makes great play of this, of the various levels of abstraction at which the Cambridge (England) analysis operates. He pooh-poohs the idea that it is the classical rate of profits that is being discussed and, taking himself into a neoclassical framework *à la* Knight, establishes to his own satisfaction that with long-run equilibrium under perfect competition there are no profits and thus only the rate of interest is being discussed. Stiglitz (1974, p. 894) uses the two terms interchangeably, so suggesting that either they are the same or that their orders of magnitude (under conditions of certainty and so on) are the same. Marshall would not have agreed; he distinguished, at least conceptually, if not always clearly (see Eshag, 1963, p. 52), between the rate of profits (capitalists' income from the use of 'capital' in production) and the rate of interest (rentier income obtained from the transfer for some time of potential command over resources) *even in long-period equilibrium*. I am indebted to Tom Asimakopulos for this point.

23 For a discussion of this and other mistaken uses, see Rowthorn (1974, pp. 73–4).

24 Similarly, the aim of the recent work on standard theorems in general equilibrium and international trade theory by Metcalfe and Steedman (1972a, 1972b, 1972c) is *not* to provide an alternative theoretical framework with which to tackle these puzzles but to show the logical slips contained in the old framework when account is taken of the Cambridge (England) critique (see, especially, 1972a, pp. 140, 155; 1972b, p. 1).

25 See Dobb (1973, pp. 263–6) for a lucid exposition of Sraffa's solution. Note that it is only a limited solution, applying to one economic system at one moment of time and so does not solve Ricardo's problem of comparisons over time.

26 These observations should serve to remind us that, though the critics of neoclassicism may be united against a common enemy, they are, in other respects, a heterogeneous collection, split into at least three camps – Neo-Keynesian, Neo-Marxian and Neo-Ricardian – with some members managing to have feet in more than one camp at the same time.

27 Amongst the recent first fruits of this approach (the description of which has now reached a steady state of Post-Keynesian) are the important paper by Asimakopulos and Burbidge (1974) on 'The Short-Period Incidence of Taxation' and Pasinetti's essays (Pasinetti, 1974a).

28 Joan Robinson (1975e, p. 398) says of the Post-Keynesian result (the rate of profits equals 'the rate of growth divided by the proportion of saving in incomes derived only from profits') that it 'is not . . . of direct application to any real problem[s] . . . belongs to the sphere of doctrine[;] . . . shows that there is no room for a theory of profits based on "marginal productivity of capital"' '.

29 We assume that sustainable stationary states are being compared. If we examine steadily growing economies, it is necessary further to assume that the Golden Rule of Accumulation, or neo-neoclassical theorem, applies, so that the maximum levels of consumption per head (c) for given rates of growth (g) have been established. This implies in turn a negative association between c and g. In the neoclassical case, maximization of c also implies that $r = g$. The negative association between c and g therefore involves, simultaneously, a negative association between c and r (see Harcourt, 1972, chapter 5).

30 Once workers save, a distinction must be made between the share of wages and the share of wage-earners in the national income. The aggregate production function version applies only to the former. The distinction itself is at the bottom of the controversies over alternative theories of the rate of profits in the Cambridge exchanges (see Harcourt, 1972, chapter 5; Kregel, 1971; Pasinetti, 1974a).

31 In a one all-purpose commodity model, relative factor supplies and the form of the production function are sufficient to determine income distribution; with more than one sector, though, demand factors – people's preferences – must be introduced in order to obtain, simultaneously, solutions for all prices and quantities (see Johnson, 1971).

32 Thus:

$$\frac{dr}{dk} = f''(k) \quad \text{and} \quad \frac{dw}{dk} = -f''(k)k;$$

$$\frac{dw}{dr} = \frac{dw}{dk} \bigg/ \frac{dr}{dk} = -k$$

and

$$E = -\frac{r}{w}\frac{dw}{dr} = \frac{rk}{w}.$$

33 Because Blaug's critique of the Cambridge critics is couched strictly within a neoclassical framework, with virtually no reference to the social relations of production, he argues that 'the problem of measuring "labour" is on all fours with the problem of measuring "capital"' (Blaug, 1974, p. 10). But capital goods *can* only be (and must be) aggregated in terms of value using their equilibrium prices, in which is contained the rate of profits, whereas an aggregate of labour in terms of man hours may be obtained by supposing relative wages to be constant and using them as weights, or sidestepped altogether, as Steedman (1975b, p. i) points out, because while there must be a uniform rate of profits (in long-period equilibrium), even when capital goods are heterogeneous, there does not have to be a uniform rate of wages unless labour is homogeneous. In a non-slave society there is an important empirical difference between 'physical' and 'human' capital and it should be recognized in the way in which economic theory, applicable to such a society, is formulated. I am indebted to Tom Asimakopulos for this point.

34 I am indebted to Tom Asimakopulos for this proof. See, also, Asimakopulos and Harcourt (1974).

35 As the consumption commodity is the only commodity in the net product, the intercept of each w-r trade-off line on the w axis shows, for *all* values of r, productivity and the maximum wage rate, w_{max}. This is not true in general as

different relative prices are associated with different values of *r* (see Harcourt, 1972, chapter 1).

36 See Harcourt (1972, chapter 4) for some very special exceptions.

37 'it is only when the same production function can be written for the consumption-good and the capital-good sector, so that they in effect collapse into one sector, that the elasticity of the . . . factor–price frontier provides a measure of the wage–profit shares in national income' (Samuelson, 1974c, p. 18).

38 In correspondence Professor Samuelson assures me that in none of his papers in this area is there intended to be *any* implication that the *transitional* paths are described by the factor price frontier envelope; only that, *if* the end result of an out-of-equilibrium transitional process, whatever is its actual path over 'time', *is* to reach a new permanent long-run equilibrium position, it is *this* position that is indicated by the factor price frontier envelope.

39 Gallaway and Shukla (1974) tried to define the sufficient conditions for a well-ordered production function because the 'upshot of the . . . criticisms of the neoclassical production function has been to call into question its very existence and all that follows from it . . . more than a trivial theoretical point' (p. 348). The condition, 'that commodity prices be positive and finite for any positive value of the interest rate' (p. 349), which is supposed to rule out reswitching and the implications of price Wicksell effects, flounders on the point that the only *economically* relevant range of rates of profits is from zero to the maximum rate that is implied by technology, and outside of which wage-rates must be negative. We know – and it has been shown conclusively by Laibman and Nell (1977) – that reswitching can occur in model economies with positive prices within this range, even though there be negative prices outside it.

40 Gallaway and Shukla's paper (1974), also Sato's (1974), to name only two, are evidence that there are still many economists who wish the results of equilibrium comparisons to conform to the neoclassical parables – and the two together to throw light on processes. Hence the great efforts recently to find those conditions under which reswitching and capital-reversing, or related phenomena, cannot occur, even though we are told they are not really required for essentially neoclassical results to hold (see Burmeister and Turnovsky, 1972; Stiglitz, 1973a, 1973b). Similarly, the destruction of the fourth parable purely by curves is sloughed off by arguing that it was not *real* neoclassical marginal productivity theory anyway (see Blaug, 1974; Johnson, 1973; Ng, 1974a, 1974b; Stiglitz, 1974).

41 Ferguson (1972, p. 175), emphasis added. The 'weak assumptions' in the circulating capital goods example of the Dobb *Festschrift* paper (Solow, 1967) are full employment, competitive pricing, and the comparison of one stationary state with another which has the same labour force but uses, at a given rate of interest, certainly more of some, and never less, circulating capital goods.

42 Joan Robinson (1964a, pp. 410–11) has remarked that this is a useful concept in a kibbutz, though not necessarily in Solow's form, but what has it to do with the rate of profits on aggregate 'capital' in a capitalist economy?

43 'Fisher demonstrated that general equilibrium analysis . . . could be extended to embrace capital theory, showing that the same principles that could be used to determine the relative prices of different commodities at a given moment of time could also be used to determine the relative prices of commodities at different points of time, and hence the rate of interest from one moment

to the next. To focus attention on the latter, he neglected the former, thus effectively confining himself to a one-commodity model. [Though] aware that [the] dichotomy was illegitimate, . . . he assumed that it would only require patience to combine his analysis with that of Walras and Pareto to form a multi-commodity inter-temporal general equilibrium theory . . . his confidence was justified . . ., for example, by Debreu [1959]' (Dougherty, 1972, pp. 1325-6).

44 This view has much – but not all – in common with Garegnani's view that a downward-sloping demand curve for aggregate value 'capital', so that aggregate 'capital' is a continuous function of the rate of profits, underlies even the most careful formulations of the traditional theory whereby 'the explanation of distribution [is] in terms of supply and demand' (Garegnani, 1970, p. 422). Rowthorn (1974) does not accept this as a criticism of general equilibrium theory (though he does accept it as a criticism of traditional aggregate theory) because it has no bearing on the existence or non-existence of equilibrium.

45 So, perhaps, Metzler (1951, p. 68) gave way too easily in his recantation.

46 It is significant that at this point in Johnson's version of the general equilibrium model in which there *is* a uniform rate of profits (see Johnson, 1973), he has to use the concept of malleable 'capital' in the production functions.

47 See Hahn and Matthews (1964, p. 881). I am indebted to Alfredo Medio for drawing this example to my attention. Though Hahn and Matthews refer to the marginal social return on investment, they are drawing on the work of Malinvaud (1953) and Koopmans (1957) in which the *same* concept is called the marginal product of 'capital'. (See also Laing 1971; Dougherty, 1972, pp. 1345-6; Ng, 1974b, pp. 126-7.)

48 Spaventa (1973) shows that they rupture the equality between the rate of profits and the rate of return on investment as well.

49 'These achievements of the Neo-Ricardian school are real and substantial . . . a complete demolition of the aggregate production function and marginal productivity based upon it . . . vulgar economy . . . is now forced to rely upon general equilibrium theory . . . far less suitable for teaching and propagandist purposes' (Rowthorn, 1974, p. 73).

50 Robinson (1974, p. 11). It would also be nice if we *could* agree that 'the controversy is over . . . that marginal productivity of capital in industry as a whole has been shown to be a meaningless expression [and that] we must look somewhere else to determine the laws which regulate the distribution of the produce of the earth among the classes of the community' (Robinson, 1951-80, vol. iv, p. 173).

51 These suggestions seem to have the blessings of both Marx and Morishima. 'Thus many contemporary economists believe it is more important to obtain a theory which can describe dynamic movements of an economy, rather than one which can elaborate consumers' preferences . . . exactly the choice which Marx made' (Morishima, 1973, p. 3).

52 I am indebted to Tetsunori Koizumi for this 'terse exposition'.

18 The theoretical and social significance of the Cambridge controversies in the theory of capital   An evaluation*

The editor has asked the contributors to discuss the theoretical and social significance of the Cambridge controversies in the theory of capital. A sharp division between these two aspects logically cannot be made for, like trend and cycle, analysis and ideology and Samuelson and Solow, they are indissolubly mixed. Nevertheless, it is a convenient division for purposes of exposition so I adopt it and deal, first, with the theoretical significance, and then with the significance, if such there be, for society. I survey the various, very differing views of the contro versies, indicating where I believe truth lies and what the ongoing implications for theory and practice both are likely to be and should be, for the two, unfortunately, have not as yet converged into one. I proceed by outlining what I take to be the gist of the various approaches; the references at the end of the paper provide the detailed evidence from which the interested reader may check whether I have been just in my presentation. The debate is, of course, a continuing one but I think that we have now reached a position where some broad generalisations and evaluations usefully may be made. I take it that the principal issues and results are familiar to readers. For those, however, who are either coming at them afresh or wish to refresh their memories, there are a number of convenient sources which, together, provide an exhausitive overview, from all points of view, of the whole controversy (see Blaug, 1974; Dobb, 1973; Hahn, 1972a, pp. 1-18, 1974, 1975b; Harcourt, 1972, 1976; Kregel, 1973; Ng, 1974b; Pasinetti, 1974a; Robinson, 1974, 1975a, 1975b, 1975c, 1975d; Rowthorn, 1974; Samuelson, 1966, 1975; Solow, 1975a; Stiglitz, 1974).

The paper is in two sections. In section I, the theoretical issues are examined and evaluated. In section II, the social significance, especially the implications for policy, is speculated on.

I

1.1 The theoretical issues resolve themselves into two groups, the first of which relates to the questions actually being asked, the second, to the appropriate methodology to be used. Endless confusion has occurred in the literature because these two underlying strands have not always sufficiently been made explicit. As to the first head, the principal questions being discussed, at least as seen by the Post-Keynesian school (the leaders of which include Joan Robinson, Kahn, Kaldor and, as a guiding spirit, Piero Sraffa), are some of those with which the great classical political economists and, of course, Marx, were concerned: 'the relation between accumulation and the distribution of the net product of industry between wages and profits' (Robinson, 1975e, p. 398), together with discussions of the origins of profits, their size (absolutely and as a rate) at any moment of time and over time, and the analogous aspects of wages. Solow recently (in his review, Solow, 1975a, of Blaug, 1974, and Pasinetti, 1974a) made clear his agreement with this evaluation. He discussed the orthodox view (the old-time religion that, according to Joan Robinson, is good enough for him) of how profits (interest) arise and what determines their size and rate in conditions of certainty and when monopoly, short-run shortages and risk have been ruled out by assumption. 'The third component of profit is the routine return to capitalist firms under tranquil conditions in the absence of monopoly' (p. 277).[1] Also connected to these questions are those which concern the concepts of natural, as the classicals had it, or normal, as Marshall would say, prices, and the relations between distribution and the relative price system where the latter are seen as the relative (natural) prices of broad classes of commodities. The distinguishing characteristics of the commodities are determined both by their ultimate uses and by the classes in society who principally are associated with those uses. These questions constitute a natural link between the works of Ricardo, Marx and Sraffa; they have received particular attention from Garegnani (1959, 1960, 1970) and Eatwell (1974).

1.2 Though the debates have been designated as recurring within the context of capital theory, in fact four related strands of theory are involved: value theory (which is absolutely central), capital theory itself, growth theory and distribution theory. Joan Robinson, who started these particular debates with her 1953 article, 'The Production Function and the Theory of Capital' (Robinson, 1953-4), was at the time searching the literature for the orthodox theories of profits and choice of technique *at the level of the economy as a whole*. She was in the process of working out the various strands of her theory of growth, her generalisation of *The General Theory*, as expressed fully in *The Accumulation of Capital* (Robinson, 1956). (The latter itself was inspired by Harrod's seminal works in this area (Harrod, 1939, 1948) and left-over business from the true Keynesian revolution.)

1.3 Growing out of the preoccupations discussed above but also intimately associated with them, is another set of issues which provides the link through to the second head of methodology. These relate to the Post-Keynesian critique of orthodox or mainstream neoclassical analysis, especially the theory of value, production and distribution which loosely comes under the head of marginal productivity theory. There have been a number of strands of this critique, emanating principally (in these contexts) from Dobb, Joan Robinson, Kaldor, Garegnani, Pasinetti and Sraffa. The critique has concerned itself, first, with the logical tenability of certain propositions thought to be associated with the traditional neoclassical approach to value and distribution, especially those theories which draw on the concepts of supply and demand as their fundamental tools. Second – here the link occurs – it has concerned itself with the methodological procedure of using (long-run) equilibrium comparisons in order to throw light on actual processes in capitalist economies as they evolve through actual historical time. Thus the theoretical contexts may be seen to be both classical and modern. They are classical, and especially Marxist, in that they are concerned with the 'laws of motion' of capitalist economies; that is to say, the historical processes of growth, with which are associated endogenous technical changes as a result of the internal workings and possibly contradictions of the system, and of transition from one mode of production to another, the latter an aspect honoured more by default than in practice or by profundity. They are modern because, with the exceptions of Harrod and (some of) the Post-Keynesian school – and, recently, Sir John Hicks (see Hicks, 1973a) – though orthodox economists have returned in the post-war period to a preoccupation with classical problems of accumulation, growth (both descriptive and optimal) and distribution, they have brought with them the tools and perspectives which were attained during their sojourn in the land of the margin (see Harris, 1975). There, they were preoccupied with a different set of problems, the properties – existence, uniqueness, stability – of an equilibrium state when the resources to be allocated by competitive markets are exogenous to the analysis itself. By contrast, Harrod and the Post-Keynesians brought with them to the renewed interest in classical and Marxist problems, the Kaleckian–Keynesian solution of the realisation problem, so that the advances in the theory of the short run of the 1930s could be integrated with the post-war developments.[2]

1.4 The neo-neoclassical economists, on the whole, have preferred explicitly to assume away the effective demand aspects. They have grafted the neoclassical analyses of allocation in situations of full employment onto their analyses of movements through 'time' due to accumulation, in which the savings dog wags the investment tail,[3] 'capital' is substituted for labour, and technical progress, whether disembodied or embodied, is usually exogenous. Initially, neoclassical growth theory was concerned principally with steady-state analysis. Very quickly, however, modifications and extensions were made as the conditions of stability were investigated outside the domain of the simple one all-purpose commodity model in which there was, in effect, perfect foresight because of the assumption of malleability of the one all-purpose commodity. The steady-state now serves merely as a reference point and as a means of flexing intellectual muscles (see Hahn, 1971; Hicks, 1975a).[4] The focus of the analysis has been, to a much greater extent, on the traverse – the initial and ultimate response of the economy to a new factor, say an innovation or an autonomous change in the saving rate, the path it is likely to follow and the possibility of it finding its way, both technocratically and, more generally, by postulating the behaviour of its economic agents, to a new equilibrium position (see Samuelson, 1975).

1.5 Bound up with the methodological issues is the further question as to which particular branch of neoclassical analysis is both relevant to the principal questions being asked and is under attack. I have argued elsewhere (see Harcourt, 1975a, 1976) that it is the neoclassical theories which, misleadingly in my view, are dubbed 'aggregative', *viz.* the aggregate production function growth models and econometric studies, much of international trade and orthodox development theory, and the rate of return model at the economy level, which are both relevant and vulnerable. Those neoclassical models which are associated with (J. R.) Hick's *Value and Capital*[5] and with the general equilibrium models of Arrow–Debreu, whatever their logical robustness (believed by Arrow and Hahn, for example, to be very great), are not designed to answer the questions at present under discussion. Rather, they are concerned with what rigorously may be said to be true of the properties of the invisible hand, another major insight and preoccupation of the classical political economists from Adam Smith on (see Arrow and Hahn, 1971; Hahn, 1973b; Arrow, 1974). The reason why it is the aggregative theories which are relevant has to do with the attempts of modern theory to tackle the classical questions, especially of the distribution of income, in the context of a class-dominated society. Perhaps it should not be necessary to stress this at the moment in an integrated capitalist world which is dominated by an inflationary crisis which is itself intimately bound up with competing class claims on national products. Admittedly, the modern scenario is much more complicated than the simple triad of landlords, capitalists and workers of the classical stage. Nevertheless, it certainly is an indispensable element of the analysis, far more relevant than an attempt to start with isolated utility-maximising, economic agents with their arbitrary initial distribution of resources, between whom power is diffused equally, which, on the whole, are the characteristics of the orthodox approach to these questions.

1.6 Yet the questions themselves have been rejected as uninteresting (Vanags, 1975, p. 335; Blaug, 1974, p. 57)[6] or ill-defined (Hahn, 1974, 1975b) and the consequent preoccupation with the *meaning*, much more important than the *measurement* of capital, has been rejected as irrelevant for neoclassical analysis and results (see Bliss, 1975; Stiglitz, 1974; Weizsäcker, 1971). We need only quote Steedman's view (in his review, Steedman, 1975b, of Blaug, 1974) conclusively to refute this point.

> Their [the Post-Keynesian theorists'] good reason [for emphasising the heterogeneity of capital goods but not of labour] lies in the fact that different types of labour do not *need* to be aggregated and can receive different wages while, in long-run equilibrium theory, capital goods have to be aggregated, in value terms, since the [rate of profits] on their value is uniform. (p. i.)

That is to say, for those who dismiss the concept of classes as too vague and woolly to be included in rigorous economic analysis and who seek for universality of principles rather than a more modest set which is tied to time and place, in which the sort of economy that the writer has in mind is explicitly specified – its institutional framework, 'rules of the game' and social relationships – the whole issue has an air of mystery and incomprehension, of being 'rather silly' and unable 'to capture the interest or imagination of economists outside the circle of immediate participants in the two Cambridges' (Vanags, 1975, p. 334).

1.7 All sides of the argument are agreed that there is much wrong with the state of orthodox economic theory at the moment;[7] but here the agreement ends – or almost, for it is also almost agreed that concentration on equilibrium states, as usually or traditionally defined, is one of the root causes of the trouble. Joan Robinson has been attacking what she considers to be the characteristics of the neoclassical concept of equilibrium and equilibrium analysis since at least 1953. Especially has she attacked what she considers to be a characteristic neoclassical methodology of attempting to analyse what are essentially processes occurring in time by comparisons of long-run equilibrium states, a methodology which allows 'time' to be modelled only in so far as it has the characteristics of space (see Bliss, 1974).[8]

1.8 We should note at this point an important argument by Garegnani. In his view, a belief in long-period gravitation towards natural prices has been shared by all economists up until *Value and Capital* (Hicks, 1939). It is this belief that has justified the use of comparisons as an analytical device for 'studying the *permanent* effects of changes in conditions of the economy' (Garegnani, 1976, p. 25). Furthermore, it is *not* this methodological procedure which is at fault, but, rather, its use *in conjunction with the concepts of supply and demand*, the characteristic procedure of neoclassical economists, including Marshall, the original Austrians, Walras and Wicksell. Garegnani (1959, 1960, 1970, 1973, 1976) has concentrated his criticisms on both the difficulties in the concepts of the supply and demand for labour and, especially, 'capital', and on the need for there to be a 'well-behaved' relationship between 'capital' and the rate of profits in order that unique and stable equilibria may both exist *and* be attained.

> It is therefore apparent that this difficulty . . . [concerns] the theory i.e. the way in which the centres of gravitation of the system are determined, and not the static *method* of analysis based on such 'centres'[,] . . . no similar difficulty arises for the classical economists who used the same method but did not determine the centres of gravitation as equilibria between supply and demand. (Garegnani, 1976, p. 36)[9]

Be that as it may, in place of this method, Joan Robinson has called consistently for a return to a predominantly Keynesian methodology whereby actual historical time is modelled by placing an economy down in history and letting it evolve under the influence of its own past historical experiences and present expectations of the future, in which environment there is an ever present uncertainty of the future, an uncertainty which, by its very nature, cannot be modelled by probability distributions and the like.[10]

1.9 In more formal terms, Pasinetti (1974a, pp. 43–4) has described the Keynesian method as being akin to the Ricardian one; the economic theorist has a duty to name which relationships between variables exhibit a one-way direction, 'such an overwhelming dependence in one direction (. . . such a small dependence in the opposite direction)', and which are so interrelated as properly to be treated as part of an interdependent system of simultaneous equations.

The characteristic consequence of this methodological procedure [which also includes singling out for consideration those variables that are thought to be most important] is the emergence in Keynes, as in Ricardo, of a system of equations of the 'causal type' or . . . of the 'decomposable type', as opposed to a completely interdependent system of simultaneous equations. (p. 44)

Joan Robinson (1975e, pp. 397–8) comments at this point:

Since the word 'causal' always raises philosophical blood pressure [for a good example, see Hahn (1974, pp. 36–7)], the point may be put more concretely: the Keynesian system is designed to show the consequences, over the immediate and further future, of a change taking place as an event at a moment of time, while the equilibrium system can only compare the differences between two positions or two paths conceived as coexisting in time, or rather outside time.

1.10 Kalecki also used a similar method, in that he divided time into short periods, each with its own past and expectations of the future, and then let the process unravel as the happenings of one short period were passed on to be the historical or initial conditions of the next, the actual events now helping to form the expectations of the next period. Thus, for Kalecki, the trend and cycle were indissolubly mixed, not separable as in statistical techniques and much neoclassical growth theory.[11] (This approach is well exemplified in Asimakopulos and Burbridge (1974), a Post-Keynesian analysis of tax incidence at the economy level, and in Asimakopulos (1977), an endogenous theory of investment in a Kaleckian model.[12]) Hicks, too, uses a similar methodology in *Capital and Time*, in order to trace out the immediate and ultimate consequences of a change (in technical possibilities) intruding itself into an existing equilibrium position. He uses a full-employment equilibrium path as the reference point from which to measure divergences as the story unfolds (see Hicks, 1975a). It is, moreover, only the early parts of the story – what Hicks calls the Early Phase – which are likely to be of relevance to an explanation of actual events in actual time.[13]

1.11 There are, of course, parallel developments in orthodox neo-neoclassical theory, in that out-of-(long-period)-equilibrium processes, and studies of transient paths, are its stock in trade, as are the methods of temporary and momentary equilibria. Where the two approaches differ from one another relates especially to their modelling of economies. In one there are still, or were at least until very recently, isolated economic agents between whom power is diffused equally, usually price-takers *in markets which clear each instant*. In the other, we have broad distinct classes, classified by their differing functions in the economy and by their different spending, saving and accumulating characteristics, models which, like Ricardo's, are 'highly simplified but . . . not arbitrary fanciful constructions like those of Debreu'.[14] Moreover, there is not the same dependence on temporary and/or momentary equilibria, in the sense of market-clearing *prices*, as the means of modelling *actual* processes.

1.12 The particular strands of the Post-Keynesian approach which has been outlined above are on the whole neglected by its critics. They have tended, rather, to concentrate on the formal results, for example, those which emerged from the reswitching debates of the mid to late 1960s (see Harcourt, 1972, chapter 4; 1976). Thus Hahn in one of his many attacks on those whom he now calls 'the reactionaries' (because he interprets them as a back-to-Ricardo movement) chooses to focus attention on Piero Sraffa's propositions (which are set out in Sraffa, 1960), usually as interpreted by Sraffa's followers. Hahn argues that the Post-Keynesian school is concerned with the wrong issues and uses the wrong arguments (see Hahn, 1975a, 1975b). He criticises Sraffa's propositions for their complete lack of operational and/or empirical content (with the exception of the assumption of a uniform rate of profits, which, he says, is patently empirically false). That is to say, we have only a set of logical propositions which are of necessity true, not even in principle capable of being falsified empirically. (Presumably such an approach is all right in the theory of optimal growth but not in a prelude to a critique of economic theory.) He is willing (now) to give Sraffa and others an alpha for demonstrating that there is no *necessary* inverse relationship between the rate of profits and the (value of) capital;[15] he is not willing to draw the further inference that Sraffa's propositions were designed as a prelude to a critique of neoclassical-type answers via supply and demand concepts to the questions of accumulation, growth and distribution with which the classical political economists were concerned. Hahn regards these as non-questions for moderns. With the same breath, though, he is willing to praise modern general equilibrium theorists for having provided a rigorous (but, on the whole, negative) set of answers to another grand question which has classical origins, namely, the ability of the invisible hand in a competitive system of isolated economic agents to bring about a satisfactory disposition of economic resources (see Arrow and Hahn, 1971; Hahn, 1973b). Yet it is this sort of theory that underlies (erroneously, evidently) Friedman and Harry Johnson's apologia and propaganda for the virtues of a free market system.[16] And, just for good measure, Hahn

(1975b, p. 362) regards every one of Sraffa's formal propositions as consistent with and, indeed, deducible from modern general equilibrium theory.

1.13 Hahn is very conscious of the rudimentary state of the economic theory which he champions, despite its great technical difficulty. He has, in several seminal articles, discussed the unlikelihood of a growing 'capitalist' economy which contains heterogeneous capital goods (though usually no recognisable capitalists or workers) going through time in a full-employment equilibrium state. He also has been concerned with the puzzles of putting money into general equilibrium models and taking the auctioneer out, so that something akin to Keynesian involuntary unemployment may be made to appear. In passing he has ridiculed the simple neoclassical models. And he has stressed the nature of an equilibrium as a situation which, *if it were to exist*, and if the assumption of maximising behaviour were to be made – 'like Marxian Economics, orthodoxy is founded on the hypothesis of the greedy, rational, self-seeking capitalist' (Hahn, 1974, p. 35) – would require, as a matter of logic, that certain simple relationships, sometimes akin to textbook marginal productivity relationships, would of necessity hold. But he is most insistent in stating that the proof of existence implies neither uniqueness nor local nor global stability and that it is the latter which are of relevance to the issues discussed in the present theoretical debates.[17] Nor will he allow anything concerning determination or explanation to be drawn from the equilibrium relations. This is a point of view with which Joan Robinson would certainly agree, for it underlies her discussions of logical and historical time and the related concepts of equilibrium and causal models respectively.[18] What Hahn is reluctant to admit – he does grant that 'the neoclassical textbook' is a fair target, hastening to add that 'textbooks [and their "vulgar theories"] are not the frontier of knowledge' (Hahn, 1975b, p. 363) – is that the very errors that he deplores in the Post-Keynesians are more to be found in a large part of the literature that goes under the name of neoclassical economies, *viz.* the simple growth models, the econometric studies of the relative contributions of 'deepening' and technical progress to productivity growth over time, and much of the orthodox theory of international trade and development. That there is much at stake has been witnessed to by the recent, in the event, abortive, attempts to defend the neoclassical propositions which underlie these constructions *by means of analyses which consist of equilibrium comparisons* (see, for example, Gallaway and Shukla, 1974).

1.14 Solow wishes to ride two horses at once. First, he takes a pragmatic approach to the simpler stories, the neoclassical parables which underlie the econometric work[19] and which are only guides to empirical work, even if there is no rigorous theory necessarily to back them up even as possibilities. (The outcome of the reswitching and capital-reversing debates is to show that the parables do not necessarily hold, even as the outcome of long-run equilibrium comparisons, let alone as a description of actual processes: see Harcourt, 1975a, pp. 315–29.) Evidently we are to treat them as correct until refuted by empirical findings.[20] But if the world is modelled by a predisposition to find certain relationships there and if certain observations are to be viewed 'as if' they were the empirical counterparts of the theoretical variables of the model, it is hard to see *how* the facts could refute them, as opposed to providing the orders of magnitude of the coefficients in the imposed relationships (see Shaikh, 1974, and Solow's reply, Solow, 1974a).[21] Second, Solow is a great proponent of highbrow rigorous theory which, like Hahn (1974) and Stiglitz (1974, pp. 898–9), he argues is independent of any relationships and concepts, especially aggregate ones, against which logical objections have been established when the simpler versions of neoclassical theory are examined.

1.15 The strongest attacks in the *present* debates or, rather, those most distressing to the protagonists involved, come not from the Post-Keynesians on the Neo-neoclassicals, nor from the Neo-neoclassicals in reply, but from the Marxist and radical economists' camp – and the attacks are on the Post-Keynesians, not the Neo-neoclassicals. (Of course, the Post-Keynesians and the Marxists and their allies are united in the attacks on the Neo-neoclassicals, though they stress somewhat different issues. It is their attitudes to each other which is under review here.)[22] Two good representatives of this aspect of the controversies are Rowthorn (1974) and Roosevelt (1977) (see, also, Medio, 1972).[23] Partly these attacks are misconceived because they sometimes fail to distinguish between the negative aspect of the Post-Keynesians' works – the critique from within, as it were, of neo-neoclassical logic – and the positive aspect whereby the Post-Keynesians try to provide an alternative approach to economic analysis, building on Marxian, Kaleckian and Keynesian underpinnings. The main thrust of the Marxists' attack relates to the (supposed) neglect of the sphere of production in Post-Keynesian analysis and the (alleged) failure also to use the concept of the mode of production, whereby the spheres of production and of distribution and exchange interrelate one with another in an organic manner. This implies both a neglect of the characteristics of the mode of production, in this case, the capitalist mode, and of an analysis of the processes whereby one mode is transformed into another. It is for this reason that the Post-Keynesians have been christened Neo-Ricardians by Marxists – Marx, of course, made a similar criticism of Ricardo. It is also a clue to the reason why relevance in economic analysis has been defined by some radical economists in recent years as that which adds to our understanding of the inevitable transition to socialism.

1.16 Roosevelt sees the Post-Keynesians (as represented, principally, by Sraffa, and Robinson and Eatwell, 1973) as falling into the same trap as J. S. Mill whereby the laws of production are universal, technical, physical matters but the laws of distribution reflect existing institutions and social relationships and are subject to fundamental changes, as well as varying as between one society and another and being, in the main, independent of production. He criticises at length what he takes to be a neglect of discussion of production as a set of social relationships as opposed to physical and technical ones. He objects to the undue concentration on the distribution of the surplus as opposed to discussions of how it is created, what determines its size and the organic relationship that exists between its production and distribution through the social relationships involved, which he takes to be the principal characteristic of the capitalist mode of production. Both Rowthorn and Roosevelt are critical of the neglect of feedback relationships between the two spheres. They argue that such relationships are a characteristic of Marxian analysis but are, in their view, conspicuous by their absence in Post-Keynesian analysis, especially that branch which emanates from and/or is inspired by Sraffa's work.

1.17 In contrast to Rowthorn and Roosevelt, Eatwell (1974) vigorously defends the Sraffian strands, regarding them as constituting important advances in *Marxian* analysis, especially in regard to the form of the problem of the link between 'values' and 'prices of production', i.e. the transformation problem. The latter is not seen primarily as a problem concerned with relative prices, of the link between commodities exchanging at their Marxian or labour value and commodities exchanging at their prices of production. Rather, it is seen as the link between surplus value, a social phenomenon that is a function of the social relations in the capitalist mode of production, and profits, as seen on the surface in the sphere of distribution and exchange, as a component of the prices of production. That is to say, it is concerned primarily with the origin of profits in the essence of the capitalist mode of production, instead of with the deviations of the prices of production from Marxian values, a secondary consideration.[24] This link Sraffa provides with his standard system and standard commodity (see Sraffa, 1960, chapters IV–VI). With these constructions, Sraffa is able to demonstrate by his wage-rate–rate-of-profits relation that, although the wage, rate of profits and relative prices of the standard and actual systems are identical (see Sraffa, 1960, p. 23), yet in the standard system the wage, rate of profits relation and the wage, surplus value relation exist, as it were, *prior to and independently of the relative prices*, i.e. the prices of production.[25] 'Sraffa's standard commodity therefore possesses all the characteristics which Marx sought in the "average commodity" which was to be the key to his solution of the transformation problem' (Eatwell, 1974, p. 302).[26]

1.18 Though Eatwell criticises Medio (1972) as well as Rowthorn in his defence of Sraffa, it does appear that Medio and Eatwell agree at least on general issues. Medio's criticism of Sraffa relates to details rather than to his general approach. Thus, Medio objects to Sraffa's assumption that the wage is paid out of the surplus rather than advanced and therefore part of the firms' capitals, as in the classical and Marxian tradition. Sraffa adopted his procedure, not without misgivings (see Sraffa, 1960, pp. 9–10) because it had the convenient by-product that the relationship between the wage (measured in terms of the standard commodity) and the rate of profits was a very simple straight-line one.[27] Medio feels that this simplification is bought at too high a price in that it obscures the Marxian insight, whereby the wage is measured in terms of labour time, so that the working day splits conveniently into the workman working, first, for himself and then for the capitalist (surplus value). Moreover, Medio argues, in the Sraffian scheme the wage is purely a distributive phenomenon, instead of being integrated into the social and technical relationships associated with the production of output and, more importantly in this context, the surplus. Marx's macroeconomic foundations of microeconomics are thus in Medio's view not sufficiently emphasised in Sraffa's formulation.[28] Sraffa is well aware of this criticism for he argues (Sraffa, 1960, p. 10) that while his treatment of the wage formally implies that wage goods are non-basics, yet their essentially basic characteristic will show up in the formation of relative prices and profits in other ways.

1.19 We may conclude that while the Marxists and radicals legitimately may take issue on the *details* of the Post-Keynesians' analysis, their general criticism that there is a neglect of the concept of the mode of production, of social relationships and of the importance of the sphere of production is not really well-founded. Marx was well known for his method of concentrating on one aspect of a large interrelated problem and putting the other aspects theoretically in cold storage, while, at the same time, stressing the importance of their interrelationships and overlaps in a complete analysis. Presumably a charitable view would allow the Post-Keynesians a similar dispensation.

II

2.1 We now consider the social significance of the controversies. The theoretical issues provide a convenient launching pad. A major result that has emerged is the view of both sides that time must be modelled seriously and that analysis of processes in an uncertain environment is the most pressing problem yet to be tackled, or, at least, tackled satisfactorily. Where the protagonists differ is over the 'vision' of the economy that will go into the model to be used. Thus, Hahn (1975b, p. 363) tells us that there is 'no Millsian complacence [in] the current mainstream theoretical literature' and that there 'have been important developments in the modelling of information, sequence, economies, uncertainty, coalitions and power. Results most damaging to neoclassical theory have recently been proved by Debreu, Sonnenschein and Mas-Collel'. Nevertheless, as Hahn himself made clear in his Inaugural Lecture (Hahn, 1973a), he still wishes to have equilibrium, albeit in a considerably modified neoclassical sense, as a central concept and Walrasian economic agents interacting in Walrasian markets, but now, of course, without the auctioneer and recontracting, but using money, as the principal actors.[29] Bliss, too, while properly aware of the limited advances which further concentration on steady-state analysis will bring, none the less wishes to take over to his studies of 'capital theory in the short run', a framework similar to that of Hahn. Thus he intends to use a *temporary equilibrium* analysis 'in which current markets and a restricted set of forward markets are clearing' (Bliss, 1974, p. 3). And, while Clower and Leijonhufvud (1975) are, at least implicitly, critical of these approaches their own suggestions concerning the essential role of traders who hold stocks seem to make them also horses of a similar stable.

2.2 The use of these approaches means that no radical changes in 'vision' are involved. Capitalism is still seen as advancing through 'a process of "deepening the structure of capital", in which the savings decision of atomistic individuals', as expressed in their inter-temporal choices between goods today and goods tomorrow, are the driving forces of the system. 'The capitalist firm is seen merely as an intermediary between the individuals as suppliers of factors and the individuals as *rentiers* consuming their lifetime income' (Harris, 1975, p. 329). Consumption is the be-all and end-all of economic life; accumulation, by contrast, is an incidental feature, a means merely to an end. Growth in the labour force and technical advances are exogenous to the system. Crises and cycles are aberrations on a process of smooth development (though something supposedly akin to Keynesian involuntary unemployment may be deduced in some versions of these models; see, for example, Malinvaud and Younès, 1977).

> There is no identifiable class of workers displaced from property in the means of production who must depend entirely on employment in capitalistic production . . . for their economic survival. It is therefore difficult to see what real historical phenomena . . . this system of thought is intended to explain. (Harris, 1975, p. 330)[30]

As Pasinetti (1974a) has pointed out, Keynes was modelling an industrial society. This is a tradition which his immediate followers and their pupils have followed. By contrast,

> much of the pre-Keynesian economic thought [which is the base on which both the Bastard Keynesians and the 'new' interpreters of Keynes – Clower and Leijonhufvud – have built] does not . . . refer to an industrial society, but to a more primitive . . . society, in which resources (. . . given) are being offered and at the same time represent the purchasing power of the single individuals . . . Pushed to the extreme, the concepts are shaped into a 'model of pure exchange' expressed precisely by a system of simultaneous equations (supply . . . and demand functions) from which prices emerge as the solutions. (p. 470)

This gives rise to the 'misleading impression . . . that all the problems of our time would disappear if only the [so-called Keynesian] "rigidities" were to be eliminated . . . [,] as if [they] were the cause and not . . . one of the . . . inherent consequences of the industrial society in which we live' (p. 48).

2.3 By contrast, the positive contributions of the Post-Keynesians are intended specifically to deal with the neglected elements which have their base in historical fact and industrial societies. Some members of the school are open to the criticism that they tend to analyse the trend independently of the cycle (e.g. Kaldor's stylised facts do not include the cycle though this has not always been true of his approach). Nevertheless, they have been attempting to provide the ingredients for a theory of growth which is *a theory of the expanded reproduction of the capitalist mode of production on a world scale*' (Harris, 1975,

p. 331). When their approach is integrated with Marxian analysis, so that we return to the boundaries of our subject, as 'more generously drawn by the classical pioneers' (Dobb, 1973, p. 11), we will have a more suitable and richer framework for the analysis of historical developments, past and future. Lest this be mistaken for a plea for economists to be techniques Luddites, it should be said that there is no suggestion that we are to scrap modern methods of technical analysis. Rather, they are to be used at the appropriate places in this different context in order to fine up and enrich the resulting analyses. (A good example of such an application is the analytical sections of Harris's paper, (Harris, 1975, pp. 331–5). I also have in mind the valuable works of Braverman (1974) and Marglin (1974) both of which throw considerable light on the detailed conditions of work, technical advances and saving in the sphere of production, aspects virtually neglected by the Neo-neoclassicals and only lightly touched upon by the Post-Keynesians.)

2.4 There are important social and policy implications of the two contrasting approaches. In a sense, it may not be too fanciful to argue that we are now at a position in time which is equivalent to, or at least has strong similarities with that prior to the publication of *The General Theory*. Then, it will be remembered, both practical men and many economists were advocating pump-priming measures for raising the capitalist world from its slump, but the authoritative theory which would explain exactly *why* there was the sustained slump *and* how these measures could remove it still waited to be written and accepted.[31] Two branches of orthodoxy dominate the discussion and implementation of policy in the capitalist world, one actually (the Bastard Keynesians), one, on the whole, potentially (the Monetarist school). (Nixon at one stage gave the latter a slight run for its money and recent United Kingdom (Conservative) and Australian (Labor) administrations have flirted with some aspects of the Monetarist recommendations.) The Bastard Keynesians are in the process, which is probably very far along, of being discredited in many capitalist countries, because of the conjunction of high rates of inflation *and* unemployment. An extreme and old-fashioned form of orthodoxy is bidding to take its place. 'Once again it is alleged that the private market economy can and will, without aid from government policy, steer itself to full employment equilibrium' (Tobin, 1975, p. 196). This is, of course, Friedman's Monetarism with its stress on the need to get markets, especially labour markets, functioning efficiently and competitively, and to remove as much as possible the discretionary role of government as well as its absorption of the community's resources. (An even more extreme view is that of von Hayek (1975) and his followers, the present von Mises revivalists, who are suspicious even of Friedman and who strangely, even incongruously, want a system of free markets, again especially labour markets, and fixed exchange rates for the capitalist world as a whole.) With this go also their attempts to show that the Keynesian revolution was but an aberration – and an abortive one at that – on the mainstream of the development of liberal economic thought from Adam Smith on. That is to say, the focus is, once again, on the primary importance of substitution and flexibility, on the quick and correct, that is, stable, response of the economy to price market signals. These forces, in a correct environment, are seen as far more powerful than the major instabilities implied by the discrepancies between saving and investment, leakages and injections, which are the central features of the Keynesians–Kaleckian and Marxist approaches.

2.5 There are attempts to replace tendencies to deficiencies or excesses in the level of effective demand with the concept of the 'natural' rate of unemployment, a concept which draws on an underlying Walrasian equilibrium in competitive markets in which the relative price system is the key method of allocation and inflation is a monetary phenomenon superimposed on the workings of the real sector. ' "Equilibrium" often allows for any steady rate of deflation or inflation, not just zero' (Tobin, 1975, p. 196). In a parallel movement, the Keynesian concept of involuntary unemployment is also being replaced, or whittled away to insignificance, by the job search literature in which is employed the belated discovery that an atomistic competitor in an uncertain world nevertheless could have some direct responsibility for setting prices which, themselves, may well not be equilibrium ones.

2.6 There are also in places glimpses of and attempts to create consensus policies embodying genuine *money* income restraints and what Joan Robinson has called 'a real social contract which would satisfy the reasonable demands of the workers for more control over their own work, more security against redundancy, better social services and so forth'. This recognises a point which Keynes (and Kalecki) clearly foresaw: that prolonged near full employment would imply inflation unless there were changing attitudes and methods of *money* wage bargaining. The Post-Keynesian critique of the marginal productivity theory of distribution, together with Sidney Weintraub's work, are especially relevant at this point. These efforts tend to be timid and unsustained, to lack confidence because the authoritative theoretical backing, though by no means completely waiting to be written, certainly does still await wide acceptance. It should also be said that amongst many of those who are attempting to provide it, there is much more ambivalence about (and/or outright hostility to) the desirability of either propping up or salvaging the capitalist mode of production than was the case when Keynes was writing *The General Theory*.[32] It is at this juncture that the Post-Keynesian contributions, both methodologically and analytically, most relevently fit into the current policy and social situation. The above scenario is one of the themes of Joan Robinson's Richard T. Ely Lecture, 'The Second Crisis of Economic Theory' (Robinson, 1972). These very fundamental and practical implications are thus an important offshoot of the seemingly esoteric theoretical exchanges of the Cambridge controversies in the theory of capital.

Notes

* *Revue d'économie politique*, vol. 87, 1977, pp. 191–215. I am especially indebted to Peter Kenyon for helpful discussions when the first draft of this paper was being written. I am also grateful to John Henry, Neil Laing, Harold Lydall, Eric Russell and Bob Wallace for their comments on a draft. As usual, I thank them all but implicate none.

1 Solow (1975a, p. 277) argued that the real dispute concerns size rather than origin but I think that this is wishful thinking. For Solow finds his clues to size in the modern versions of Fisherian theory; 'the preferences of investors and savers, . . . the alternative forms of wealth available to them', while the Post-Keynesian theory has its roots in the Marxian concepts of exploitation and surplus value allied with the Keynesian–Kaleckian solutions of the realisation problem, i.e. 'mainly [in] the investment decisions of profit-seeking firms, not . . . the intentions to save of thrifty householders (Robinson, 1975e, p. 397).

2 'Keynes's theory of effective demand, which has remained so impervious to reconciliation with marginal economic theory, raises almost no problem when directly inserted into the earlier discussions of the Classical economists. Similarly, . . . the post-Keynesian theories of economic growth and income distribution, which have required so many artificial assumptions in the efforts to reconcile them with marginal productivity theory, encounter almost no difficulty when directly grafted on to Classical economic dynamics' (Pasinetti, 1974a, p. ix).

3 'Keynes's intellectual revolution was to shift economists from thinking normally in terms of a model of reality in which a dog called *savings* wagged his tail labelled *investment* to thinking in terms of a model in which a dog called *investment* wagged his tail labelled *savings*' (Meade, 1975a, p. 82).

4 Similarly, in the initial stages, Post-Keynesian theory was preoccupied with Golden Age analysis, as a preliminary flexing of muscles prior to tackling the much harder problems of actual growth processes.

5 Hicks has recently reminded us, as a result of my denseness, that the 'non-neoclassic' John Hicks of *A Theory of Economic History* and *Capital and Time* is J.R.'s uncle, who is not all *that* well pleased with his nephew (see Hicks, 1975, p. 365).

6 'The great mystery of the modern theory of distribution is, actually, why anyone regards the share of wages and profits in total income as an interesting problem. It has after all little practical relevance.' To this view, happily *and* relevantly, may be contrasted Alice Rivlin's recent 'political prediction', in her 1975 Richard T. Ely Lecture (Rivlin, 1975), 'that income shares . . . are going to become a major focus of policy debate in the next few years' (p. 1).

7 'the present orthodoxy is in serious need of revision and perhaps of revolution . . . the theory of dis-equilibrium is in considerable disarray as is the theory of intertemporal allocation in the face of uncertainty' (Hahn, 1974, p. 37).

8 A similar conclusion, albeit in a rather different and more limited context, recently has been stated by Clower (1975, p. 12). Referring to the finest modern flowering of neoclassical analysis, namely, general equilibrium (or Neo-Walrasian) theory, Clower says: '[The] existing body of Neo-Walrasian analysis rests upon assumptions that preclude its use for explicit analysis of either disequilibrium trading processes or monetary exchanges. . . . [It] is closed to extensions in certain crucial directions including . . . those . . . that would permit explicit formal analysis of Keynesian short-run adjustment processes . . . precisely the kind of processes about which economists must be able to speak with scientific authority if their science is to be anything more than a body of idle speculation and a breeding ground for charlatans and quacks.'

9 It is, of course, natural for Marxists to defend the traditional equilibrium concept, for most of vol. I of *Das Kapital* uses this methodology, yet refutes the use of supply and demand concepts as the surface phenomena of vulgar economy (see Rowthorn, 1974). I am indebted to John Henry for this point.

10 'The Keynesian method is to describe a set of relationships (intended to correspond to what are believed to be the relevant features of the economic system) and to trace the effects in the immediate and further future of a change taking place as an event at a moment of time' (Robinson, 1975f, p. 92).

11 'In fact, the long-run trend is but a slowly changing component of a chain of short-period situations; it has no independent entity' (Kalecki, 1968, p. 263).

12 See, also, Harcourt (1965a) for an early example.

13 '"Convergence to equilibrium" has been shown to be dubious . . . also unimportant. Even at the best, it will take a long time; and in most applications before that time has elapsed, something else . . . will surely have occurred' (Hicks, 1975a, p. 366).

14 Robinson (1975f, p. 92). Hahn thinks Marx would have been scornful of the Post-Keynesians – those whom Hahn calls 'reactionaries' – because they define classes by the orders of magnitude of their saving propensities. 'The reactionaries take differences in the propensity to save as their characterisation of class – how Marx would have scoffed!' (Hahn, 1975a, p. 92). That may be; certainly his present-day followers are rather scornful, though not for this reason (see paras 1.15–1.19). But how much more scornful Marx would have been of Hahn's own peculiarly sophisticated brand of Vulgar Economy.

15 'The neo-Ricardians, by means of the neoclassical theory of the choice of technique, have established that capital aggregation is theoretically unsound. Fine. Let us give them an alpha for this' (Hahn, 1975b, p. 363). This is a resolution of a major area in favour of the critics, a resolution that surprised at least one commentator. 'Economists have looked for this simple relationship, one of the main propositions of neoclassical economics, for a century; but now it is

generally recognized that the property did not always hold. . . . Cambridge U.K. had been right on this point' (Malinvaud, 1977, p. 174). Malinvaud adds, wrongly in my view, that he does not think the consequences are 'very profound'.

16 It is at this point that Garegnani's (nearly) unique stance is significant. For, as we saw in para. 1.8, he wishes both to defend a well-established methodology *and* to deduce the disquieting conclusion that when it is allied with the neoclassical emphasis on supply and demand, insuperable logical difficulties associated principally with the treatment of 'capital' prevent the approach from providing a viable theory of accumulation and distribution. 'Thus, after following in the footsteps of traditional theory and attempting an analysis of distribution in terms of "demand" and "supply", we are forced to the conclusion that a change, however small, in the "supply" or "demand" conditions of labour or capital (saving) may result in drastic changes of r and w . . . would even force us to admit that r may fall to zero or rise to its maximum . . ., without bringing to equality the quantities supplied and demanded of the two factors. . . . No such instability [has] ever [been] observed. . . . In order to explain distribution, [we] must rely on forces other than "supply" and "demand"' (Garegnani, 1970, p. 426). The response of those more favourably disposed towards traditional neoclassical theory (and its modern offshoots) has been either to evade the conclusions (Friedman, Johnson), or to change the questions, or the methodology, or both. Garegnani's lesson from the Cambridge controversies is thus a head-on confrontation, a full frontal attack, *even in terms of the long-run comparisons.*

17 The abstract equilibrium tells us what value[s] the unknowns must have if there is to be equilibrium; it does not tell us anything of any economic process which establishes such values' (Hahn, 1974, p. 36, n. 4).

18 'There is much to be learned from *a priori* comparisons of equilibrium positions, but they must be kept in their logical place . . . cannot be applied to actual situations . . .. In a model depicting equilibrium positions there is no causation. It consists of a closed circle of simultaneous equations . . .. At any moment in logical time, the past is determined just as much as the future. In an historical model, causal relations have to be specified. Today is a break in time between an unknown future and an irrevocable past. . . . Movement can only be forward' (Robinson, 1962, pp. 25–6).

19 For a list of the parables, see Harcourt (1975a, p. 316).

20 'The mainstream replies that this is only a crude simplification made for the purpose of applying the theory to real numbers, and so is to be judged pragmatically and not by the standards of rigorous analysis' (Solow, 1975a, p. 277).

21 'It merely shows how one goes about interpreting given time series if one starts by *assuming* that they were generated from a production function and that the competitive marginal-product relations apply' (Solow, 1974a, p. 121, emphasis in original).

22 The use of Keynes's name makes Marxists and radicals suspicious, for they (rightly) see Keynes as wishing to preserve the capitalist system by ridding it of its short-run effective demand deficiencies. They also suspect that something of this attitude – here they are on less firm ground – has affected the Post-Keynesian approach to the analysis of the longer-run developments of capitalist economies.

23 Roosevelt (1977, n. 2) acknowledges the important influence of Medio and Rowthorn's work on his own.

24 The exchanges between Samuelson (1974a, 1974b) and Baumol (1974a,

1974b) on the transformation problem also centre on these basic distinctions.

25 This, incidentally, gives a rigorous meaning to the classical view that 'distribution precedes value' (Harcourt, 1975b, p. 342) which Hahn (1975b, p. 361) finds not merely mistaken but also incomprehensible. Sraffa thus bridges satisfactorily both Ricardian with Marxian thought *and* these together with modern thought. As with Ricardo of old, his editor gives 'the primary emphasis of his theory' to the proposition 'that a rise in wages would reduce profits equivalently [but] he [is] by no means blind to its differential effect on prices' (Dobb, 1975, p. 329).

26 Meek (1967, pp. 175–8) made a similar point many years ago in his classic review article of Sraffa's book (originally published simultaneously in the June and Spring 1961 issues of the *Scottish Journal of Political Economy* and *Science and Society*, respectively). It was, however, obscured by his exposition in which he treated the transformation problem as being directed more towards an explanation of the deviations of the 'prices of production' from 'values'. Harcourt and Massaro (1964b, pp. 453–4), in arguing that Sraffa had rehabilitated the labour theory of value, also pitched it in these terms rather than in the more correct terms, from the point of view of an interpretation of Marx, of the fundamental explanation of the origin of profits, themselves a surface phenomenon.

27 On Sraffa's analysis when the wage is advanced, see Roncaglia (1974).

28 'The theory of *value* performs [an] important function within the Marxian analysis of capitalism. It links Marx's "macroeconomic model" which shows the mechanism of the system setting some basic relationships between a limited number of variables, with his "microeconomic model" of interindustry competitive relationships' (Medio, 1972, p. 330).

29 [An] economy is in equilibrium when it generates messages which do not cause agents to change the theories which they hold or the policies which they pursue' (Hahn, 1973a, p. 28).

30 Harris's paper has influenced greatly the views I have taken in the present section.

31 With hindsight, Harry Johnson (1975) is now arguing that *The General Theory* is yet another example of unnecessary English originality. He feels, moreover, that its effects are pernicious, for it drew on the unique United Kingdom experience, a special case that was nevertheless easily explainable in orthodox terms, as the basis for an unnecessary and incorrect general theory of how capitalism works.

32 In commenting on a draft of this paper, Harold Lydall described the political attitude of the Cambridge Post-Keynesians as 'a sort of "bastard Marxism" [which will get] short shift from "true" Marxists [though its proponents serve] a useful purpose as intellectual fellow travellers, whose main function is to undermine faith in capitalism and any other kind of market economy'.

19 Non-neoclassical capital theory*

The editor of this issue has asked me to write on the characteristics of non-neoclassical capital theory, as exemplified by the contributions of the Cambridge, England, school. Like 'capital' itself (even in the neoclassical tradition), non-neoclassical capital theory is not a homogeneous commodity. Nevertheless, I shall try to outline approaches to the theory of capital which are shared in varying degrees by a number of prominent critics of orthodox neoclassical capital theory such as is contained in the writings of Arrow and Hahn (1971), Ferguson (1969, 1972), Samuelson, Solow and, most recently, Bliss (1975). Obviously, the emphasis which the individual authors place on certain points differs but the various strands are, I believe, recognizable in their contributions. I draw principally on the contributions of Joan Robinson, Sraffa, Dobb, Kaldor, Pasinetti, Garegnani, Mathur and Nuti, from the Cambridge school itself, and also on Hicks (in his recent neo-Austrian phase; see Hicks, 1970, 1973, 1975a), Kregel (1972, 1973, 1976a) and Lowe (1976).

The first general point to make is that the major influences on these writers are the classical political economists, especially Ricardo, and, of course, Marx (who, while he inherited the classical tradition, also radically added to and altered it). In some instances, Keynes too is a major influence, as Kregel (1976a) recently has reminded us. Though in the end they are critical of Wicksell's approach, he nevertheless is the most respected and influential of the neoclassical writers. Marshall's influence also may be discerned, especially on the English contributors. We examine in detail below the significance of these influences. The second general point is that, if only because of the classical tradition which it shares, non-neoclassical capital theory must be regarded as indissolubly integrated with value, distribution and growth theory, and especially with the analysis of the origin of profits in the capitalist mode of production, a point that is both central and of obvious Marxist origin. Of course, orthodox capital theory is also integrated with these other branches and is concerned with the nature of profits and interest but the emphasis and the answers and the form of analysis itself are very different (see, for example, Bliss, 1975, chapter 15). The third general point is that in non-neoclassical theory, 'capital' as a concept is like love, a many splendoured thing. In particular, it is an all-pervading concept instead of being just a category, for example, a third factor of production, sometimes treated as if it were a primary factor, as in the neoclassical tradition.

These three general themes permeate the discussions that follow.

I

The concept of capital dominated classical economic thought.[1] Not only did it (in its technical production aspects) embrace virtually the whole range of economic goods — wage goods, raw materials and stocks of all kinds, and durable capital goods — but it was also intimately associated with the social relationships which characterized the economy. The latter is made especially clear in Marx's work where it was the combined emergence of the capitalist and working classes which gave rise to the overall concept of capital in his system. Furthermore, his reclassification of capital goods into variable and constant capital was vital to his view of the essential characteristics of the capitalist mode of production and of the origin of profits in the surplus labour and surplus value that was associated with it. (Marx considered that Ricardo's — in Marx's view — less fundamental classification of capital goods into circulating and durable capital goods constituted the principal stumbling block in the way of Ricardo being able clearly to perceive why profits arose. The return in some instances by modern non-neoclassical writers to the Ricardian classification and their (alleged) neglect of the sphere of production has been criticized strongly by some modern Marxists; see, for example, Rowthorn, 1974; Roosevelt, 1977.)

Marx was, of course, perfectly well aware of the impact on labour productivity that the accumulation of capital goods technically made possible — few economic historians have documented the process in more telling detail. Nevertheless, for him, as for the modern writers, the social aspects were far more fundamental, *viz*. that the monopoly of the means of production by the capitalist class made it possible for them to exploit this technological fact of life and extract surplus labour from the working class, influencing greatly their conditions of work and life styles generally in the process. As the latter were deprived of direct access to the means of production, they had no alternative but to sell their labour power to the capitalists. It was this social relationship in the sphere of production which was the clue both to the creation of profits and to the further accumulation of capital goods which were the *raison d'être* of the capitalist system. Labour was thus the only *socially relevant* factor. In this tradition, non-neoclassical capital theory takes as its basic model a capitalist system (sometimes competitive, sometimes not) in which clear-cut social classes may be discerned and for which profit-making and the accumulation of capital goods are ends in themselves, necessary, but not always sufficient, for actual survival. The principal goal of non-neoclassical capital theory is to aid an analysis in detail of the 'laws of motion' of such an economy as it reproduces and expands over actual historical time.

Marx developed another aspect of capital by examining the process in more detail. He distinguished between capital in the form of money, then in commodities involved in the production process, and then in money again, if the production of commodities made possible by the investment of capital goods, including variable capital goods, i.e. the advance of wage goods, in the production process, was saleable. In Marx, as in the work of the classical political economists, the sequence nature of production was highlighted — first, the production period in which wages were advanced and the two elements of constant capital, raw materials and durable assets, were used, *then* the exchange period. Out of the latter arose both the possibility of further accumulation and expansion as the cycle was repeated and, of course, the possibility of contradiction and crises associated with the realization problem. All of these strands find expression in modern non-neoclassical theory: the emphasis on labour's contribution and its payment (so that the wage fund in a modern guise becomes again an important ingredient of the story), the sequence nature of production processes, the fact that one aspect of the investment process is the commitment of money capital as a hostage to fortune in an uncertain world.

Joan Robinson, for example, has frequently emphasized the strategic role of the real wage[2] in capital and growth theory, its effect on both the *amount* and type of investment which may be done. The real wage not only affects the size of the potential surplus available, it also affects the amount of labour time that a given surplus may command in the capital goods trades. The minimum real wage associated with the inflation barrier, i.e. the level below which the wage-earners cannot be pushed, limits the size of the potential surplus. Within that limit, accumulation leads and the real wage is the residual when activity, output and prices are determined. In her view these effects are far more important than a third effect, the bearing of the real wage on the choice of techniques of production, the aspect on which the neoclassical tradition has tended to concentrate. (Drawing initially on Wicksell, Joan Robinson has discussed the latter in considerable detail, but she now confines the results to the sphere of doctrinal debate.) She has, moreover, used the classical notion of working-capital funds that are needed to back up advanced wages in the periodic cycle of production as a technical reason for overthrowing, even on its own ground, the neo-classical proposition that the wage equals the marginal product of labour. (The equality in fact should be between the marginal product of labour, on the one hand, and the wage *plus* the interest on the additional finance required to advance the wage of the additional wage-earner, on the other.)[3] Pasinetti and Garegnani also have highlighted the patterns of the labour structure of production in their contributions, as have Hicks (1970, 1973, 1975a) and Nuti (1970).

Sraffa (1960), it is true, departs from the classical tradition whereby the wage is advanced. Instead, he treats it as paid out of the surplus at the end of the production period. This, however, is done merely for technical convenience, in order to obtain a simple linear relationship between the rate of profits and the wage in the standard system, $r = R(1 - w)$, where r = rate of profits, R = maximum rate of profits and w = wage (measured as a proportion of the standard net product) (see Sraffa, 1960, pp. 22 ff). The object of the exercise is to illustrate some Ricardian-*cum*-Marxian problems – the antagonism between the real wage and the rate of profits, the possible independence of distribution from value, at least at a point in time, and the relationship of this property to Marx's transformation problem. Thus Sraffa is able to demonstrate by the above relationship that, although the wage, rate of profits and relative prices of the standard and actual systems are identical, yet in the standard system the wage–rate of profits relation (and, it could be added, the wage–surplus value relation) exist, as it were, *prior to and independently of the relative prices*, i.e. the prices of production. As Eatwell (1974, p. 302) comments, 'Sraffa's standard commodity therefore possesses all the characteristics which Marx sought in the "average commodity" which was to be the key to his solution of the transformation problem.' As well as giving a rigorous meaning to the classical view that distribution precedes value (in context, if not in time), Sraffa bridges satisfactorily both Ricardian with Marxian thought and these together with modern thought. Moreover, from the point of view of production and capital theory, the whole analysis may be done with the wage advanced and no major proposition is affected in any essential way (though, of course, the simple linear

relationship between the wage and the rate of profits no longer holds)
(see Roncaglia, 1974).

Also associated with the discussion above is Sraffa's procedure of regarding the whole of the wage as paid out of the surplus, rather than
distinguishing between that part of the wage which is taken up by the
necessaries, 'the ever-present element of subsistence' (Sraffa, 1960, p.9)
or classical natural price of labour power, and the wage-earners' share in
the surplus over and above the necessaries and the replacement of the
means of production used up in the production process. The size of
the latter may be interpreted as an index of the intensity of, and relative
strengths of the two sides in, the class struggle at any moment of time.
The objections raised to it by some modern Marxists, e.g. Medio (1972),
Rowthorn (1974) and Roosevelt (1977), is that it treats the length of
the working day and the other conditions of production in the sphere
of production as exogenous to the system and so concentrates only on
exercises in the sphere of distribution and exchange, in particular, on
the impact on the prices of production of 'changes' in distribution.
Moreover, it obscures the Marxian insight whereby the wage is measured
in terms of labour time, so that the working day splits conveniently
into the workman working first for himself and then for the capitalist.
But Sraffa's concentration on particular issues is *not* equivalent to
arguing that the other factors are unimportant or unacceptable, it is
merely to argue that they have been put in cold storage as not being
relevant to the particular problem in hand.[4]

Both Nuti (1970) and Hicks (1970, 1973, 1975a) take a sequential
view of individual (and economy-wide) production processes which is
both classical and Austrian in origin. Only labour inputs per period and
final commodity output are shown explicitly, i.e. co-operating machines
and work in progress, though known to be at work in the background,
do not make actual appearances. The production process is presented in
terms of the time profiles of inputs and outputs. This technical apparatus allows a discussion of the ability of a decentralized economy to
move through a transitional phase to a new equilibrium following a
technical innovation in the methods of production. In addition, of
course, a whole series of comparative dynamic propositions may be
ground out by use of this model, all of which can be shown to be consistent with the results of more orthodox models. Nevertheless, by
undertaking the analysis within this alternative framework, additional
insights may be gained.[5]

An important contribution by Pasinetti (1973) also arises from a
consideration of the labour structure of production; it leads to an

analysis which throws additional light on the transformation problem and Marx's theory of value generally, including the composition of the prices of production as they are traced back through the production system, as well as on the role of the time structure of production in a multisectoral growth model. Pasinetti is concerned to discuss the concept of vertical integration from a theoretical point of view. His principal tool of analysis is Sraffa's device of sub-systems (see Sraffa, 1960, p.89, Harcourt and Massaro, 1964a). A sub-system is an ingenious device whereby the total direct and indirect labour content of a particular commodity in a given production and technical situation may be obtained immediately, without resort to the alternative device of 'reduction to dated quantities of labour' (Sraffa, 1960, chapter VI). Its relationship to vertical integration will become clear in what follows.

Suppose that we consider an economic system of circulating commodities, each one of which is produced in a single commodity industry, i.e. the model which underlies much of classical political economy. (The device is, nevertheless, a general one, applicable to joint production systems, including the case of fixed capital.)[6] In the actual economic system we suppose there to be produced over a given production period, a gross product of such size and composition as to provide a net product, i.e. a surplus of commodities over and above those which serve to replace the used-up means of production and, we may say for our purposes, necessary wage goods as well. With this particular level of production will be associated a given amount of labour units, distributed in a technically determined way between each industry as its direct labour content. We wish to find, though, the direct and indirect labour content of each particular commodity in the net product. Therefore, we construct notionally a system in which the net product contains one (or more) units of the commodity that we are interested in *but no other*. That is to say, the notional levels of activity in the other industries are such as only to allow the production of sufficient of each to replace the amounts of each used up as means of production in the sub-system as a whole. Then, obviously, the *total* amount of labour associated with the sub-system is the direct and indirect labour content of the commodity that constitutes its net product. A sub-system thus shows up *directly* the total labour requirements and what Pasinetti calls the composite commodity requirements of a unit of any final good. Moreover, we have rearranged our way of looking at the production process so as to form a series of 'notional' vertically integrated activities, one for each commodity. We also have 'redistributed' the total labour force employed in the economy into its vertically integrated components, as obtained from the sub-system corresponding to each commodity in the original net product. The same process also may be repeated, as many times as we like, for the 'composite commodity' of each sub-system. It is this approach and variations on it that Pasinetti exploits in order to discuss the implications of the theoretical concept of vertical integration for value, distribution, capital and growth theory.

We mentioned above that the sub-system device was a general one, as applicable to joint production systems as to single commodity ones, and that the interest in joint production mostly lay in its relevance for the case of fixed capital. Sraffa's device of treating one period older durable capital goods as commodities jointly produced with the other commodities of each production process has, as he says himself, classical origins (see Sraffa, 1960, pp. 94–5). It is an approach which is now receiving greater attention as the joint production sections of Sraffa's book are becoming more familiar and more people are examining them (see, for example, Schefold, unpublished, Morishima, 1973, 1974; Steedman, 1975a). The approach is, of course, von Neumann's as well. Burmeister (1974) has shown how von Neumann's framework may be generalized in order to take in other approaches to capital theory, so that the method itself has, in his view,[7] a foot in both the non-neoclassical and neoclassical camps. The implications of joint production for Marx's theory of the origin of profits recently has been discussed by Morishima (1973, 1974) and Steedman (1975a), and for Marx's theory of depreciation by Steedman and Hodgson (1977), with seemingly damaging effect for Marx's theory of profits. Thus, it seemed possible to show, by use in effect of sub-systems, that negative surplus value could be associated with positive profits, so that we have a counter example to the 'Fundamental Marxian Theorem'. However, at least in the circulating-commodity case, it may be shown, provided only that some very reasonable economic constraints are accepted, that these damaging implications of joint production for the Marxian theory of profits may be circumvented (see Cheok, Davis, Harcourt and Madden, 1976; Morishima, 1976; and Steedman, 1976). The puzzles associated with the fixed capital case evidently still remain (see Howard and King, 1975, pp. 157–60). There are two main puzzles: first, that the labour values of a commodity are not unique when two equiprofitable techniques are in operation, i.e. switch point cases. Second, when the number of products and number of processes in a joint product system do not match, the system is either underdetermined or overdetermined so that both the prices of production *and* labour values remain unknown.

II

As we have mentioned, non-neoclassical capital theory is intimately associated with the classical notion of the surplus of commodities over and above the necessaries and means of production, and the respective amounts of labour associated with each collection (which, in Marx's hands, became the crucial ingredient of his theory of the origin of profits). The re-emergence of the surplus concept (vanished during the neoclassical era to the shadowy subjective underworld of consumers' and producers' surplus) in recent years, the basis of cost–benefit analysis, is a significant aspect of the theory. It obviously has relevance for questions relating to planning the development of an economy and also for those questions which are concerned with an economy's own capacity and ability to develop, that is to say, to have on tap at each stage of a development sequence, the requisite quantities of commodities needed. These themes preoccupy both Hicks (1970, 1973) in his study of the transition process following a technical innovation, and Lowe (1976) in his new book on the structure of production in a capitalist economy. In this book Lowe uses a fixed-coefficients model and is

> concerned with the almost totally neglected problem of the adjustment of a growing system using fixed-capital goods to a change in its parameters and, in particular, with the issue of 'traverse' . . . from a given to a higher or a lower rate of growth. (Nell, 1976, p. 290)

The neglect has not been complete, however. In the early 1960s, Mathur (1965) made a most thorough study of these themes within a context of planning for steady growth, that is to say, within a context of analysing the paths which an economy could and should take when changing markedly its composition of physical capital goods. (He argued that his analysis would illuminate the process of development of a mixed economy as well, provided only that the government acted in such a way as 'correctly' to influence both the amount and the composition of the investment expenditures of private businessmen and their use of resources generally (p. 11).)[8] Mathur grafted the von Neumann-Sraffa analysis onto the contributions of Joan Robinson in particular. One advantage of von Neumann's approach for Mathur was that the wage was viewed as advanced rather than as paid out of the surplus, as in Sraffa's formulation. This provided a framework in which, in Mathur's view, Marxian prices and values (and also Wicksell effects) could the better be understood.

The questions are two: first, *can* the economy physically, i.e. technocratically, get from one position — for example, a level of activity and/or rate of growth – to another following the intrusion of new factors? Second, if it is technically a physical possibility (Lowe's book and Hicks's work throw doubt even on this; see also Nell, 1975), is it likely that a decentralized economy will work in such a way as to give the appropriate signals which ensure that the appropriate path will be followed step by step? A significant part of Joan Robinson's work has been to criticize the assumption that such transitions *are* either feasible or possible (and to suggest that the concept of malleable capital was a way of avoiding these puzzles). It is these considerations which lie behind her emphasis on the importance of the distinction between changes – actual processes – and differences – comparisons of equilibrium states, together with her criticism that neoclassical capital and growth theory has *not* kept these distinctions clearly in mind. Samuelson (1975) makes it clear that in his work he has done so, whatever may be said of his followers who have faith. Thus, he argues, the differences that remain between him and Joan Robinson and the post-Keynesians generally relate to judgment and to vision, that is to say, differing beliefs about the existence in actual economies of the processes modelled in theoretical ones, and also about the efficacy of market forces, signals and substitution possibilities. It is no accident that in their capital theory neoclassical economists put emphasis on substitution possibilities, either by using simple neoclassical models, or by looking at individual processes with fixed coefficients but allowing the composition of output to change in response to demand changes. Non-neoclassical theorists tend more to emphasize rigidities and fixity both in the small and in the large and are much less inclined to accept that time heals all wounds.

Finally, in this context, we should note Solow's criticism (1974b) of what he calls the longitudinal approach to capital and growth theory of Hicks whereby the disappearance of machines and raw materials becomes vital. For, he argues, we need to know, when discussing transitions, the extent of *ex post* substitution present, i.e. the range of intensity over which existing machines may be run in their present activities and also the possibilities of shifting them from one activity to another. We need also to make explicit the roles (and extent) of markets for financial assets of firms and second-hand markets for durable capital goods. These points recently have been raised to positions of central importance in Davidson (1972) and in Minsky's (1975) interpretation of the basic message of the *General Theory* – that it is a theory of cyclical fluctuations in which cash flows and the asset/liability structure of capitalist firms as well as capital stock adjustment processes are the key to fluctuations.

Joan Robinson also was concerned originally to measure capital as real capital (capital in terms of commodities deflated by the real wage) because she was trying to see whether it was possible to make sense of capital as a one-dimensional factor of production in the *neo-classical setting of the aggregate production function*. As I argued in Harcourt (1972, pp. 21–2) her measure did reflect meaningfully the technical aspects of capital in a production function – the technical source of output flows.[9] However, it does not satisfy the requirement of being a measure which is independent of distribution and prices, a point which, of course, is central to both Joan Robinson and Sraffa's critique of the neoclassical doctrine and approach. There are two other factors associated with this discussion. The first is the Keynesian-*cum*-Marshallian view that capital has at least two aspects – free or money capital seeking profitable investment opportunities and the subsequent capital goods, the hard objects which are the specific forms in which the money outlays have been made hostages to fortune and which must take the chance of actual cash flows disappointing the expectations held when the investments were planned and made. The other factor has been the long argument about the need to find a unit in which capital could be measured which was independent of distribution and prices, in order that supply and demand concepts, including a well-behaved relationship between the rate of profits and the 'quantity' of capital, could be used in an explanation of profits and profits share. It is true that the neoclassical approach as represented by the modern general equilibrium theorists denies that such a measure is needed in a general equilibrium framework. The non-neoclassical critics reply that it *is* needed *if* the quantity of capital is to play a meaningful role in a demand and supply explanation (see Garegnani, 1970; Harcourt, 1976).

Here Joan Robinson and Garegnani's work come together.[10] Garegnani (1959, 1960, 1970, 1973) has shown that the measurement problem was common to both the classicals (Ricardo, Marx) and the neoclassicals (Walras, Wicksell), i.e. to the inventors, or at least the main innovators of the surplus approach and to those who rejected it in favour of a marginalist, especially marginal productivity, approach. The measurement problem of the first tradition arose out of Ricardo's efforts to measure the surplus that was to be distributed, with which was associated his theory and measurement of the rate of profits on capital. Garegnani argues that the solution to Ricardo's problem is to be found in the use of the concept of the average period of production. In the other strand, however, as is now well known, the problem proves insuperable, in so far as obtaining an *independent* measure of the 'quantity' of capital is a central aim of the analysis.

III

Within non-neoclassical capital theory is another strand that is classical — the return to making capital the central concept of capital theory together with making growth and distribution over time the central problems of economic theory. As we have seen above, it involves the view, common to both Marx and Keynes, that profit making and capital accumulation are ends in themselves. For Keynes, they were in the last analysis a way of life for businessmen; for Marx, they were the means of survival in a ruthlessly competitive environment (and not always achievable at that). Both saving and investment become class phenomena, dictated by the reproducing and expanding nature of the system, rather than being the means to the end of maximizing individuals' satisfactions through present and future consumption plans. (There is, of course, more than a vestige of the individual's role left in Keynes's psychological underpinnings of the aggregate consumption function. This is not so in Kalecki and Joan Robinson's versions which are Marxian in origin.) The approach replaces the principal preoccupations of the neoclassicals who have put prices at the centre and, at least for a while, the allocation of *given* scarce resources between competing ends at a *point* in time as the central problem of analysis. (One thinks of Jevons and Walras.) The concept of capital also shrank in several dimensions as a result, becoming more a technological concept virtually unconnected with social relationships. For example, each individual economic agent, now the basic variable of the analysis, arbitrarily could be endowed with resources at the beginning of the period and it was the allocation and the maximization (of satisfaction) aspects of the workings of the economy which were concentrated on. Witness also Solow's view (1963) that, paradoxically, it is often easier to understand capitalism by thinking about socialism. Moreover, in Walras's hands, for example, as Eagley (1974) has shown, capital goods have become only durable assets, while raw materials and wage goods have become associated instead with financial and income flows.

In Irving Fisher's hands, capital goods *as such* disappeared and capital accumulation was analysed in terms of consumption foregone. The latter went into a black box of productive transformation over time, as given technically by the investment opportunity curve, ultimately to emerge as consumption goods in the future, the amounts being guided by technical possibilities, the markets for money loans and the psychological time preference of the agents (see Dougherty, 1972). The principal focus of interest became the inter temporal price

system, especially its allocative properties and accompanying relationship to efficiency, a far cry from the swashbuckling and ruthless accumulators of capital and receivers of profits in the classical and Marxian
stories. The analysis of production processes in sequence disappeared
(at least for a while), as did the distinction between the production and
exchange periods. Simultaneity of solution in a general equilibrium system took their place. Moreover, as we have seen, when sequences did
reappear, they were associated with the efficiency properties of inter-
temporal *prices* rather than with the categories of the classical tradition
(see Bliss, 1975). Furthermore, not only did prices become the central
concept, both in the static allocative version and in the inter-temporal
one, but also they were often market prices, usually competitive ones
which served to clear existing markets. This again is in contrast to the
natural prices of the classical political economists and the prices of
production of Marx, those centres of gravity determined by sustained
and fundamental forces, of which the market prices were but imperfect
indexes, being subject to the short-run whims of transitory demand and
supply factors.[11] These trends have been reversed to varying degrees
within the body of non-neoclassical capital theory, especially in the
contributions of Sraffa and Garegnani. The latter, indeed, has made
these considerations not only central to his criticisms of neoclassical
theory but also to his disagreement with some aspects of Joan Robinson's contributions and criticisms of neoclassical theory (see Garegnani,
1976). Non-neoclassical theory has also witnessed a re-emergence of the
classical concept of competition as the dynamic allocator of investment
funds over time through the tendency to establish uniform rates of
profit in all activities, as opposed to the neoclassical concept in which is
emphasized market-clearing prices that are the parameters to which
individual price-takers look in Walrasian markets (see Roncaglia, 1977).

Finally, we come to the role of Keynes in non-neoclassical capital
theory, an important point that recently has been unearthed by Kregel
(1976a) as a result of his examination of the historical background to
both capital theory, especially the start of the Cambridge–Cambridge
debates, and Harrod's theory of growth. This discovery ties in neatly
with Pasinetti's thesis (see Pasinetti, 1974a, pp. 43–4) that Keynes's
basic methodology had more in common with Ricardo's than with
that of his immediate neoclassical forebears, e.g. Marshall and certainly
Walras (Keynes knew little in detail, and thought even less, of Walras).
The methodology incorporates the view that the economic theorist
has a duty to single out the most important variables and freeze out
others by assumption, so that there emerges 'a system of equations of

the "causal type" . . . as opposed to a completely interdependent system of simultaneous equations', which is a characteristic of the neoclassical tradition. Furthermore, the economic theorist needs

> to specify which variables are sufficiently interdependent as to be best represented by simultaneous relations, and which . . . exhibit such an overwhelming dependence in one direction (and such a small dependence in the opposite direction) as to be best represented by one-way-direction relations.

(Even more was this procedure characteristic of Kalecki and his example and influence are very marked in non-neoclassical capital, distribution and growth theory, especially in the work of Joan Robinson and her closest followers.) This procedure is also related to a recurring theme in the writings of the late Maurice Dobb, whose last statement on it may be found in Chapter 1 of *Theories of Value and Distribution* (1973). Dobb was insistent that to neglect a discussion of directions in a system of interdependent relations was to refuse to accept the (necessary) responsibility of a theorist to provide 'an *explanation*, in the sense of depicting the situation as an economic process that works in a certain way and is capable of being acted upon and influenced' (p. 8, emphasis in original). Dobb (p. 9) quotes with approval Mathur's view that causal relations are present in an equilibrium situation even if the latter is described by a set of simultaneous equations. Thus, every 'equation depicting an economic relation has got one or two direction signs, which we neglect to print, but must not be lost sight of when we analyse the solution of simultaneous equations' (Mathur, 1965, p. 70).

Returning to Keynes's immediate influence in these areas, it is to be found, first, in the discussion of measurement problems which initially were thought to be the main bone of contention (though we now know that it was the meaning (of capital) which was at stake). In *The General Theory*, Keynes distinguished two fundamental units of measurement, in so far as the analyst was concerned with the aggregate behaviour of the system as a whole. Keynes thought it impossible to measure (in a way that made them comparable) different quantities of capital (or, indeed, real income) at different points of time. He settled instead for use of the quantity of money-value and the wage unit as the fundamental units, an approach which has been followed in recent years by Asimakopulos in particular. 'The first of these is strictly homogeneous, and the second can be made so' (Keynes, 1971-9, vol. vii, p. 41); he thus reserved 'the use of vague concepts . . . the quantity of output as a whole, the quantity of capital equipment as a whole' (p. 43) for historical comparisons where approximations and imprecision are more acceptable.[12]

Keynes was also sympathetic to the classical–Marxian notion that labour was the only socially relevant factor of production, a view which we have seen is also represented in Joan Robinson's attempt to see if *any* sense could be made of the neoclassical tradition (that came immediately through J. R. Hicks) of capital as a one-dimensional factor of production in the aggregate production function. The non-neoclassical criticisms of marginal productivity theory also find echoes in Keynes who, because of his concern with uncertainty and expectations, always distinguished between physical and value productivity and rejected outright the idea that capital as a factor of production was productive in any sense that was meaningful in determining its return, see Kregel (1976a, p. 49). This view is associated of course with Keynes's argument that the barter economy of neoclassical tradition was unsuitable for an analysis of overall employment and production in a monetary economy. Thus his rejection of Say's Law carried with it the rejection of many other neoclassical propositions concerning, for example, capital, interest and profits: hence his liquidity preference theory of interest, a monetary phenomenon, and his linking of profits to expected monetary returns on physical assets.

IV

In conclusion, it is necessary to point out that we should not stress too much the detailed differences between orthodox and non-neoclassical capital theory. Thus, for example, in both Jevons and Böhm-Bawerk, emphasis was laid on labour (and land) and on the importance of time as the source of the productivity of capital goods and of interest. (The former view of time was attacked by Keynes and is now much modified or even abandoned.) Moreover, orthodox economists have done a great deal of work on dynamic processes and recently again on sequence analysis (see Hahn, 1973a), though, again, prices, usually market prices, have been the basic variables. What remains as the essential difference is therefore that orthodox theory is technocratic, concerned with inputs and outputs, prices and efficiency, in a world of individual economic agents, the maximization of whose satisfaction under constraints is the driving force and *raison d'être* of the system. Social relations are only shadowy reflections of their real-world counterparts, if there at all, whereas for non-neoclassical capital theory, as for Marx, they are *the* essentials of the theory, together with the reproducing and expanding nature of the process of capital accumulation. Thus it is no surprise to learn that Bliss (1975, p. 352), in concluding what must certainly stand as the most impressively original and substantial exposition of the *equilibrium theory of capital*, presents it 'as an alternative to the Marxian system' in that it

> does not show the distribution of income to be the outcome of a uni-directional chain of causes starting from the rate of exploitation. [Rather it] shows the distribution of income to be the outcome of the balancing of a large number of mutually interacting forces.

Notes

* *World Development*, vol. 7, no. 10, October 1979, pp. 923–32. I thank, but in no way implicate, Gautam Mathur, Neil Laing, Alessandro Roncaglia and Luigi Pasinetti for their comments on a draft of this article. I am also especially indebted to Gautam Mathur for his patience and forebearance while waiting for the final product.

1 A recent outstanding exposition of this view is Eagley (1974).

2 This must not be taken to imply that wage-earners are able to control the level of real wages actually achieved. As with Keynes, Joan Robinson argues that a central feature of the analysis of the capitalist process is that the wage bargain is made in money terms.

3 Even in the case of a continuous process this proposition holds, so that my criticism of Joan Robinson and Kregel on this point in Harcourt (1973, p. 1269) is wrong. However, my general point that 'even if the simple equality be destroyed, the maximizing principle which is basic to the marginalist view, far from being refuted by the proposition, is in fact consistent with it' (p. 1269) still stands.

4 See Harcourt (1977a) and Roncaglia (1977) for an elaboration of these points.

5 Burmeister (1974) discusses these various approaches and their reconciliation in considerable technical detail.

6 'The interest of Joint Products does not lie so much in the familiar examples of wool and mutton, or wheat and straw, as in its being the genus of which Fixed Capital is the leading species' (Sraffa, 1960, p. 63).

7 Burmeister's view contrasts starkly with that of Mathur (1965), see pp. 6–11 for a succinct statement why. Mathur argues vigorously that the von Neumann (and Sraffa) models, despite their 'apparent similarities' to 'aggregative neoclassical economics', are 'quite inconsistent with these for all practical purposes'. By contrast, 'post-Keynesian macro dynamics is . . . compatible with the analyses of Sraffa and von Neumann' which even though they 'look different . . . are of the same nature'. The differences between Burmeister and Mathur may be due, partly at least, to the fact that Mathur has more in mind than Burmeister, the characteristics and properties of the Solow–Swan aggregative neoclassical growth models, in which certain very simple neoclassical propositions are essential for the arguments that are developed with their aid.

8 Professor Chakravarty recently reminded me that von Hayek analysed a similar problem, albeit by rather different methods, in the early 1930s.

9 It has also been shown (by Read, 1968, and Rymes, 1968, 1971) that the real capital measure picks up adequately, as Solow's neoclassical measure and

method do not, the total impact of technical innovations in an economy characterized by commodity interdependence such as is characteristic of Sraffa's model. Essentially, if commodities are produced by commodities, measures of technical progress that treat the production process as a one-way flow from factors to final products will fail to pick up the feedback effects of technical progress from one activity to another (see Harcourt, 1972, pp. 86–7).

10   We should note, though, Joan Robinson's view that it is the *meaning*, not the *measurement*, of capital, which is the central issue; indeed, this is the principal theme of this essay.

11   This has not always been the case, for the major battleground between the two Cambridges has used as centre-pieces models in which prices of production containing a uniform rate of profits play a prominent role.

12   Keynes's insistence on exactness in theoretical work (as opposed to practical measurement) is also shared by Sraffa; see, for example, his comments on this issue at the Corfu conference in capital theory, as quoted by Sen (1974, p. 33) and Joan Robinson, as demonstrated by her many discussions of when it is or is not possible to define in an exact manner concepts such as the rate of profits and the value of capital.

20 On theories and policies*

There are at least three schools of thought which may be said to underlie current debates on policy, two of which, though they start from different theoretical premises, nevertheless largely inform our present [late 1976 but pre-devaluation] policy stances.[1] They also reflect the philosophy of the leaders of the present government, in so far as they could be said to have a coherent and consistent philosophy. The third school departs from the former two both in theoretical analysis and policy prescription. The three schools are, respectively, the monetarists (which have their greatest though by no means exclusive influence in the Reserve Bank); the Bastard Keynesians (which by and large is the stance of the Treasury though there are also aspects of it in the often eclectic approach of the Reserve Bank economists, just as there are some monetarist elements in Treasury thinking); and the Post-Keynesians. The Post-Keynesian school is the group of theorists who draw directly on the work of Keynes himself. The most influential members include Joan Robinson and Richard Kahn (that is to say, the people who actually worked with Keynes after he had published the *Treatise* and when he was writing *The General Theory*), and their followers and contemporaries, for example, Nicholas Kaldor. The other major influences are Michal Kalecki, and Marx and the classical political economists, especially as the latter have been interpreted through Piero Sraffa's and Maurice Dobb's edition of and writings on Ricardo, and through Sraffa's own original works, most importantly the *Production of Commodities* (1960). These are, of course, broad judgments which try to discern major stances and trends, and to identify dominant themes. Clearly neither Reserve Bank nor Treasury officials are homogeneous or abstract labour power.

The Friedman view

Milton Friedman's monetarist philosophy, which has a great influence on aspects of the Reserve Bank's approach, has its ideological roots in

315

Smithian liberalism. It involves a policy of non-intervention, except for the creation and/or preservation of competitive institutions and relatively simple rules for the monetary authorities to follow, together with a much more modest role for the public sector than is the case at the moment. Its theoretical basis also lies in one aspect of the Smithian vision (another aspect leads to Marx and the Post-Keynesians), that of the efficacy and efficiency of the invisible hand, as achieved through the market-clearing properties of freely fluctuating prices in individual markets. The line goes through Walrasian general equilibrium rather than through Marshall, which is more the tradition of the second school in Australia, especially Melbourne, of the Prest era anyway, though not, of course, in the U.S.A. Friedman's life work may be seen from one aspect as a concerted effort to pick off, decade by decade, the principal props of Keynes's system – the rival consumption functions; the relative impact of money versus investment on overall activity and prices; the liquidity preference theory of interest versus Friedman's capital theory; monetary versus fiscal policy; the relative importance of balance sheets *vis-à-vis* income and expenditure accounts; and so on. He wishes to reveal the so-called Keynesian revolution as an abortive aberration on the mainstream of economic theory and, incidentally, make the world safe for free men. (Harry Johnson has been a most prolific, indeed obsessive, expositor of this view. For obvious reasons, Friedman has been more muted, not least because, as Patinkin has argued and Friedman has conceded, Friedman's 'restatement' of the quantity theory has Keynesian innovations and attitudes in it.)

The practical implications of Friedman's views include an attack on detailed, and often variable, government intervention on fiscal matters, especially the irresponsibility and dishonesty of taxation through inflation in order to move resources into the public sector, a commitment to simple but sustained monetary rules, and encouragement of attempts to create flexible competitive institutions so that the real world may be made to work as if it were a Walrasian system. The latter is especially true of the attitude to labour markets, where a dislike of minimum wage regulations goes hand in hand with humanitarian plus efficiency support for comprehensive retraining and relocating schemes, coupled with the advocacy of the need for great increases in information flows. Allied with these views and the monetarist's version of the quantity theory of money is the central importance that is given to the role of expectations, especially wage-earners' and businessmen's expectations about the future course of prices *vis-à-vis* their money wage receipts or payments. In particular, Friedman (and Hayek) believe that an economy, left to itself, could find its way to that level of employment where individual labour and product markets clear at the appropriate prices (the natural rate of unemployment), a process that is being continuously frustrated by misguided attempts to run the economy below the natural rate, so creating accelerating inflation. Consequently, practical policy implications must involve intermittent spells of unemployment. The object of this is to create a new climate of more moderate expectations about prices and wages so that the 'correct' relative wage and price structures may be perceived, undistorted by the overall inflationary veil. Furthermore, from such situations the economy's markets may grope for the 'correct' relative price structure from above the natural rate, as it were, without perpetrating new bouts of accelerating inflation. Hence we have had Reserve Bank support for the Treasury's short, sharp shock thesis (which seems to have been maintained for rather a long time now), its opposition to 'excessive' public sector spending and deficit, its belief in the primacy of curing inflation, and its lukewarm attitudes to the wage indexation experiment. (A Fried-manite variant would be, of course, indexation of everything so that the relative price system always would be revealed, regardless of the overall absolute rate of inflation. Hayek, by contrast, wants a return to a regime of fixed exchange rates in order to impose strict monetary disciplines on governments – or, failing that, have them give up al-together issuing money unless they are shown to be responsible in their behaviour. Otherwise, more acceptable counterfeiters are to take over.) It should be noted that the theoretical underpinnings of the monetarist position – do but leave well alone and all will be well – are not sup-ported by the findings of the modern mathematical work on general equilibrium theory, in particular, the ability of a competitive capitalist economy to grope successfully to an equilibrium, an equilibrium, more-over, which even if it exists, may not be either unique or locally or globally stable (see, for example, Hahn, 1973b). The monetarists' answer is, of course, that the proof of the pudding is in the eating and that their relatively simple, causal models *are* supported by *their* abundant empirical findings.

The bastard Keynesians

The Bastard Keynesians share a similar microeconomic foundation to that of the monetarists – markets which behave *as if* they were Wal-rasian competitive ones – but part company with them on the ability of a capitalist economy left to itself to find its way, even sluggishly, to a full employment equilibrium. That is to say, they accept, correctly in my view, that Keynes's revolutionary contribution was to demonstrate the possibility of underemployment rest states, through the development of the theory of effective demand, as Kregel recently has reminded us (see Kregel, 1976b). Hence they see a role for government intervention of a macroeconomic nature, such as the Treasury has long been accustomed to do. The Hicks–Hansen *IS–LM* analysis is their main tool of analysis. It is un-Keynesian without quotes;[2] nevertheless Keynes himself in *The General Theory* is not entirely free of blame for the microeconomic foundations, though they are Marshallian not Walrasian.[3] Thus Joan Robinson has described Keynes's and the true Keynesian approach, as exemplified in chapter 21 of *The General Theory*, as follows:

> We [the 'British Keynesians'] started from the concept of the Marshallian short-period situation, in which fixed plant, business organisation and the training of labour are all given, and can be more or less utilised according to the level of effective demand. A short-period supply curve relating the level of money prices to the level of activity (at given money-wage rates) led straight from Marshall to the *General Theory*. (Robinson, 1969b)[4]

Whether we use the Marshallian micro model of Keynes or the Walrasian micro model of the Bastard Keynesians, we have an underlying rationale for the control of both unemployment and inflation centrally to rest in the hands of the Treasury through fiscal policy (aided, no doubt, by consultations with their junior partners at the Reserve Bank). The emphasis, though, is on control of the levels of real demands, so that as the product markets work themselves out, derived demands for labour show up in job vacancies plus relative wage movements. These imply, overall, a level of money wages which, given the (short-run) level of productivity, is consistent with reasonable price stability, especially in relation to rates of increase of prices among our trading rivals.

There is, moreover, an element of Keynes's closed economy model in the argument that a cut in real wages is the only way effectively to raise employment, i.e. that a lower real wage is needed in order that the economy may move down the aggregate marginal product of labour curve towards the intersection of the demand and supply curves for labour (which signifies full employment in the labour market). This is, of course, a position which is not achievable automatically by the unaided workings of the capitalist system when there is a failure of effective demand. (In an open economy the lower real wages will also affect imports and exports.)

The microeconomic aspects of the above analysis imply that it is the product wage (the money wage deflated by the price of the products which businessmen sell) which is – in the model – the relevant one for the real wage, marginal product comparison by the profit-maximizing, cost-minimizing businessmen. It is not, in the model, the real wage as seen by the wage-earners (i.e. their money wages deflated by an index of the prices of the commodities which they habitually consume). Yet the call in Australia in 1976 for a cut in real wages, which are said to be too high, has consistently been based on the latter, which is inappropriate even in terms of the theoretical model which props up the analysis. The appropriate calculations which are needed to see whether in fact wages are too high (we would still need to ask, relative to what?) would be figures for the export sector wage, the import-competing sector wage, the non-traded goods sector wage and so on. To my knowledge, these calculations have never been done, or at least made public. In any event, it would be necessary also to take into account the feedback repercussions on aggregate demand of the means whereby the cuts were brought into effect, an old-fashioned maxim of Keynes which rather seems to have been forgotten in recent discussions.

Supposing such a cut in real wages to have been secured without adverse consequences on planned spending then, the argument goes, there would be the added advantages of (i) allowing the bulk of Australian exports to sell at prices which, though set abroad, nevertheless would promise profits at home, (ii) reducing our demand for imported goods at any given level of activity, and (iii) raising profits' share in output to a level which, at least indirectly, would encourage a rise in the level of planned investment expenditure. There is no place here for either union power or indexation – hence the unswerving hostility to the latter, and the advocacy by the Treasury of the short, sharp shock thesis (and now the sustained variant) in order to blunt the former. The above theoretical underpinnings thus have the advantage of keeping economic power firmly in the Treasury's hands (despite the creation in 1976 of a separate Department of Finance), so adding weight to a natural human tendency to hold on to what has been achieved already and to ward off interlopers. The severity, indeed savagery, of its practical implications for many Australian citizens reflects in part the isolation of the decision-makers in Canberra from the human aspects of their decisions. It also reflects the contempt which practical men of affairs in the Treasury (and industry) have for academic criticism and developments. These are considered to be airy-fairy stuff of no practical importance – except, of course, as Frank Davidson once remarked, for those theories of the three years or so when the decision-makers themselves were under-graduates. Then, just for once, theory magically provided the necessary structures of thought which the decision-makers have retained for ever after. (This phenomenon is not confined to decision-makers.)

Post-Keynesianism

Post-Keynesianism, as mentioned, has its roots in Keynes, Kalecki, Sraffa, Marx and the classical political economists. In recent years some have tended to take the Kaleckian road rather than the road that Keynes either had taken or may have meant to take – this is especially true of Joan Robinson and her closest followers. It *is* the appropriate road for analysing the present Australian situation, for a number of reasons. First, its microeconomic foundations are to be preferred as being more relevant and realistic. In the Kaleckian framework, an explicit role is given to the administered price sector, usually identified with manufacturing. The typical firm is pictured as having a reverse L shaped marginal (equals average variable) cost curve, implying a physical limit to production at any moment of time, with actual levels of production usually below this limit. A distinction is made between direct (factory floor) labour and indirect labour (the managing director, supervisory staff and Mrs Mops who will be there as long as the firm does not close down, and so regardless of short-run fluctuations in production).[5] This has the important implication that as output levels are raised in the short run, overall labour productivity rises, so that it is possible to obtain a shift to profits without there being any change in prices or the size of the mark-up on average variable costs (at normal levels of output) and the costs themselves (the mode of pricing which is taken to be characteristic of this section of industry). The shift to profits has important consequences for the level of private investment expenditure. The other sectors of the economy are viewed as more conventionally competitive, with Marshallian-type demand and supply forces interacting to set prices in markets which are characterized by price-taking by the individuals in them. (Hicks has dubbed these distinctions as fix price and flex price respectively.) A theory of the size of the mark-up completes the story – in Kalecki's models, the degree of monopoly, in more recent developments, a link between investment expenditure plans and the resulting finance required is invoked in order to determine its size within the constraints imposed by the extent of the competitive nature of the industry, the level of activity and so on.

Second, within the framework, a macro theory of distribution emerges at the same time as a theory of the short-run level of activity. This is especially relevant for today's problems because it focuses directly on the inflationary consequences of inconsistent income distribution demands which are a prominent feature of the present (and past) inflationary puzzles. Third, the framework is explicitly one of political economy, reflecting Kalecki's Marxist background and also Keynes's view that theory was valuable only in so far as it threw light on current problems and contributed in detail to the formation of policy. It involved, moreover, an explicit recognition of what Kalecki called the political trade cycle and the class struggle over distributive shares. He recognized very early on (as did Joan Robinson and Richard Kahn) that sustained full employment was an open-ended invitation to inflationary pressures through rises in the (efficiency) money wage rate so that periodic interruptions of it would be needed in order 'to discipline the workers'. (The interruptions also would need to be timed vis-à-vis election dates.) Stability of the money wage was the clue to the stability of the whole system. Since Kalecki – and the Post-Keynesians – regard the periodic bouts of unemployment as savage and uncivilized, they, very early on again, sought alternative ways of influencing the overall level of the money wage and, thus, given the underlying micro foundations, the overall price level: hence Joan Robinson's remark, initially in the mid 1930s, that incomes policy was her middle name.

A further desirable property of the Kaleckian version of the central propositions of *The General Theory* is that it is set in a model of cyclical growth, a model of motion, the happenings of one short period influencing the behaviour of the next: 'the long-run trend is but a slowly changing component of a chain of short-period situations; it has no independent entity' (Kalecki, 1968, p. 263). Furthermore, the model is explicitly set in a class context where the producing, spending and saving behaviours of broad sociological groups are differentiated and explained. (In Australia, one immediately thinks of exporters, manufacturers and wage-earners as a preliminary broad classification.) Moreover, the process of development over time is seen as a reproducing and expanding one (not necessarily steadily, of course) in which profit-making and capital accumulation are ends in themselves, not means to the end of maximizing the satisfactions of individuals through the patterns of their lifetime consumption. Again Kalecki is to be preferred to Keynes, in that Keynes has individual psychological underpinnings to his aggregate consumption function so that saving is discussed in terms of individuals' choices between the present and the future, rather than as a function of what particular classes are meant to do and are able to do, which is a characteristic of Kalecki's approach, and which, in my view, is the more relevant and realistic model of the process of accumulation in capitalist economies.

The above views have fundamental implications for the attitudes which will be taken to economic policy in general, especially when allocation over time is no longer seen to be the necessary product of an efficient price system. (Thus it could be argued that the recent clash over the company taxation portions of the Mathews Committee Report may be explained in terms of two very different 'visions' of how society may be thought of as working. One view is Chicago, the other is Keynesian–Marxist in spirit.) Of course, it must be pointed out that the Post-Keynesian model as a method of theory nevertheless can encompass a wide range of political attitudes and ideologies – from Keynes plus compassion through Crosland socialism and Wedgwood Bennery to a Marxist restructuring of the whole society. Hence, it has also been criticized as principally a closed economy model, so that when open economy puzzles have been considered, there has tended to be a rather *ad hoc* advocacy of specific controls.

Keynes has often been criticized for making the money wage level exogeneous to his system, for examining the implications of changes in money wages but not asking first how they came about and whether there was an endogenous process involved in it all. There is some merit in the criticism, as far as Keynes himself is concerned, though it could be said in his defence that an assumption of relative constancy made more sense as a practical starting point when he was writing *The General Theory* than it would in the post-war world. Moreover, there is an endogenous story told in Book V of *The General Theory*, though it is never spelt out very fully or far,[6] and the question of sustained full employment and the money wage is barely discussed. Nevertheless, as Paul Davidson and Sidney Weintraub have documented in detail, Keynes was fundamentally correct in seeing the central importance of efficiency wage stability for the stability of the system as a whole and his immediate followers – Kahn and Joan Robinson, for example – have carried on the analysis of the implications of this fundamental insight in very great detail indeed.[7] In recent years they have been joined by Hicks, (1974, lecture III; 1975b) and Phelps Brown, who see an important part of the post-war inflationary problem as founded in sociological and historical learning patterns, allied with deeply ingrained notions of 'fair' wages (which include a notion of a 'fair' rate of increase). This implies that long-established relativities are hallowed, and any major rupturings produce havoc. Phelps Brown has also stressed even more what he believes to be the inflationary consequences of what he sees as the shift in the balance of power to unions (Phelps Brown, 1971, pp. 12-13; 1975).

One advantage that Keynes had over Kalecki in the development of the Post-Keynesian tradition was that Keynes was first and foremost a monetary economist, so that *The General Theory* was a major modification of Keynes's intended magnum opus, the *Treatise*. Much of the latter's monetary analysis was still regarded by Keynes as relevant, to be taken as given as a background to *The General Theory*. Hyman Minsky has made this the central theme of his interpretations of *The General Theory* (Minsky, 1975), as has Paul Davidson in *Money and the Real World* (Davidson, 1972). Minsky shows that the rich balance-sheet analysis of firms and households of the *Treatise*, together with the new developments of *The General Theory*, imply that the main model of *The General Theory* is a theory of the (real and monetary) cyclical development of the economy. The cycles arise from the implications of disappointed expectations concerning cash flows, the accompanying distorted balance-sheet patterns relative to income and expenditure accounts, themselves the products of changing states of confidence and expectations, and the reactions of firms and households to them and to their effects on the markets for financial assets. This is not to say that Kalecki ignored monetary factors. The principle of increasing risk is still a relevant part of the story and his two-sided link between profits and investment, whereby the former are both the inducement for and the means to enable, directly and indirectly, the financing of investment, are the basic ingredients of the Post-Keynesian theory of investment. The Minsky-Davidson-Keynes-Kalecki strands together may be seen as constituting the outline of a plausible alternative story to that of the monetarists (and to that of Tobin) in trade cycle analysis and the role of monetary policy.

Finally, Kalecki's approach to the theory of investment is preferable to Keynes's, for it explicitly deals with plans, construction and final implementation, explicitly taking account of the time lapses between them. As we have seen, this allows the economic process to be modelled as the happenings of one short period growing out of another. Kalecki was prepared to be more cavalier than Keynes in his treatment of time. Keynes in the end thought it best to give up trying to handle time processes in analytical detail (even though he had done this successfully in the *Treatise*). He settled instead for the theory of effective demand, the possibility of underemployment equilibria (rest states), ignoring in order to make this central point (and also because he believed it was not possible to find a 'determinate time unit') lags, processes and feedback phenomena, especially amongst expectations.

Policy approaches

With the above as background let us finally turn to a discussion of policy approaches, both of recent years and for the future. In general, the events of recent years, especially the behaviour of the Liberal-Country Party coalition when in opposition and its method of coming to power, culminating in the Governor General's actions of 11 November 1975, make very poor the chances of conservative governments in Australia being able successfully to implement policies which would be consistent with Post-Keynesian analysis, even if they wished to, which clearly they do not. Moreover, the experiences of the Whitlam government while in office also make for scepticism about the chances of a social democratic government implementing successfully a 'Keynes plus compassion' policy such as that attempted by Labor. This reflects not only Labor's inexperience and, at times, incompetence, silliness and lack of resolution, and the extraordinarily difficult general problems faced by the Labor administration, but, more importantly, fundamental and deep-seated power sources in the political and economic structure of Australian capitalism. These together imposed constraints which virtually ruled out the Labor government's ability to act in certain ways. The constraints are set by both domestic and overseas business interests, by the power struggles and differing ideologies within the Labor and trade union movements themselves, by what the Federal and State public services themselves will tolerate, and by the privately controlled media, all of which militate against fundamental changes in the public–private sector split, or major redistributions of wealth and income.[8] The 'animal spirits' of Australian business are so susceptible to policies which it feels to be against its own interests (whether its perceptions are right or not is another matter) and its ability to act by reducing investment spending is so effective, as to make the room for manoeuvre by a Whitlam-type government extremely limited indeed. The practical alternative, therefore, may be a reversion to a Lewis-type policy (Lewis, 1976a and 1976b) whereby private consumer spending leads in both recovery and in sustained growth (in the latter, accompanied by private investment spending), aided by a restructured tax system, with the public sector taking an increasingly modest role in the provision of goods and services.

Another alternative approach whereby the socialist nettle, such as is outlined in Stuart Holland's *The Socialist Challenge* (Holland, 1975) suitably modified for Australian conditions, is grasped, seems far from being an election winner, or at least as being perceived as such by those who make policy and political decisions in the A.L.P. It seems unlikely, then, that there is yet another alternative, that of creating in Australia consensus policies embodying genuine *money* income restraints and what Joan Robinson has called 'a real social contract which would satisfy the reasonable demands of the workers for more control over their own work, more security against redundancy, better social services and so forth'.[9]

But, if this alternative were possible, what forms would it take? As far as maintaining a high level of employment and a satisfactory rate of growth is concerned (its composition will need attention, too, but that is another story for the moment), the single most important institutional change required in Australia is the creation of effective machinery with which to ensure that, by and large, we obtain the level and rate of change of prices which is acceptable, largely independently of measures designed to affect the level of employment and the rate of economic growth and its composition. Post-Keynesian theory suggests that there is a wide range of the level of activity over which money wages and prices may be regarded as independent of the level of activity, at least for quite substantial periods of time. It is *this* proposition that needs to be exploited. Of course, we already have gone rather haltingly and reluctantly towards establishing such a set of institutions, with the introduction of pre-tax and now post-tax indexation procedures. These constitute in effect a form of incomes policy which is historically and sociologically suited to the Australian industrial environment. Indexation is understood and by and large trusted by our wage-earning groups, and present attempts by the government and its advisers to smash it seem tragically ill-advised. As argued elsewhere (Harcourt, 1974), it is the major reform that can remove the overriding anxiety of each wage-earning group in a period of inflation that its absolute real income may be eroded. In its absence, each group of necessity pitched its money wage demands towards the upper limit of what was considered to be feasible, and employers individually were inclined to acquiesce, with the result that the overall outcome was to give an intolerably high level and rate of increase of overall money wages and therefore prices. This led inevitably to savage fiscal and monetary policies designed to bring the rates down, policies that proved ineffectual in their aims and disastrous and tragic in their by-products. It was a weakness of the initial arguments for indexation, in so far as they were concerned with tackling inflation, that they were coupled with egalitarian considerations. Thus flat rate adjustments other than at the bottom end of the scale were advocated in order to narrow differentials. Another major weakness, given the inflation rates that had been experienced and which were to come, was not immediately to couple pre-tax indexation with post-tax indexation.

Of course, indexation by itself is not a panacea. It needs to be coupled with a relativities *plus* productivity element, that is to say, a wage fund over and above that already spoken for by the indexation procedure proper. Its size would be determined by considerations such as whether the economy is in a transition state, as far as the creation of new institutions is concerned, or whether it has reached its new ongoing path, with the institutions securely established. The fund would allow ruptured relativities to be restored (not necessarily at one fell swoop),[10] for relativities to change if seemingly irresistible forces suggest that this is desirable, and for all groups to receive money wage increases which would allow them to absorb their share of any general rise in prosperity that is implied by the underlying trend in national productivity, if and when the latter is resumed.[11] What needs to be appreciated is that the same *real* gains may be realized by employed persons by a myriad of money wage and price combinations, but that only a small range of them is consistent with the other aims of high employment, reasonable growth and remaining competitive *vis-à-vis* our main overseas rivals. The quid pro quo for the *money* wage restraint involved would be the provision of goods and services through the public sector which is beneficial in particular to the wage-earning sectors and their children. Such, of course, was the rationale of much of Labor's programme. This means that by wage-earners foregoing unduly inflationary pressures on money wage levels and, indeed, at times being prepared to make some sacrifice in the rate of increase of their real take-home pay, the government in return would be in a position to ensure jobs and redistribute resources in a more egalitarian manner, while at the same time maintaining activity at a level which ensures that adequate investment is undertaken, and profits earned, by the private sector.

Finally, governments must put forward explicitly coherent and integrated policies, the framework and broad targets of which are fully explained to all relevant sectors. Then, they must show a determination to stick to them regardless of the inevitable flak from the various interested groups who may be adversely affected, at least in the short run and sometimes permanently. Inflexibility, of course, must not be made the only virtue. There should be minor detailed alternatives and some room for manoeuvre. Nevertheless, resolution and defined objectives, of which all are made aware, are definitely needed and have been conspicuously absent in the policies of governments of recent years.

Notes

* A slightly amended version of a paper published as chapter 4 of John Nieuwenhuysen and Peter Drake (eds.), *Essays in Australian Economic Policy*. Melbourne, Melbourne University Press, 1977.

Amongst the many reasons why I am grateful for having been a student of Wilfred Prest, two stand out in the present context. First, it was Wilfred who first introduced me to capital theory (in the Final Division Class of 1952-3). Second, as it was his wont to do good works by stealth, in 1968 Wilfred recommended me to Mark Perlman as a possible replacement when Perlman was let down at quite an advanced stage of proceedings by the person whom he originally had asked to survey recent developments in capital theory for the newly established *Journal of Economic Literature*. What became my sustained interest in capital theory led naturally on to the adoption of a Post-Keynesian stance on matters of political economics, a stance that seems most relevant to the current discussions of indexation and other measures as means of tackling stagflation in Australia. For comments on a draft of this paper I am extremely grateful to John Burbidge, Jon Cohen, Ronald Henderson, Mervyn Lewis, Ian McLean and the editors. They must be completely absolved, though, from responsibility for *any* views expressed here.

1 Mervyn Lewis has pointed out that there is a fourth school which may be dubbed 'structuralist' and which considers macro policy from an essentially orthodox micro basis. Members include F.H. Green, R.G. Gregory and the I.A.C. economists. Although their influence on policy may have been considerable, it is not discussed in this paper.

2 The best short account of why is the Appendix to Donald Moggridge's Fontana *Modern Masters* biography of Keynes (Moggridge, 1976). The basic reason is the non-independence of the *LM* and *IS* curves. They interrelate through the medium of interrelated and changeable expectations, so that movements of one (or along one), unless very marginal, inevitably imply movements, not always predictable, of the other. 'If both curves shift, there is no clear prediction possible . . . as to what the final outcome will be' (p. 166).

3 Three years later, in his *Economic Journal* comment on Dunlop's and Tarshis's findings on real and money wages over the cycle, Keynes changed his position and enunciated what must be one of the earliest statements of the normal cost pricing hypothesis that now is characteristic of the microeconomic foundations of Post-Keynesian theory (see Keynes, 1971-9, vol. vii, Appendix 3, pp. 406-12). No doubt it was all in Marshall anyway.

4 Putting the two strands, Hicks-Hansen and Marshall, together, the model may be set out in terms of two simple diagrams which allow the price level to be introduced explicitly (see Harcourt, 1980, pp. 155-6).

5 Of this group, cleaners are probably the most vulnerable in situations of sustained unemployment.

6 This was in keeping with Keynes's method in his book, as he wrote to Hicks (see Moggridge, 1976, p. 92), of not 'pursuing anything very far, [his] object being to press home as forcibly as possible certain fundamental opinions — and no more'.

7 In particular, I would refer readers to Kahn's masterly paper, 'On Rereading Keynes' (Kahn, 1974). Kahn's analysis of the roles of money and money wages in Keynes's own thought and in the Post-Keynesian tradition is absolutely authoritative. Incidentally, he outlines a package deal which in essentials corresponds to the analysis and policies most favoured in this paper (see especially pp. 30–2).

8 There are other ratchet-type effects which put (some) constraints on *cuts* in expenditure, e.g. the education lobby, and structural changes, e.g. the protectionist lobby.

9 Press release of public lecture in Adelaide, April 1975. Joan Robinson was clearly pessimistic about the chances of such a policy actually coming about; nor was her heart in it anyway, for she would prefer to see society restructured on much more radical lines. However, James Meade and his happy band of intelligent radicals seem much more confident of success, as indeed we all might be, if only our worlds were exclusively inhabited by civilized, humane and enlightened James Meades, and we had as much confidence as he has in the Bastard Keynesian aspects of his analysis (see Meade, 1975b).

10 The danger is that the recent inflationary experience, together with plateau and/or partial indexation procedures, may have so ruptured previously long-established norms that, now, no consensus may be established as to what *is* the structure which ought to be restored. Moreover, there may no longer be that measure of good will with which to allow a new pattern either to be agreed upon or arrived at.

11 Even if productivity growth *is* zero, it may still be necessary to have a fund with which to tackle the inherited stock of ruptured relativities over a transition phase. Of course, a successful attack on inflation itself should allow productivity to start growing again.

Part VI
Intellectual biographies

21 Eric Russell, 1921-77
A great Australian political economist*

I

I am greatly honoured to be asked to give the 1977 Newcastle Lecture in Political Economy. Last year Professor Youngson kicked off the series with a fine evaluation of the contributions of the first great political economist, Adam Smith (Youngson, 1976). This year I want to discuss the contributions of Eric Russell to Australian political economy. This is a sad and a proud task; sad, because Eric was my friend and my mentor. I valued his good opinion more than anyone else's, as did all his friends — and now he is gone, dying suddenly on 26 February this year. It is a proud task, because it was a unique privilege to have known and worked with Eric and now, I hope, to contribute towards ensuring that his achievements live on. But I would not wish this to be a solemn occasion. Eric was the wittiest and happiest of men, enthusiastic and alive, loving and lovable, properly angry when he had to be, but polite, courteous, modest, a great man at a party, a superb sportsman, and I would like some of that atmosphere to be here as we look at his work.

II

Eric was born in 1921. His father was a station master in the Victorian Railways, so that the young Russells (there were four children) moved round a lot in Victorian country areas. Nevertheless, his secondary schooling was in Melbourne — Eric was a product of the vintage years of Melbourne High School — and he went on to the University of Melbourne during the war years, obtaining first class honours in Arts and Economics. History, philosophy, economics, theatre and literature were his intellectual loves. An early important influence on him was the late George Paul, the Cambridge philosopher who was then at Melbourne. After the war, Eric went to King's, Cambridge, where he read for Part II of the Economics Tripos and obtained a first in the company of Frank Davidson, Harry Johnson, Robin Marris, I.G. Patel and Aubrey

Silberston. He was supervised by Gerald Shove and Richard Kahn; he saw the great Keynes in action once (when, I understand, Keynes rather went after Joan Robinson). Eric was also one of the small chosen band that attended Wittgenstein's lectures at Cambridge. Returning to Australia, he taught at Melbourne, Sydney and the University of New England (it was New England University College then) before coming to Adelaide in 1952 to join his old friend and contemporary, Peter Karmel.[1] Eric stayed there for the rest of his life, except for three spells of study leave at Oxford (1960) and the L.S.E. (1967 and 1976). He was promoted to Reader in 1958, appointed to the newly created second Chair of Economics in 1964 and became Chairman in 1966. This is not the place to assess his achievements as Chairman and University of Adelaide man generally. Suffice it to say here that they were splendid. What I want to do today is to speak of Eric Russell, the political economist.

Why do I describe Eric as a political economist? He certainly was *not* that comfortable with *some* aspects of the political economy movement in Australia today, especially those elements that tend to be dogmatic and strident in tone. Yet he *was* a political economist in the best sense of the word – he was always conscious of the political and institutional settings of any economic problem and he was interested in economics only in so far as it bore directly or indirectly on policy issues. In all the major policy issues of the post-war period Eric's was always one of the first and wisest voices (despite the fact that he published very little: see Harcourt, 1977b), and his analysis of a problem was *never* confined to what the orthodox would regard as the *economics* of it. That is to say, it was not confined to those factors which could be contained under the umbrella of maximization or minimization under constraints. No, as the late Maurice Dobb has it (Dobb, 1973), like the classical pioneers, Eric was prepared to draw more generous boundaries in order to include whatever factors from whatever 'discipline' as long as they were relevant to, and illuminating of, the problem in hand. (He was very strict about the responsibility attached to those who offered advice and he himself was extremely careful and cautious, always shaping out and making explicit where framework and fact ended and judgment, values and ideology entered in policy matters, or where they could not be unentwined.)

As a result, Eric's economics was a splendid blend of many traditions. His historical perspective always made him conscious of those sustained and fundamental forces stressed by the classical political economists, especially by Ricardo, as well as of dynamic historical processes, the different strengths of which served to differentiate both economies and epochs one from another. From the classicals and Marx, he took note of social relationships, of classes and their clashes, of contradictions and either their exacerbation or their elimination by endogenous economic processes, for Eric had a healthy respect, given the appropriate circumstances, for the survival power of the body economic and politic. From the orthodox, he took a thorough knowledge of substitution possibilities, especially over longer periods of time – he put the energy crisis into perspective as a result, while at the same time recognizing it, increasingly so in recent years, as a most serious and dangerous problem. He also took from them the relevance and usefulness of supply and demand analysis in the discussions of devaluation, fixed versus floating exchange rates, and similar problems. From Keynes and Keynes's followers he took the basic insight that capitalism was a production system in which money, and financial institutions generally, played an indispensable role. Finally, from this same Keynesian tradition, together with his own instinctive sympathies and understanding, economics was to Eric, I believe, a moral science in which a sense of relevance and moral purpose was always central and to which he brought a willingness to use intuition and judgment, as well as the more conventional methods of economic analysis, to acknowledge that a changing universe was its proper subject (see Chick, 1975).

III

I wish now to illustrate these general points by considering in some detail Eric's contributions in three areas, between which, however, there are unifying threads and strands. The first is Eric's seminal paper (written jointly with James Meade) which was published in the *Economic Record* in April 1957 (Meade and Russell, 1957). This paper sets out Eric's basic views on *how* the Australian economy works, what the social relationships and relevant institutions are, how the domestic price level is formed and how Australia as a small open economy responds to external happenings. This paper represents the 'vision' which Eric took with him into all his discussions of Australian economic problems. He amended and updated it through the years but, nevertheless, it represents the foundations of his thinking. The story of how the paper came to be written is fascinating, and I have been able to reconstruct some of it from the evidence provided in his papers, in which is included his correspondence with James Meade. (The latter, incidentally, is a model of civilized and honest communication and response.)

The Meade–Russell paper sets the scene for perhaps his most important contribution: his work on an Australian wages and, latterly, incomes policy, especially his submission of evidence to the Arbitration Commission in 1959 (Russell, 1959), his important paper in *Australian Economic Papers* in 1965 (Russell, 1965) which was capped off by a talk which he gave to the South Australian teachers of economics in 1971 (Russell, 1971), and his version of the Adelaide Plan which was delivered as a public lecture in Unley Town Hall in 1974.

The final illustration is Eric's Presidential address to Section 24 of A.N.Z.A.A.S. in 1972, 'Foreign Investment Policy – What Role for the Economist?' (Russell, 1978). Ostensibly it was on the debates about foreign investment in Australia and on what an economist might be expected to contribute to the arguments. It gave Eric an opportunity to set out his views on methodology, the value of economic theory and the use of empirical evidence.

IV[2]

The Meade–Russell paper had its origin in Trevor Swan's then unpublished but already famous Swan diagram of external and internal balance, with its zones of economic unhappiness and ambiguous signals as to which instruments to use in order to hit what targets. Swan's analysis initially derived from Meade's great works on international economic policy (Meade, 1951, 1955) which in those days were, rightly, everybody's Bible (despite Harry Johnson's savage review of vol. I, 'The Taxonomic Approach to Economic Policy': Johnson, 1951). Nevertheless, Eric sensed that, in the form which Meade originally gave to his models and which Swan adopted, they belonged to, as Eric said, 'another world'; that they were in certain important respects inapplicable as models which purported to catch the crucial features of the Australian economy. Eric therefore prepared for a staff–student seminar in 1953 some notes in which he wrote down what he considered to be the critical characteristics of the Australian economy for the sorts of puzzles that were then demanding the full attention of Australian policy-makers and academic economists alike. (The immediate puzzle was the great wool boom of the early 1950s which was associated with the extraordinary demands for raw materials for stock-piling which accompanied the Korean war.) These notes formed the background to Eric's teaching of honours students in subsequent years. When Meade (who was spending six months at the A.N.U.) came to Adelaide, he and Eric talked about these issues. Meade was so impressed by Eric's

approach that when he returned to Canberra he wrote a paper which
included orthodox models, such as he himself was accustomed to use,
which gave formal content to Eric's ideas and which brought forth
Eric's results. (In the opening note to this first draft, Meade writes:
'The analysis in this note was prompted by a discussion with Mr. E.
Russell . . . who suggested most of the ideas to me, though I do not
want to hold him responsible for the conclusions which I have drawn
from them.') In a letter to Eric (6 September 1956) which accompanied
the note, Meade mentions that Dick Downing would like to publish the
note in the *Economic Record*. Meade, like Barkis, was willing but had
one reason for hesitation: 'With my usual inability to distinguish between my own and other people's ideas, I think that it is quite possible
that every idea in the note is yours; [moreover, if Eric had in preparation
a paper on the same subject] I would not want to go ahead with my
note.' He asked for Eric's views on this and any comments on the
analysis itself. In a letter of 8 September 1956 (addressed from the
L.S.E.), Meade writes: 'another thought has occurred to me. It would
give me great pleasure if you would be willing to sign something on the
lines which I sent you jointly with me'.

Eric responded with a very full letter, only a draft of which remains
in his files.[3] Eric ended by saying that he would like to add his name to
Meade's on the paper – 'your offer is a most generous one' – but not as
it then stood. He suggested three possible courses of action:

1. Meade to publish his note as it was, with Eric following on in a later
   issue of the *Record*, 'setting out . . . the judgements involved in the
   policy recommendations'.
2. 'What I would like the best. In a joint article list, without deciding
   the issue, what factors would have to be taken into account in making
   a policy judgement. That is, present the article as a theoretical
   analysis, clarifying the Australian dilemma and giving a plausible
   framework in which economists and policy makers can make qualitative and political judgements.' (This particular approach to advice
   Eric always scrupulously followed himself. As he said in his A.N.Z.
   A.A.S. Presidential address, if 'there are no simple truths . . . suitable
   for painting on a banner, it is proper to point this out . . . a fault to
   pretend otherwise. If to do so is academic, so much the better for
   academic studies': Russell, 1978, p. 193.)
3. Add a footnote to Meade's paper to the effect that certain estimates
   were still a matter of judgment.

Meade responded immediately (15 November 1956) with a revised
note 'which simply omits all policy arguments' as he 'would very much

like to turn the note into a joint note . . . because . . . it is clear from your notes of 1953, that the basic idea is yours rather than mine'. This became the Meade–Russell paper as published; it 'include[d] only what [they] both wish[ed] to say – a neutral model with all policy implications suppressed' (E.A.R. to R.I.D., 26 November 1956).[4] Eric added:

> Something like it should have been put in the *Record* in 1952–3. A more interesting example for analysis in 1956 would be to work out the implications of an exchange rate variation on reduction in money wage rates relative to prices. The model would be the same . . . the questions would have a less old-fashioned look – especially today!!

Why did not Eric publish his ideas earlier on and on his own? What were the essential characteristics of the Australian economy, as he saw them, which made him feel that the Swan–Meade keys were to open doors to 'another world' and that he did not want to accept the policy implications of the first draft of Meade–Russell? There were two 'general reasons' why Eric had not published before. First, Swan had not published his paper(s), the ideas of which were nevertheless very influential in getting the Arbitration Commission to 'set a wage which would contribute to "internal balance" by setting an appropriate relationship between Australian and world prices'. They also underlay the abandonment in 1953 of the automatic cost-of-living adjustment.

> The economic rationale was in Swan's papers. . . . Secondly, to do the trick properly would require that [the analysis] be related in a strict way to traditional theory. Ad hoc models in crude arithmetic (not . . . accompanied by a tight mathematical analysis) cannot budge an accepted theoretical system.

'Therefore', Eric wrote to Meade, 'your article from my point of view is doubly excellent. It sets out a relevant model of the Australian economy and it is related to your own previous work . . . very important that you should have done it.'

The features of the Australian economy which Eric identified in his 1953 notes and which Meade incorporated, albeit in a Meadean neoclassical form, in the Meade–Russell paper are, first, the ratio of exports to national income is very high; second, Australian exports (at the time) were predominantly agricultural and pastoral so that they had a very low elasticity of supply in the short run. (Eric made a qualification about metals and also added that this was true more in aggregate than being necessarily so for any one commodity.) The implications were that with fluctuations in world incomes, there were wide fluctuations in export prices. (Thus, one of the favourite exercises given to first-year Adelaide students in macroeconomics is to get them to work out the multiplier consequences of a change in the *value* of exports as opposed to a change in their *volume*. The latter is the more usual exercise in that students usually are given an exercise which is based on the model which was first developed by Joan Robinson in 1937 when she 'opened' the model of *The General Theory*, having in mind no doubt an exporter of manufactures such as the United Kingdom: Robinson, 1937b). Third, there is a tendency for the *home* price of commodities that are exportable ('exportables') to move in sympathy with the prices of exports. (Eric added the qualification that home price schemes, such as were prevalent in the 1950s and earlier, may weaken the link in the short run. Nevertheless, there is constant pressure on such schemes because of the need to keep some balance between the controlled and uncontrolled prices.) These characteristics, taken together, imply balance of payments problems, a tendency to induced income fluctuations and a tendency for the distribution of incomes as between rural and urban areas to fluctuate widely.

Next, we take account of the link between the consumer price index (then the C series) and the facts that a high proportion of wages and salaries are adjusted for variations in it, that from time to time there are adjustments to the 'real' basic wage, and that there is a 'remarkably strong tradition of pricing in the domestic market . . . by [a] constant percentage mark-up on wage and material costs'.

It is these features taken together which make it especially difficult for policy-makers to achieve widely acclaimed objectives – high levels of employment without inflation (no excess demand), relative stability of general prices, equity in income distribution between wages and gross profits, between urban and rural incomes, balance of payments equilibrium, and the use of the price mechanism in the allocation of resources between primary and other production and between home production, exports and import replacement. 'In fact these demands on policy makers are mutually inconsistent.'

The particular problem which Meade analysed was the process that is set in train by a rise in demand for the exports of a small country that exports mainly primary products, the wage-earners of which country consume a basket in which the prices of 'exportables' and imports figure prominently and whose money wages are linked either formally or informally to a cost-of-living index. The analysis is done in neoclassical terms – relative factor intensities determine marginal products which in turn help to determine real income shares — rather than in terms of Eric's model. The latter, in effect, incorporated the Kaleckian version of the main propositions of *The General Theory*, allied with Kalecki's microeconomic foundations, especially in manufacturing industry, and macro theory of distribution, suitably modified to take into account the Australian class structure, history and institutions, together with a realistic assessment of what the traditional workings of market mechanisms could and could not be expected to achieve.[5] In any event, the story that emerges from both approaches is the now only too familiar one of the rise in export demand (or a devaluation) ultimately making the balance of payments weaker because of the consequent reaction of money wages and prices to the income distribution initially implied, and the consequent changes in the demand for imports and, these days, the reactions of speculators with respect to the capital account.

V

We now move to the debate about wages policy in the 1960s. This was already in Eric's mind when he was corresponding with Meade. He had been asked to give evidence, or at least advice, about the South Australian living wage, and he took as the background his views on how the Australian price level adjusted in order to bring about a distribution of income that was 'liveable with'. Moreover, in the 1950s he worked extraordinarily hard for the wage-earners' cause, especially in advising Bob Hawke on the content of his A.C.T.U. briefs. In 1959 Eric prepared a theoretical paper (he was one of the first Australian academic economists ever to go into the witness box on behalf of the trade unions) and the late Wilf Salter prepared the empirical estimates of productivity. Eric believed that at a minimum the wage-earning sectors of Australian society were entitled to share in *effective* productivity gains, and therefore that effective productivity based on longer-run underlying trends, and ignoring temporary fluctuations, was the appropriate concept which the Commission should have in mind in determining the capacity of the economy to pay wages. Eric's was a significant intellectual contribution in that the argument about wages was never the same again, at least not until very recently!

His views on effective productivity and the Commission were at the forefront of his thinking when he returned to the question of a wages policy for Australia in his 1965 *Australian Economic Papers* article.[6] The Commission had 'explicitly in the basic wage case of 1961 and

1964 and the margins case of 1963 . . . followed the principle of adjusting *real* wages for productivity' (Russell, 1965, p. 1). By contrast, a number of economists — Eric lists Hancock, Karmel, Downing, Isaac, Cockburn and Whitehead — had been urging the Commission 'to set award wages in such a way that average money earnings increase at the same rate as the average productivity of the work force' (p. 1). By the 1965 judgment their combined influences, both directly and through employers' counsel, had been successful. 'The majority judgement . . . rejected the principles of the 1961 basic wage judgement; explicitly denied that price increases gave grounds for increasing minimum wages . . . [and] returned to the principle-without-content, that the wage should be the highest that the economy has capacity to pay' (pp. 1-2). Eric's paper explores 'in the Australian context' the implications of adjusting money wages for productivity. His objective was to provide a rationale for the Commission's past reluctance to accept the economists' advice, and to project some of the difficulties that may follow from the 1965 policy being adopted.

The first aspect that is discussed is the mechanism by which the economists' rule is said to achieve price stability. Two essential links are concentrated on, that between awards and earnings, and that between costs and prices. Only if these are invariably stable relationships which can be depended upon will the Commission's decisions do the trick, so that the choice of a lower rate of increase of award rates 'will have no "real" economic consequences other than those that might flow from worsened industrial relations' (p. 3). As to the second strand of the argument, Eric seemingly forgoes one of the major strands of his own (earlier) argument, *viz.* the constant mark-up hypothesis which underlies the argument for the stability of the aggregate gross profit margin in manufacturing industry. I say 'seemingly' for he made the simplifying assumption of a constant mark-up, I suspect, first, because it was the *simplest*, most plausible assumption for catching the characteristics of the manufacturing sector, and, second, because using it allowed the model-builder to bring out in stark relief the role of the price of exportables and imports *vis-à-vis* the achievement of *domestic* price stability. Moreover, he added, it is wrong, in searching for a rule for price stability, to generalize the characteristics of manufacturing industry where there are grounds for expecting stable margins (though Eric notes the exceptions too) to other administered prices such as medical services, rent, power and transport services.

The Meade–Russell model is most in evidence in section IV of the 1965 paper where Eric analyses the implications of a productivity-only rule for a 'trading nation', and also of some variants of it, for example, the domestic productivity *plus* export prices rule, which received some support from Hancock and Karmel, and which is equivalent to the effective productivity *plus* internal prices rule – in 'the timeless world of algebra' but not as practical policies where they are 'wildly at odds'. The first rule would entail tying money wages to the most volatile component in the Australian price structure whereas the latter 'damps the adjustment process', an essential ingredient for any practical policy (Russell, 1965, p. 18).

In the paper, Eric attempted to work out the effects on prices, money and real wages and the distribution of income of following the productivity rule. (The essential function of adjusting money wages for prices as well as productivity with a fixed exchange rate is to raise the internal price level in step with world prices, thereby averting a re-distribution of incomes towards the export sector; it 'might also be a first approximation to an appropriate balance-of-payments adjust-ment': p. 19.) Unfortunately, in the article he made a statistical error in the calculations. (He deflated Australian costs by home production instead of by the volume of goods available in Australia.) Donald White-head (1966) picked up the error and, correcting for it, argued that Eric had been hoisted with his own petard, especially as Eric had argued that in this 'area . . . numbers are the essence of the problem' (p. 15). Donald certainly was correct, as far as this particular strand of Eric's argument was concerned.[7] Despite this, the overall soundness of his arguments remains intact. The Commission serves both a useful and a realistic function if it arranges that money wages rise in such a way that the Australian price level keeps in step with prices in the 'relevant' over-seas markets. In this way, the authority of the Commission is not eroded, and when overseas events *do* demand some departure from the role because of a disequilibrium in the balance of payments, the Com-mission *then* is in a position to make its decisions consistent with those of government policies as a whole. The relevance of Eric's judgment, written twelve years ago, has recently been reaffirmed by the main thesis of Deputy President Isaac's 1977 Giblin Memorial Lecture (Isaac, 1977).

Thus, to Eric, wages policy was as much a political as an economic problem. Indeed, as Peter Karmel has written, 'the notion that there were unique solutions derived from economics angered him' (Karmel, 1977, p. 160). This same insight is shown in Eric's contribution – a major one – to the 1974 so-called Adelaide Plan. Then, on a platform provided by the Liberal Movement in the Unley Town Hall (a rather incongruous speaking format for an old 'Leftie'), Eric stressed the need to find consensus, to reach people's sense of fair play, to show that sacrifices are both necessary – that the problems were serious and real – and would be shared, before the problem of inflation could be brought under control – and, most important, unemployment avoided. Hence the various ingredients involved: indexation of money wages in return for restraint on *over* indexation payments, taxes on excess profits and/or on those who paid excess increases in wages (sweetheart agreements), the possibility of making greater profits by increasing efficiency or selling more output. There was, moreover, always his desire to work through the institutions that already existed, to appeal to the sociological and historical background which people understood and with which they were comfortable. There was also the attempt to use the carrot and stick technique in order to induce and cajole the actual decision-makers to take the directions desired, rather than to use administrative fiat. Finally, there was the overlay of pragmatism and common sense allied with humility, modest aims and a modest assessment of the likelihood of success in a complex area.

VI

Eric's agnosticism and modesty, both about his own analysis (where it was unnecessary) and about what economic analysis may be expected to achieve (where it was), were displayed in the areas just discussed, and, perhaps most clearly and at their best, in his Presidential address to A.N.Z.A.A.S. in 1972 (Russell, 1978). He took as his subject, Foreign Investment Policy – What Role for the Economist?. He felt that an economist might 'disentangle some of the elements in the public debate . . . identify those matters of theory and fact where . . . an economist [might] speak with some special authority' (p. 193). He mentioned in passing the reaction to the Treasury paper, *Overseas Investment in Australia*, published just after his own topic had been 'embedded in the A.N.Z.A.A.S. brochures', that it 'was "academic" . . . offered no conclusions for policy' on which he offered the comments that I have already quoted (p. 335 above).

Eric chose three areas in order to illustrate how economic theory and assumptions are used in making decisions:
1. The balance of payments costs for the home country of foreign investment.
2. Whether foreign investment will add to the net real income of residents of the borrowing country.

3. Whether the price offered by foreigners and accepted for Australian assets is a proper price.

The focus was on 'what evidence [economists] offer or *can* offer about the realism and the relevance of the . . . models they use' (p. 194). In the discussions under the first head, in which Eric criticized both the Treasury and the Vernon Committee discussions of this point, it is made clear that the essential judgment relates to whether or not the free market solution is always the most efficient, least painful one. Thus the Treasury, in declaring that there is little or no *special* balance of payments cost of foreign investment,

> argues that if the exchange rate is at the right level domestic policies . . . well managed . . . the relation between prices and incomes in Australia and overseas will ensure that the balance of payments and the resources of the economy will adjust to the investment of foreign funds; . . . the remittance of foreign earnings . . . will be achieved with 'ease'. (pp. 197–8)

Eric comments: 'The basic confidence of the Treasury Paper is in the efficacy and speed of working of the market mechanism' – quick response and adjustment from eager and alert businessmen, mobile and self-interested labour, ample responsive supplies of the required skills and investment funds, quick adaption of existing land and capacity to new market opportunities.

'To believe the contrary, . . . that the response of business is sluggish . . . that the process of change [is] resisted by ignorance and defensive, conventional responses, is not "an assumption" [but] a different claim about the way the economy works in fact' (p. 198). The Vernon Report, for example, '(and the enormous tradition that it reflects) finds the market a weak instrument for securing coherent, overall objectives' (p. 198).

How, asks Eric, are we to judge between these views?

> Just because economists construct . . . explore the implications of models that highlight price/output relationships, it does not follow that economists *must*, or *can* with authority judge, that the Australian economy will, in fact, adapt quickly . . . painlessly to small changes in relative prices. Whether theories mirror the world will not be determined by an appeal to the theories. (p. 199)

The free market advice is not based on special studies of particular countries – it is 'an all purpose advice' which allows the economist to 'start talking as he gets off the plane' (p. 199). Or, sometimes, it is a second best: 'From Adam Smith to Harry Johnson the pro-market view has relied both on confidence in the beneficence of the invisible hand and doubts about the quality of the state apparatus' (p. 199).

In discussing additions to the net real income of residents, Eric proceeds by assuming away any transitional or adjustment problems associated with foreign investment occurring (such as had been the essence of the matters discussed under the previous head). He argues that 'of necessity, the enquiry must be deductive, must appeal to general theoretical reasoning . . . [for what] *is* at issue is how well based are the theoretical models and how do we judge this when we use them to make policy prescriptions' (p. 200). At the centre of this particular argument is the neoclassical proposition that profits on a unit of capital are a measure of the increase in output that the increase in capital brings about, i.e. it depends upon the validity of the marginal productivity theory of distribution. Eric then launched into an attack on the theory and its applications that does Joan Robinson proud. The upshot of the discussion is nevertheless that 'the answer is not to be arrived at by a closer examination of the theory but . . . by a judgement about the way that markets and market pressures, in fact, work' (p. 201). 'Economic theory does not tell us that competition is the case. It explores the implications of *assuming* that competition is the case' (p. 201). Again, the crucial point is the need to form a view about the way the world actually works.

Finally, we come to a passage which illustrates the acuteness of Eric's mind and, especially, his critical powers.[8] In talking about the prices paid by foreigners for Australian assets during the investment process, Eric speculated about the *nature* of the prices so paid and the possibility that some of the pressure for controls on foreign investment might spring from a belief that prices arrived at in the market might be less than the 'true worth' of the assets. He added:

The economist's paradigm market case is Wicksteed's thrifty housewife who moves among the familiar market stalls, comparing the lettuce and the cabbages, noting their well-displayed prices and at last selecting her basket of greens. After watching her, it would indeed be strange to wonder, 'but did she really prefer the goods that she in fact bought?' No, in this case, with *all* the evidence fresh and crisp before her, what she does *is* what she prefers. But we slip over to other cases where doubt is proper [and the] slide from 'He does so-and-so' to 'He prefers so-and-so' to 'so-and-so is *to be* preferred', [though it may be] almost instantaneous, [is also misleadingly treacherous]. The essence of the matter is, of course, the information that is available to the parties. (p. 203)

Eric was sceptical about Meade's judgment that the market is 'the most efficient and rapid calculating machine yet devised for the solution of . . . complicated economic riddles' (Meade, 1956, p. 243). But he was also sceptical of uncritical and empty platitudes about replacing the market by planning, and he was sympathetic towards 'economists [who] tend to favour an eclectic set of policies that largely continue the practice of the past' in the present situation, for example,

> an admixture of interventions in international transactions, monetary and fiscal policy changes, *ad hoc* attempts to restrain the rate of change of money wages through arbitration tribunals, from time to time changes in the exchange rate, some compromise about the objective of price stability . . . untidy, discretionary, changing as the world monetary system changes. (p. 206)

He ended the paper by saying 'that one's view of the way the world works will tend to cohere with one's values and political judgements' (p. 206).

VII

Eric's own values were admirable and his political judgments sound. Because of his own superb mind, he sometimes saw more issues, interconnections and subtleties in situations than ordinary mortals would have been capable of, so that he sensed conspiracies or saw plots which in fact were not always present. But generally and overall, he was spot on and we can only be thankful that large numbers of students, who were inspired by him and his approach, are now able to lend wise counsel in those places where decisions are made.

Eric hated injustice and underprivilege – he was at once a most dispassionate and passionate person. He valued friendship, he loved fun, good food and drink, playing squash and 'make-up' games (beach cricket and tennis), the entertainment of yer average Australian – the footy, the races – the interplay of congenial minds. His economics was always directed towards removing those obstacles in the way of others achieving such ends, if they wanted to. In the process he made the subject live marvellously for his pupils and his colleagues. As Peter Karmel said, 'it was Eric who kept facing us with the wider issues of the human condition [just as it was he who reminded] us of the limitations of our discipline' (Karmel, 1977, p. 160).

Eric was my friend and my mentor. Much of what I think is too personal to be said in a public lecture or written in a published tribute. Nevertheless, I hope that I have managed to give you a glimpse of why he so influenced those who knew him and of why we loved him.

Notes

* The 1977 Newcastle Lecture in Political Economy given at the University of Newcastle on 4 October 1977. I was greatly helped in preparing this lecture by the research assistance of Anne Madden.

1 Peter Karmel writes: 'In the early 1950s at Adelaide . . . new professors could . . . secure one or two additional posts. My time came in 1951, and I felt enormously flattered and happy when I discovered that Eric was prepared to come to Adelaide as senior lecturer in 1952' (Karmel, 1977, p. 159).

2 This section is based upon the papers and correspondence about Meade–Russell that I have found among Eric's papers. I am indebted to James Meade for additional information and his own recollections of events.

3 I am hoping that James Meade has the actual letter in his papers: a search of them – they are stored at the L.S.E. – currently is being done.

4 In a letter to me (15 August 1977) Meade comments (following his discussion of the events in the text): '[When] I got Eric actually to sign on the dotted line, this was regarded as the greatest achievement of my six months in Australia!'

5 In his Presidential address to A.N.Z.A.A.S., Eric repeatedly stressed the central importance of deciding whether flexibility or rigidity characterizes the production and exchange spheres of the economy concerned when choosing between particular views and their associated implied or explicitly recommended policies (see pp. 341–3).

6 This paper was originally given at A.N.Z.A.A.S. in Hobart in August 1965.

7 Eric never published a reply to Donald but I have found in his papers drafts of a reply in which, while he concedes the immediate point, he nevertheless re-asserts the fundamental soundness of his approach and views.

8 In Peter Karmel's tribute in *Australian Economic Papers* to Eric, his class-mate at the University of Melbourne and subsequently close colleague and friend at Adelaide, we read: 'Eric was the widest read of the group and acknowledged as having the most critical mind' (Karmel, 1977, p. 159).

22 Joan Robinson*

Joan Robinson is the rebel with a cause *par excellence*. She has been at the forefront of most major developments, some of them revolutionary, in modern economic theory since the late 1920s. Joan Robinson has always believed passionately in her subject as a force for enlightenment and she has coupled this belief with an equally passionate hatred of social injustice and oppression. She has thrown in her lot with the wretched of the earth, whether they be the unemployed of the capitalist world in the 1930s, or the poverty-stricken and militarily oppressed of the Third World in the post-war era, or students cheated of the living fire by their professors in the 1970s.

Joan Robinson was born on 31 October 1903 into an upper-middle-class English family characterized by vigorous dissent and independence of mind. Her great-grandfather was F.D. Maurice, the Christian Socialist; her father was Major-General Sir Frederick Maurice, the victim of the infamous Maurice debate in 1918. He subsequently became Principal of what is now Queen Mary College in the University of London. Her mother was Helen Margaret Marsh, the daughter of Frederick Howard Marsh, Professor of Surgery and Master of Downing at Cambridge. An uncle was Edward Marsh, civil servant, patron of the arts and scholar. Joan Robinson was educated at St Paul's Girls' School and Girton College, Cambridge, where she was Gilchrist Scholar. She read for the Economics Tripos, 1922–5, graduating in 1925 with second class honours ('a great disappointment'). She married Austin Robinson, the Cambridge economist, in 1926. After a period in India, the Robinsons returned to Cambridge in 1929. Joan joined the Cambridge Faculty as a Faculty Assistant Lecturer in Economics in 1931; subsequently she became a University Lecturer in 1937, Reader in 1949 and Professor in 1965. She was elected to a Professorial Fellowship at Newnham and made an Honorary Fellow of Girton in 1965, and of King's in 1979 and Newnham in 1971. She 'retired' from her Chair in 1971, remaining as active as ever. Cambridge has always been her geographical as well as her intellectual home, but she is an intrepid and enthusiastic traveller, regularly visiting places as disparate as China and Canada. She is as excited now by the prospect of a visit anywhere as when she first went to India in the 1920s.

Joan Robinson has an incisive mind which allows her to cut to the heart of the matter, to see the logical fallacy of an intricate theoretical argument or the political realities of a complicated situation. She has the facility, which has increased with the years (it started from a high base), of distilling the essence of the matter in a few sharp crystal-clear sentences, each one of which is the tip of an iceberg of knowledge and thought. She is able to make sense of technical literature, even though she is virtually innocent of mathematical training, because of a combination of superb intuition with equally superb logical powers. (One of her favourite sayings is: 'As I never learnt mathematics, I have had to think.') These qualities explain why she is an outstanding theoretician. They also explain why her political analysis and judgments are sometimes simplistic and distorted, by-products of that ability to abstract and simplify which marks the good theoretician. Hers is also one of the toughest minds in the trade; she neither avoids nor minds confrontation. Here is the late Harry Johnson's description of a visit by her to Chicago (not recommended as a place for the timid).

> Once she came to Chicago to talk to my students there; they looked at her and decided, 'Well, we'll certainly show this old grandmother where she gets off' . . . They picked their heads up off the floor, having been ticked off with a few well-chosen blunt squelches. . . .
> (Johnson, 1974, p. 30)

Her barbs are spiced with a robust and civilized sense of humour, combined, it must be said, with what John Vaizey calls 'bleak Cambridge rudeness'.

> They [the professors of M.I.T.] now admit . . . that there is no logical reason why the pseudo-production function should be [well behaved]. They just assume that it is so. After putting the rabbit into the hat in full view of the audience it does not seem necessary to make so much fuss about drawing it out again. (Robinson, 1966a, p. 308)

'The purpose of studying economics is not to acquire a set of ready-made answers to economic questions, but to learn how to avoid being deceived by economists' (Robinson, 1951–80, vol. ii, p. 17). 'This model was described as a parable. A parable, in the usual sense, is a story drawn from everyday life intended to explain a mystery; in this case it is the mystery which is expected to explain everyday life' (Robinson, 1977c, p. 10). As we shall see, she has the ability to cast off and start anew; she is no respector of vested interests, certainly not her own, though at any moment of time she will argue fiercely in defence and in favour of her current position.

An original thinker, Joan Robinson is punctilious in documenting her mentors and sources of inspiration. Four close associates hold pride of place: Keynes, Piero Sraffa, Michal Kalecki and, over many years, Richard Kahn, whose 'remorseless logic [has been] an ideal complement to her innovative enthusiasm' (Eatwell, 1977, p. 64). In the Foreword to her first big book *The Economics of Imperfect Competition* (Robinson, 1933a, p.*v*), she writes:

> Of not all the new ideas, however, can I definitely say that 'this is my own invention'. In particular I have had the constant assistance of Mr. R.F. Kahn. The whole technical apparatus was built up with his aid and many of the major problems . . . were solved as much by him as by me.

In the Preface to her *magnum opus, The Accumulation of Capital* (Robinson, 1956, p.*vi*): 'As so often, it was R.F. Kahn who saw the point that we were groping for and enabled us to get it into a comprehensible form.' Piero Sraffa was the inspiration for at least two of her major contributions: *The Economics of Imperfect Competition* (much of the analysis of which she was later to reject: 'to apply the analysis to the so-called theory of the firm, I had to make a number of limitations and simplifications which led the argument astray' — Robinson, 1933a, 2nd edition, 1969, p. *vi*), and her contributions to the theory of value, distribution, capital and growth. She says of Sraffa: 'I worked out a theory of imperfect competition, inspired by Sraffa's article [Sraffa, 1926]' (Foreword by Joan Robinson to Kregel, 1973, p.*x*). In her 'generalisation of the *General Theory*', especially in considering the meaning of the rate of profits, she says: 'Piero Sraffa's interpretation of Ricardo provided the most important clue and the long-delayed publication of his book *The Production of Commodities by Means of Commodities* put into a sharp form the ideas that I had been groping for' (Robinson, 1951–80, vol. iv, p. 125). Her debt, as of us all, to Keynes is documented in many places; Kalecki's influence is discussed below. Of other contemporaries, we should also mention Ester Boserup, Harrod, Kaldor, Myrdal, Pigou and Shove, whose 'teaching in Cambridge for many years past . . . influenced the whole approach to many problems of economic analysis' (Robinson, 1933a, p. *vi*).

Of the greats of the past, Joan Robinson has been most influenced by Ricardo, Marx, Marshall and Wicksell. She finds herself today far more in tune with the former two than the latter two and, indeed, her lasting contribution to the subject, I venture to predict, will be seen as helping to form a unified system of political economy that is classical-cum-Keynesian-Kaleckian in inspiration, directly applicable to the analysis of, and policy prescriptions for, problems of the modern world. She admires Wicksell, not so much for his contributions or approach, as for his candour and honesty, which she contrasts with Marshall's attitudes. 'Unlike Marshall, . . . Wicksell is very candid. When he cannot get an answer he admits the difficulty. This I found very helpful; I gave great credit to Wicksell — not for getting an answer but for seeing the problem' (Robinson, 1951–80, vol. iv, pp. 125, 259). Of Marshall she says: 'The more I learn about economics the more I admire Marshall's intellect and the less I like his character' (p. 259).

> Marshall had a foxy way of saving his conscience by mentioning exceptions, but doing so in such a way that his pupils would continue to believe in the rule. He pointed out that Say's Law . . . breaks down when there is a failure of confidence [but] this was mentioned by the way. It was not meant to disturb the general faith in equilibrium under laissez faire. (Robinson, 1973, p. 2)

'Both [static and dynamic] elements were present in his thinking and he showed great agility in appealing, in each context, to whichever would best suit his purpose of presenting a mollifying picture of the private-enterprise economy' (p. *ix* of Foreword in Kregel, 1973).

Her first major work was *The Economics of Imperfect Competition* (1933a). There is a delightful story concerning Joan at this time. Quite a fuss was being made of her because of her book. Mary Marshall (Alfred's widow) congratulated her at a garden party and promised to tell Alfred, dead then nine years, that he was wrong to claim that women could not do original work in economic theory. In writing the book, Joan Robinson was inspired by Sraffa's 1926 *Economic Journal* article and his 'sacrilege in pointing out inconsistencies in Marshall . . . [who] *was* economics' when she came up to Cambridge in 1922. As Joan Robinson has come to see it, the inconsistencies related to a deep-seated conflict in Marshall's *Principles* between the analysis which is purely static and the conclusions drawn from it which apply to an economy developing through time with accumulation going on. As Sraffa saw it at the time and, we conjecture, Joan Robinson also, the inconsistencies related to the internal logic of static partial equilibrium analysis, especially the dilemma of reconciling the simultaneous existence of falling supply price and competition. Looking back forty years later, Joan Robinson states that her 'aim was to attack the internal logic of the theory of static equilibrium and to refute, by means of its own arguments, the doctrine that wages are determined by the marginal productivity of labour' (p. x of the Foreword to Kregel, 1973).

The latter part of the statement reflects hindsight and present attitudes. It cannot be sustained by either her stated objectives at the time or by the work she subsequently did in the same areas up to the 1940s, especially her papers on 'Euler's Theorem' (1934a), 'What is Perfect Competition?' (1934b) and 'Rising Supply Price' (1941), that 'excellent article . . . which has not attracted the attention . . . it eminently deserves' (Viner, 1953, p. 227). Probably Keynes (in his report on the book to Macmillan in November 1932) comes closest to the correct assessment. He refers to 'a very considerable development of the theory of value in the last five years', developments to be found in journals and in 'oral discussion at Cambridge and Oxford', and to the fact that there is 'no convenient place' in which may be found

> a clear statement of the nature of modern technique, or a summary of the recent work on the subject. Mrs. Robinson aims at filling this gap . . . has done it very well. . . . The book will be for a little while to come an essential one for any serious student of the modern theory of value.

In *The Economics of Imperfect Competition*, Joan Robinson explores systematically the implications for firms in a competitive environment of facing downward-sloping demand curves for their products, so that the profit-maximizing prices and quantities are determined by the intersections of their marginal cost and marginal revenue curves. This analysis illuminated the real world facts (alluded to by Sraffa) that businessmen felt it was demand conditions rather than rising costs which limited their sales, and that firms could still make profits with plants running well below capacity, facts that were incomprehensible within the framework of the Marshallian–Pigovian theories that preceded it.

Joan Robinson subsequently refuted (in the Preface to the second edition – Robinson, 1933a, 2nd edition 1969, p. vi) the approach of the book because of her dissatisfaction with the static method, its inability to handle time. She regarded as a 'shameless fudge' the notion that businessmen could find the 'correct' price by a process of trial and error, because it assumed that the equilibrium position towards which a firm is tending at any point in time is independent of the path it is *actually* taking. Thus she subjected her own analysis to what she regards as the most fundamental criticism of the general methodology of analysis by comparison of static equilibrium positions, a critique which she had developed in other areas in the ensuing years. She still approves of the section in the book on price discrimination but is distressed that the negative lessons of the book, especially the attack on the marginal productivity theory of wages within the confines of its own theoretical framework, have been ignored while the weaknesses have been frozen into orthodox teaching.

At the same time, Joan Robinson was playing a significant part in the formation and propagation of what has come to be known as the Keynesian revolution. Keynes was attempting theoretically to explain why the capitalist world at that time (the early 1930s) had fallen into a deep and sustained slump, in the process, as it turns out, mounting 'a powerful attack on equilibrium theory'. As now has become clear from the publication of vols XIII and XIV of *The Collected Writings of John Maynard Keynes* (edited by Donald Moggridge), the most influential people persuading Keynes both to modify and to expand the analysis in his 1930 *Treatise on Money* (Keynes, 1930) and helping to develop his ideas by both criticisms and contributions, included Harrod, Kahn, Meade, Sraffa and Austin and Joan Robinson. The last five constituted the 'Circus' which argued out the *Treatise* and helped in the formulation of what was to become *The General Theory*. Reading the fascinating exchanges as Keynes moved towards the final draft of *The General Theory* (Keynes, 1936), it is clear that he respected and valued Joan Robinson's contributions and judgment. She herself was important, both for her critical grasp and for her expository powers in making the new theory widely accessible to students and others. Her little book *Introduction to the Theory of Employment* (1937b) is still one of the most lucid accounts that we have of the essentials of Keynes's theory, as are her 'Essays 1935' (Robinson, 1951–80, vol. iv, part 2). Furthermore, she was one of the first to extend Keynes's analysis to an open economy.

In her essay 'Kalecki and Keynes' (1951–80, vol. iii, pp. 92–3), Joan Robinson describes how in the early years of the depression, Keynes, who was groping for a theory of employment (which he ultimately was to find in his theory of effective demand, the possibility of sustained under-employment equilibria or rest states), set Kahn to work out properly the impact of a rise in investment on employment and saving in order to back up Keynes's argument supporting Lloyd George's scheme for public works. Kahn's famous article on the multiplier came out in 1931. The *Treatise* went to the printers for the last time in September 1930. It contained no theory of employment, being concerned mainly with fluctuations in the general level of prices, though it did have the 'highly significant conception' of a relationship between investment and saving via profits. There followed a great bout of argument that churned over these ideas for three years. Austin Robinson (1977, p. 35) tells us that by the end of 1931 'the *questions* [which] the *General Theory* set out to answer' had begun to be asked by Keynes and his junior colleagues. 'In 1933 [Joan Robinson] published [an] interim report [Robinson, 1933b] which clears the ground for the new theory but does not supply it.' That, of course, had to wait until the publication of *The General Theory* itself early in 1936. Even then, they had 'moments when [there was] some trouble in getting Maynard to see what the point of his revolution really was. . . . [However,] when he came to sum it up [in Keynes, 1937] after the book was published he got it into focus' (Robinson, 1973, p. 3). For Joan Robinson, the central themes of *The General Theory* were the theory of effective demand in which is integrated a theory of money and the interest rate, a theory of the general price level, and an analysis of the impact of an uncertain future on the present which occurs through investment expenditure, so locking Keynes's analysis securely into actual historical time.

Significant though her contribution to Keynesian (of *The General Theory*) analysis has been, the most significant step in her thought occurred when she decided to graft Marx onto Keynes (partly through the influence of Michal Kalecki, a Polish Marxist contemporary who independently discovered the main proposition of *The General Theory*). She herself dates this at 1940, though with Piero Sraffa and Maurice Dobb as colleagues and her interest in generalizing *The General Theory*, it seems plausible to conjecture that her interest was aroused even earlier. 'In 1940, as a distraction from the news, I began to read Marx . . . . For me, the main message of Marx was the need to think in terms of history, not of equilibrium' (p. x of Foreword to Kregel, 1973). Again hers is a view which benefits from hindsight; it was Harrod's work *Towards a Dynamic Economics* (1948), which she reviewed in 1949, that really brought this message home. She thus found in Marx what she also found in Keynes (and, fudged, because of its uncomfortable implications, in Marshall). For, as she has said elsewhere of the Keynesian revolution, 'on the plane of theory, the revolution lay in the change from the conception of equilibrium to the conception of history; from the principles of rational choice to the problems of decisions based on guess-work or on convention' and 'once we admit that an economy exists in time, that history goes one way, from the irrevocable past into the unknown future, the conception of equilibrium based on the mechanical analogy of a pendulum swinging to and fro in space becomes untenable' (Robinson, 1973, pp. 3, 5). Thinking in terms of history also involves always asking what sort of society (and its accompanying institutions) is being examined and what social relationships rule in it. It involves, moreover, distinguishing between theories which deal with logical time and those which deal with historical time. 'Logical time can be traced from left to right on the surface of a blackboard. Historical time moves from the dark past behind it into the unknown future in front' (Robinson, 1977a, p. 57). Analyses in logical time are at best the flexing of intellectual muscles, sometimes in a framework in which to sort out doctrinal puzzles, usually as a preliminary to the real thing, the analysis of processes occurring in historical time. This approach also implies that economics is very much a 'horses for courses' discipline, rather than a general theory into which particular situations may be fitted as special cases.

Her book on Marx (Robinson, 1942) is still one of the best introductory pieces to be found, despite its idiosyncrasies and even though, or, perhaps, because in places it contains heresies that continue to infuriate the faithful. Especially is this true of her attitude to the labour theory of value, which has hardened over the years. Thus:

we are told that it is impossible to account for exploitation except in terms of *value*, but why do we need *value* to show that profits can be made in industry by selling commodities for more than they cost to produce, or to explain the power of those who command finance to push around those who do not? (Robinson, 1977a, p.51)

To learn from Marx's ideas we do not have to remain 'stuck in the groove that led him to them'. Nevertheless, the book was not written 'as a criticism of Marx [but] to alert my bourgeois colleagues to the existence of penetrating and important issues in *Capital* that they ought not to continue to neglect' (Robinson, 1977a, p. 50). It abounds in insights and produces a lucid sketch of the skeleton that sustains Marx's system, a skeleton that is too often obscured by the flesh of Hegel, by polemic and by the lack of time and health to polish and rewrite that characterizes much of Marx's own writing. All in all, therefore, it is a constructive and sympathetic critique of Marx's work. The same may be said of her subsequent writings on Marx, attitudes which contrast with the impatience she sometimes shows towards Marxists themselves.

The book led Joan Robinson into her two main preoccupations of the post-war period: on the positive side, the attempt to provide a 'generalisation of the *General Theory*, that is, an extension of Keynes's short-period analysis to long-run development' (Robinson, 1956, p.*vi*), principally to be found in *The Accumulation of Capital* (1956) and interpretative books and articles that have grown up around and from it — *Exercises in Economic Analysis* (1960), *Essays in the Theory of Economic Growth* (1962b), *Economic Heresies* (1971b). A further influence on the way may well have been Rosa Luxemburg's book (1913), also called *The Accumulation of Capital*, to which Joan Robinson contributed the Introduction to the 1951 English edition (Robinson, 1951–80, vol. ii, pp. 59–73). Joan Robinson's own work provides us with a Keynesian-Marxist framework (derived in structure from Kalecki's adaptation of the Marxian schemes of reproductions) with which to interpret the process of growth in capitalist economies and to tackle the grand problems of classical political economy: the possibilities of growth in output per head and the course of the distribution of the national product between broad classes in capitalist societies as capital goods are accumulated over time, influenced principally by the nature of the 'animal spirits' of the societies' businessmen, combined with population growth and technical advances. In this area she shares with Harrod and, possibly, with Kaldor and Pasinetti, the most influential contributions from the Keynesian school to the modern theory of economic growth and distribution.

The Accumulation of Capital sometimes has been misunderstood. Joan Robinson starts the analysis with an examination of the conditions necessary for steady growth, a search for the characteristics of what she calls Golden Ages. Too often this has been taken for descriptive analysis rather than the careful setting out of logical conditions and relationships, one of the principal purposes of which, as is hinted at by the very name, is to show how unlikely it is that they will ever be realized in fact. 'I used the phrase "a golden age" to describe smooth, steady growth with full employment (intending thereby to indicate its mythical nature)' (Robinson, 1962b, p. 52). In the subsequent clarifications and expansions of her findings she has emphasized more the lessons of the later chapters on the short period and the interconnections of short periods over time. She also has reiterated what she stated in the original work, that the sections on the choice of techniques of production at the level of the economy as a whole occupy more space than their importance (as opposed to their difficulty) warrants. Moreover, they relate principally to the realm of doctrinal debate associated with the vast literature on the aggregate production function rather than to that of positive analysis.

The second strand is associated with her sustained attack on the currently received paradigm of economics, the neoclassical theory of value, production and distribution. This has been centred in the last twenty-five years in the theory of capital, mainly because of her celebrated article 'The Production Function and the Theory of Capital' (Robinson, 1953-4), which started off what have become known as the Cambridge controversies in the theory of capital. 'Cambridge' refers to the fact that the main protagonists in the controversies have all been associated either temporarily or permanently with the two Cambridges – Cambridge, England, and Cambridge, Mass., where M.I.T., and Samuelson and Solow, are situated. On the surface the argument has tended to evolve around whether or not it is possible to measure 'capital' as a factor of production, what units to use, is there a unit that is independent of distribution and prices, and what sense, if any, may be made of the proposition that the marginal product of capital equals the rate of profits? But, as Joan Robinson has stressed again and again, the argument has not really anything to do with the problem of measuring and valuing 'capital', as opposed to the *meaning* of 'capital', but with the attempt by those she dubs the 'Bastard Keynesians' to reconstruct 'pre-Keynesian theory after Keynes'.

> It has nothing to do either with measurement or with capital; it has to do with abolishing time. For a world that is always in equilibrium there is no difference between the future and the past, there is no history and there is no need for Keynes (Robinson, 1973, p. 6)

– or Marx.

> The controversies over so-called capital theory arose out of the search for a model appropriate to a modern western economy, which would allow for an analysis of accumulation and of the distribution of the net product of industry between wages and profits. . . . Long-run accumulation became the centre of interest, [so making] it necessary to come to grips with concepts of the quantity of capital and the rate of profit in the economy as a whole. (Robinson, 1977c, pp. 5, 6-7)

Joan Robinson sees the response to her criticisms as the outcome of an ideological tide that reacts continually against the damaging criticisms of Marx, Keynes and Sraffa, that attempts to create an economic theory which by implication at least tends to support the *status quo*, in particular, democratic capitalist free market institutions and, in at least some influential quarters, a doctrine of *laissez faire*.

Here, it must be said, Joan Robinson has tried to get too many targets in her sights at one time. The groups most favourably disposed to *laissez faire*, Friedman and the Chicago school, and their burgeoning offshoots elsewhere, have been vigorously attacking what *they* take to be the exposed flanks of the American or 'Bastard' Keynesians who are led from M.I.T. and Yale, while Joan Robinson has been attacking what she takes to be other vulnerable areas. The attacked themselves could, with justice, claim that not only are they staunch advocates and defenders of middle-of-the-road to leftish Keynesian policies but also that they have provided a considerable amount of the ammunition that over the years has been used to destroy the more grandiose claims that may be made for a free-rein market economy as an efficient allocator of resources and maximizer of community welfare. As Tobin (1973, p. 106, n. 1) remarks, '[Samuelson's] work on the theory of public goods . . . is only an outstanding example of the attention modern theorists, in America and overseas, have paid to the allocative failures of *laissez faire*.' Thus, Joan Robinson's simplicity of vision may be faulted in detail but there is, nevertheless, considerable validity in her general argument: hence the irritation and anger that she arouses, especially in conservative academic and political circles.

In the debates, she has been tenacious and consistent, returning again and again to the theme that orthodox equilibrium analysis is incapable of handling the essential facts of a capitalist economy, namely, that it exists in real historical time, that it is investment decisions by capitalist businessmen (and not the saving decisions of households) which are the dynamic driving force of the economy, that uncertainty and unrealized expectations about the future are inescapable facts of life which *must* find a place in any theory of the development of a capitalist economy over time, that

> interest [is] the price that a businessman pays for the use of finance to be committed to an investment [while] profit [is] the return that he hopes to get on it, [and that] wage rates are settled in terms of money [while] the level of real wages depends upon the operation of the economy as a whole. (Robinson, 1977c, p. 5)

An index of her success in these endeavours is that both Samuelson (in the *Quarterly Journal of Economics*, 1975) and Hahn, in a number of places, including his Inaugural Lecture (Hahn, 1973a) have either explicitly or implicitly conceded the validity of many of her claims. Tobin, in an otherwise rather pained review of *Economic Heresies* (Robinson, 1971b) and the two Cambridges' debates, nevertheless praises her for her repeated stress on the treatment of expectations and her objection that 'Walrasian general equilibrium, even when enlarged to postulate markets in all commodities in all contingencies at all future dates, is no real solution' (Tobin, 1973, p. 109). Sir John Hicks, having repudiated aspects of those versions of Keynesian theory which are peculiarly associated with him through his 1937 *Econometrica* paper, 'Mr. Keynes and the "Classics"' (Hicks, 1937), now takes approaches which parallel closely those of Joan Robinson (see, for example, Hicks, 1976, 1977). In addition, along with others, especially Piero Sraffa, Joan Robinson has exposed the logical inconsistencies in those versions of neoclassical theory which attempt to provide a theory of distribution which could take the place of classical, especially Ricardian, theory and also, of course, of Marxian theory. These particular criticisms came to a head in the reswitching and capital-reversing debates of the mid 1960s. The debates themselves were the culmination of earlier discussions concerning whether certain results which were rigorously true of simple one-commodity neoclassical models would continue to be so in more complex heterogeneous capital good models. Joan Robinson now regards these particular criticisms and results as 'unimportant' (Robinson, 1975a). She prefers to rest the weight of her critique on her more general methodological arguments, together with her stress on the indispensable need always to postulate what are the social relationships and institutions of the economy being modelled and at what stage in its history is the analytical story taken up. Finally, in her Richard T. Ely Lecture to the American Economic Association Meeting in 1971 (a personal triumph in which the main room overflowed into subsidiary ones and for which she received a standing ovation), Joan Robinson identified a second crisis in economic theory (the first being its inability to handle the interwar slump), the lack of a suitable framework with which to tackle the terrible problems of modern economic life – poverty, racism, urban puzzles and pollution, excessive population growth and war.

Her latest word on all this – to date, of course – is her comprehensive paper, 'What are the Questions?' (Robinson, 1977d). She starts by arguing that ideology and economic analysis are indissolubly mixed and that the dominant ideology exerts disproportionate power in the discipline at any moment of time, and she quotes Benjamin Ward (1972, pp. 29–30) in support. This leads her to savage Robbins's definition of economics when it is set in the context of a capitalist economy:

> The question of scarce means with alternative uses becomes self contradictory when it is set in historical time, where today is an ever-moving break between the irrevocable past and the unknown future. At any moment, certainly, resources are scarce, but they have hardly any range of alternative uses. (Robinson, 1977d, p. 1322)

She deplores a major distinction that is made in modern orthodox economics, that between micro and macro. One cannot exist without the other, for

> micro questions . . . cannot be discussed in the air without any reference to the structure of the economy in which they exist [or] to the processes of cyclical and secular change. Equally, macro theories of accumulation and effective demand are generalizations about micro behaviour. . . . If there is no micro theory, there cannot be any macro theory either. (p. 1320)

Moreover, the macro setting for orthodox micro theory is a kind of vague Say's Law world which, until very recently anyway, is *not* the macro world that is analysed in *its* own separate compartment.

We must also mention her contributions to the theory of international trade. As we saw, she was amongst the first systematically to apply the Keynesian mode of thought to the problems of an open economy; she wrote a seminal article on the theory of the foreign exchanges (Robinson, 1937a), and in her Inaugural Lecture *The New Mercantilism* (Robinson, 1966c) and lectures at Manchester University (reprinted in vol. iv of her collected works, Robinson, 1951–80) she applied her general critiques of orthodox theory to the special area of international trade and suggested alternative avenues of approach. We should also mention a half-way house paper (Robinson, 1946–7) in which she critically expounds the classical theory of international trade as it came down from Marshall, in order 'to try to see what basis it offers for the belief in a natural tendency towards equilibrium' (p.98).

She returns to this theme again in 'What are the Questions?', pointing out that Ricardo (in 'the famous story which begins with England and Portugal both producing both cloth and wine') was the first to commit the cardinal sin (in her eyes) of analysing a process going on through time by the comparison of two equilibrium positions, an invalid procedure that is, as we have seen, the centre-piece of her critique of orthodoxy. (Ricardo, as a pioneer, is absolved.) It must be said that Samuelson, whom, along with Solow, she has criticized repeatedly for doing this, courteously but firmly denies it, producing chapter and verse in support (Samuelson, 1975). Furthermore, Garegnani, an influential ally of Joan Robinson and Piero Sraffa in their attack on neoclassical theory, also takes issue with her on this point. He argues that comparisons of long-run positions (not, note, equilibrium ones, for equilibrium is a notion that is intimately related to supply and demand) *are* fundamental to economic methodology. However, the neoclassicals err when they try to incorporate the method with *their* overriding emphasis on the forces of supply and demand. *Their* theories, he argues, then run into insuperable logical difficulties, especially in the depiction of the demand curve for 'capital' and the consequent existence and stability of long-run equilibrium positions (see Garegnani, 1959, 1970, 1976). That is to say, Garegnani wishes to preserve the tradition that began with the classicals of relating key concepts – for example, natural prices – to sustained and fundamental forces. He feels that Joan Robinson's attack on orthodoxy threatens this tradition also. Joan Robinson also wishes to retain the key classical concepts but to scrap the method.

There is a puzzle that often emerges in discussions of Joan Robinson's contributions, namely, the lack of empirical work by her of at least the conventional kind. The answer probably lies in two areas: first, she principally has been concerned with fundamental theoretical questions, the necessary setting out of definitions, concepts and logical relationships, the provision of a framework which must precede good empirical work. Second, her close associates over the years – Kahn and, of course, Keynes and Kalecki – were applied economists in the old-fashioned sense *par excellence*. They made it their business to know intimately the institutions, the historical sequences and the orders of magnitude of particular situations and they had a feel for the limits of particular policy recommendations. Joan Robinson's work, therefore, often was complementary to theirs as was theirs to hers. Moreover, much of her theoretical work *is* based on Marshallian-type empirical generalizations, that is to say, broad qualitative statements which constitute either the basis for the development of a logical argument or the puzzles that are to be explained by theoretical reasoning.

Joan Robinson's admiration for and extensive writings on the Chinese experiment are well known, probably to a wider audience than those for any of her other works. She is always stimulating, full of insights, putting a complicated and changing scene into a manageable framework. Her writing in this area contains a leaven of advocacy, a conscious effort to try to offset what she believes to have been the unsympathetic critiques of Chinese policies which emanated from orthodox circles. In addition, she has written extensively on the theoretical and practical aspects of planning in socialist societies, based on her experience with, and criticisms of, the Russian and Eastern European experiments.

Her championing of Kalecki's independent discovery of the main propositions of *The General Theory* is well known from a number of delightfully written and absorbing articles. (We mention, especially,

Robinson, 1976 and 1977b; the latter is also a fine introduction to, and exposition of, Kalecki's analysis of capitalism.) Moreover, time is confirming her judgment that '[in] several respects Kalecki's version is more robust than Keynes'' (Robinson, 1977b, p. 10). Nor has she neglected the involved intellectual's task of communicating to a wider circle than those within her discipline. She contributed a charming and influential book, *Economic Philosophy* (Robinson, 1962a), to the New Thinkers' Library in 1962. (It is, perhaps, too Popperian for most Marxists' taste.) Allen & Unwin have twice persuaded her to try her hand at books for a wide audience – *Economics: An Awkward Corner* (Robinson, 1966b), which diagnosed Britain's economic ills, and *Freedom and Necessity* (Robinson, 1970b), which is a model for a challenging introductory course in the social sciences – if only the teacher were Joan Robinson.

Last, but certainly not least, her concern for students and what they are taught has been evidenced in a number of areas. Generations of Cambridge undergraduates and research students have paid their tribute to a demanding but devoted supervisor, as a perusal of the prefaces of books by former students will show. She has lectured all over the world to students, often at their request, and she never refuses an invitation from students, if it is humanly possible for her to get there. In 1973 she wrote, with John Eatwell, a new type of textbook, *An Introduction to Modern Economics*, which she fervently hoped would herald a new dawn in the teaching of Economics. It is splendid in conception but rough in execution. It is too ambitious – she tries to distil into one work for first-year students her life-long ponderings and even the cream of the British intelligentsia whom she and Eatwell are accustomed to teach find it more than hard going. In addition, it is a long time since either author has taught first-year students of *any* calibre so that they have overestimated the absorption effect. Nevertheless, it is a noble experiment which should not be ignored by the hidebound, the pedestrian and the timid. Let it also be hoped that it serves to produce the 'generation well educated, resistent to fudging, imbued with the humility and the pride of genuine scientists [making] contributions both to knowledge and to the conduct of affairs that no one need be ashamed of' (Robinson, 1951–80, vol. iii, p. 6). But whatever the outcome of this particular venture, Joan Robinson herself has much more than fulfilled her own modest aim of doing 'a little good here and there to set in the scales against all the harm' (Robinson, 1951–80, vol. iii, p. 6).

Note

* A version of this essay appears in David L. Sills (ed.), *International Encyclopaedia of the Social Sciences, Biographical Supplement*, New York, Free Press, 1979, vol. 18, pp. 663–7. I thank most sincerely but in no way implicate Tom Asimakopulos, M.C. Bradbrook, John Burbidge, Jon Cohen, Phyllis Deane, Robert Dixon, John Eatwell, Peter Groenewegen, Donald Harris, John Hatch, Susan Howson, Bruce McFarlane, Ian McLean, Donald Moggridge, Mark Perlman, Lorie Tarshis, John Vaizey, David Vines and Trevor Wilson for their help and/or their comments on a draft. The letter from John Maynard Keynes to Harold Macmillan is quoted with permission from Lord Kahn.

23 Occasional portraits of the founding Post-Keynesians Lorie Tarshis (or, Tarshis on Tarshis by Harcourt)*

From time to time we intend to publish in the *JPKE* portraits – or sketches, if you like – of some of the original Post-Keynesians, a loose term designed to cover those people who were pupils of and/or worked with and/or were strongly influenced by Keynes, and whose work continues to reflect this influence. A most appropriate person to include in the series is Lorie Tarshis. So on Friday 13 June 1980 I spent a most enjoyable day talking to Lorie at the Ontario Economic Council, 81 Wellesley Street, Toronto, where, as a youthful 69, he is Research Director.

I say 'appropriate' because Lorie went to Keynes's lectures at Cambridge in the early 1930s when Keynes was drafting *The General Theory*. He previously had had a thorough grounding in the *Treatise* and Cambridge-style economics generally at the Department of Political Economy of the University of Toronto, principally through Wynne Plumptre and Vincent Bladen; he played a significant role in the conversion of Abba Lerner to Keynesian economics; and he published in 1947 (with Houghton Mifflin) the first explicitly Keynesian textbook in the U.S.A., *The Elements of Economics*. As we shall see, Lorie and the book were disgracefully treated. Nevertheless, to Lorie's great joy and proper quiet pride, he still meets people at conferences who tell him that the Keynesian section of the book (Part 4, of 250 pages) was – and is – the best introduction to Keynesian fundamentals that they have ever come across. Finally, throughout his professional life, during which he has made significant contributions to the development of Keynesian thought, especially to the too much neglected aggregate supply side (see Tarshis, 1979) and to our understanding of international monetary puzzles, Lorie has built on and extended his thorough training in the economics of Keynes. What follows is based on my notes (all forty-two pages of them) of our conversation which spread over five hours, and which we both enjoyed very much, no doubt because, as Lorie quipped, we were both talking about one of our favourite subjects.

Lorie was born in Toronto in 1911; he lived for much of his child-hood in the Annexe in Kendal Avenue, in a house close enough for him now to punt a ball from there onto the front garden of our mutual friends, Jon and Paola Cohen. His father, Dr Singer, was a general practitioner, possibly the first Jew to graduate in medicine from the University of Toronto — certainly old people who remember him with respect and affection have said this to Lorie. Dr Singer was the City Coroner, which, though a mark of distinction for a hard-working young G.P., was also, as we shall see, to have tragic consequences. Lorie's mother, 'a very beautiful woman', was the daughter of comfortable, middle-class, non-practising Jewish parents. Neither side of Lorie's family lived completely, or even predominantly, within the Jewish community and Lorie himself, in a city supposedly at that time noted for discrimination, was never aware of it, numbering amongst his school and university friends people from both communities.

After a sheltered girlhood, educated at Loretta Abbey and for two years at a finishing school in Germany, Lorie's mother married at 18. Lorie was born when she was 19 and his sister, thirteen months later. In 1915 there was a typhoid epidemic in Toronto. Dr Singer con-tracted the disease, possibly through his post of City Coroner, and died, leaving Lorie's mother a widow at 22, with two small children and a third on the way, a son who died in infancy. With her upbringing, she was quite ill-equipped to cope, except by marrying again. This she did, marrying Mr Tarshis, whose name Lorie was to take. Lorie was very fond of him and always refers to him as 'Dad'. The remarriage unjustly estranged Lorie's mother from most of the Singer family — a very large and influential one though her own parents and family were most supportive. It seems to have been a happy marriage (his mother died in the mid 1940s, his 'Dad' in the late 1960s) and certainly Lorie speaks with affection of them both.

In this family of wealthy, Jewish, middle-class people, Lorie had relatives who supported and appreciated the arts — theatre, opera, ballet, painting, the orchestra — as well as being in the professions or, as in the case of his step-father, in business. Mr Tarshis was a retailer and wholesaler, first in typewriters, then in building materials and conveyor-belts (Lorie's step-brother — there were two children of the second marriage — only relinquished control of the family business on Front Street a couple of years ago). Thus Lorie's strong love for, and extensive knowledge of paintings, sculpture, books (his passion is Blake), music and live theatre come naturally from his family back-ground. In Inga, his charming wife, herself deeply cultured and whose background is embedded in knowledge and appreciation of the arts (she is a singer and her father was an antiquarian bookseller in Rome), Lorie has the ideal companion for the rich and satisfying private life of culture which unobtrusively characterizes the Tarshises.

Lorie was educated at Huron Street Primary School (innocently pronounced 'urine'); at the University of Toronto School, at which were nurtured the intellectual *and* sporting elite of Toronto, happily overlapping sets; and at the University of Toronto. He was always good at his work — got high grades, as we Canajians say — got on well with his teachers, and did well at sport, especially ice hockey and squash, because of his excellent co-ordination. (Today he still beats most people on the Scarborough squash courts and is one of Heather Mackay's prize pupils at the Toronto Squash Club. Once he gets to the front court you might as well 'give it away'.) He himself wished to be a doctor, partly because it had been his father's profession, but he knew it would cause 'Dad' some heartache (because of the attitude of the Singer family to Lorie's mother and also because G.P.s in those days worked extremely hard for extremely modest incomes). Lorie's mother and 'Dad' worried about him as impractical, unlikely to survive in the rough and tumble of the real world, or even to learn how to tie unaided his own shoe laces. As Lorie tells it, he was a shy child, younger than the others in his class, and in adolescence most of his friendships with girls were 'in his mind'. Nevertheless he was quietly determined to have his own way (a characteristic that is still present), should the need arise. But it did not.

Lorie's step-father had arranged for Lorie to go to a camp run by Taylor Statten whom 'Dad' and Lorie had heard speak at a fathers' and sons' night. The hackneyed reason for this was to make a man of him which in 'Dad's' view their joint attendance at boxing matches had not. So Lorie spent a number of happy summers at a camp for 250 or so boys (there were girls at a 'sister' camp on an island about a mile away, with patrol boats to keep the boys at a distance) where he came under Statten's influence. Statten immediately took a great interest in him. For two years, Lorie was a camper, then he was on the staff as a 'counsellor in training'. Through Statten he met a U.S. guidance counsellor who quizzed the intending university student concerning what he wished to do. Lorie said 'medicine' and mentioned that math was probably his best subject. 'Oh, you don't want to waste your time on medicine then; do economics where it will come in more useful.' All Lorie knew about economics was the Wall Street boom (it was 1927) so, being a well brought up young Canadian, he said, 'Yes, Sir, thank

you, Sir' – and so Lorie Tarshis the economist was conceived. (Lorie
thought he would make a million quickly and retire early.)

Lorie went to the Department of Political Economy at the University of Toronto at a most exciting time for economics. The greatest
influences on Lorie were Wynne Plumptre, Vincent Bladen, Donald
Macgregor, Harold Innis, and Harry Cassidy, a labour economist who
took his pupils as observers to meet both sides during a strike, and to
listen to debates at Queen's Park. Plumptre had just returned from
Cambridge. He was a superb teacher. He looked younger than his pupils,
who called him by his first name from the beginning (a rare event in
those or even – dare I say it? – these days), and he had the bright ones
round for beer and conversation on Sunday nights. Plumptre brought
copies of the *Treatise* with him from Cambridge for his pupils and
Lorie's third year was spent immersing himself in its pages. He 'understood it thoroughly though not enough then to see its flaws'.

Vincent Bladen's exciting course was on advanced economic theory:
a lot of Adam Smith, of course, but the students also were encouraged
to read the journals – and in the examination to write about what *they*
had read. Thus Lorie read Sraffa (1926) and all the follow-ups in the
pages of the *Economic Journal* up to the symposium on increasing
returns and the representative firm, and wrote his exam answer –
'students should attempt one or more questions' – on that. Lorie took
Innis's fourth-year course on Canadian economic history; he agrees
with Vincent Bladen that Harold Innis was 'a great educator though a
terrible teacher, inaudible, notes always in a mess'.

Lorie says that throughout his life he has been blessed with close
friends who have been quite extraordinary people. (His friends could
well reply that they have been privileged to know an extraordinary
person in Lorie.) One of his closest friends at the U. of T., and subsequently at Cambridge until his death, was Bill Walker, who was 'a
top quality Toronto society person but very nice'. Lorie tells a harrow-
ing tale of the aftermath to Bill (who was at Cambridge but playing ice
hockey on the Continent) and a companion climbing Mont Blanc in
two days – an unheard of feat in those days. Walker got gangrene in his
frost-bitten toes and Lorie had to get him from the Continent to Cambridge by train and ferry without his legs falling below the horizontal.

At the U. of T. Lorie was an active student in Hart House Debates
and in sports generally. He was runner up in the Rhodes scholarship,
then a most prestigious award. The disappointment of missing out was
lessened when an elector told him that they had not given it to him
(but to a close friend of his who subsequently became a distinguished

lawyer in Toronto) because Oxford was not a good place for economics. They wanted Lorie to go to Cambridge and they knew that he was to get a Massey scholarship in order to be able to do so – a degree of paternalism with which I am not sure Lorie would agree, either then or now. But just as well for economics.

So, in September, 1932, Lorie with eleven other young Canadians, eleven of them from Toronto, headed for Cambridge, Oxford and London on a ship which Walker and Tarshis had done the leg work in selecting, the principal criterion being the maximum time on board. It was Cunard's *Aurania*, laughingly called a liner, but so much like an island ferry that Lorie's mother burst into tears when she saw them off.

Lorie went to Trinity because Wynne Plumptre had arranged that he – and Bob Bryce, a mining engineering graduate of the U. of T. who was to read economics at Cambridge at St John's, and who became 'a very close friend' – would see as much of Keynes as they wished, especially through Keynes's P.E. Club, of which they both became members. At Trinity, Plumptre reckoned Lorie would have contact with Maurice Dobb, Dennis Robertson and Piero Sraffa. Lorie was an affiliated student which meant he could read for the Economics Tripos in two years. He went, each year, to all of Keynes's lectures and his notes of them are still coveted by aspiring historians of thought. His supervisors included Maurice Dobb, Dennis Robertson – 'always friendly and warm, then and after' – and Colin Clark. He got a First in a remarkable year for Firsts which included Bob Bryce, Sid Butlin (with whom he was supervised by Dennis Robertson in most of his first two years), Brian Reddaway and V.K.R.V. Rao (with whom Lorie became firm friends), and he then enrolled for a Ph.D.

As we mentioned, Lorie was a member of the Keynes Club. He remembers Richard Kahn as its secretary and responsible for the tea, 'damn strong and bitter', and plum cake. He also remembers leaving one evening behind Keynes and Sraffa; Keynes teased Sraffa: 'I say, Piero, is there anything to this Marx chappie?' Sraffa was a regular attender. He usually said nothing until near the end when the other members waited eagerly for what was usually the keynote question, often the knockdown blow for the whole argument, delivered in a slightly querulous tone. Austin and Joan Robinson were there sometimes, and Keynes would bring visitors from time to time: Schultz of the hog cycle, Douglas of Cobb–Douglas, who nearly took Lorie to Chicago for his graduate work. Lorie also remembers Maurice Dobb as scrupulous in keeping his political views from his pupils – and as teaching Marshallian economics – and that Keynes never referred to his younger colleague's commitment to the Communist Party.

Keynes's lectures, says Lorie, were much taken up with definitions of terms — saving, investment, user cost, profits, income — the necessary preliminary tasks through which Keynes was to sort out his own mind and provide himself with the apparatus for his new theory. Lorie thought that the lectures were expanding and elaborating the *Treatise* though from a different slant, i.e. applying the principles there to the new problem of the levels of output and employment as a whole. Vincent Bladen has a slightly different account: 'he [Lorie Tarshis] tells of attending his first lecture from Keynes and being bewildered when Keynes announced that this course which was said to be on the theory of money would in fact be on the theory of output as a whole. The *General Theory* had been conceived' (Bladen, 1978, p. 182). The new stuff itself was very compressed, occurring towards the end of the series of seven to eight lectures which Keynes gave each year. Nevertheless, when *The General Theory* came out in February 1936 (Lorie and some others were given advance copies on Friday so that they could read it on Saturday and discuss it with Keynes on Sunday before the book itself was published on Monday), Lorie recognized everything in it and felt familiar and at home with it all and, of course, knew of things — e.g. the theory of the co-operative economy — which were omitted from the final draft. However, he still finds new insights and nuances, even on his n^{th} reading of *The General Theory* today.

Lorie stayed on in Cambridge for two more years in order to keep his six terms for the Ph.D. degree. He was senior research scholar at Trinity (a prestigious award though he did not know this at the time). Through the young Canadians in London with whom he had travelled to England, Lorie met Paul and Allen Sweezy (Paul then was an ardent and belligerent defender of Hayek) and Abba and Arthur Lerner (also Hayek fans). Lorie got Lerner to visit Cambridge many times and they argued through the respective merits of the works of their heroes. Abba used to arrive at lunchtime at Lorie's room in Trinity. His lunch consisted of Marmite sandwiches, a peculiar English and Australian tradition (the Australian equivalent is Vegemite), and Lorie would leave the room and meet Abba *after* lunch because he could not take the smell of Marmite. At least in the after-lunch discussions Lorie triumphed for Abba became — and remained — a convinced and ardent Keynesian.

Lorie's dissertation, *The Determinants of Labour Income*, was an examination of the share of wages in the national income combined with a study of the determinants of real wages. His aim [was] to deal with certain problems of functional distribution in a way consistent with recent findings ... in respect to the behaviour of the individual firm [the theories of imperfect competition and of the short period associated particularly with Joan Robinson and Richard Kahn] and in respect of the functioning of the whole economy [Keynes's *General Theory*, of course]. (Preface, p. i)

His supervisor was Colin Clark; but as Lorie wanted to work on U.S. data, about which Clark knew little, and because the U.K. data was not suitable, and also because Clark was not a theoretician, it was mainly a 'do it yourself' job. Nevertheless, his acknowledgments in the Preface – 'I am grateful for the advice and stimulus afforded me by Mr. R.F. Kahn, Mr. P. Sraffa and Mr. D.H. Robertson': p. iv) – justify Plumptre's decision to send Lorie to Trinity, knowing that he also would have access to the economists in King's. In fact, Lorie wrote most of it when he went to Tufts to his first teaching job in the autumn of 1936. There, he used the U.S. data from the N.R.A. and T.N.E.C. and developed a theoretical framework. Though the latter lacked the elegance and simple power of Kalecki's work on similar lines – Lorie had not yet learnt how to make simple, illuminating assumptions in order to get clear but relevant, simple results – it was essentially an independently discovered version of Kalecki's macro theory of distribution, with considerably more empirical work – 'and it [was] correct'. Lorie also was influenced by Gardner Means and others then working on mark-up pricing and he included these ideas in his theoretical framework, looking for the relationship between average and marginal labour costs and the gap between price and cost as a clue to distribution. He did not use the reverse L shaped cost curve and so had more complicated marginal, average relationships with which to deal, possibly a legacy from his early training in these areas. (The same mastery of these relationships and the details associated with them may be found in his 1979 paper: Tarshis, 1979.)

Out of Lorie's doctoral research (he knuckled down to write it when he realized that a Ph.D. was the trade union ticket in the U.S. – in Cambridge there had been other diversions and the usual spell of research student blues when Lorie wondered whether he would ever write anything and, even if he did, whether it would be worth reading) came the famous 1939 *Economic Journal* note on the course of real wages over the cycle. This, together with Dunlop's article on the same issue (Dunlop, 1938), convinced Keynes that he should abandon the Marshallian perfectly competitive micro foundations of *The General Theory* and led to one of the earliest statements of the normal cost pricing hypothesis, now a hallmark of Post-Keynesian theory. Lorie got a shock when he discovered that real wages did not move as Keynes had predicted in *The General Theory*. But it did not cause him to lose faith in Keynes or his general theory: he recognized that Keynes had used the Marshallian foundations partly in order to avoid clouding the main issue with the orthodox by bringing in the imperfect competition revolution at the same time as his own revolution. Keynes, after all, had read Joan Robinson's *Economics of Imperfect Competition* for Macmillan, so certainly knew *all* about it, or at least as much as would fit into the twenty minutes which Gerald Shove argued was necessary in order to understand the theory of value. Others were not so sanguine. Always lukewarm believers, or not believers at all, they pounced on the Dunlop–Tarshis results in order completely to dismiss Keynes. Keynes himself wrote quickly to Lorie in positive terms about the note, and accepted it 'as is' — an appropriate response to the little men waiting in the wings for the great one to stumble. With the proceeds received for the article, Lorie bought life membership of the Royal Economic Society, which, given his long life, has proved a very handsome return on his investment.

The examiners of his Ph.D. dissertation were John Hicks and Mrs Holland; the oral took most of the day with a break for luncheon — and the examiners were far more nervous and ill at ease than the examinee! Most of the questions asked for elaboration and/or explanation — there were no critical questions. Hicks especially was kind and supportive, though many of the findings could not have been *that* congenial to the author of *The Theory of Wages*. At the end of the oral they told him he was Dr Tarshis and Lorie and his mother-in-law, who was visiting Cambridge, bought his Ph.D. robes that same afternoon. Lorie met Kalecki at this time. Lorie arrived in England two days before the actual oral and was introduced to Kalecki who then was working in the U.K. They quickly got into an animated and serious discussion as they realized that they were working along similar lines. Lorie found him 'amazingly quick'; he agrees that Kalecki was not noted for his social graces and that he had a voice 'like a screeching tyre'. He formed a lasting respect and affection for him.

Despite its originality and importance, Lorie's Ph.D. dissertation was never published. The first — and only — publisher whom he tried rejected it, not because of its merit or even because of its style (which could have been rectified), but because of an adverse report by a reader who was an envious contemporary.

Before we leave Lorie's Cambridge years, we add a postscript which arises from some questions raised by Austin Robinson, who read a draft of this paper. Austin asked whether Lorie 'was interested in the development of the multiplier which was going on while he was at Cambridge' and: 'In what directions in his working life did he develop the original ideas of *The General Theory*, e.g. did he try to open the system that was initially a closed system in his work on foreign trade?'

In answer to the first query, Lorie writes:

> Yes, but probably I thought – as I remember it – that most of it was pretty obvious. I remember D.H.R. questioning me over and over how S could remain equal to I during the multiplier process and I tried to explain it in terms of a MPC which temporarily strayed from its 'true' short-term value, or in terms of lags. (I still do one or the other – quite ambidextrous!)
>
> As to 'opening' K's model: I imagine that it was the hundreds of times that I had heard, while studying in Toronto, that Canada was an *open economy* – . . . it was that and some other matters that Innis made much of – that made me critical and doubtful of the facile application of the general theory, as it was gradually taking shape, to Canada; so Bob [Bryce] and I often made use of what later was called the Marginal Propensity to Import to reduce the value of the Multiplier.

At Tufts Lorie was greatly influenced by Frederick St Leger (Buzz) Daly, a friend who had been at Statten's camp and who also had been a favourite pupil of Vincent Bladen at the U. of T. Daly was five years senior to Lorie; he had been a great football player and Lorie had hero-worshipped him. He never wrote anything for publication and, indeed, never finished his Ph.D. at Harvard; Daly was a 'Shove-like figure', 'a slow intelligence', punctilious, modest and the best, most patient, teacher Lorie ever encountered. At Tufts, they had offices opposite one another in a very narrow corridor and Lorie remembers the stream of students that flocked in; he would hear Daly explaining in very great and careful detail the answers to their questions. Lorie and Daly played squash together, walked together, drove together. Lorie was more a follower of Keynes than Daly who, nevertheless, and characteristically, was very honest in his efforts to get hold of Keynes's message.

Lorie considers it 'a super bit of luck for him' to have been at Tufts at this time; to live in Cambridge and to go to Harvard for seminars where he met Paul Samuelson and met up again with Paul Sweezy (whose then wife, Maxine, was also teaching at Tufts) – and also with Walter and Bill Salant. Walter was a friend from Lorie's Cambridge days. Lorie met and heard Mason, Schumpeter and Hansen (who alone of the senior people was a Keynesian, or, at least, one who, after his thoughtful review of the *Treatise*, thoroughly understood Keynes. Seymour Harris was a Keynes enthusiast but, at least in those days, an embarrassment too). It was Bob Bryce and Lorie Tarshis as much an any of the younger people who brought Keynes to Harvard. Even Samuelson was more interested in microeconomics.[1]

Nor was Lorie's influence confined to theory and academia. Following the 1930s depression, in 1936 the United States G.N.P. accelerated upwards, then in the late spring of 1937 it started to fall. Lorie was one of a small group in and around Harvard – Paul and Maxine Sweezy, Walter Salant, Emile Despres, Richard Gilbert, John Wilson – who got together to write a 'tract for the times' on fiscal policy as they realized that nothing was being done, yet a decline into another depression was close. The book, *An Economic Program for American Democracy*, sold extraordinarily well. The authors were attacked, but to be a left-winger, even a Communist, in those days was not what it later was to become. Roosevelt's advisors were influenced by the book – all sorts of nuances in the 1938 budget made it clear that it had had its effect on policy. Tufts got into some trouble over the book – withdrawal of bequests that otherwise would have been provided in some wills?

During the Second World War Lorie became, in effect, a 'boffin' in the U.S. air force (the Ninth Bomber Command in Libya). After Pearl Harbor, Lorie, who was working at Tufts, received a 'we want you' telegram from F.D.R. (as did everyone, but Lorie like many others did not know this at the time). He responded by becoming a U.S. citizen (on 23 March 1942) so that he could join the war effort. He first spent a fruitless and frustrating year in Washington working on a committee headed by the legendary Frank Coe and which also included Lauchlin Currie. Lorie acted as the go-between for Canadian firms that could provide munitions for the U.S.A., contacting officials who were already in the pay of U.S. firms for U.S. orders! Then, through the good offices of a physicist friend, Dick Roberts, who could not go himself because of research associated with radar on which he then was working and with whose family Lorie then was staying, Lorie joined an outfit in the air force which advised on bombing raids and other puzzles. In the outfit Lorie chummed up with another extraordinary person, an academic engineer by trade, George Housner, who also was, in one of Lorrie's favourite expressions, 'very bright'. In the outfit Lorie learnt an important methodological lesson: if you ask a silly question, you'll get a silly answer. Constant confirmation of this led Lorie and George by the end of the war to have a very low opinion indeed of the U.S. military intelligence – Lorie and George, of course, provided the silly answers!

Nevertheless, they also solved some very tricky problems during their years in the air force and Lorie learnt a lot about the methodology of natural scientists in the process. Indeed, I suspect from the enthusiasm with which he recounts them, and his memory today of the details of the problems and their solutions, that inside Lorie is a frustrated applied mathematician only waiting to get out. In addition, when George and Lorie 'liberated' Rome, they also met Inga who subsequently was to become Lorie's second wife.

After the war, Lorie moved to California, to Stanford. (He tells an amusing tale of getting an offer from The Leland Stanford *Junior* University and thinking he'd gone from a small school – Tufts – to a tiny one.) However, he first returned to Tufts for a year, though he was thoroughly browned off with the place, partly because of the ultra conservative views of the then President, partly because of their shabby treatment of Buzz Daly (who did not return from the war – he contracted pneumonia after joining a parachute unit). The offer from Stanford came before the war but there was a mix-up in timing, so he went back to Tufts in order to help them out.

Lorie started to write his textbook in the spring of 1946; he became very excited about it and had offers from two publishers. He settled for Houghton Mifflin – 'a master stroke' – because they had a superb editor who taught Lorie how to write. (His Ph.D. dissertation was written – like a Ph.D. dissertation.) The book itself was written at great speed – and out of order, which did not make things easy for the Houghton Mifflin reader who was not an economist. At one stage Lorie was writing three chapters at once – one dictated, one typed and one in longhand. A wonderful howler nearly got through. At that time – perhaps still – Houghton Mifflin was a very conservative New England publishing house. Lorie had dictated that the aim of the economic system is 'to maximize the output of goods and services' which somehow got through to the galleys as 'to maximize the output of good conservatives'. Lorie carried it to Stanford with him in September 1946 in its final draft. He had signed in May 1946 and the book was out, eleven months later, with Lorie having worked like a fiend over the previous summer and at Stanford 'which nearly killed him'. At Stanford he was teaching classes of up to 250 students – previously his classes had never exceeded 15 – at the same time as he was completing the book.

While Lorie was teaching at Williams the following summer, he began to get disquieting calls from Boston about attacks on his book. At the beginning it had taken off well with scores of departments prescribing it. It was Part 4, the 250 or so pages on Keynes, which caused the trouble. It was a straightforward account of the fundamentals, containing the aggregate supply function as well as the aggregate demand function — always an emphasis of Lorie's. The aggregate supply function was shown as a required price, output and employment relationship rather than as a required receipts, output and employment relationship — 'perhaps the easier way to do it'. The President of Williams stood firm. His economists told him that it was a good book, he told the trustees that it was to be prescribed and he defended the employ-· ment of Lorie himself. It was an anti-new dealer, Merwin K. Hart, who led the attack through the offices of a writer, Rose Wilder Lane. Her attack was sent to every trustee of every university in the country, warning against the book. Bill Buckley, Jr., took up the attack later, devoting a chapter in *God and Man at Yale* to Lorie's book, quoting vigorously out of context. While Lorie had belonged to the Socialist Club at Cambridge (as well as to the Marshall Society, hardly a hotbed of Reds), he was sufficiently under the influence of Keynes both to want and to believe it possible to make capitalism work. Ken Galbraith played an important role in getting the A.E.A. to stand up for Lorie and academic freedom generally. Lorie says he got a lot of support from the profession itself, even if some of it consisted of people saying how embarrassed they were to be required by their trustees to take his book off their reading lists. With *some* people for friends. . . . The upshot was Lorie's book sold respectably at 10,000 or so a year, did well in Europe and especially in Sweden, but it was never the best-seller it otherwise would and should have been. (Not one copy was sold in Canada.)

Now began over twenty happy years at Stanford, where Lorie taught the first-year course to undergraduates and the first-year graduate macro course. He was Chairman for many years and again was especially happy and lucky with his colleagues — as they were with him. His closest friends were Bernard Haley, Tibor Scitovsky (in 1981 there will be a new macro text, published by Oxford University Press and written jointly by Tibor Scitovsky and Lorie), Ed Shaw, Moe Ambramovitz, Jack Gurley, Ken Arrow, Paul Baran, Mel Reder, Paul David, Ronald McKinnon and, especially, Emile Despres. Lorie thought Despres a superb economist, and considers that he is the joint author of every good post-war article on international economics and international money, and on development economics, even though he wrote very little directly himself. Lorie first met him at Tufts and got him to Stanford when he was Chairman and Despres was at Williams. Because of his slim *curriculum vitae*, publications section, Lorie enlisted the aid of Paul Samuelson in order to persuade the pedestrian number-counters of the wisdom of their choice. Samuelson wrote: 'Since Stanford cannot have Adam Smith they should do the next best thing and take Emile Despres.'

Lorie's interest in international monetary matters began with a joint project that he and Paul Baran started. (Lorie finished it as Baran moved onto other projects, including writing *Monopoly Capital* with Paul Sweezy.) Lorie's work here has been an extension of the Keynes model, partly influenced by Shaw's work on the role of money. Since 1971 he has worried about the disastrous implications of the growth of the Eurodollar market – 'the financial San Andreas fault, we know there will be an earthquake but we don't know when'. The growth it-self has led to a stock, the size of which dwarfs the capitalist world's share of M_1 or M_{1A} or M_2. Moreover, when things start to go there only will be hours, not weeks, to bail out the banks and countries affected. The point about banks, says Lorie, is that they always think their assets and liabilities are properly matched with one another until they suddenly realize that their assets are starting to fade away but not so their liabilities – and, then, the whole pack of cards topples unless there is a central bank to hold them up – which there is not in the Eurodollar market.

Lorie's association with Stanford ended in 1971. Sickened by the Vietnam war, worried about political trends and the growing illiberalism in the U.S.A., Lorie wrote to his old mentor, Vincent Bladen, asking him to let him know if any jobs were coming up in Canada. The result was a call from Wynne Plumptre, back from Ottawa as Principal of Scarborough College of the U. of T., asking Lorie to join the College as Chairman of Social Sciences. Lorie agreed to go for one year; in the event he stayed for two as acting Chairman of Social Sciences, then stayed permanently, excited at the prospect of building up an eco-nomics department within the Division of Social Sciences at Scar-borough. The rest – for Scarborough – is history. Lorie left a flourish-ing department of young and very bright – and nice – scholars when he retired in 1978, to go to the Ontario Economic Council as Research Director. He still lectures one day a week at Scarborough, giving an introductory course and a Keynes course, where the undergraduates are introduced to his love of his master's works by going steadily through them, with each student talking and writing on a selection of his or her choice from them.

Lorie Tarshis is a modest, unassuming man. During his life he has had more than his share of injustice and unhappiness but these have not soured him — he is too balanced and mature a person, too much at ease with himself and aware of his own worth, to allow the machinations of lesser people to get him down. Secure in a supremely happy marriage, surrounded by appreciative friends, young and old, loved, respected, with his company much sought after, Lorie looks forward as eagerly now as when a young student at the U. of T. or at Cambridge to his daily game of squash (where he'll win if he can) and to planning a seminar, or writing a position paper for the Council. He brings to the task the enthusiasm of a youngster and the wisdom and experience of a sage and his papers read as incisively now as when he first 'learnt to write' from that excellent editor at Houghton Mifflin. Yet, as all through his life, it is by personal contact in discussion, criticism and enthusiastic support that Lorie has his greatest influence. He is an old-fashioned teacher *par excellence*.

Through students and colleagues, the essential soundness of Keynes's message and approach has been imparted in the U.S.A. and Canada, quietly and unobtrusively but with conviction and persuasion, not least by Lorie Tarshis. He reserves his ire, his anger and scorn, which can be withering, for the stupid and the insensitive and the inhumane, who, failing to see the soundness of the approach, unwittingly push capitalism towards the abyss from which Keynes tried to rescue it well over forty years ago. I suppose the acid test for Lorie is whether you think that, in this world of ours, causality runs from employment to the real wage, or vice versa. If you think the former, you share Lorie Tarshis's 'vision' and may enjoy the privilege of his friendship and concerned companionship.

Notes

* I am indebted to Don Campbell, Jon Cohen, Joan Harcourt, Donald Moggridge and Austin Robinson for their comments on a draft of this essay.

1 Lorie subsequently added in writing some further memories of Harvard. 'By the time I finished and got my first job near enough to Harvard to enable me to sit in on Harvard Seminars I had (not alone, but I only remember *me*, naturally) worked out the more obvious extensions of the G.T. Come to think of it, Harvard was so empty in 1936–37 of people who properly understood Keynes — apart from Bob Bryce — that going it alone was almost mandatory. I got more out [of] my students in that first year than from Harvard's best. In the second year matters improved; Emile Despres and Bill Salant came back for a year, I got to know Dick Gilbert, by then Paul Sweezy had moved from Hayek to Keynes, and theory and policy could be discussed without our getting bogged down in "Well how can I be equal to S if I save and put the money under the mattress?" I should have mentioned Alvin Hansen too, whose seminar I attended.'

Part VII
Conclusion
The social science imperialists

Conclusion
The social science imperialists*

Introduction

I am greatly honoured to have been asked to give the 1978 Academy Lecture, not least because, I understand, I was rushed into the First Team when the person originally selected declined to play. Casual empiricism leads me to suggest that the Academy Lecture, like the Marshall Lectures in Economics at Cambridge, *can* be the end of a person's reputation. If that should be so this evening, I ask my fellow Fellows to save their assessments (for my ears anyway) until we are between the fish and the main course. Hunger makes me aggressive so that, if they were to do otherwise, I might hit first and start talking after.

I take as my subject the social science imperialists, by whom I mean, of course, that leading species of the large genus social scientists to which I belong, the economists. The title was suggested to me by Lester Thurow's recent paper 'Economics 1977' (Thurow, 1977). 'If the early 1960s were the golden age of economics when economists were perceived as knowing all the "right" answers, the late 1970s are the age of economic imperialism' (Thurow, 1977, p. 79). We economists, it seems, have taking ways. When I was young (some of you may know that I have now entered the category of elder statesman, being the only member of the Academic Board of the *Journal of Post Keynesian Economics* under 70, also I've retired from playing Aussie Rules), we were taught that economics was an aspect of *all* life, that equilibrium was just equilibrium, that economics was neutral between ends – and that it certainly was *not* political economy. (Jevons, who disliked Ricardo, the labour theory of value and trade unions and would have disliked Marx had he heard of him, made great play on all this.) The great leap forward occurred, evidently, when the discipline ceased to be political economy and became economics.

The most persuasive purveyors of these views, as presented to us by Jean Polglaze in first-year lectures for potential honours students at Melbourne University, were Philip Wicksteed and Professor, now Lord,

Robbins. Both the admirable Wicksteed, whose presentation of the neo-classical subjective theory of value in *The Common Sense of Political Economy* (Wicksteed, 1910) was as clear as his family life, also presented in the same book, was exemplary, and Robbins were particularly severe on Carlyle and Ruskin, who regarded economics as the dismal science, the pig philosophy, as a subject sordid, mean and unworthy. (James Meade recently has reminded us that in the light of recent findings economics now may be viewed not as the dismal science but as the gay science.)

These particular views meant that while the practical applications of the discipline for a while at least would continue to relate to 'mankind in the ordinary business of life', *in principle* an economic decision was involved *whenever* a choice situation arose; as Robbins put it, whenever scarce means had to be allocated between alternative and competing ends.[1] The point of Wicksteed's view was that the ends themselves could be lofty or base and, moreover, it was not the economist's business to inquire which. Rather, the economist's job was to illuminate the allocation process itself. Thus, whether you were deciding whether directly to save your mother-in-law from drowning, or go for help or a ladder, the height of the river bank above the water being a key constraint; or whether as a student to stay longer in bed or get up and attend a lecture; or how to distribute a given supply of milk between a hungry infant and a cat recovering from poisoning, the same principles were involved. The law of diminishing marginal utility (later refined to diminishing marginal rate of substitution) allowed the same light to be shed. Economic imperialism (of a new order) had begun.

A general theory of social behaviour

The conservative elements in our trade today, those who think that Adam Smith's laying on of hands has come down to them alone, have tossed old Marshall overboard. I think especially of Becker and the Chicago school generally, also the new Libertarians and the Hayek–von Mises revival. They have taken up Wicksteed's illustrations in deadly earnest, extending the analysis first to marriage, then to divorce and then, finally, to the economics of extra-marital activity (they were never strong on sequence analysis). Now they are on to suicide and crime, including the economics of capital punishment. If by hanging one extra person rather than imprisoning them for life, the probability of murder occurring is reduced, capital punishment is justified. We even have, God help us, a straight-faced discussion of the optimum rate of whipping in Fogel and Engerman's massive study of the economics of American slavery, *Time on the Cross* (Fogel and Engerman, 1974). 'Planters sought not perfect but optimal submission . . . different concepts. Planters strove to use force not cruelly, but optimally.'[2] Too few lashes were ineffectual, too many, counter-productive; ergo: there's an optimal amount in between, the exact amount varying, no doubt, according to time and place, sex, age and marital status of the slave concerned. Again, we have the economics of racial and sexual prejudice. Blacks (or women) are paid less than whites (or men) because their characteristics are a negative argument in a prejudiced employer's utility function. As Thurow says, '[We] think of [ourselves] as having a better analytical apparatus for studying these phenomena than other social scientists' (Thurow, 1977, p. 79). Who can doubt this after reading the following matchless profundity?

> [Becker] assumes that persons marry when the utility expected from marriage exceeds the utility expected from remaining single. . . . natural to assume further that couples separate when the utility expected from remaining married falls below the utility expected from divorcing and possibly remarrying. One way to reconcile the relatively high utility expected from marriage at the time of marriage and the relatively low utility expected at the time of dissolution is to introduce uncertainty and deviations between expected and realized utilities; . . . persons separating presumably had less favourable outcomes from their marriage than they expected when marrying. (Becker *et al.*, 1977, p. 1142)

You will be glad to know that the 'case for a common theoretical approach to all social behaviour would be greatly strengthened if the same theory is applicable to employee turnover and termination of friendships' (Becker *et al.*, 1977, p. 1185).

Mathematical economics and econometrics

I have mentioned the Libertarians' analysis and their formidable backlash in modern times. (As to places, not least here at the A.N.U. though, as yet, we have not elected any to the Academy.) But theirs is not the only recent reaction to the domination since the 1870s of neoclassical economics. Together with them, we have witnessed over the last ten to fifteen years or so the radical economists' reaction, together with a resurgence of interest in Marxist and classical political economy itself, a return, as the late Maurice Dobb put it, to the boundaries 'more generously drawn by the classical pioneers' (Dobb, 1973, p. 11). We must also discuss the increasing use of mathematics in the subject and the rise of econometrics. The former has its roots partly in the 1870s' development – the subjective theory of value, the concept of the margin and the central importance of marginal changes associated with choice were ideal vehicles for the use of the differential calculus (though Menger thought otherwise). This, no doubt, is one reason why mathematics took on so. Nevertheless, the really revolutionary take-off dates from the publication of Samuelson's *Foundations* (Samuelson, 1947) and the impetus to economic theory and the mathematical method which it gave, the enhanced status which it bestowed and the attractions it had for the bright young things, especially in America, who could follow a first degree in math with a Ph.D. in economics, flocking to M.I.T. and its surrogates to do so. This movement was at the height of its influence and power in the early 1960s, when Samuelson and Solow reigned supreme and unchallenged. American society was tranquil enough and 'Keynesian' economic policies seemingly successful enough, to avoid any disquieting matters of social conscience breaking through into the mathematical training of fledgling social scientists.

Samuelson claimed to have revolutionised *and* unified the method and the discipline by showing that all substantive propositions grew out of two general principles: maximisation or minimisation under constraints and the correspondence principle, the interconnection between statics and dynamics. Together, they provided the basis for operationally meaningful theorems over the whole span of economics. As one far-out convert and fan of P.A.S. put it to me: 'I never read the greats. If what they had to say is not valuable it will not be in the *Foundations*; if what they had to say *is* valuable, it will be said better in the *Foundations*.' In those days mathematical economics and theoretical economics were intertwined, almost synonyms, indissolubly mixed. Now it is not so. With the advent of top line mathematicians in their own right in the discipline (the mathematics of the *Foundations* is regarded as somewhat clumsy and inelegant), Samuelson and his cohorts have to be content with being theoretical economists. Mathematical economists are in a class of their own, their only connection with matters economic occurring when the analysis starts, in the sense that they write let p = price and q = quantity before the manipulation starts.

Samuelson, whose influence on teaching both through his famous first-year text and the methods that came to be adopted in graduate schools, inspired by the approach of the *Foundations*, in recent years has been relegated to the Reserves. The mathematical economists proper have taken over as the First Team (though they have no one to play against). There has been, moreover, the rejection by the more socially aware – and brightest – graduate students from the mid 1960s on. Prior to this, the M.I.T. approach tended to be accepted uncritically as the best. The pressing problems of American society, indeed world capitalist societies, and the Vietnam war combined to create a generation desperately unhappy with both the problems discussed and analysed, and with the methods used. So Samuelson received the Nobel Prize for economics just when what he had so successfully created was beginning to experience a serious challenge, a not atypical occurrence for recipients of Nobel Prizes in economics. So, also in a manner not uncommon for imperialists, the taking over of another discipline may have ended with the expropriated becoming the expropriators. Latterly, of course, the radical wing itself has lost momentum and currently is on the defensive, not against a Samuelsonian comeback (though he has shown admirable flexibility in his reappraisal) so much as against the right-wing backlash, the resurgence of the free market Libertarians in economic policy and in related fields of political analysis. I think in particular of the Chicago economists and their offshoots, and of Buchanan and Tullock at Virginia.

The situation is more complicated in the sphere of econometrics and quantitative methods generally. Many of the presidential addresses in the U.S.A. and U.K. in recent years have taken the form of lament for economics and, more particularly, econometrics. We may mention Henry Phelps Brown (1972) and David Worswick (1972) as examples, also the Lord Kaldor (1972). These addresses led Hahn (1973b, p.322) to comment that economists 'do not grow bitter gracefully', a psychological explanation of the paradox that 'so much of this literature . . . is so bad [even though] some of the authors are so distinguished'.[3] Nevertheless, quantitative methods have grown apace and so has the employment of econometric models not only in academia but also in the public domain, the policy-making bodies of the various Treasuries or equivalent departments and other government departments.

The purpose of, and the justification for, econometric models have changed subtly in the process as Thurow, for one, has pointed out. Initially, it had been hoped that econometric methods might provide independent tests of the validity of theoretical models, as well as providing empirical orders of magnitude of key parameters in the models. Could 'clearly specified theory . . . be statistically verified [?] Was the theory supported by the data?' (Thurow, 1977, p. 83). But, now, we have reached a position where the former objective has been (must be?) scrapped. 'In the end conclusive tests did not prove to be possible'

(Thurow, 1977, p. 83). It is only if we assume beforehand that the world is as depicted in the particular specifications of our models, that the resulting econometric estimates make any sense, have any meaning. But they by themselves do not allow us to say that our specification has been verified as correct in the first instance. This comes out clearly, for example, in the Shaikh–Solow exchange over the aggregate production function and Shaikh's humbug production function. 'It merely shows [says Solow] how one goes about interpreting given time series if one starts by *assuming* that they were generated from a production function and that the competitive marginal-product relations apply' (Solow, 1974a, p. 121).

Psychology and economic theory

The subjective theory of value itself has been under fire over the years, first, within its own confines and, lately, from outside, as it were. Within its own confines, as is well known, there was a great struggle to get away from the concept of cardinally measurable utility, which gave rise, first, to the great indifference curve revolution (we are all ordinal now) and then to the concept of revealed preference. Eric Russell had some wise words to say on this last and related matters in his 1972 Presidential Address to Section 24 of A.N.Z.A.A.S. and I quote them now:

> The economist's paradigm market case is Wicksteed's thrifty housewife who moves among the familiar market stalls, comparing the lettuce and the cabbages, noting their well-displayed prices and at last selecting her basket of greens. After watching her, it would indeed be strange to wonder, 'but did she really prefer the goods that she in fact bought?' No, in this case, with *all* the evidence fresh and crisp before her, what she does *is* what she prefers. But we slip over to other cases where doubt is proper [and the] slide from 'He does so-and-so' to 'He prefers so-and-so' to 'so-and-so is *to be* preferred', [though it may be] almost instantaneous, [is also misleadingly treacherous.] The essence of the matter is, of course, the information that is available to the parties. (Russell, 1978, p. 203)

Australians Duncan Ironmonger and Kelvin Lancaster (who now teaches at Columbia) carried the refinements even further by looking at demand as demand, not for commodities as such, but for a desired bundle of characteristics which the commodities provide.[4]

Recently Tibor Scitovsky has stood back completely and led the community of economists into the realm of modern psychology. (The psychologists tell me that the psychology is not *that* modern.) I refer to his challenging book, *The Joyless Economy* (Scitovsky, 1976), for the writing of which he had a great deal of trouble obtaining financial support (moral: write an article). He also suffered much opposition from his colleagues while writing it. 'Economists are deeply divided into the Establishment and its radical-left critics, but they were like a harmonious and happy family in their unanimous hostility to my ideas.' Scitovsky 'took comfort in [this reaction as it fitted] in so well with one of [his] main points . . . : . . . man wants novelty but cannot take, and gets disturbed by, too much of it' (Scitovsky, 1976, p. *xv*). The basic questions he addressed himself to are why the arrival of affluence leaves us all feeling so flat, so dissatisfied – he lives in the U.S.A. and has a U.S. viewpoint but with suitable adjustments for sociological and historical differences his reasoning may be applied to Europe and to Australia – and why conventional economics seems unable to throw much light on the phenomenon. Why has 'a whole generation of young Americans become disaffected and disappointed with the way of life and high standard of living of their parents' generation [?]' (Scitovsky, 1976, p. *vii*). He finds the answer in the psychological speculation that we crave both comfort *and* stimulation, and if we do not get the mix right, because after a point they are mutually exclusive, with excess comfort characterising the American way of life, we emerge as the disenchanted, unhappy lot that we are. The theory has great attraction for your mainstream economists because it stresses the inevitable choice situation, the need to discern a trade-off relationship and choose the optimum position made available by its presence.[5]

In his splendid *Social Limits to Growth* (Hirsch, 1977), the late Fred Hirsch finds a related if not exactly identical explanation of the paradox of affluence, distributional compulsion and reluctant collectivism in his concept of positional goods – positions or jobs that we all may aspire to but of which there is only a limited supply, *either* for Ricardo, Chapter 1-type reasons *or* because trying to increase the supply would destroy their attractiveness in the process. Not least of the victims of the present secular age has been the dethronement of the Professor-God by the creation of multi-chair departments. Again, the increase over recent years in the number of Fellows of our illustrious Academy has led some of us older ones to raise our eyebrows and shake our heads, to say that things are not what they used to be.

Radicals and Marxists

Turning now to the radical reaction, the most obvious manifestation has been the resurgence of interest in and, indeed, the respectability of, Marxist studies. I suppose that Marx managed to linger on during the Cold War and McCarthy era in politics and philosophy departments but he received very short shrift in economics departments. One of the cracks that Samuelson, for example, most regrets having made (because it now tends to cut him off from serious dialogue with modern Marxists) is the remark in his Presidential Address to the American Economic Association in 1961 to the effect that in matters of economic theory Marx was 'a minor post-Ricardian' (Samuelson, 1962b, p. 14). (This is rather like saying that P.A.S. himself is a minor pre-Keynesian – *after* Keynes.) Again, another 'heavy' is on record as saying that no Marxist economist could be employed in a university economics department because if anyone accepted the labour theory of value then, if they were honest, they could not be intelligent – and *vice versa*. All this is now a thing of the past – token Marxists are to be found everywhere – and some of them are even willing to jettison the labour theory of value, at least in its quantitative form; see, for example, Steedman (1977). Dick Downing in his review (Downing, 1973) of Benjamin Ward's *What's Wrong with Economics?* (Ward, 1972) (Ward wrote when optimism about reform and reappraisal was still possible, *i.e.* in the early 1970s) characterised modern neoclassical economics as techniques without relevance as opposed to Marxist economics, which has relevance but no techniques. While some of the modern revival of interest in Marx takes the form of Billy Graham-type reverence for the sacred texts, by far the major part of it is concerned to provide high-powered relevant analysis of current problems, as well as rigorous – and vigorous – critiques of the orthodox and a scholarly re-evaluation of Marx's own work in the light of modern discoveries, advances and translations. This is not only to be found in Piero Sraffa's and Ian Steedman's work but also in the work of Rowthorn and Shaikh and, particularly, in the work of Bowles and Gintis (1977, 1978). (We should pause at this point to pay a tribute to two of the most influential of modern scholars of Marx, alas no longer with us, who kept on when the going was hard: Maurice Dobb and Ronald Meek.) Bowles and Gintis, both Harvard trained, have an understanding of the orthodox and an array of techniques which make them extremely formidable critics of orthodoxy. All strands of Marxists' analysis are present in their work – historical examples, abstract models, philosophical and epistemological concepts, the role of classes, the concept of the mode of production, the notion of contradiction, the influence of ruling-class ideology on institutions in order to preserve hierarchical structures and produce the sort of labour force needed in the sphere of production of the capitalist mode. Their orthodox training allows them also to produce abstract technical models, the most impressive of which to date is their demonstration that the labour theory of value, properly interpreted, rigorously may survive the existence of heterogeneous labour *and* the inability to find a unit with which to reduce the different types to a single aggregate. This rigorous approach is even more characteristic of the so-called Neo-Ricardian school, most of whom nevertheless claim allegiance to Marx. Here, despite disclaimers to the contrary, the notion that truth comes only in the guise of a mathematical model holds much stronger sway. Especially is this true of Steedman's work, summarised in *Marx After Sraffa*, which has incurred the wrath not only of the Billy Graham Marxists, who don't matter, but also of your serious, analytically talented and open-minded ones, such as Shaikh and Rowthorn, who do.[6]

The Post-Keynesians

Sandwiched uncomfortably in between the Marxists proper and all strands of the orthodox is the Post-Keynesian school of which I know most, since I identify with it more than with any other group. (Frank Hahn, 1975b, has gone so far as to describe me as 'a well-known salesman' of it.) This is the group that most clearly traces itself back to Keynes, Marshall and Cambridge generally. Its elder statespersons are Richard Kahn, Joan Robinson, and also Nicholas Kaldor. Piero Sraffa provides a special contribution as does the late Michal Kalecki. Through the latter two, Ricardian and Marxist influences are introduced and a more pure brand of Keynesian revolution than appears in the textbooks is created. In Joan Robinson's view, anyway, Keynes never succeeded completely in throwing off the effects of his neoclassical forebears, especially Marshall, and, moreover, his political temperament was such that as he grew older he dropped back into ways of thought that, politically, were less and less acceptable to his younger, more radical colleagues. Michal Kalecki, by contrast, was always a convinced socialist, with a healthy contempt for both capitalism *and* the Stalinist brand of communism. His political and analytical attitudes fit more comfortably with the attitudes of those who established the Post-Keynesian school.

As I said, this group has been attacked from both sides. Perhaps the most picturesque attack from the Marxist side comes under Frank Roosevelt's title of 'Cambridge Economics as Commodity Fetishism' (Roosevelt, 1977). Rowthorn also had a go at them (and the orthodox) in a paper originally entitled 'Vulgar Economy' (Rowthorn, 1974). Their supposed sin is an obsessive concentration on the sphere of distribution and exchange to the neglect of the sphere of production and the social relationships contained therein – the very points for which Marx criticised Ricardo so strongly. The attacked feel themselves to be rather ill-used, since in their work they have stressed the role of institutions, the need for knowledge of the 'rules of the game', and past historical and sociological influences as being the very essence of proper economic analysis. Indeed, they are the ones *par excellence* who return to those boundaries 'more generously drawn by the classical pioneers'. This is so partly because they view economics very much as a horses for courses discipline, rather than as a set of universal principles that may illuminate *any* time and place, the 'all purpose advice' that allows the economic advisor, as Eric Russell put it, to 'start talking as he gets off the plane' (Russell, 1978, p. 199). Eric had in mind your market men, of whom we have had our fair share lately, with visits from the Friedmans, Parkin and Laidler, and, of course, our own home-grown variety.

Workers and thinkers

Our imperialist tendencies have even extended to the provision (by Frank Hahn) of an economic theory of the writing of *Festschrifts*.

> A Festschrift . . . gives pleasure to the man honoured . . . a token of esteem. But . . . it has . . . disadvantages. Most potential contributors reserve their . . . best papers for journals so that they may be widely read. . . . [When] on occasion they do not do so, their contribution may well be lost. . . . [Rarely] do Festschrifts find a large readership . . . a Nash equilibrium: if most people send their best papers to journals, . . . it is rational for any one person to submit his less good efforts to Festschrifts . . . rational for few people to sample the book. But while, as Marshall would have said, there may be a tendency to such an equilibrium, any given collection . . . may not be an equilibrium collection. (Hahn, 1978, p. 578)

I mention before dinner this piece of after-dinner brilliance because Hahn goes on to discuss a number of issues which divide mathematical economists from political economists, or as Mirrlees would have it, the *workers* in the scientific tradition from the *thinkers* in the scholastic tradition (Mirrlees, 1973, p. *xxi*). This constitutes a great gulf which threatens to widen, to the detriment of the discipline itself. It is illustrated by two papers in the Georgescu–Roegen *Festschrift* which Hahn singles out for comment, one to praise, the other to blame. Hahn says we must be on our guard against 'taking grand ideas on a trip through economics' (Hahn, 1978, p. 579) because the 'large questions [may be beyond our] capacity to provide clear and coherent arguments' (Hahn, 1978, p. 578). The illustration is the treatment of time in economics. Samuelson takes a small problem: time seems to go faster as we grow older. He 'proceeds, not in generalities or high-falutin speculation, but by getting down to the hard work of making the idea precise enough so that it [could] be both tested and used in further theorizing'. Hahn adds: 'It is precisely this stretching of the intellectual muscle that one misses in Hicks's piece, which is cast in the form of a reminiscence of the development of his ideas on time' (Hahn, 1978, p. 578).

Now Hicks has changed very considerably his view of the role of time and how it may be modelled, becoming progressively more modest and cautious in his aims and critical of what could be gained in the understanding of actual processes by use of the temporary equilibrium method which he presented in *Value and Capital*. Nevertheless, between *Value and Capital* (1939) and *Capital and Time* (1973) (*Capital and Growth* appeared in 1965), there has been *no* slackening of Hicks's intellectual muscle — each book is as rigorous as the others, the claims are less in the later ones because the author has reached a deeper understanding of the complexities and difficulties of the problems he is tackling. Surely then it is not improper for him to stand back and draw some general lessons from the specific pieces of analysis that he has undertaken. Hahn himself has helped us by doing just that in 'The Winter of Our Discontent' (Hahn, 1973b) and other papers. Why he is not able to allow Hicks to do this too *and* at the same time rightly give Samuelson his due, I am at a loss to know, unless he still does believe that truth can come only in the guise of a mathematical model. It is not the fault of economists that the future is uncertain, unknowable, yet businessmen must make decisions within such an environment, and economists have to analyse them. If to do so means using on occasions 'casual and speculative argument', as Mirrlees calls the analysis in Keynes's *General Theory*, then so much the better for speculative argument. Nor is it possible to agree with Mirrlees (1978, p. 157) that 'economists [have] avoided doing the hard work for forty years'. Rather, it may be that those in the true Keynesian tradition have managed to avoid, as Kahn (1977, p. 386) says of Malinvaud's book to which Mirrlees was referring, 'the effect[s] which the study of orthodox economic theory can have upon a powerful mind'.

Economics and biology

I move now to the last set of evidence of our imperialistic tendencies that I have time for: Marshall thought that biology rather than physics should be 'the Mecca of the economist'. He stressed the organic nature of the body economic and politic, interrelated processes which moved forward, often blotting out the possibility of returning along the paths by which the advances were made. (This is the message of Marshall's famous Appendix H of *The Principles*, placed in an appendix because, on Joan Robinson's interpretation, anyway, its message seriously undermined the ideological stance of the text of *The Principles*.) Similarly, Marxist economists react vigorously to attacks on the labour theory of value just because they do not regard it as an appendix to the Marxist body of thought, that is to say, as an organ that has outlived its usefulness and may be removed without causing any complications for the entire system, but as a vital organ, the removal of which could lead to the death of the rest of the organism. The biological analogy recently has arisen in different contexts, in which the Volterra predator–prey model of 'the symbiosis of two populations – partly complementary, partly hostile' is seen as having an illuminating application to economic puzzles. The most impressive example is Goodwin's model of cyclical growth (Goodwin, 1967). The shares of wages and profits fluctuate over the cycle but exhibit a long-run constancy, all the outcomes of the inherent conflict and complementarity of workers and capitalists, which are reflected in the levels and shares of wages and profits, and their resulting impacts on accumulation and employment.

The most recent application is in an entirely different area (well, perhaps not entirely). It employs the predator–prey model, the work done on the optimum rate of fishing, which is itself part of the literature on common property resources, in order to analyse mugging in modern American cities. I refer here to a highly entertaining and illuminating paper by Philip Neher (1978). 'The muggery', says Neher,

> is a geographic place where muggers and muggees transfer wealth from the latter to the former. Such transfers involve the allocation of time and money, so it seems natural to view mugging as an economic activity with the agents on both sides maximizing subject to constraints . . . two features in common with the open sea fishery.
>
> (1) Muggers and muggees stand in a fundamental *predator–prey relationship* to each other. . . .
> (2) As prey, muggees are a *common property resource* from the point of view of an individual mugger. Over-mugging can occur for the same reasons as over-fishing. (Neher, 1978, p. 437)

Neher analyses the free entry muggery and the controlled muggery. He asks: 'should society prefer competitive, free entry mugging over the same activity organized by a farsighted manager?' He comes up with one judgment: 'If one places a sufficiently high value on having viable urban neighbourhoods, organized mugging is to be preferred. Well-organized and managed muggers will not drive their prey to extinction . . . legitimate economic activity will survive' (Neher, 1978, p. 442). Neher uses his analysis to make the important but obvious point that the market may be deficient in organising production when 'predator-prey and common property relationships are particularly important, and where the prey has the property of being capital from the predator's point of view' (p. 444).

Evaluation

I now sum up: modern economics and economists are in a state of flux. (Thurow prefaced his paper with a quote from *A Tale of Two Cities*: 'It was the best of times, it was the worst of times . . .'.) On the one hand, the young Turks (*and* the not so young, one at least is the oldest *enfant terrible* in the trade) are still wedded to the application of more and more rigour and *some* sections of this group are allying this with a non-interventionist stance on policy, or, rather, an anti-government and anti-bureaucrats stance. Their theoretical studies of economic systems and political and bureaucratic behaviour lead them to argue anew for Smithian liberal principles, of getting back to the magic of the market, as it says on the bags of the fruit stalls in Adelaide's Central Market. In this they join some of the old men of the tribe, for example, von Hayek and Friedman, both currently cult figures, though I suspect Hayek and the younger Friedman think Milton is a bit of a bolshie – he thinks the state should provide the police force and the currency.

On the other hand, there are other old men of the tribe – I think of Phelps Brown (1972) and Worswick (1972), also Roll (1978) and Cairncross, Galbraith (1973) and the late R.A. Gordon (1976) – who want us to return to historical studies, for economics to take on again the flavour of moral philosophy which Cambridge in particular gave it, and which so influenced Keynes's approach. They are sceptical of the value of the move towards more and more complex econometric work in the applied area and mathematics in the theoretical area. Then we have the small, embattled and scattered band of Post-Keynesians trying to drive their critical message home *and* provide positive alternatives. These are now more empirical in character, to be found principally in the writings of the Cambridge D.A.E. group and the *Cambridge Journal* in the United Kingdom and the recently established *Journal of Post Keynesian Economics* in the U.S.A. It would be silly to say that they have had *that* much impact, but there are some straws in the wind, not least that the recent issues of *Challenge* are devoted in part to expositions of their modest contributions and approach (see Eichner, 1978; Cornwall, 1978; Kenyon, 1978; Kregel, 1978; Moore, 1978; Chase, 1978; Burbidge, 1978; Appelbaum, 1979; Roncaglia, 1979). Moreover, some of the leading American Keynesians – Okun, Solow, Tobin, Heller, Lerner – have joined with Wallich and Weintraub in the advocacy of what in effect is a Post-Keynesian package deal of policies with which to attack stagflation.

The Marxists are at least holding their own; their construction of rigorous theories is accorded begrudging respect by the orthodox and the present crisis in the capitalist world also is helping them to survive and attract students. Finally, though the mainstreamers have had their confidence shaken, they still dominate the economics academy as a whole, tending probably to move to a more non-interventionist stance than formerly, to advocate a greater use of the price mechanism together with carrot and stick interventions of the sort advocated by Marshall and Pigou long ago. Partly this is because modern studies of the state and the bureaucracy make them sceptical of Keynes's belief that the 'presuppositions of Harvey Road' would continue to guide our public servants.

For myself, I still find the puzzles considered by the classicals, the Marxists and the Keynesians, the fascinating ones, and the horses for courses approach advocated by Joan Robinson, the most attractive approach. I'm also not a techniques Luddite, so that I welcome the help which both mathematical and econometric techniques can provide within the context of this general approach. Nevertheless, I'm under no illusions as to how few will join me in this stance. But, then, I'm no stranger either to belonging to a minority group.

I wish you all good appetites. If anyone would care to join me in a pre-dinner run in order to shake up their livers in preparation for the coming assault on them, I leave from University House entrance in ten minutes' time.[7]

Notes

* *Politics*, vol. XIV, no. 2, November 1979, pp. 243–51. The Annual Lecture of the Academy of the Social Sciences in Australia, given on Tuesday, 14 November 1978, and reprinted here by kind permission of the Academy of the Social Sciences in Australia. In writing the lecture I was greatly helped by hearing Fred Gruen's 1978 Joseph Fisher Lecture, 'Australian Economics 1967–77' (Gruen, 1979), and reading Glenn Withers's *Australian Quarterly* paper, 'The State of Economics' (Withers, 1978). Needless to say, they are not responsible for any of my errors or libels. I have left the lecture as it was presented. My objectives were to be understood by non-economists *and* interesting, or at least irritating, to my own kind. The lecture and I are the victims of Australian isolation and the lags that accompany it. Waiting for me on my return to Adelaide after the Annual Meeting of the Academy was the May 1978 issue of the *American Economic Review*, virtually all of which consisted of papers relating to my topic.

1 'Economics is the science which studies human behaviour as a relationship between ends and scarce means which have alternative uses' (Robbins, 1935, p. 16).

2 Quoted by John Anthony Scott in his review article of *Time on the Cross* (Scott, 1974, p. 57).

3 No doubt the prior offering by Leontief (1971) and subsequent offerings by Galbraith (1973) and the late R.A. Gordon (1976) would have served merely to harden his view.

4 Ironmonger (1972); Lancaster (1966). Ironmonger's book is based upon his Cambridge Ph.D. dissertation, written a decade or so earlier, so that he has not received the recognition due to him for his original contribution.

5 Economics is riddled with big trade-offs – that between equity and efficiency (Okun), unemployment and inflation (now discredited!), business success and marital happiness (see *Fortune Magazine*).

6 For a discussion of these issues see Harcourt and Kerr (1978).

7 There was one taker, *not* a Fellow.

Bibliography

Anderson, W.H.L. (1964), *Corporate Finance and Fixed Investment: An Econometric Study*, Boston, Harvard University Press.

Appelbaum, E. (1979), 'Post-Keynesian Theory: The Labor Market', *Challenge*, vol. 21, no. 6, January–February, pp. 39–47.

Arrow, K.J. (1974), 'General Economic Equilibrium: Purpose, Analytic Techniques, Collective Choice', *American Economic Review*, vol. lxiv, no. 2, June, pp. 253–72.

Arrow, K.J., Chenery, H.B., Minhas, B.S., and Solow, R.M. (1961), 'Capital-Labor Substitution and Economic Efficiency', *Review of Economics and Statistics*, vol. XLIII, no. 3, August, pp. 225–50.

Arrow, K.J., and Hahn, F.H. (1971), *General Competitive Analysis*, San Francisco, Holden-Day; Edinburgh, Oliver & Boyd.

Asimakopulos, A. (1969), 'A Robinsonian Growth Model in One-Sector Notation', *Australian Economic Papers*, vol. 8, no. 12, June, pp. 41–58.

Asimakopulos, A. (1970), 'A Robinsonian Growth Model in One-Sector Notation – An Amendment', *Australian Economic Papers*, vol. 9, no. 15, December, pp. 171–6.

Asimakopulos, A. (1975a), 'A Kaleckian Theory of Income Distribution', *Canadian Journal of Economics*, vol. 8, no. 3, August, pp. 313–33.

Asimakopulos, A. (1975b), 'The Price Policy of Firms, Employment and Distribution: A Comment', *Australian Economic Papers*, vol. 14, no. 25, December, pp. 261–2.

Asimakopulos, A. (1977), 'Profits and Investment: A Kaleckian Approach', in G.C. Harcourt (ed.), *The Microeconomic Foundations of Macroeconomics*, London, Macmillan, pp. 328–42.

Asimakopulos, A., and Burbidge, J.B. (1974), 'The Short-Period Incidence of Taxation', *Economic Journal*, vol. 84, no. 334, June, pp. 267–88.

Asimakopulos, A., and Harcourt, G.C. (1974), 'Proportionality and the Neoclassical Parables', *Southern Economic Journal*, vol. xl, no. 3, January, pp. 481–3.

Atkinson, A.B., and Stiglitz, J.E. (1969), 'A New View of Technological Change', *Economic Journal*, vol. 79, no. 315, September, pp. 573–8.

Ball, R.J. (1964), *Inflation and the Theory of Money*, London, Allen & Unwin.

394

Baran, P., and Sweezy, P. (1966), *Monopoly Capital, An Essay on the American Economic and Social Order*, New York, Monthly Review Press.

Bardhan, P.K. (1969), 'Equilibrium Growth in a Model with Economic Obsolescence of Machines', *Quarterly Journal of Economics*, vol. 83, no. 2, May, pp. 312–23.

Barna, T. (1957), 'The Replacement Cost of Fixed Assets in British Manufacturing Industry in 1955', *Journal of the Royal Statistical Society*, Series A (General), vol. 120, Part I, pp. 1–36.

Baumol, W.J. (1974a), 'The Transformation of Values: What Marx "Really" Meant (an Interpretation)', *Journal of Economic Literature*, vol. xii, no. 1, March, pp. 51–62.

Baumol, W.J. (1974b), 'Comment', *Journal of Economic Literature*, vol. xii, no. 1, March, pp. 74–5.

Becker, G.S., Landes, E.M., and Michael, R.T. (1977), 'An Economic Analysis of Marital Instability', *Journal of Political Economy*, vol. 85, no. 6, December, pp. 1141–87.

Bharadwaj, K.R. (1963), 'Value Through Exogenous Distribution', *Economic Weekly*, vol. xv, 24 August, pp. 1450–4.

Bharadwaj, K.R. (1972), 'Marshall on Pigou's *Wealth and Welfare*', *Economica*, vol. 39, no. 153, February, pp. 32–46.

Bharadwaj, K.R. (1978a), *Classical Political Economy and Rise to Dominance of Supply and Demand Theories*, R.C. Dutt Lectures (1976), New Delhi, Orient Longman.

Bharadwaj, K.R. (1978b), 'The Subversion of Classical Analysis: Alfred Marshall's Early Writing on Value', *Cambridge Journal of Economics*, vol. 2, no. 3, September, pp. 253–71.

Bitros, G.C., and Kelejian, H.H. (1974), 'On the Variability of the Replacement Investment Capital Stock Ratio: Some Evidence from Capital Scrappage', *Review of Economics and Statistics*, vol. 56, no. 3, August, pp. 270–8.

Bladen, V.W. (1978), *Bladen on Bladen, Memoirs of a Political Economist*, Toronto, University of Toronto.

Blaug, M. (1968), *Economic Theory in Retrospect*, London, Heinemann, 2nd edition.

Blaug, M. (1974), *The Cambridge Revolution: Success or Failure? A Critical Analysis of Cambridge Theories of Value and Distribution*, London, Institute of Economic Affairs.

Bliss, C.J. (1968a), 'On Putty-Clay', *Review of Economic Studies*, vol. 35(2), no. 102, April, pp. 105–32.

Bliss, C.J. (1968b), 'Rates of Return in a Linear Model', Cambridge, mimeo.

Bliss, C.J. (1970), 'Comment on Garegnani', *Review of Economic Studies*, vol. xxxvii (3), no. 111, July, pp. 437–8.

Bliss, C.J. (1974), 'Capital Theory in the Short-run', Buffalo, mimeo.

Bliss, C.J. (1975), *Capital Theory and the Distribution of Income*, Amsterdam, North Holland; New York, American Elsevier.

Bosworth, B. (1971), 'Patterns of Corporate External Financing', *Brookings Papers on Economic Activity*, no. 2, pp. 253–79.

Boulding, K.E. (1971), *Collected Papers*, vol. 1 (ed. F.R. Glahe), Colorado, Colorado Associated University Press.

Bowles, S., and Gintis, H. (1977), 'The Marxian Theory of Value and Heterogeneous Labour: A Critique and Reformulation', *Cambridge Journal of Economics*, vol. 1, no. 2, June, pp. 173–92.

Bowles, S., and Gintis, H. (1978), 'Professor Morishima on Heterogeneous Labour and Marxian Value Theory', *Cambridge Journal of Economics*, vol. 2, no. 3, September, pp. 311–14.

Braverman, H. (1974), *Labor and Monopoly Capital. The Degradation of Work in the Twentieth Century*, New York, Monthly Review Press.

Bruno, M., Burmeister, E., and Sheshinski, E. (1966), 'The Nature and Implications of the Reswitching of Techniques', *Quarterly Journal of Economics*, vol. lxxx, no. 4, November, pp. 526–53.

Burbidge, J.B. (1978), 'Post-Keynesian Theory: The International Dimension', *Challenge*, vol. 21, no. 5, November–December, pp. 40–5.

Burmeister, E. (1974), 'Synthesizing the Neo-Austrian and Alternative Approaches to Capital Theory: A Survey', *Journal of Economic Literature*, vol. xii, no. 2, June, pp. 413–56.

Burmeister, E., and Turnovsky, S.J. (1972), 'Capital Deepening Response in an Economy with Heterogeneous Capital Goods', *American Economic Review*, vol. lxii, December, pp. 842–53.

Champernowne, D.G. (1953–4), 'The Production Function and the Theory of Capital: A Comment', *Review of Economic Studies*, xxi, pp. 112–35.

Chase, R.X. (1978), 'The "Ruth Cohen" Anomaly and Production Theory', *Challenge*, vol. 21, no. 5, November–December, pp. 32–9.

Cheok, A., Davis, K., Harcourt, G.C., and Madden, P. (1976), 'Surplus Value, Profits and Joint Production', mimeo, Adelaide.

Chick, V. (1975), 'Come Back, Keynes', *Times Higher Educational Supplement*, 31 January, p. ii.

Clark, J.B. (1889), 'The Possibility of a Scientific Law of Wages', *Publication of the American Economic Association*, vol. iv, pp. 36–63.

Clark, J.B. (1891), 'Distribution as Determined by a Law of Rent', *Quarterly Journal of Economics*, vol. v, pp. 289–318.

Clower, R. (1975), 'Reflections on the Keynesian Perplex', *Zeitschrift für Nationalökonomie*, vol. 35, pp. 1–24.

Clower, R., and Leijonhufvud, A. (1975), 'The Coordination of Economic Activities: A Keynesian Perspective', *American Economic Review, Papers and Proceedings*, vol. lxv, no. 2, May, pp. 182–8.

Cornwall, J. (1978), 'Post-Keynesian Theory: Macrodynamics', *Challenge*, vol. 21, no. 2, May–June, pp. 11–17.

Davidson, P. (1972), *Money and the Real World*, London, Macmillan.

Davidson, S. (1957), 'Depreciation, Income Taxes and Growth', *Accounting Research*, vol. 8, no. 3, June, pp. 191–205.

Debreu, G. (1959), *Theory of Value. An Axiomatic Analysis of Economic Equilibrium*, Cowles Foundation Monograph No. 17, New York, John Wiley.

De Lorme, C.D., and Rubin, P.H. (1975), 'A Theory of the Determination of the Mark-up Under Oligopoly: A Comment', *Economic Journal*, vol. 85, no. 337, March, pp. 148–9.

Del Punta, V. (1970), 'Sterility of the "Cambridge School" Criticism of the Marginal Productivity Theory', Selected paper (No. 5, 1971), from *Rivista di Politica Economica*, pp. 1–42.

Dobb, M.H. (1973), *Theories of Value and Distribution since Adam Smith. Ideology and Economic Theory*, Cambridge, Cambridge University Press.

Dobb, M.H. (1975), 'Ricardo and Adam Smith', in A.S. Skinner and T. Wilson (eds), *Essays on Adam Smith*, Oxford, Clarendon Press, pp. 324–35.

Dougherty, C.R.S. (1972), 'On the Rate of Return and the Rate of Profit', *Economic Journal*, vol. lxxxii, no. 328, December, pp. 1324–50.

Dow, J.C.R. (1956), 'Analysis of the Generation of Price Inflation. A Study of Cost and Price Changes in the United Kingdom, 1946–1954', *Oxford Economic Papers* (New Series), vol. 8, no. 3, September, pp. 252–301.

Downing, R.I. (1973), 'Review of Ward, Benjamin (1972), *What's Wrong with Economics*', Basic Books, New York and London, *Journal of Economic Literature*, vol. xi, no. 2, June, pp. 539–40.

Dunlop, J.T. (1938), 'The Movement of Real and Money Wage Rates', *Economic Journal*, vol. xlviii, September, pp. 413–34.

Eagley, R.V. (1974), *The Structure of Classical Economic Theory*, New York, Oxford University Press.

Eatwell, J.L. (1974), 'Controversies in the Theory of Surplus Value: Old and New', *Science and Society*, vol. xxxviii, no. 3, Autumn, pp. 281–303.

Eatwell, J.L. (1977), 'Portrait: Joan Robinson', *Challenge*, vol. 20, pp. 64–5.

Eatwell, J.L. (1979), *Theories of Value, Output and Employment*, London, Thames Papers in Political Economy.

Eckstein, O., and Fromm, G. (1968), 'The Price Equation', *American Economic Review*, vol. 58, no. 5, part 1, December, pp. 1159–83.

Eichner, A.S. (1973), 'A Theory of the Determination of the Mark-Up Under Oligopoly', *Economic Journal*, vol. 83, no. 332, December, pp. 1184–200.

Eichner, A.S. (1974), 'Determination of the Mark-Up Under Oligopoly: A Reply', *Economic Journal*, vol. 84, no. 336, December, pp. 974–80.

Eichner, A.S. (1975), 'A Theory of the Determination of the Mark-Up Under Oligopoly: A Further Reply', *Economic Journal*, vol. 85, March, pp. 149–50.

Eichner, A.S. (1976), *The Megacorp and Oligopoly*, Cambridge, Cambridge University Press.

Eichner, A.S. (1978), 'Post-Keynesian Theory: An Introduction', *Challenge*, vol. 21, no. 2, May–June, pp. 4–10.

Eshag, E. (1963), *From Marshall to Keynes. An Essay on the Monetary Theory of the Cambridge School*, Oxford, Basil Blackwell.

Ferguson, C.E. (1969), *The Neoclassical Theory of Production and Distribution*, Cambridge, Cambridge University Press.

Ferguson, C.E. (1972), 'The Current State of Capital Theory: A Tale of Two Paradigms', *Southern Economic Journal*, vol. xxxix, no. 2, October, pp. 160–76.

Fisher, F.M. (1970), 'Aggregate Production Functions and the Explanation of Wages: A Simulation Experiment', Working Paper 61, Department of Economics, M.I.T.

Fisher, F.M. (1971), 'The Existence of Aggregate Production Functions: Reply', *Econometrica*, vol. xxxix, no. 2, March, p. 405.

Fisher, I. (1930), *The Theory of Interest*, New York, Macmillan.

Fogel, R.W., and Engerman, S.L. (1974), *Time on the Cross: The Economics of American Negro Slavery*, vol. I, Boston, Little, Brown.

Galbraith, J.K. (1973), 'Power and the Useful Economist', *American Economic Review*, vol. 63, no. 1, March, pp. 1–11.

Gallaway, L., and Shukla, V. (1974), 'The Neoclassical Production Function', *American Economic Review*, vol. lxiv, no. 3, June, pp. 348–58.

Garegnani, P. (1959), 'A Problem in the Theory of Distribution from Ricardo to Wicksell', unpublished Ph.D. dissertation Cambridge University.

Garegnani, P. (1960), *Il Capitale nelle Teorie della Distribuzione*, Publicazioni della Facoltà di Economica e Commercio dell' Università di Roma XII Milano, Dott A. Guiffre Editore.

Garegnani, P. (1966), 'Switching of Techniques', *Quarterly Journal of Economics*, vol. lxxx, no. 4, November, pp. 554–67.

Garegnani, P. (1970), 'Heterogeneous Capital, the Production Function and the Theory of Distribution', *Review of Economic Studies*, vol. xxxvii, no. 3, pp. 407–36, and 'A Reply', p. 439.

Garegnani, P. (1973), 'Summary of the Final Discussion', in J.A. Mirrlees and N.H. Stern (eds), *Models of Economic Growth*, London, Macmillan.

Garegnani, P. (1976), 'On a Change in the Notion of Equilibrium in Recent Work on Value and Distribution: A Comment on Samuelson,' in M. Brown, K. Sato and P. Zarembka (eds), *Essays in Modern Capital Theory*, Amsterdam, North Holland, pp. 25–45.

Godley, W.A.H., and Nordhaus, W.D. (1972), 'Pricing in the Trade Cycle', *Economic Journal*, vol. 82, no. 327, September, pp. 853–82.

Goodwin, R.M. (1967), 'A Growth Cycle', in C.H. Feinstein (ed.), *Socialism, Capitalism and Economic Growth: Essays Presented to Maurice Dobb*, Cambridge, Cambridge University Press, reprinted in E.K. Hunt and J.G. Schwartz (eds) (1972), *A Critique of Economic Theory: Selected Readings*, Harmondsworth, Middx, Penguin Books, pp. 442–9.

Gordon, R.A. (1976), 'Rigor and Relevance in a Changing Institutional

Setting', *American Economic Review*, vol. 66, no. 1, March, pp. 1–14.

Grant, J.McB., and Mathews, R.L. (1957), 'Accounting Conventions, Pricing Policies and the Trade Cycle', *Accounting Research*, vol. 8, no. 2, April, pp. 145–64.

Grant, J.McB., and Mathews, R. (1958), *Inflation and Company Finance*, Sydney, The Law Book Company of Australasia.

Gruen, F.H. (1979), 'Australian Economics, 1967–1977', *Australian Economic Papers*, vol. 18, no. 32, June, pp. 1–20.

Hahn, F.H. (1971), 'Introduction', in F.H. Hahn (ed.), *Readings in the Theory of Growth*, London, Macmillan, pp. vii-xv.

Hahn, F.H. (1972a), *The Share of Wages in the National Income. An Enquiry into the Theory of Distribution*, London, Weidenfeld & Nicolson.

Hahn, F.H. (1972b), 'Notes on Vulgar Economy', Cambridge, mimeo.

Hahn, F.H. (1973a), *On the Notion of Equilibrium in Economics. An Inaugural Lecture*, Cambridge, Cambridge University Press.

Hahn, F.H. (1973b), 'The Winter of Our Discontent', *Economica*, vol. xl, no. 159, August, pp. 322–30.

Hahn, F.H. (1974), 'Back to Square One', *Cambridge Review*, vol. 96, pp. 34–7.

Hahn, F.H. (1975a), 'Comment', *Cambridge Review*, vol. 96, p. 92.

Hahn, F.H. (1975b), 'Revival of Political Economy: The Wrong Issues and the Wrong Argument', *Economic Record*, vol. 51, no. 135, September, pp. 360–4.

Hahn, F.H. (1978), 'Review of Tang, A.M., Westfield, F.M. and Worley, J.S. (eds) (1976), *Evolution, Welfare and Time in Economics: Essays in Honor of Nicholas Georgescu-Roegen*', Heath, Lexington Books, Lexington, Mass. and Toronto, *Journal of Economic Literature*, vol. xvi, no. 2, June, pp. 578–9.

Hahn, F.H., and Matthews, R.C.O. (1964), 'The Theory of Economic Growth: A Survey', *Economic Journal*, vol. lxxiv, no. 296, December, pp. 779–902.

Hall, M. (1967), 'Sales Revenue Maximization: An Empirical Examination', *Journal of Industrial Economics*, vol. 15, no. 2, April, pp. 143–56.

Harcourt, G.C. (1963), 'A Critique of Mr. Kaldor's Model of Income Distribution and Economic Growth', *Australian Economic Papers*, vol. 2, no. 1, June, pp. 20–36, reprinted as essay 6 in this collection.

Harcourt, G.C. (1964), 'Review of B.S. Minhas, *An International Comparison of Factor Costs and Factor Use*', Amsterdam, North-Holland, 1963, *Economic Journal*, vol. lxxiv, no. 294, June, pp. 543–5.

Harcourt, G.C. (1965a), 'A Two-sector Model of the Distribution of Income and the Level of Employment in the Short Run', *Economic Record*, vol. xli, pp. 103–17, reprinted as essay 7 in this collection.

Harcourt, G.C. (1965b), 'The Accountant in a Golden Age', *Oxford Economic Papers*, vol. 17, no. 1, March, pp. 66–80, reprinted as essay 4 in this collection.

Harcourt, G.C. (1966a), 'Cash Investment Grants, Corporation Tax and

Pay-out Ratios', *Bulletin of the Oxford Institute of Economics and Statistics*, vol. 28, pp. 163–79.

Harcourt, G.C. (1966b), 'Biases in Empirical Estimates of the Elasticities of Substitution of C.E.S. Production Functions', *Review of Economic Studies*, vol. xxxiii (3), no. 95, July, pp. 227–33, reprinted as essay 10 in this collection.

Harcourt, G.C. (1967), 'Cash Investment Grants, Corporation Tax and Pay-out Ratios: A Correction', *Bulletin of the Oxford Institute of Economics and Statistics*, vol. 29, pp. 87–93.

Harcourt, G.C. (1968), 'Investment-Decision Criteria, Investment Incentives and the Choice of Technique', *Economic Journal*, vol. 78, March, pp. 77–95, reprinted as essay 11 in this collection.

Harcourt, G.C. (1969a), 'Some Cambridge Controversies in the Theory of Capital', *Journal of Economic Literature*, vol. vii, no. 2, June, pp. 369–405.

Harcourt, G.C. (1969b), 'Investment-Decision Criteria, Capital-Intensity and the Choice of Techniques', in J.T. Dunlop and N.P. Fedorenko (eds), *Planning and Markets: Modern Trends in Various Economic Systems*, New York, McGraw-Hill, pp. 190–216.

Harcourt, G.C. (1972), *Some Cambridge Controversies in the Theory of Capital*, Cambridge, Cambridge University Press.

Harcourt, G.C. (1973), 'The Rate of Profits in Equilibrium Growth Models: A Review Article', *Journal of Political Economy*, vol. 81, no. 5, September–October, pp. 1261–77.

Harcourt, G.C. (1974), 'The Social Consequences of Inflation', *Australian Accountant*, vol. 44, no. 9, October, pp. 520–8.

Harcourt, G.C. (1975a), 'The Cambridge Controversies: The Afterglow', in M. Parkin and A.R. Nobay (eds) (1975), pp. 305–34.

Harcourt, G.C. (1975b), 'Decline and Rise: The Revival of (Classical) Political Economy', *Economic Record*, vol. 51, no. 135, September, pp. 339–56.

Harcourt, G.C. (1976), 'The Cambridge Controversies: Old Ways and New Horizons – or Dead End?', *Oxford Economic Papers*, vol. 28, no. 1, March, pp. 25–65, reprinted as essay 17 in this collection.

Harcourt, G.C. (1977a), 'The Theoretical and Social Significance of the Cambridge Controversies in the Theory of Capital: An Evaluation', *Revue d'économie politique*, vol. 87, pp. 191–215, reprinted as essay 18 in this collection.

Harcourt, G.C. (1977b), 'Eric Russell, 1921–1977: A Memoir', *Economic Record*, vol. 53, no. 144, December, pp. 467–74.

Harcourt, G.C. (1980), 'A Post-Keynesian Development of the "Keynesian" Model', in E.J. Nell (ed.), *Growth, Profits and Property. Essays in the Revival of Political Economy*, Cambridge, Cambridge University Press, pp. 151–64.

Harcourt, G.C. (1981), 'The Sraffian Contribution: An Evaluation', in M.C. Howard and I. Bradley (eds), *Classical and Marxian Political Economy: Essays in Honour of R.L. Meek*, London, Macmillan, forthcoming.

Harcourt, G.C., and Kerr, P.M. (1978), 'On Some Central Issues in Ian

Steedman's *Marx After Sraffa'*, paper presented at the Seventh Conference of Economists, Macquarie University, August–September 1978.

Harcourt, G.C., and Laing, N.F. (1971) (eds), *Capital and Growth. Selected Readings*, Harmondsworth, Middx, Penguin Books.

Harcourt, G.C., and Massaro, V.G. (1964a), 'A Note on Mr. Sraffa's Sub-Systems', *Economic Journal*, vol. lxxiv, no. 215, September, pp. 715–22, reprinted as essay 12 in this collection.

Harcourt, G.C., and Massaro, V.G. (1964b), 'Mr. Sraffa's Production of Commodities', *Economic Record*, vol. xl, no. 91, September, pp. 442–54, reprinted as essay 13 in this collection.

Harris, D.J. (1973), 'Capital, Distribution, and the Aggregate Production Function', *American Economic Review*, vol. lxiii, no. 1, March, pp. 100–13.

Harris, D.J. (1974), 'The Price Policy of Firms, The Level of Employment and Distribution of Income in the Short Run', *Australian Economic Papers*, vol. 13, no. 22, June, pp. 144–51.

Harris, D.J. (1975), 'The Theory of Economic Growth: A Critique and Reformulation', *American Economic Review*, Papers and Proceedings, vol. lxv, no. 2, May, pp. 329–37.

Harrod, R.F. (1939), 'An Essay in Dynamic Theory', *Economic Journal*, vol. xlix, March, pp. 14–33.

Harrod, R.F. (1948), *Towards a Dynamic Economics: Some Recent Developments of Economic Theory and their Application to Policy*, London, Macmillan.

Harrod, R.F. (1961), 'Review of P. Sraffa, *Production of Commodities by Means of Commodities. Prelude to a Critique of Economic Theory*, 1960', *Economic Journal*, vol. 71, no. 284, December, pp. 783–7.

Hayek, F.A. von (1975), *Full Employment at any Price?*, London, Institute of Economic Affairs.

Hazledine, T. (1974), 'Determination of the Mark-Up Under Oligopoly: A Comment', *Economic Journal*, vol. 84, December, pp. 967–70.

Hicks, J.R. (1932), *The Theory of Wages*, London, Macmillan.

Hicks, J.R. (1937), 'Mr. Keynes and the "Classics"; A Suggested Interpretation', *Econometrica*, vol. 5, pp. 147–59.

Hicks, J.R. (1939), *Value and Capital. An Inquiry into some Fundamental Principles of Economic Theory*, Oxford, Clarendon Press.

Hicks, John (1965), *Capital and Growth*, Oxford, Clarendon Press.

Hicks, John (1969), *A Theory of Economic History*, Oxford, Clarendon Press.

Hicks, John (1970), 'A Neo-Austrian Growth Theory', *Economic Journal*, vol. lxxx, no. 318, June, pp. 257–81.

Hicks, John (1973), *Capital and Time. A Neo-Austrian Theory*, Oxford, Clarendon Press.

Hicks, John (1974), *The Crisis in Keynesian Economics*, The 1974 Yrjö Jahnsson Lectures, Oxford, Basil Blackwell.

Hicks, John (1975a), 'Revival of Political Economy: The Old and the

New', *Economic Record*, vol. 51, no. 135, September, pp. 365-7.

Hicks, John (1975b), 'What is Wrong with Monetarism', *Lloyds Bank Review*, no. 118, October, pp. 1-13.

Hicks, John (1976), 'Some Questions of Time in Economics', in A.M. Tang, F.M. Westfield, and J.S. Worley (eds), *Evolution, Welfare, and Time in Economics: Essays in Honor of Nicholas Georgescu-Roegen*, Lexington, Heath, Lexington Books, pp. 135-51.

Hicks, John (1977), *Economic Perspectives: Further Essays on Money and Growth*, Oxford, Clarendon Press.

Hirsch, F. (1977), *Social Limits to Growth*, London and Henley, Routledge & Kegan Paul.

Hirshleifer, J. (1958), 'On the Theory of Optimal Investment Decision', *Journal of Political Economy*, vol. lxvi, pp. 329-52.

Hirshleifer, J. (1970), *Investment, Interest and Capital*, Englewood Cliffs, Prentice-Hall.

Holland, S. (1975), *The Socialist Challenge*, London, Quartet Books.

Howard, M.C., and King, J.E. (1975), *The Political Economy of Marx*, Harlow, Longman.

Hudson, H.R., and Mathews, R.L. (1963), 'An Aspect of Depreciation', *Economic Record*, vol. 39, no. 86, June, pp. 232-6.

Ironmonger, D.S. (1972), *New Commodities and Consumer Behaviour*, Cambridge, Cambridge University Press.

Isaac, J.E. (1977), 'Wage Determination and Economic Policy', Giblin Memorial Lecture, A.N.Z.A.A.S., Melbourne.

Johnson, H.G. (1951), 'The Taxonomic Approach to Economic Policy', *Economic Journal*, vol. lxi, December, pp. 812-32.

Johnson, H.G. (1971), *The Two-Sector Model of General Equilibrium*, the Yrjö Jahnsson Lectures, 1970, London, Allen & Unwin.

Johnson, H.G. (1973), *The Theory of Income Distribution*, London, Gray-Mills Publishing.

Johnson, H.G. (1974), 'Cambridge in the 1950s: Memoirs of an Economist', *Encounter*, vol. xlii, January, pp. 28-39.

Johnson, H.G. (1975), 'Keynes and British Economics', in M. Keynes (ed.), *Essays on John Maynard Keynes*, Cambridge, Cambridge University Press, pp. 108-22.

Jorgenson D.W. (1965), 'Anticipations and Investment Behaviour', in *The Brookings Quarterly Econometric Model of the United States*, Chicago, Rand McNally.

Kahn, R.F. (1959), 'Exercises in the Analysis of Growth', *Oxford Economic Papers*, vol. xi, no. 2, June, pp. 143-56.

Kahn, R.F. (1974), 'On Re-reading Keynes', Fourth Keynes Lecture in Economics, *Proceedings of the British Academy*, vol. 60, Oxford University Press.

Kahn, R.F. (1977), 'Malinvaud on Keynes', *Cambridge Journal of Economics*, vol. i, no. 4, December, pp. 375-88.

Kaldor, N. (1956), 'Alternative Theories of Distribution', *Review of Economic Studies*, vol. xxiii, pp. 83-100.

Kaldor, N. (1957), 'A Model of Economic Growth', *Economic Journal*, vol. lxvii, December, pp. 591-624.

Kaldor, N. (1959), 'Economic Growth and the Problem of Inflation – Parts I and II', *Economica*, vol. xxvi, August and November, pp. 212-26, 287-98.

Kaldor, N. (1961), 'Capital Accumulation and Economic Growth', in F.A. Lutz and D.C. Hague (eds) (1961), pp. 177-222.

Kaldor, N. (1966), 'Marginal Productivity and the Macroeconomic Theories of Distribution', *Review of Economic Studies*, vol. 33, no. 4, October, pp. 309-19.

Kaldor, N. (1970), 'Some Fallacies in the Interpretation of Kaldor', *Review of Economic Studies*, vol. 37, no. 1, January, pp. 1-7.

Kaldor, N. (1972), 'The Irrelevance of Equilibrium Economics', *Economic Journal*, vol. 82, no. 328, December, pp. 1237-55.

Kaldor, N., and Mirrlees, J.A. (1962), 'A New Model of Economic Growth', *Review of Economic Studies*, vol. 29, June, pp. 174-92.

Kalecki, M. (1937), 'The Principle of Increasing Risk', *Economica*, vol. 4, November, pp. 440-7.

Kalecki, M. (1968), 'Trend and Business Cycles Reconsidered', *Economic Journal*, vol. lxxviii, no. 310, June, pp. 263-76.

Kalecki, M. (1971), *Selected Essays on the Dynamics of the Capitalist Economy: 1933-1970*, Cambridge, Cambridge University Press.

Karmel, P. (1977), 'Eric Alfred Russell', *Australian Economic Papers*, vol. 16, no. 29, December, pp. 159-60.

Katzner, D.W., and Weintraub, S. (1974), 'An Approach to a Unified Micro-Macro Economic Model', *Kyklos*, vol. 27, pp. 482-510.

Kay, J.A. (1976), 'Accountants, too, Could be Happy in a Golden Age: The Accountant's Rate of Profit and the Internal Rate of Return', *Oxford Economic Papers*, vol. xxviii, no. 3, November, pp. 447-60.

Kay, J.A. (1978), 'Accounting Rate of Profit and the Internal Rate of Return, a Reply', *Oxford Economic Papers*, vol. xxx, pp. 469-70.

Kenyon, P. (1978), 'Pricing in Post-Keynesian Economics', *Challenge*, vol. 21, no. 3, July-August, pp. 43-8.

Keynes, J.M. (1930; 1958-60), *A Treatise on Money*, 2 vols, London, Macmillan. Vol. 1, *The Pure Theory of Money*; vol. 2, *The Applied Theory of Money*.

Keynes, J.M. (1936), *The General Theory of Employment, Interest and Money*, vol. vii of *The Collected Writings of John Maynard Keynes*, London, Macmillan, for the Royal Economic Society, 1973.

Keynes, J.M. (1937), 'The General Theory of Employment', *Quarterly Journal of Economics*, vol. 51, February, pp. 209-23.

Keynes, J.M. (1971-9), *The Collected Writings of John Maynard Keynes*, vols. I-XXIX, edited by D.E. Moggridge, for the Royal Economic Society, London, Macmillan.

Koopmans, T.C. (1957), *Three Essays on the State of Economic Science*, New York, McGraw-Hill.

Kregel, J.A. (1971), *Rate of Profit, Distribution and Growth: Two Views*, London, Macmillan.

Kregel, J.A. (1972), *The Theory of Economic Growth*, London, Macmillan.

Kregel, J.A. (1973), *The Reconstruction of Political Economy, An Introduction to Post-Keynesian Economics*, London, Macmillan.

Kregel, J.A. (1976a), *Theory of Capital*, London, Macmillan.

Kregel, J.A. (1976b), 'Economic Methodology in the Face of Uncertainty: The Modelling Methods of Keynes and the Post-Keynesians', *Economic Journal*, vol. 86, no. 342, June, pp. 209–25.

Kregel, J.A. (1978), 'Post-Keynesian Theory: Income Distribution', *Challenge*, vol. 21, no. 4, September–October, pp. 37–43.

Krimpas, G.E. (1974), *Keynes' General Theory*, Athens.

Kuznets, S. (1952), 'Long-term Changes in the National Income of the United States of America Since 1870' in S. Kuznets (ed.), *Income and Wealth*, Series II, International Association for Research into Income and Wealth, Cambridge, Bowes & Bowes.

Laibman, D., and Nell, E.J. (1977), 'Reswitching, Wicksell Effects and the Neoclassical Production Function', *American Economic Review*, vol. 67, no. 5, December, pp. 878–88.

Laing, N.F. (1971), 'Trade, Growth and Distribution: A Study in the Theory of the Long Run', in G.C. Harcourt and N.F. Laing (eds) (1971), pp. 343–7.

Lancaster, K.J. (1966), 'A New Approach to Consumer Theory', *Journal of Political Economy*, vol. 74, no. 2, April, pp. 132–57.

Lanzillotti, R.F. (1958), 'Pricing Objectives in Large Companies', *American Economic Review*, vol. 48, no. 5, December, pp. 921–40.

Leontief, W. (1971), 'Theoretical Assumptions and Nonobserved Facts', *American Economic Review*, vol. 61, no. 1, March, pp. 1–7.

Levhari, D. (1965), 'A Nonsubstitution Theorem and Switching of Techniques', *Quarterly Journal of Economics*, vol. lxxix, no. 1, February, pp. 98–105.

Levhari, D., and Samuelson, P.A. (1966), 'The Nonswitching Theorem is False', *Quarterly Journal of Economics*, vol. lxxx, no. 4, November, pp. 518–19.

Levine, D.P. (1980a), 'Aspects of the Classical Theory of Markets', *Australian Economic Papers*, vol. 19, no. 34, June, pp. 1–15.

Levine, D.P. (1980b), 'Production Prices and the Theory of the Firm', *Journal of Post Keynesian Economics*, vol. iii, no. 1, Autumn, pp. 88–99.

Levine, H.S. (1960), 'Comment' on Robert W. Campbell, 'Soviet Accounting and Economic Decisions', in Gregory Grossman (ed.), *Value and Plan*, Berkeley, University of California Press, pp. 96–7.

Lewis, M.K. (1976a), 'The Case for Tax Cuts', *Australian Financial Review*, 19 October, pp. 2, 3, 5.

Lewis, M.K. (1976b), 'The Cuts Need Not be Inflationary', *Australian Financial Review*, 20 October, pp. 9, 11.

Lowe, A. (1976), *The Path of Economic Growth*, New York, Cambridge University Press.

Lutz, F.A., and Hague, D.C. (1961) (eds), *The Theory of Capital*, London, Macmillan.

Luxemburg, R. (1913) (1964), *The Accumulation of Capital*, English edn, London, Routledge & Kegan Paul; American edn, New York, Monthly Review Press (Joan Robinson wrote the Introduction to the

1951 English translation. The book was first published in German).

Mabry, B.D., and Siders, D.L. (1967), 'An Empirical Test of the Sales Maximization Hypothesis', *Southern Economic Journal*, vol. 33, no. 3, January, pp. 367–77.

Malinvaud, E. (1953), 'Capital Accumulation and Efficient Allocation of Resources', *Econometrica*, vol. xxi, no. 2, April, pp. 233–68.

Malinvaud, E. (1977), 'Discussion of Koopmans' Paper', in G.C. Harcourt (ed.), *The Microeconomic Foundations of Macroeconomics*, London, Macmillan, p. 174.

Malinvaud, E., and Younès, Y. (1977), 'Some New Concepts for the Microeconomic Foundations of Macroeconomics', in G.C. Harcourt (ed.), *The Microeconomic Foundations of Macroeconomics*, London, Macmillan, pp. 62–85.

Marglin, S.A. (1974), 'What do Bosses do? The Origins and Functions of Hierarchy in Capitalist Production', *Review of Radical Political Economics*, vol. vi, no. 2, Summer, pp. 60–112.

Marris, R. (1964), *The Economic Theory of 'Managerial' Capitalism*, London, Macmillan.

Marshall, A. (1890), *Principles of Economics* (8th edition, 1920), London, Macmillan.

Mathews, R.L. (1962), *Accounting for Economists*, Melbourne, F.W. Cheshire.

Mathews, R.L. and Grant, J. McB. (1957), 'Accounting Conventions, Pricing Policies and the Trade Cycle', *Accounting Research*, vol. 8, no. 2, April, pp. 145–64.

Mathews, R.L., and Grant, J. McB. (1958), *Inflation and Company Finance*, Sydney, The Law Book Company of Australasia.

Mathur, G. (1965), *Planning for Steady Growth*, Oxford, Blackwell.

Meade, J.E. (1951), *The Theory of International Economic Policy, Vol. I, The Balance of Payments*, Oxford, Oxford University Press.

Meade, J.E. (1955), *The Theory of International Economic Policy, Vol. II, Trade and Welfare*, Oxford, Oxford University Press.

Meade, J.E. (1956), 'The Price Mechanism and the Australian Balance of Payments', *Economic Record*, vol. 32, November, pp. 239–56.

Meade, J.E. (1961), *A Neoclassical Theory of Economic Growth*, London, Allen & Unwin.

Meade, J.E. (1963), 'The Rate of Profit in a Growing Economy', *Economic Journal*, vol. lxxiii, no. 292, December, pp. 665–74.

Meade, J.E. (1966), 'The Outcome of the Pasinetti-Process: A Note', *Economic Journal*, vol. lxxvi, no. 301, March, pp. 161–5.

Meade, J.E. (1975a), 'The Keynesian Revolution', in M. Keynes (ed.), *Essays on John Maynard Keynes*, Cambridge, Cambridge University Press, pp. 82–8.

Meade, J.E. (1975b), *The Intelligent Radical's Guide to Economic Policy. The Mixed Economy*, London, Allen & Unwin.

Meade, J.E., and Hahn, F.H. (1965), 'The Rate of Profit in a Growing Economy', *Economic Journal*, vol. lxxv, no. 298, June, pp. 445–8.

Meade, J.E., and Russell, E.A. (1957), 'Wage Rates, the Cost of Living and the Balance of Payments', *Economic Record*, vol. xxxiii, no. 64, April, pp. 23–8.

Means, G.C. (1972), 'The Administered Price Thesis Reconfirmed', *American Economic Review*, vol. 62, no. 3, June, pp. 292–306.

Medio, A. (1972), 'Profits and Surplus-Value: Appearance and Reality in Capitalist Production', in E.K. Hunt and J.G. Schwartz (eds), *A Critique of Economic Theory. Selected Readings*, Harmondsworth, Middx, Penguin Books, pp. 312–46.

Meek, R.L. (1964), 'Ideal and Reality in the Choice Between Alternative Techniques', *Oxford Economic Papers*, vol. 16, pp. 333–54.

Meek, R.L. (1967), *Economics and Ideology and Other Essays. Studies in the Development of Economic Thought*, London, Chapman & Hall.

Merrett, S. (1964), 'Capital, Profit and Bonus in Soviet Industry', *Economica*, vol. 31, no. 124, November, pp. 401–7.

Metcalfe, J.S., and Steedman, I. (1972a), 'Reswitching and Primary Input Use', *Economic Journal*, vol. lxxxii, no. 325, March, pp. 140–57.

Metcalfe, J.S., and Steedman, I. (1972b), 'Heterogeneous Capital and the Heckscher-Ohlin-Samuelson Theory of Trade', Nice, mimeo.

Metcalfe, J.S., and Steedman, I. (1972c), 'The Golden Rule and the Gain from Trade', Nice, mimeo.

Metzler, L.A. (1951), 'The Rate of Interest and the Marginal Product of Capital: A Correction', *Journal of Political Economy*, vol. lix, no. 1, February, pp. 67–8.

Minhas, B.S. (1963), *An International Comparison of Factor Costs and Factor Use*, Amsterdam, North Holland.

Minsky, H.P. (1975), *John Maynard Keynes*, New York, Columbia University Press.

Mirrlees, J.A. (1973), 'Introduction', in J.A. Mirrlees and N.H. Stern (eds), *Models of Economic Growth*, London, Macmillan.

Mirrlees, J.A. (1978), 'Review of Malinvaud, Edmond (1977), *The Theory of Unemployment Reconsidered*, Oxford, Basil Blackwell', *Economic Journal*, vol. 88, no. 349, March, pp. 157–9.

Moggridge, D. (1976), *Keynes*, Fontana *Modern Masters*, Collins.

Moore, B.J. (1978), 'A Post-Keynesian Approach to Monetary Theory', *Challenge*, vol. 21, no. 4, September–October, pp. 44–52.

Morishima, M. (1966), 'Refutation of the Nonswitching Theorem', *Quarterly Journal of Economics*, vol. lxxx, no. 4, November, pp. 520–5.

Morishima, M. (1973), *Marx's Economics. A Dual Theory of Value and Growth*, Cambridge, Cambridge University Press.

Morishima, M. (1974), 'Marx in the Light of Modern Economic Theory', *Econometrica*, vol. 42, no. 4, July, pp. 611–32.

Morishima, M. (1976), 'Positive Profits with Negative Surplus Value — A Comment', *Economic Journal*, vol. 86, no. 343, September, pp. 599–603.

Neher, P.A. (1978), 'The Pure Theory of Muggery', *American Economic Review*, vol. 68, no. 3, June, pp. 437–45.

Neild, R.R. (1963), 'Pricing and Employment in the Trade Cycle: A Study of British Manufacturing Industry', *National Institute of Economic and Social Research Occasional Paper*, no. 21.

Nell, E.J. (1967), 'Theories of Growth and Theories of Value', *Economic Development and Cultural Change*, vol. xvi, no. 1, October, pp. 15–26.

Nell, E.J. (1975), 'The Black Box Rate of Return', *Kyklos*, vol. 28, pp. 803–26.

Nell, E.J. (1976), 'An Alternative Presentation of Lowe's Basic Model', appendix to A. Lowe (1976).

Nevin, E. (1963), 'The Cost Structure of British Manufacturing, 1948–1961', *Economic Journal*, vol. lxxiii, no. 292, December, pp. 642–64.

Ng, Y.K. (1974a), 'Harcourt's Survey of Capital Theory (Review Article)', *Economic Record*, vol. 50, no. 129, March, pp. 119–29.

Ng, Y.K. (1974b), 'The Neoclassical and the Neo-Marxist-Keynesian Theories of Income Distribution: A Non-Cambridge Contribution to the Cambridge Controversy in Capital Theory', *Australian Economic Papers*, vol. 13, no. 22, June, pp. 124–32.

Norman, N.R. (1973), 'The Economic Effects of Tariffs on Industry', unpublished Ph.D. Thesis, University of Cambridge.

Nuti, D.M. (1969), 'The Degree of Monopoly in the Kaldor–Mirrlees Growth Model', *Review of Economic Studies*, vol. 36, no. 2, April, pp. 257–60.

Nuti, D.M. (1970), 'Capitalism, Socialism and Steady Growth', *Economic Journal*, vol. lxxx, no. 317, March, pp. 32–57.

Nuti, D.M. (1974), 'On the Rates of Return on Investment', *Kyklos*, vol. xxvii, pp. 345–69.

Parkin, M., and Nobay, A.R. (1975) (eds), *Contemporary Issues in Economics*, Manchester, Manchester University Press.

Parkinson, J.R. (1955), 'The Terms of Trade and the National Income 1950–1952', *Oxford Economic Papers* (New Series), vol. 7, no. 2, pp. 177–96.

Pasinetti, L.L. (1962), 'Rate of Profit and Income Distribution in Relation to the Rate of Economic Growth', *Review of Economic Studies*, vol. xxix, pp. 267–79.

Pasinetti, L.L. (1964), 'A Comment on Professor Meade's "Rate of Profit in a Growing Economy"', *Economic Journal*, vol. lxxiv, no. 294, June, pp. 488–9

Pasinetti, L.L. (1966a), 'Changes in the Rate of Profit and Switches of Techniques', *Quarterly Journal of Economics*, vol. lxxx, no. 4, November, pp. 503–17.

Pasinetti, L.L. (1966b), 'The Rate of Profit in a Growing Economy: A Reply', *Economic Journal*, vol. lxxvi, no. 301, March, pp. 158–60.

Pasinetti, L.L. (1966c), 'New Results in an Old Framework', *Review of Economic Studies*, vol. xxxiii (4), no. 96, October, pp. 303–6.

Pasinetti, L.L. (1969), 'Switches of Technique and the "Rate of Return" in Capital Theory', *Economic Journal*, vol. lxxix, no. 315, September, pp. 508–31.

Pasinetti, L.L. (1970), 'Again on Capital Theory and Solow's "Rate of Return"', *Economic Journal*, vol. lxxx, no. 318, June, pp. 428–31.

Pasinetti, L.L. (1972), 'Reply to Mr. Dougherty', *Economic Journal*, vol. lxxxii, pp. 1351–2.

Pasinetti, L.L. (1973), 'The Notion of Vertical Integration in Economic Analysis', *Metroeconomica*, vol. xxv, pp. 1-29.

Pasinetti, L.L. (1974a), *Growth and Income Distribution, Essays in Economic Theory*, Cambridge, Cambridge University Press.

Pasinetti, L.L. (1974b), 'A Reply to Dr. Nuti on the Rate of Return', *Kyklos*, vol. xxvii, pp. 370-3.

Penrose, E.T. (1959), *The Theory of the Growth of the Firm*, Oxford, Basil Blackwell.

Pesaran, M.H. (1974), 'A Dynamic Inter-Industry Model of Price Determination – A Test of the Normal Price Hypothesis', Department of Applied Economics, University of Cambridge, Reprint Series, no. 401.

Phelps Brown, E.H. (1971), *Collective Bargaining Reconsidered*, Stamp Memorial Lecture, London.

Phelps Brown, E.H. (1972), 'The Underdevelopment of Economics', *Economic Journal*, vol. 82, no. 325, March, pp. 1-10.

Phelps Brown, E.H. (1975), 'A Non-monetarist View of the Pay Explosion', *Three Banks Review*, no. 105, March, pp. 3-24.

Phelps Brown, E.H., and Weber, B. (1953), 'Accumulation, Productivity and Distribution in the British Economy, 1870-1938', *Economic Journal*, vol. lxiii, June, 263-88.

Pickering, J.F. (1971), 'The Prices and Incomes Board and Private Sector Prices: A Survey', *Economic Journal*, vol. 81, no. 322, June, pp. 225-41.

Prais, S.J. (1955), 'The Measure of Income for Shareholders and for Taxation', *Accounting Research*, vol. 6, no. 3, pp. 187-201.

Prest, A.R. (1950), 'Replacement Cost Depreciation', *Accounting Research*, vol. 1, no. 4, pp. 385-402.

Quandt, R.E. (1961), 'Review of P. Sraffa, *Production of Commodities by Means of Commodities. Prelude to a Critique of Economic Theory*, 1960', *Journal of Political Economy*, vol. 69, p. 500.

Ramsey, F.P. (1928), 'A Mathematical Theory of Saving', *Economic Journal*, vol. xxxviii, December, pp. 543-59.

Read, L.M. (1968), 'The Measure of Total Factor Productivity Appropriate to Wage-Price Guidelines', *Canadian Journal of Economics*, vol. 1, no. 2, May, pp. 349-58.

Reder, M.W. (1961), 'Review of P. Sraffa, *Production of Commodities by Means of Commodities. Prelude to a Critique of Economic Theory*, 1960', *American Economic Review*, vol. 51, no. 4, September, pp. 688-95.

Rivlin, A.M. (1975), 'Income Distribution – Can Economists Help?', Richard T. Ely Lecture, 1975, *American Economic Review, Papers and Proceedings*, vol. lxv, no. 2, May, pp. 1-15.

Robbins, L. (1935), *An Essay on the Nature and Significance of Economic Science*, 2nd edition, London, Macmillan.

Robinson, Austin (1977), 'Keynes and his Cambridge Colleagues', in D. Patinkin and J.C. Leith (eds), *Keynes, Cambridge and the General Theory*, London, Macmillan, pp. 25-38.

Robinson, J. (1933a), *The Economics of Imperfect Competition* (2nd edition 1969), London, Macmillan.

Robinson, J. (1933b), 'The Theory of Money and the Analysis of Output', *Review of Economic Studies*, vol. i, pp. 22–6.

Robinson, J. (1934a), 'Euler's Theorem and the Problem of Distribution', *Economic Journal*, vol. xliv, September, pp. 398–414.

Robinson, J. (1934b), 'What is Perfect Competition?', *Quarterly Journal of Economics*, vol. xlix, November, pp. 104–20.

Robinson, J. (1937a), *Essays in the Theory of Employment* (2nd edition 1947), Oxford, Basil Blackwell.

Robinson, J. (1937b), *Introduction to the Theory of Employment* (2nd edition 1969), London, Macmillan.

Robinson, J. (1941), 'Rising Supply Price', *Economica*, vol. viii, February, pp. 1–8.

Robinson, J. (1942), *An Essay on Marxian Economics* (2nd edition 1966), London, Macmillan.

Robinson, J. (1946–7), 'The Pure Theory of International Trade', *Review of Economic Studies*, vol. xiv, pp. 98–112.

Robinson, J. (1949), 'Mr. Harrod's Dynamics', *Economic Journal*, vol. lix, March, pp. 68–85.

Robinson, J. (1951–80), *Collected Economic Papers*, 6 vols. Oxford, Basil Blackwell.

Robinson, J. (1953–4), 'The Production Function and the Theory of Capital', *Review of Economic Studies*, vol. xxi, pp. 81–106, partly reprinted in J. Robinson (1951–80), vol. ii.

Robinson, J. (1956), *The Accumulation of Capital* (2nd edition 1969), London, Macmillan.

Robinson, J. (1960), *Exercises in Economic Analysis*, London, Macmillan.

Robinson, J. (1961), 'Prelude to a Critique of Economic Theory', *Oxford Economic Papers*, vol. 13, no. 1, February, pp. 53–8.

Robinson, J. (1962a), *Economic Philosophy*, London, C.A. Watts.

Robinson, J. (1962b), *Essays in the Theory of Economic Growth*, London, Macmillan.

Robinson, J. (1964a), 'Solow on the Rate of Return', *Economic Journal*, vol. lxxiv, no. 294, June, pp. 410–17.

Robinson, J. (1964b), 'Pre-Keynesian Theory After Keynes', *Australian Economic Papers*, vol. 3, nos. 1–2, June–December, pp. 25–35.

Robinson, J. (1966a), 'Comment on Samuelson and Modigliani', *Review of Economic Studies*, vol. xxxiii (4), no. 96, October, pp. 307–8.

Robinson, J. (1966b), *Economics: An Awkward Corner*, London, Allen & Unwin.

Robinson, J. (1966c), *The New Mercantilism: An Inaugural Lecture*, Cambridge, Cambridge University Press.

Robinson, J. (1969a), 'A Further Note', *Review of Economic Studies*, vol. 36, April, pp. 260–2.

Robinson, J. (1969b), 'Review of A. Leijonhufvud, *On Keynesian Economics and the Economics of Keynes*, 1968', *Economic Journal*, vol. lxxix, no. 315, September, pp. 581–3.

Robinson, J. (1970a), 'Capital Theory up to Date', *Canadian Journal of Economics*, vol. iii, no. 2, May, pp. 309–17.

Robinson, J. (1970b), *Freedom and Necessity*, London, Allen & Unwin.

Robinson, J. (1971a), 'The Existence of Aggregate Production Functions: Comment', *Econometrica*, vol. xxxix, no. 2, March, p. 405.

Robinson, J. (1971b), *Economic Heresies: Some Old-Fashioned Questions in Economic Theory*, London, Macmillan.

Robinson, J. (1972), 'The Second Crisis of Economic Theory', Richard T. Ely Lecture, 1972, *American Economic Review, Papers and Proceedings*, vol. lxii, no. 2, May, pp. 1–10.

Robinson, J. (1973) (ed.), *After Keynes*, Oxford, Basil Blackwell.

Robinson, J. (1974), *History versus Equilibrium*, London, Thames Polytechnic.

Robinson, J. (1975a), 'The Unimportance of Reswitching', *Quarterly Journal of Economics*, vol. lxxix, no. 1, February, pp. 32–9.

Robinson, J. (1975b), 'Reswitching: Reply', *Quarterly Journal of Economics*, vol. lxxxix, no. 1, February, pp. 53–5.

Robinson, J. (1975c), 'Introduction 1974: Reflections and Reminiscences', in J. Robinson (1951–80), vol. ii, 2nd edition, pp. iii–xii.

Robinson, J. (1975d), 'Introduction 1974. Comments and Explanations', in J. Robinson (1951–80), vol. iii, 2nd edition, pp. iii–xiv.

Robinson, J. (1975e), 'Review of L.L. Pasinetti, *Growth and Income Distribution. Essays in Economic Theory*, 1974', *Economic Journal*, vol. 85, no. 338, June, pp. 397–9.

Robinson, J. (1975f), 'Letter to Editor', *Cambridge Review*, vol. 97, pp. 91–2.

Robinson, J. (1976), 'Michal Kalecki: A Neglected Prophet', *New York Review of Books*, 4 March, pp. 28–30.

Robinson, J. (1977a), 'The Labour Theory of Value', *Monthly Review*, vol. 29, pp. 50–9.

Robinson, J. (1977b), 'Michal Kalecki on the Economics of Capitalism', *Oxford Bulletin of Economics and Statistics*, vol. 39, no. 1, February, pp. 7–17.

Robinson, J. (1977c), 'Qu'est-ce que le capital?', in A. Heertje (ed.), *Cambridge Controverse sur la théorie du capital. Aspects sociaux et économiques, Revue d'économie politique*, Editions Sirey, Paris, pp. 165–79.

Robinson, J. (1977d), 'What are the Questions?', *Journal of Economic Literature*, vol. xv, no. 4, December, pp. 1318–39.

Robinson, J. (1978), 'Morality and Economics', *Challenge*, vol. 21, no. 1, March–April, pp. 62–4.

Robinson, J., and Eatwell, J.L. (1973), *An Introduction to Modern Economics*, London, McGraw-Hill.

Robinson, J., and Naqvi, K.A. (1967), 'The Badly Behaved Production Function', *Quarterly Journal of Economics*, vol. lxxxi, no. 4, November, pp. 579–91.

Robinson, R. (1974), 'Determination of the Mark-Up Under Oligopoly: A Comment', *Economic Journal*, vol. 84, December, pp. 971–4.

Roll, E. (1978), 'Has Economics a Future? Dim Prospects for a Dismal Science', *Encounter*, vol. 51, no. 1, July, pp. 8–14.

Roncaglia, A. (1974), 'Labour-Power, Subsistence Wage and the Rate of Wages', *Australian Economic Papers*, vol. 13, no. 22, June, pp. 133–43.

Roncaglia, A. (1977), 'The Sraffian Revolution', in S. Weintraub (ed.), *Modern Economic Thought*, Oxford, Basil Blackwell, pp. 163–77.

Roncaglia, A. (1979), 'Sraffa and the Reconstruction of Political Economy', *Challenge*, vol. 21, no. 6, January–February, pp. 48–53.

Roosevelt, F. (1977), 'Cambridge Economics as Commodity Fetishism', in J. Schwartz (ed.), *The Subtle Anatomy of Capitalism*, Santa Monica, California, Goodyear, pp. 412–57.

Rose, H. (1965), *Disclosure in Company Accounts*, 2nd edition, IEA, Eaton Paper 1.

Rothschild, K.W. (1947), 'Price Theory and Oligopoly', *Economic Journal*, vol. 57, September, pp. 299–320.

Rowthorn, R.E. (1972), 'Vulgar Economy', Cambridge, mimeo.

Rowthorn, R.E. (1974), 'Neo-Classicism, Neo-Ricardianism and Marxism', *New Left Review*, no. 86, pp. 63–87.

Russell, E.A. (1959), '1959 Basic Wage Case: Statement of Evidence by Eric Alfred Russell', Adelaide, mimeo.

Russell, E.A. (1965), 'Wages Policy in Australia', *Australian Economic Papers*, vol. 4, nos. 1–2, June–December, pp. 1–26.

Russell, E.A. (1971), 'Australian Incomes Policy', Adelaide, mimeo.

Russell, E.A. (1978), 'Foreign Investment Policy – What Role for the Economist?', *Australian Economic Papers*, vol. 17, no. 31, December, pp. 193–206.

Rymes, T.K. (1968), 'Professor Read and the Measurement of Total Factor Productivity', *Canadian Journal of Economics*, vol. i, no. 2, May, pp. 359–67.

Rymes, T.K. (1971), *On Concepts of Capital and Technical Change*, Cambridge, Cambridge University Press.

Salter, W.E.G. (1960), *Productivity and Technical Change*, Cambridge, Cambridge University Press.

Salter, W.E.G. (1962), 'Marginal Labour and Investment Coefficients of Australian Manufacturing Industry', *Economic Record*, vol. 38, no. 82, June, pp. 137–56.

Salter, W.E.G. (1965), 'Productivity Growth and Accumulation as Historical Processes', in E.A.G. Robinson (ed.), *Problems in Economic Development. Proceedings of a Conference held by the International Economic Association*, London, Macmillan.

Samuelson, P.A. (1947), *Foundations of Economic Analysis*, Cambridge, Harvard University Press.

Samuelson, P.A. (1962a), 'Parable and Realism in Capital Theory: The Surrogate Production Function', *Review of Economic Studies*, vol. xxix, pp. 193–206.

Samuelson, P.A. (1962b), 'Economists and the History of Ideas', *American Economic Review*, vol. 52, no. 1, March, pp. 1–18.

Samuelson, P.A. (1966), 'A Summing Up', *Quarterly Journal of Economics*, vol. lxxx, no. 4, November, pp. 568–83.

Samuelson, P.A. (1971), 'Understanding the Marxian Notion of Exploitation: A Summary of the So-Called Transformation Problem between Marxian Values and Competitive Prices', *Journal of Economic Literature*, vol. ix, pp. 399–431.

Samuelson, P.A. (1972), 'The Economics of Marx: An Ecumenical Reply', *Journal of Economic Literature*, vol. x, pp. 51–7.

Samuelson, P.A. (1973), 'Samuelson's "Reply on Marxian Matters"', *Journal of Economic Literature*, vol. xi, pp. 64–8.

Samuelson, P.A. (1974a), 'Insight and Detour in the Theory of Exploitation: A Reply to Baumol', *Journal of Economic Literature*, vol. xii, pp. 62–70.

Samuelson, P.A. (1974b), 'Rejoinder: Merlin Unclothed, a Final Word', *Journal of Economic Literature*, vol. xii, pp. 75–7.

Samuelson, P.A. (1974c), 'Interest Rate Determinations and Oversimplifying Parables: A Summing Up', Buffalo, mimeo.

Samuelson, P.A. (1975), 'Steady-State and Transient Relations: A Reply on Reswitching', *Quarterly Journal of Economics*, vol. lxxxix, no. 1, February, pp. 40–7.

Samuelson, P.A., and Modigliani, F. (1966a), 'The Pasinetti Paradox in Neoclassical and More General Models', *Review of Economic Studies*, vol. xxxiii (4), no. 96, October, pp. 269–301.

Samuelson, P.A., and Modigliani, F. (1966b), 'Reply to Pasinetti and Robinson', *Review of Economic Studies*, vol. xxxiii (4), no. 96, October, pp. 321–30.

Samuelson, P.A., and Weizsäcker, C.C. von (1971), 'A New Labour Theory of Value for Rational Planning Through Use of the Bourgeois Profit Rate', *Proceedings of the National Academy of Science, U.S.A.*, vol. lxviii, pp. 1192–4.

Sato, K. (1974), 'The Neoclassical Postulate and the Technology Frontier in Capital Theory', *Quarterly Journal of Economics*, vol. lxxxviii, no. 3, August, pp. 353–84.

Schefold, B. (unpublished), *Mr. Sraffa on Joint Production*.

Schultz, T.P. (1974), 'Review of H.G. Johnson, *The Theory of Income Distribution, 1973*', *Journal of Economic Literature*, vol. xii, June, pp. 483–4.

Schumpeter, J.A. (1954), *History of Economic Analysis*, London, Allen & Unwin.

Scitovsky, T. (1976), *The Joyless Economy. An Inquiry into Human Satisfaction and Consumer Dissatisfaction*, Oxford, Oxford University Press.

Scott, J.A. (1974), 'Review of Fogel, R.W. and Engerman, S.L. (1974), *Time on the Cross: The Economics of American Negro Slavery*, Little, Brown & Company, Boston', *Challenge*, vol. 17, no. 5, November–December, pp. 53–62.

Sen, A.K. (1963), 'Neo-Classical and Neo-Keynesian Theories of Distribution', *Economic Record*, vol. 39, no. 85, March, pp. 53–64.

Sen, A.K. (1974), 'On Some Debates in Capital Theory', *Economica*, vol. xli, August, pp. 328–35.

Sen, A.K. (1978), 'On the Labour Theory of Value: Some Methodological Issues', *Cambridge Journal of Economics*, vol. 2, no. 2, June, pp. 175–90.

Shaikh, A. (1974), 'Laws of Production and Laws of Algebra: The Humbug Production Function', *Review of Economics and Statistics*, vol. lvi, no. 1, February, pp. 115–20.

Shaikh, A. (1977), 'Marx's Theory of Value and the "Transformation Problem"', in J. Schwartz (ed.), *A Subtle Anatomy of Capitalism*, California, Goodyear.

Smith, K.R. (1969), 'The Effect of Uncertainty on Monopoly Price, Capital Stock and Utilization of Capital', *Journal of Economic Theory*, vol. 1, June, pp. 48–59.

Smithies, A. (1962), 'Comment on Solow', *American Economic Review, Papers and Proceedings*, vol. 52, no. 2, May, pp. 91–2.

Solow, R.M. (1956), 'A Contribution to the Theory of Economic Growth', *Quarterly Journal of Economics*, vol. lxx, no. 1, February, pp. 65–94.

Solow, R.M. (1957), 'Technical Change and the Aggregate Production Function', *Review of Economics and Statistics*, vol. xxxix, no. 3, August, pp. 312–20.

Solow, R.M. (1963), *Capital Theory and the Rate of Return*, Professor Dr F. De Vries Lectures, 1963, Amsterdam, North Holland.

Solow, R.M. (1967), 'The Interest Rate and Transition between Techniques', in C.H. Feinstein (ed.), *Socialism, Capitalism and Economic Growth. Essays Presented to Maurice Dobb*, Cambridge, Cambridge University Press, pp. 30–9.

Solow, R.M. (1970a), *Growth Theory: An Exposition*, The Radcliffe Lectures delivered at the University of Warwick, 1969, Oxford, Clarendon Press.

Solow, R.M. (1970b), 'On the Rate of Return: Reply to Pasinetti', *Economic Journal*, vol. lxxx, no. 318, June, pp. 423–8.

Solow, R.M. (1974a), 'Laws of Production and Laws of Algebra: The Humbug Production Function: A Comment', *Review of Economics and Statistics*, vol. lvi, no. 1, February, p. 121.

Solow, R.M. (1974b), 'Review of John Hicks, *Capital and Time. A Neo-Austrian Theory*, 1973', *Economic Journal*, vol. 84, March, pp. 189–92.

Solow, R.M. (1975a), 'Cambridge and the Real World', *Times Literary Supplement*, 14 March 1975, pp. 277–8.

Solow, R.M. (1975b), 'Brief Comments', *Quarterly Journal of Economics*, vol. lxxxix, no. 1, February, pp. 48–52.

Solow, R.M., and Stiglitz, J.E. (1968), 'Output, Employment and Wages in the Short Run', *Quarterly Journal of Economics*, vol. lxxxii, no. 4, November, pp. 537–60.

Spaventa, L. (1973), 'Notes on Problems of Transition Between Techniques', in J.A. Mirrlees and N.H. Stern (eds), *Models of Economic Growth*, London, Macmillan, pp. 168–87.

Sraffa, P. (1925), 'Sulle relazioni fra costo e quantità prodottà', *Annali i economica*, vol. ii, no. 1, pp. 277–328.

Sraffa, P. (1926), 'The Laws of Return Under Competitive Conditions', *Economic Journal*, vol. 36, December, pp. 535–50.

Sraffa, P. (1930), 'A Criticism', in 'Increasing Returns and the Representative Firm: A Symposium', *Economic Journal*, vol. xl, March, pp. 89–92, 93.

Sraffa, P. (1951–5) (ed.), with the collaboration of M.H. Dobb, *The Works and Correspondence of David Ricardo*, 10 vols, Cambridge, Cambridge University Press.

Sraffa, P. (1960), *Production of Commodities by Means of Commodities. Prelude to a Critique of Economic Theory*, Cambridge, Cambridge University Press.

Sraffa, P. (1962), 'Production of Commodities: A Comment', *Economic Journal*, vol. lxxii, no. 286, June, pp. 477–9.

Steedman, I. (1975a), 'Positive Profits with Negative Surplus Value', *Economic Journal*, vol. 85, no. 337, March, pp. 114–23.

Steedman, I. (1975b), 'Critique of the Critic', *Times Higher Education Supplement*, 31 January 1975, p. i.

Steedman, I. (1976), 'Positive Profits with Negative Surplus Value: A Reply', *Economic Journal*, vol. 86, September, pp. 604–8.

Steedman, I. (1977), *Marx after Sraffa*, London, New Left Books.

Steedman, I., and Hodgson, G. (1977), 'Depreciation of Machines of Changing Efficiency: A Note', *Australian Economic Papers*, vol. 16, no. 28, June, pp. 141–7.

Stiglitz, J.E. (1973a), 'The Badly Behaved Economy with the Well-Behaved Production Function', in J.A. Mirrlees and N.H. Stern (eds), *Models of Economic Growth*, London, Macmillan, pp. 117–37.

Stiglitz, J.E. (1973b), 'Recurrence of Techniques in a Dynamic Economy', in J.A. Mirrlees and N.H. Stern (eds), *Models of Economic Growth*, London, Macmillan, pp. 138–67.

Stiglitz, J.E. (1974), 'The Cambridge–Cambridge Controversy in the Theory of Capital: A View from New Haven: A Review Article', *Journal of Political Economy*, vol. lxxxii, no. 4, July–August, pp. 893–903.

Swan, T.W. (1956), 'Economic Growth and Capital Accumulation', *Economic Record*, vol. xxxii, November, pp. 334–61.

Tarshis, L. (1939a), 'The Determinants of Labour Income', unpublished Ph.D. dissertation, Cambridge, Cambridge University Library.

Tarshis, L. (1939b), 'Changes in Real and Money Wages', *Economic Journal*, vol. xlix, March, pp. 150–4.

Tarshis, L. (1947), *The Elements of Economics. An Introduction to the Theory of Price and Employment*, Cambridge, Mass., Houghton Mifflin.

Tarshis, L. (1979), 'The Aggregate Supply Function in Keynes's *General Theory*', in M.J. Boskin (ed.), *Economics and Human Welfare, Essays in Honour of Tibor Scitovsky*, New York, Academic Press, pp. 361–92.

Thurow, L.C. (1977), 'Economics 1977', *Daedalus*, vol. 106, no. 5, Autumn, pp. 79–94.

Tobin, J. (1973), 'Cambridge (U.K.) versus Cambridge (Mass.)', *Public Interest*, vol. xxxi, Spring, pp. 102–9.

Tobin, J. (1975), 'Keynesian Models of Recession and Depression', *American Economic Review, Papers and Proceedings*, vol. lxv, no.

2, May, pp. 195–202.

Vanags, A.H. (1975), 'Discussion', in M. Parkin and A.R. Nobay (eds) (1975), pp. 334–6.

Viner, J. (1953), 'Supplementary Note (1950)', in K.E. Boulding and G.J. Stigler (eds), *Readings in Price Theory*, London, Allen & Unwin, pp. 227–32.

Walsh, V., and Gram, H. (1980), *Classical and Neoclassical Theories of General Equilibrium. Historical Origins and Mathematical Structure.* New York, Oxford University Press.

Ward, B. (1972), *What's Wrong with Economics?*, New York and London, Basic Books.

Weizsäcker, C.C. von (1971), 'Ende einer Wachstumstheorie? Zu Hajo Reises Missverständnissen über die "Neoklassische" Theorie', *Kyklos*, vol. xxiv, pp. 97–101.

Whitehead, D.H. (1966), 'Professor Russell on Wages Policy: A Comment', *Australian Economic Papers*, vol. 5, no. 2, December, pp. 224–9.

Wicksteed, P.H. (1910), *The Common Sense of Political Economy*, London, Routledge (1933 edition, edited by L. Robbins).

Wiles, P. (1951), 'Corporate Taxation Based on Replacement Cost', *Accounting Research*, vol. 2, no. 1, pp. 77–82.

Winston, G.C. (1974), 'The Theory of Capital Utilization and Idleness', *Journal of Economic Literature*, vol. 12, no. 4, pp. 1301–20.

Withers, G. (1978), 'The State of Economics', *Australian Quarterly*, vol. 50, no. 4, December, pp. 74–80.

Wood, A. (1975), *A Theory of Profits*, Cambridge, Cambridge University Press.

Worswick, G.D.N. (1972), 'Is Progress in Economic Science Possible?', *Economic Journal*, vol. 82, no. 325, March, pp. 73–86.

Wright, F.K. (1978), 'Accounting Rate of Profit and the Internal Rate of Return', *Oxford Economic Papers*, vol. xxx, no. 3, pp. 464–8.

Wright, J.F. (1975), 'The Dynamics of Reswitching', *Oxford Economic Papers*, vol. xxvii, no. 1, March, pp. 21–46.

Yordon, W.J. (1961), 'Industrial Concentration and Price Flexibility in Inflation: Price Response Rates in Fourteen Industries, 1947–1958', *Review of Economics and Statistics*, vol. 43, no. 3, August, pp. 287–94.

Youngson, A.J. (1976), 'Adam Smith and the Omnipresent State', Australian National University Research or Occasional Paper no. 27, ISBN 0 7259 0247 7, Department of Economics, The University of Newcastle.

Official Publications

Board of Trade Journal, (United Kingdom), H.M.S.O., London.

Company Income and Finance, 1949–1953 (1956), London, Cambridge University Press, November.

Company Income and Finance, 1949–1953 (1957), London, National

Institute of Economic and Social Research.

Investment Appraisal (1965), London, National Economic Development Council.

National Income Statistics: Sources and Methods (1956), London, Central Statistical Office.

National Income and Expenditure of the United Kingdom (1957), H.M.S.O., London.

Report of the Committee on Turnover Taxation (1964), Cmnd. 2300, H.M.S.O., London.

United Kingdom Census of Production for 1951, H.M.S.O., London.

95th–99th *Reports of the United Kingdom Commissioners of Inland Revenue*, 1952–6, H.M.S.O., London.

Index

417